```
┌─────────────────────────┐
│   HANDMADE              │
│   SAMPLE                │
│                         │
│  DATE _____   │
│  SIZE  _____  │
│  TITLE _____  │
│  NUMBER_____   │
│  ARTIST_____   │
└─────────────────────────┘
```

2001
THE ONE SHOW
ADVERTISING'S BEST PRINT, DESIGN, RADIO, TV
VOLUME 23

THE ONE CLUB FOR ART & COPY

Bob Barrie
PRESIDENT

Mary Warlick
EXECUTIVE DIRECTOR/EDITOR

Tiffany Meyers
EDITOR

Diane Louvel
Steve Marchese
PRODUCTION EDITORS

BOOK DESIGN

John Boone
David Oakley
COVER DESIGN

Edwin Laguerre
SENIOR DESIGNER

Trevor Van Brook
DESIGNER

Peter Smallman
Allen Goldman
Young Hee Park
Kristin Payne
Odvar Daley
DIVIDER PAGES, IMAGE ZONE INCORPORATED

CD-ROM

Kevin Swanepoel
PROGRAMMING AND PRODUCTION
ONE CLUB INTERACTIVE

Todd Gaffney
PRODUCTION
ONE CLUB INTERACTIVE

Alan Alston
Farancois Naudé
Type01
PROGRAMMING

PUBLISHED AND DISTRIBUTED BY

The One Club for Art and Copy
32 East 21st Street
New York, NY 10010
TEL: 212-979-1900
FAX: 212-979-5006
EMAIL: oneclub@inch.com
WEBSITE: www.oneclub.com

Copyright © 2001 as a collection by The One Club for Art & Copy, Inc. All rights reserved. No part of this book may be reproduced in any way by any means whatsoever without express permission in writing from the owners.

First Printing
ISBN 0-929837-15-0

PRODUCTION AND SEPARATION BY AVA Book Production Pte. Ltd.
EMAIL: production@avabook.com.sg

A note on the alphanumeric identification system in this volume: The digits that appear in the credits for each entry comprise a unique pencil and merit award number. An "A" at the end of uniuqe numbers represents One Show winners. A "D" at the end of unique numbers represents One Show Design winners.

TABLE OF CONTENTS

Board of Directors	**vi**
President's Message	**vii**
One Show Judges	**viii**
One Club Members	**ix**
Creative Hall of Fame	**xiii**
Gold, Silver and Bronze Awards	**1**
One Show	**2**
College Competition	**68**
One Show Design	**70**
Best of Show	**85**
Judges' Choice for Best of Show	**89**
Gold On Gold	**107**
Print Merit Awards	**127**
Consumer Newspaper	**128**
Consumer Magazine	**159**
Outdoor	**225**
Guerilla	**239**
Trade	**250**
Collateral	**273**
Multi-Media	**294**
Design Merit Awards	**297**
Public Service & Political Merit Awards	**373**
Print	**374**
Radio	**414**
Television	**416**
Radio Merit Awards	**421**
Television Merit Awards	**439**
College Merit Awards	**491**
College Compitition	**492**
Young Creative Professional Competition	**505**
Index	**510**

THE BOARD OF DIRECTORS

Bob Barrie
FALLON/MINNEAPOLIS
PRESIDENT

Tod Seisser
SAATCHI & SAATCHI/NEW YORK
VICE PRESIDENT

Earl Cavanah
LOWE LINTAS & PARTNERS/NEW YORK
TREASURER

David Baldwin
MCKINNEY & SILVER/RALEIGH

Jamie Barrett
FALLON/NEW YORK

Rick Boyko
OGILVY & MATHER/NEW YORK

John Butler
BUTLER SHINE & STERN/SAN FRANCISCO

Lee Clow
TBWA/CHIAT/DAY/LOS ANGELES

Nick Cohen
MAD DOGS & ENGLISHMEN/NEW YORK

John Doyle
YOUNG & RUBICAM/IRVINE

Cliff Freeman
CLIFF FREEMAN AND PARTNERS/NEW YORK

John Hegarty
BARTLE BOGLE HEGARTY/NEW YORK

Woody Kay
PAGANO SCHENCK & KAY/BOSTON

Jim Mountjoy
LOEFFLER KETCHUM MOUNTJOY/CHARLOTTE

Ernie Schenck
FREELANCE

Steve Simpson
GOODBY SILVERSTEIN & PARTNERS/SAN FRANCISCO

PRESIDENT'S MESSAGE

Welcome to this year's One Show Annual.

Please allow me to give you an idea of just how complicated the preparations for this rather fat book have become.

Once upon a time, The One Club simply gathered together a few New Yorkers to judge a few hundred ads in a room in downtown Manhattan, put on a one-night show and published a paperback book of the winners.

In 2001, things are a bit different. A record 20,000 total entries were judged, depending on category, in locations as diverse as San Francisco (radio), Barcelona (print and TV), New York (new media) and Santa Fe (design) by judges from London, Boston, South Africa, Portland, Singapore, Richmond, Brazil and, oh yeah, Manhattan. The resulting two shows form the pillars for five full days of great events and activities... and ultimately, this annual.

The success of this monumental effort is a tribute to The One Club's Executive Director, Mary Warlick, and her tireless staff. They've made my job easy. So, as I now finish up my three-year term as President of the club and hand it over to the capable, caring and cute John Butler, I'm confident that The One Club and all it encompasses will endure as American advertising's most respected organization.

At least by those who took home a gold pencil in the latest One Show...

Thanks for your support all these years. I know it will continue.

Now, enjoy some ads.

Bob Barrie
President, The One Club for Art and Copy.

THE ONE SHOW JUDGES

Joe Alexander
THE MARTIN AGENCY/RICHMOND

Janet Champ
FREELANCE/PORTLAND

Henry Cocciolo
LEAGAS DELANEY/SAN FRANCISCO

David Droga
SAATCHI & SAATCHI/LONDON

Sean Ehringer
LEAGAS DELANEY/SAN FRANCISCO

Fabio Fernandes
F/NAZCA S&S/SÃO PAULO

Richard Foster
ABBOTT MEAD VICKERS.BBDO/LONDON

Kara Goodrich
ARNOLD WORLDWIDE/BOSTON

Gerry Graf
BBDO/NEW YORK

Johan Kramer
KESSELSKRAMER/AMSTERDAM

Rick McQuiston
WIEDEN + KENNEDY/PORTLAND

Kevin Roddy
FALLON/NEW YORK

Jon Soto
TBWA/CHIAT/DAY/SAN FRANCISCO

Ellen Steinberg
FREELANCE/NEW YORK

Monica Taylor
WIEDEN + KENNEDY/PORTLAND

Joyce King Thomas
MCCANN-ERICKSON/NEW YORK

Susan Treacy
TBWA/CHIAT/DAY/SAN FRANCISCO

Paul Venables
GOODBY SILVERSTEIN & PARTNERS/
SAN FRANCISCO

Matt Vescovo
FALLON/NEW YORK

Stacy Wall
HUNGRY MAN/NEW YORK

Graham Warsop
THE JUPITER DRAWING ROOM
(SOUTH AFRICA)/JOHANNESBURG

THE RADIO JUDGES

Chris Landi
FALLON/NEW YORK

Ron Henderson
THE RICHARDS GROUP/DALLAS

Adam Chasnow
CLIFF FREEMAN & PARTNERS/NEW YORK

Matt Ashworth
PUBLICIS & HAL RINEY/SAN FRANCISCO

Ryan Ebner
BUTLER SHINE & STERN/SAN FRANCISCO

Marty Donohue
HILL HOLLIDAY CONNORS
COSMOPULOS/BOSTON

Tim Roper
MULLEN/WENHAM

Steve Dildarian
GOODBY SILVERSTEIN & PARTNERS/
SAN FRANCISCO

Jeff Odiorne
ODIORNE WILDE NARRAWAY & PARTNERS/
SAN FRANCISCO

ONE SHOW DESIGN JUDGES

John Doyle
ONE SHOW DESIGN CHAIR
YOUNG & RUBICAM/IRVINE

Graham Clifford
GRAHAM CLIFFORD DESIGN/NEW YORK

Joe Duffy
DUFFY DESIGN/MINNEAPOLIS

Keith Helmetag
CHERMAYEFF & GEISMAR/NEW YORK

Jennifer Sterling
JENNIFER STERLING DESIGN/
SAN FRANCISCO

Robert Wong
MARCHFIRST/NEW YORK

MEMBERS

Abadi, Michael
Abbott, Jeffrey
Abraham, Geoffrey W.
Achda, Imdan
Aggarwal, Ekta
Alaie, Darius Edward
Alkouti, Saudi
Alpern, Blythe
Altabet, Elyse
Altschuler, Olivia
Amichay, Gideon
Anderson, Stephanie
Aragao, Marcelo
Asher, Larry
Avenius, Brian

Backlund, Kristina
Bade, John
Baier, Chris
Bailine, Adam
Banks, Steve
Bassett, Steve
Bautista, Steve
Bayless, Tim
Becker, Kris
Bell, Greg
Bellanca, Brian
Bennett, T. J.
Bentley, Roger
Berger, Danielle
Berkeley, Joe
Bernstein, David
Berta, Colleen
Bertuccio, Eric
Bhatia, Rahul
Bigar Kahn, Dominique
Bijur, Arthur
Bildsten, Bruce
Blau, Barry
Bond, Mindy
Boone, John
Boscia, Eric
Bossio, Peter
Bradley, Clarence
Brewer, Scott
Brokaw, Bill
Brown, Mark
Brown, St. Clair Alfonso
Brunelle, Tim
Bryson, Jane
Burkhart, Jon
Butterworth, Amy

Cadman, Larry
Cahill, Andrew
Calabretta, Alex
Callen, Steve

Canal, Ileana
Ceo, Marco
Chadwick, Chad
Chan, Jennifer
Chang, Soo Mean
Chanhyok, Park
Cheng, Chung-Mau
Chin, Jeremy
Christensen, Greg
Chung, Tom
Churchill, Chris
Cleveland, Bart
Cole, Christopher
Comstock, Michael
Cook-Tench, Diane
Cormier, Andrea
Cosentino, August
Courtright, Jim
Cox, Michael
Crandall, Court
Crane, Steve
Crifasi, Jack
Cruze, Gari
Curcuru, Phyllis
Curi, George
Curry, Chris
Curtis, Hal

D'Avanzo, Joanne
Darby, Kieth
Dauzier, Douglas
David, Adam
Davis, Bill
Davis, LaRonda
De la Rosa, Alan
DeBerry, Renee
DeGregorio, Tony
Dellovo, Laura
DeVito, John
DeVito, Sal
Dodson, Joel
Donohue, Marty
Doppelt, Steve
Dowret, Arnell
Duffy, Joe
Dunn, Andrew

Eastwood, Matt
Eggert, Philipp
Ellenson, Richard
Ellis, Belinda
Eng, Jason
Ennis, Gary
Ernelindo, Marcelo

Farris, John
Fawcett, John

Fernandez, Carlos
Ferrell, John
Finzi, Sylvia
Fischvogt, Matt
Foley, Dave
Foley, Tim
Frank, Sam
Freeman, Cliff
Freidberg, Kevin
Fremgen, Robert

Gabriel, Tom
Galvah, Mauricio
Ganton, Mark
Gardiner, David
Gardner, Beth
Gardner, Tom
Garrone, Lisa
Gatti, Joe
Gerdes, Richard
Gilbert, John Gavin
Ginsberg, Frank
Glassman, Jason
Gleason, Kenneth
Godsil, Max
Goldgeier, Dan
Goldstein, Adam
Goldstein, Mark
Goldstrom, Mort
Gordon, Mitch
Grabowski, Lori
Graybill, Jeff
Greenberg, Allan
Gregory, John
Grey, Norm
Growick, Philip
Guiffrida, Gina

Hafner, Monica
Hallock, Matthew
Hallowell, Trace
Harrington, John
Hathiramani, Jackie
Hayward, Blaise
Helfrey, Dave
Herbert, Roy
Herz, Rony
Hester, Lee
Hinkle, Woody
Hively, Charles
Holloway, Dave
Holton, Curt
Hopper, Charlie
Hord, Jim
Hough, Hugh
Hughes, Mike
Hunt, Jackie

MEMBERS

Hunter, Jason
Huntley, Diane
Hurni, Roger
Hynes, John

Iannarelli, Peter
Ingimundarson, Sveinn
Ives, Nik

Jacobs, Christopher
Jacobs, Harry
Jacobson, Per Robert
Jeffrey, Bob
Jennings, Kathy
Jenson, Kristine
Johnson, Anthony A.
Johnson, Marcus
Johnson, Mark
Jones, Stephen

Kagan, Tal
Kamsler, Stephen
Kane, Charles
Kao, Grace
Kaufman, Richard
Kelly, Tom
Kho, John
Kidwell, Jeff
Kim, Joanne
King, Paul
Kintanar, Richard
Kislowski, Leon
Korus, Renee
Kosloski, Jeff
Krouse, Neal

Lafeliece, Jonathan
Lai, Ming
Lally, John
Leahy, Joe
Lee, Deborah
Lee, Eun-Jung
Lee, Jane
Lee, Seung
Lehmann, Robert
Lemmon, Todd
Leon, Chag-Chag
Lewis, Warren
Liben, Susan
Lipkin-Balser, Lisa
Lipstein, Jenny
Liu, Mindy
Liu, Steven
Lockett, Damon
Loew, Dave

Lopresti, Frank
Lutter, John

MacDonald, D. Matthew
Maiorino, Chris
Makarechi, Sharoz
Malhan, Madhu
Mambro, Jamie
Mandelbaum, Ken
Manier, Bradley
Mann, Kevin
Mannion, John
Marino, Louis
Marks, Lawrence
Marsh, Julie
May, Richard
Mayes, Michael
McAllister, Cal
McCarthy, Joseph
McNaughton, Cameron
McPhillips, Jay
Melillo, John
Mendelis, Mark
Meo, Frank
Merrick, Tom
Meza, Richars
Michelson, R. Scott
Miller, Chris
Miller, Don
Miller, Renee
Mongkolkasetarin, Sakol
Moore, Sara
Morgan, Melvin
Mori Ikezaki, Mauricio
Morris, Jacob
Mortimore, Scott
Mountjoy, Jim
Munisteri, Cathy
Myers, Richard

Neely, Jeff
Nelson, Jay
Nemali, Arun K.
Ney, Joseph
Nicoli, Ruiz
Norman, Tom
Northrop, Ronald P.

Oberlander, Bill
Odell, Rip
Oravetz, Peter
Ordansa, Ron
Otnes, Professor Cele

Pantano, Dick

Park, Sam
Patel, Babita
Patterson, Paul
Paul, Kimberly
Peralta, José Luis
Perkins, Ricky
Perone, Christopher
Petsas, Dimitrios
Piszko, Paul
Plazonja, Jonathan
Pool, Jill
Porter, Kim
Price, Tim
Provencher, Sylvian
Pullar, Dave

Quitoni, Lisa

Rawowsky, Corey
Reilly, Jo
Ricciardi, Lisa
Richardson, Allen
Richardson, Hank
Riddle, Todd
Robertson, Michael
Rojas, Lilia
Rosen, Gary
Rotenberg, Rosanne
Rotter, Jessica
Roy, Amy
Rudig, Ann

Sabarese, Ted
Sainato, Vinny
Sander, Vicki
Sannia, Ho
Sardo, Sal
Saulnier, Anne
Savage, Emma
Saxon, Robert
Schenck, Ernie
Scheuer, Glenn
Scheyer, Dennis
Schlegel, Chris
Schmidt, Lee
Schoen Brunn, Gail
Schroeder, Jill
Schwabenland, Michael
Schwegler, Heinz
Scully, John
Seisser, Tod
Sheahan, Molly
Sheehan, Mike
Sheppard, Lori
Shields, Paul
Sibih, Desi

MEMBERS

Silva Vasquez, German
Singer, Richard
Slaff, Lauren
Sloan, Pat
Slosberg, Robert
Smith, Jr., David
Solomon, Mo
Solomon, Richard
Staluppi, Joseph
Stanton, Todd
Stefanides, Dean
Stelzer, Michael
Stephens, Eric
Stone, Marcia
Storrs, Scott
Supple, Jack
Swanson, Jennifer
Swartz, Steve
Sweet, Leslie
Szorenyi, Emese

Talamu, Jan
Tanen, Norman
Tang, Willie
Tarulli, Matthew
Taylor, Blake
Teevens, Kevin
Temp, Rick
Tersch, Kayvalyn
Terzis, Nick
Teschner, Danielle
Thomas, Greg
Thompson, Rob
Toch, Laura
Topuzes, Thomas
Tozzi, Vincent
Trillo, Imma
Trippetti, Mark
Tsiavos, Staz
Tsukerman, Roman
Tyler, Amy

Ungar, Tom
Unger, Peter

Van Bloem, Peter
Vaynerman, Paul
Venables, Paul
Vensel, Amy
Vick, Carol
Vick, Ed
Vieth, Danielle
Vine, Larry
Vitiello, Michael
Vitro, John

Wagner, Elaine
Waites, William Ernest
Wakabayashi, Dennis
Wald, Judy
Ward, Michael
Warren, Bob
Weech, Karen
West, Robert Shaw
Whitten, Nat
Wilcox, Ron
Williams, Steve
Williams, Tim
Winter, Stewart
Wojnarowski, Stefen
Wolk, Alan
Wong, Charles Tze Ho
Wong, David A.

Yamazaki, Betsy
Young, Marvin

Zagorski, Joe
Zator, Lynette
Zostak, Dean
Zucker, Mat

CREATIVE HALL OF FAME

THE CREATIVE HALL OF FAME 2001

A Message from the President

Every couple of years, the Board of Directors of The One Club faces a tough decision: Is it time again to add a new member to that elite list our predecessors boldly named "The Creative Hall of Fame?" Or, is no one currently worthy? We feel no real pressure to add one. Or two. Or three. Or none, for that matter.

The One Club believes that the Hall of Fame is truly an important part of our industry. As the driving force behind the One Show, we recognize that saluting great work is not just a year-to-year task. We also believe that a lifetime of lifting the creative standards for all of us should be celebrated.

So this whole induction matter, as you might guess, is not taken lightly.

A committee is formed, opinions are tossed, options are considered, arguments are made, votes are taken, and occasionally an inductee or two emerges from this gauntlet of cynical adfolk unscathed. And the names are always, well, impressive.

Leo Burnett was the first, in 1961. Dan Wieden and David Kennedy were the most recent, back in 1999. And in between were sprinkled the likes of Bill Bernbach, Phyllis Robinson, Bob Levenson, Mary Wells Lawrence, Carl Ally, Helmut Krone, Hal Riney, Roy Grace and Lee Clow.

Heady company, huh?

Each inductee had spent a lifetime creating, promoting and inspiring work that rose far above the banality of the advertising status quo of their day. Each created work that became an enduring part of our culture. And, more often than not, each was a pretty terrific human being.

This year we honor two men who easily satisfy all three of these criteria.

Especially that last one. One is from England, the first since some guy named Ogilvy squeaked through back in '65, and the other is our very first inductee from the southern United States.

Please join me in honoring the 35th and 36th members of The Creative Hall of Fame: Congratulations, David and Harry. You did good.

Bob Barrie
President/The One Club

A Message from the Executive Director

Since its inception in 1961, the Copywriters Hall of Fame, later to become the Creative Hall of Fame, has been judicious in the selection of nominees. As President of The One Club, Bob Barrie, notes in this book, it is a process known for its qualitative judgement rather than its frequency. The first person inducted was Leo Burnett, a copywriter who changed the face of advertising in the 40s and 50s. His legacy is an agency name and an advertising culture distinctive to Chicago. Among the great talents who followed in his stead, Bernbach defined an era in New York, Clow helped us all love LA, and Wieden and Kennedy together put Portland on the advertising map. The two gentlemen who have been nominated for the first Creative Hall of Fame in the 21st century continue the tradition of extending their influence far beyond the creative output of an agency.

The One Club is particularly proud to honor two men who have had such a significant influence on creative advertising. David Abbott has left an indelible mark on the style, wit and intelligence of a whole school of British advertising. Harry Jacobs launched a creative movement in the southern United States that redefined the traditional boundaries of creative influence. On behalf of the Board of Directors of The One Club and its members, I welcome the newest inductees to the Creative Hall of Fame.

Mary Warlick
Executive Director/The One Club

DAVID ABBOTT, ABBOTT MEAD VICKERS.BBDO

When I think of David Abbott, I think of mince beef or potatoes or some other rather prosaic foodstuff. This is not a reference to his visual appearance, which, as it happens, is dapper to the point of perfection. No, it is the produce featured in ads written by David for Sainsbury's, a brand that he helped build into the biggest, most well-regarded supermarket chain in the country.

The Sainsbury's campaign was the first in a category characterized by dull yet insistent ads, which treated women shoppers as human beings with brains in their heads—people who cared about what they bought, even, my God, considered it important in their lives.

Prior to David's campaign, price ruled. Why? Because research said that women only ever used price as a reason to trudge to one shop rather than another. Research may have spoken but David Abbott's instincts begged to differ.

What followed was a significant piece of UK advertising history and very quickly became a lesson to everyone in advertising wherever they lived.

Know your product, respect your audience, trust your intuition. Watch how people buy things, even listen if you can. By all means think about their deep-seated motivations but don't get entwined in them. Treat your audience as you would like to be treated.

These rules are regularly spouted by so-called leaders of the advertising industry. Very few of these titans believe in them, particularly in the face of a demanding client or a repitch. Even fewer live by them and build a highly successful agency in the process.

David Abbott is one of the few.

But how did he manage to succeed where so many have failed? What qualities did he possess which allowed him to dignify this often undignified business?

First and foremost David is a great advertising writer, a definition substantiated by reams of work spanning four decades, all of which bares the indelible stamp of an intelligent and enquiring mind.

His British Volkswagen ads, created at DDB London in the late 60s, lived with the best of that remarkable campaign. His later work for Volvo, The Economist and the RSPCA all displayed his almost unique ability to create ads which were always 'appropriate'; never gratuitous in their use of eye-catching headlines or visuals and where the product was invariably king.

Undoubtedly his most enduring achievement is the agency he created with Peter Mead and Adrian Vickers. During the glitzy, and in the end, rather shabby, 80s, the advertising industry in the UK flattered itself that it was at the very hub of commercial and political life. Admen and women inveigled their way onto the high table and bragged about it, although they were less forthcoming about their actual contributions.

Quietly, and following an altogether different tack, Abbott Mead Vickers stole past their flash and faintly ridiculous competitors to become the No.1 agency in the third most important advertising market in the world. No takeovers. No knighthoods. No PR-obsessed antics in an attempt to spin their way to dominance.

AMV not only became the biggest agency, it was the only agency to have been led to that position by a creative person: David Abbott. And though his partners were always on hand and contributed greatly to the agency's success, AMV was always known as 'David's agency.'

This is his most important legacy.

Many creative people can write great campaigns, some can run terrific departments. But to turn those skills into a business, to be disciplined and commercial on behalf of staff and clients alike indicates qualities rarely, if ever, attributed to anyone in a creative department.

What was achieved at AMV has only happened at a handful of agencies in the history of modern advertising. It should inspire art directors and copywriters everywhere. It should teach them not to hide behind the wall of cynicism about clients' lack of understanding or appreciation. It should encourage them to put their own heads above the parapet, in the belief that their skills and insights, their unusual almost quirky talent for mass communication could create an agency that one day may be as good as the agency David built.

In another and much more eloquent eulogy to David's career than this one, Tony Brignull suggested that while many copywriters claimed the blood of Bill Bernbach ran in their veins, only David Abbott would pass a blood test.

If DDB taught us all what advertising could be, David Abbott and AMV accepted that baton with enthusiasm and ran with it.

David's work stands, above all, for intelligence and humanity—rare qualities in a human being, let alone a transient piece of communication. And it is because he cajoled, argued, fought, charmed, probably engaged in hand to hand fighting to uphold those simple virtues, that his entry to The Creative Hall of Fame is so thoroughly deserved.

Tim Delaney
Leagas Delaney
London 2001

Or Buy a Volvo
Volvo, 1982

Doggy Bag
RSPCA, 1989

Frustrating
BT, 1994

Kissinger
The Econcmist, 1996

Abbott Under Car
Volvo, 1983

I Never Read...
The Econcmist, 1988

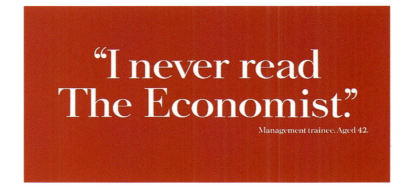

xvii

HARRY JACOBS, THE MARTIN AGENCY

Harry Jacobs has always been bigger than the business he's in.

Don't get me wrong. Advertising's great: It's big and grand. It's just that Harry Jacobs is bigger and grander. If advertising was a person at a party, it might well be the person you want to hang around with (certainly ahead of politics and insurance and dentistry), but it may not be the one you want to take home to mother.

Harry, on the other hand, is both fun at a party—and my mother loves him. She loves him because he's elegant and he stands tall and he always laughs hard at a good joke. She can see—like everyone can see—that he's a gentle man of great integrity, high standards and remarkable taste. Mom may not know much about art direction or creative leadership, but she knows a good dresser when she sees one—and Harry in a sweater looks better dressed than the rest of us in our best tuxes. To top it all off, Mom can't talk about Harry without telling everyone how handsome he is. (Frankly, I don't see that last point, but if he landed Bobbi, he must have something going for him.)

Mom doesn't know that he was once a jazz drummer, a graphic artist at the Pentagon and a world-class airplane modeler. She doesn't know that he once whipped the whole creative department at the pool hall and carried around the nickname "The Stick" for about three weeks. But she does know if you get him talking about Bobbi or their kids or their growing army of grandchildren, he'll go on forever. And she knows that if you run into Harry the first question he has for you doesn't have anything to do with advertising or business, it has to do with you and your kids and how are you doing, really? Things like that mean a lot to a mom.

Big as he is, Harry has never stooped to make an ad. Instead, he lifts the ads to a higher level.

For one thing, he makes them bigger. Although he's made some bang-up small space ads over the years, when we think of Harry, we all think of vast double truck monsters that, in Harry's hands, somehow seem bigger than the newspaper itself.

He also makes ads simpler. When you're Harry's creative partner, you don't spend much time actually making ads. Instead, you concentrate on strategy, on making sure everything gets right to the point.

In honing the message to its simplest, clearest elements, Harry makes more outlines than a high school English teacher. He increases his odds by exploring multiple directions—but each one is picked clean of all extraneous baggage. (Sounds obvious, doesn't it? Then why do most of us struggle with this challenge every day?)

But most of all, Harry lifts ads to a higher level with the most elegant, inevitable design you can imagine. When Harry was finished with an ad, it was impossible to imagine it art directed any other way.

And here's what's more amazing. That simple, elegant, gorgeous, big way of thinking was contagious. Westbrook caught it. And Torchia and Feuerman and Tench and DiSesa and Helm and Sullivan. While it's all most creative directors can do to turn out an occasional great ad, Harry was turning out great creative leaders. Harry's disciples went out and became creative directors at Chiat and Fallon and Wieden and McCann and JWT and numerous places large and small. And whether they acknowledged it or not, all those agencies learned the pain of knowing that nothing they did was ever quite good enough because in the back of their creative director's mind was this horrible, unrelenting question: What would Harry think of it?

All of us at The Martin Agency know how lucky we are to have had so much of that Jacobs magic sprinkled on us. We are who we are because he is who he is.

Now Harry's in The Creative Hall of Fame. It's not his first hall of fame, incidentally, and it probably won't be his last. But this one's special. This is writers and art directors and creative directors coming together to say thank you. I'm the one who had the honor of telling him about this. He was shocked (which he shouldn't have been) and so choked up he couldn't speak.

Once upon a time, young copywriter and future Hall of Famer, Tom McElligott, wrote Harry a note in which he articulated his career goal. He said he wanted to be like Harry.

Don't we all, Tom.... Don't we all.

Mike Hughes
The Martin Agency
Richmond 2001

Natural Death
EMD, 1982

Committed
Jacobs Morgan &
Westbrook, 1975

Boo
Vepco, 1979

Haul Derrière
Mercedes-Benz, 1994

Modern Jazz Quartet
Signet, 1989

Mountain
Barnett, 1984

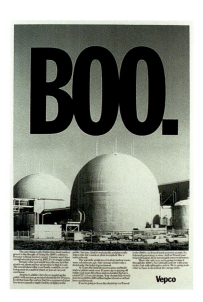

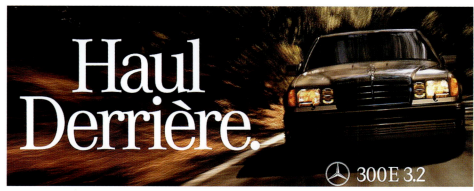

GOLD, SILVER, BRONZE

GOLD, SILVER, BRONZE

SILVER AWARD
Newspaper Over 600 Lines: Single

ART DIRECTORS
Suthisak Sucharittanonta
Prapaipim Prayongyam

WRITERS
Al Jackson
Neil French

PHOTOGRAPHER
Alex Kai Keong

CLIENT
Guinness

AGENCY
Ogilvy & Mather/Singapore

ID 010002A

BRONZE AWARD
Newspaper Over 600 Lines: Single

ART DIRECTORS
Chris Poulin
Libby DeLana

WRITER
Ted Jendrysik

PHOTOGRAPHER
Ulf Skogsberg

CLIENT
Drinks.com

AGENCY
Mullen/Wenham

ID 010003A

GOLD, SILVER, BRONZE

GOLD AWARD
Newspaper Over 600 Lines:
Campaign

ART DIRECTORS
Chris Poulin
Libby DeLana

WRITER
Ted Jendrysik

PHOTOGRAPHER
Ulf Skogsberg

CLIENT
Drinks.com

AGENCY
Mullen/Wenham

ID 010004A

GOLD, SILVER, BRONZE

SILVER AWARD
Newspaper Over 600 Lines: Campaign

ART DIRECTOR
Craig Smith

WRITER
Andy Greenaway

ILLUSTRATOR
Yau Wai Kin

PHOTOGRAPHER
Roy Zhang

CLIENT
Asia Pacific Breweries

AGENCY
Ogilvy & Mather/Singapore

ID 010005A

Also won:

MERIT AWARD
Outdoor: Campaign

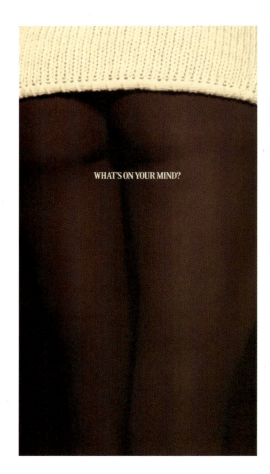
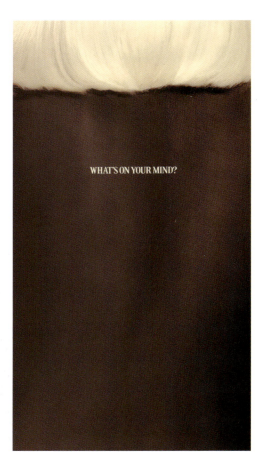

GOLD, SILVER, BRONZE

BRONZE AWARD
Newspaper Over 600 Lines:
Campaign

ART DIRECTOR
Heloise Jacobs

WRITERS
Gavin Williams
Brendan Jack
Vanessa Norman

PHOTOGRAPHER
David Prior

CLIENT
Nike

AGENCY
The Jupiter Drawing Room
(South Africa)/Johannesburg

ID 010006A

GOLD, SILVER, BRONZE

GOLD AWARD
Newspaper 600 Lines or Less: Single

ART DIRECTORS
Moe Verbrugge
Maya Rao

WRITERS
Maya Rao
Moe Verbrugge

CLIENT
Museum of Contemporary Art

AGENCY
TBWA/Chiat/Day/Los Angeles

ID 010007A

Reading the Paper, 2001
Ink on hands
Courtesy of The Museum of Contemporary Art, Los Angeles

SILVER AWARD
Newspaper 600 Lines or Less: Single

ART DIRECTOR
Dan O'Donnell

WRITERS
Eivind Ueland
Chris DeCarlo

CLIENT
Boston Herald

AGENCY
Hill Holliday Connors Cosmopulos/Boston

ID 010008A

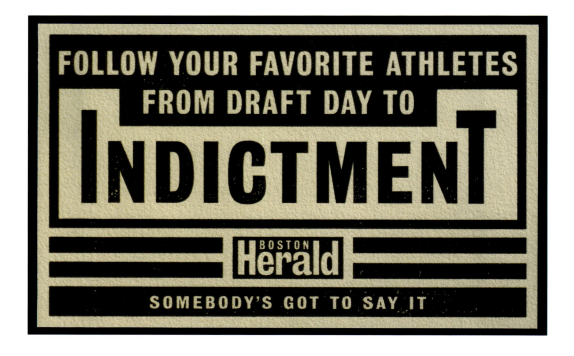

GOLD, SILVER, BRONZE

BRONZE AWARD
Newspaper 600 Lines or Less: Single

ART DIRECTOR
Julian Pugsley

WRITER
Jim Garaventi

PHOTOGRAPHER
William Huber

CLIENT
Cozone.com

AGENCY
Mullen/Wenham

ID 010009A

Buy a notebook computer, get a free Xerox laser printer.

SILVER AWARD
Magazine B/W Full Page or Spread: Single

ART DIRECTOR
Steve Back

WRITER
Steve Back

PHOTOGRAPHER
Tiziano Magni

CLIENT
Findus

AGENCY
Grey Worldwide/London

ID 010010A

GOLD, SILVER, BRONZE

BRONZE AWARD
Magazine B/W Full Page
or Spread: Single

ART DIRECTOR
Steve Back

WRITER
Steve Back

PHOTOGRAPHER
Tiziano Magni

CLIENT
Findus

AGENCY
Grey Worldwide/London

ID 010011A

GOLD AWARD
Magazine Color Full Page
or Spread: Single

ART DIRECTOR
Don Shelford

WRITER
Dave Weist

PHOTOGRAPHERS
Jeff Mermelstein
Bill Cash
Stock

CLIENT
Volkswagen of America

AGENCY
ARNOLD Worldwide/Boston

ID 010012A

SILVER AWARD
Magazine Color Full Page or Spread: Single

ART DIRECTORS
Bradley Wood
Sean Ehringer

WRITER
Steve Morris

ILLUSTRATOR
John Burgoyne

PHOTOGRAPHER
Mark Borthwick

CLIENT
Adidas Olympics

AGENCY
Leagas Delaney/San Francisco

ID 010013A

BRONZE AWARD
Magazine Color Full Page or Spread: Single

ART DIRECTOR
Don Shelford

WRITER
Dave Weist

PHOTOGRAPHERS
Stock
Bill Cash

CLIENT
Volkswagen of America

AGENCY
ARNOLD Worldwide/Boston

ID 010014A

GOLD, SILVER, BRONZE

SILVER AWARD
Magazine B/W Full Page
or Spread: Campaign

ART DIRECTOR
Steve Williams

WRITER
Adrian Lim

PHOTOGRAPHER
Chris Steele-Perkins

CLIENT
Olympus Optical

AGENCY
Lowe Lintas/London

ID 010015A

GOLD, SILVER, BRONZE

BRONZE AWARD
Magazine B/W Full Page
or Spread: Campaign

ART DIRECTOR
Steve Back

WRITER
Steve Back

PHOTOGRAPHER
Tiziano Magni

CLIENT
Findus

AGENCY
Grey Worldwide/London

ID 010016A

GOLD, SILVER, BRONZE

GOLD AWARD
Magazine Color Full Page or Spread: Campaign

ART DIRECTOR
Don Shelford

WRITER
Dave Weist

PHOTOGRAPHERS
Jeff Mermelstein
Bill Cash
Stock

CLIENT
Volkswagen of America

AGENCY
ARNOLD Worldwide/ Boston

ID 010017A

GOLD, SILVER, BRONZE

GOLD AWARD
Magazine Color Full Page
or Spread: Campaign

ART DIRECTORS
Erik Vervroegen
Karin Barry

WRITER
Wendy Moorcroft

PHOTOGRAPHER
Mike Lewis

CLIENT
Seychelles

AGENCY
TBWA Hunt Lascaris/
Johannesburg

ID 010018A

GOLD, SILVER, BRONZE

SILVER AWARD
Magazine Color Full Page
or Spread: Campaign

ART DIRECTORS
Bradley Wood
Sean Ehringer

WRITER
Steve Morris

ILLUSTRATORS
Sean Ehringer
Tim Caton
John Burgoyne

PHOTOGRAPHER
Mark Borthwick

CLIENT
Adidas Olympics

AGENCY
Leagas Delaney/
San Francisco

ID 010019A

GOLD, SILVER, BRONZE

SILVER AWARD
Magazine Color Full Page
or Spread: Campaign

ART DIRECTORS
Roger Camp
Mike McCommon

WRITERS
Mike McCommon
Roger Camp

PHOTOGRAPHERS
Lauren Greenfield
Stefan Ruiz

CLIENT
Discovery.com

AGENCY
Publicis & Hal Riney/
San Francisco

ID 010020A

15

GOLD, SILVER, BRONZE

BRONZE AWARD
Magazine Color Full Page
or Spread: Campaign

ART DIRECTORS
Sean Farrell
Phil Covitz

WRITER
Maya Rao

PHOTOGRAPHER
William Huber

CLIENT
Nike

AGENCY
Goodby Silverstein &
Partners/San Francisco

ID 010021A

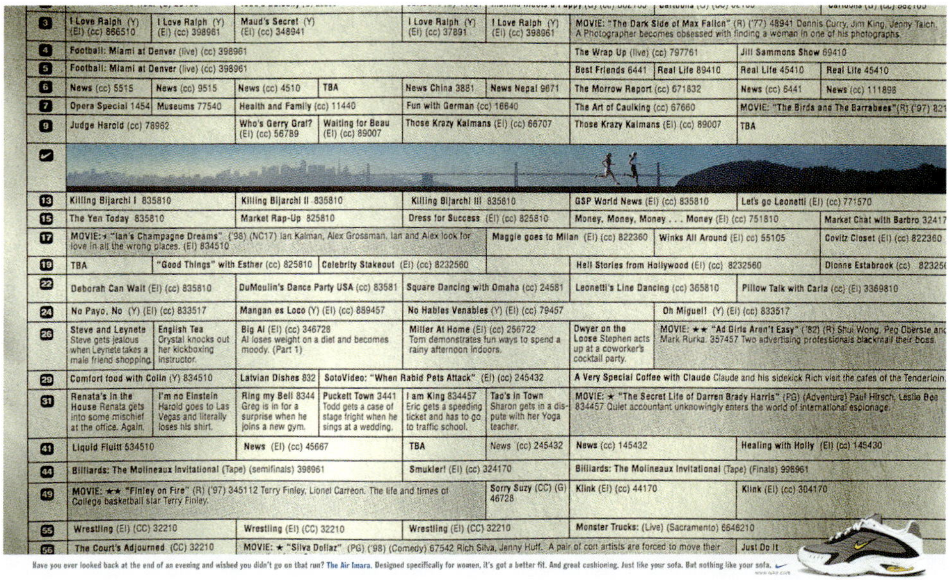

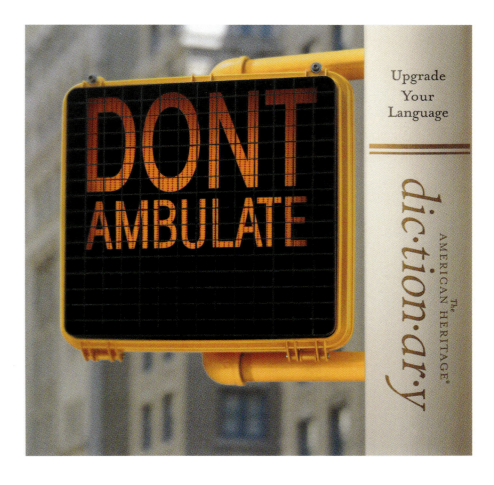

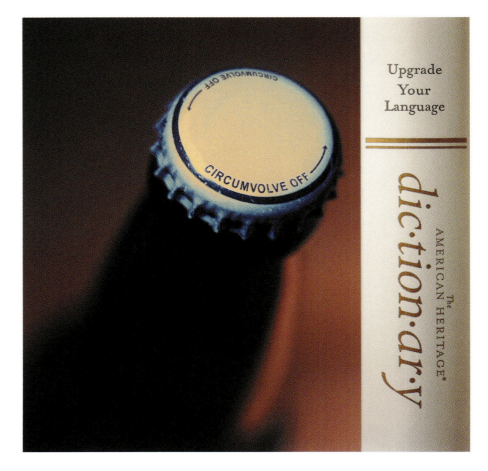

GOLD, SILVER, BRONZE

GOLD AWARD
Magazine Less Than a Page
B/W or Color: Single

ART DIRECTOR
Paul Laffy

WRITER
Brian Hayes

PHOTOGRAPHER
Dan Nourie

CLIENT
American Heritage Dictionary

AGENCY
Mullen/Wenham

ID 010022A

GOLD AWARD
Magazine Less Than a Page
B/W or Color: Single

ART DIRECTOR
Paul Laffy

WRITER
Brian Hayes

PHOTOGRAPHER
Dan Nourie

CLIENT
American Heritage Dictionary

AGENCY
Mullen/Wenham

ID 010023A

17

GOLD, SILVER, BRONZE

SILVER AWARD
Magazine Less Than a Page
B/W or Color: Single

ART DIRECTORS
Eric King
Andy Azula

WRITERS
Harold Einstein
Jim Haven

PHOTOGRAPHER
Hunter Freeman

CLIENT
Wall Street Journal

AGENCY
Goodby Silverstein &
Partners/San Francisco

ID 010024A

BRONZE AWARD
Magazine Less Than a Page
B/W or Color: Single

ART DIRECTORS
Jeff Lubow
Calvin Chu
Paul Smith
Josh Nichols
Peter Gatto

WRITERS
Jeff Lubow
Geoff MacDonald

PHOTOGRAPHER
Gus Butera

CLIENT
SciFi Channel

AGENCY
SciFi Channel/New York

ID 010025A

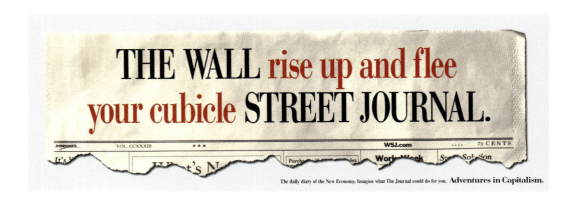

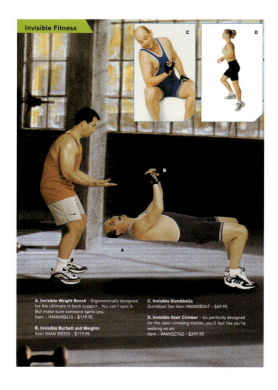

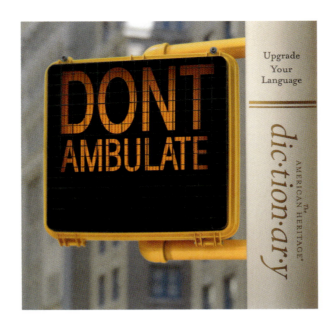

GOLD, SILVER, BRONZE

SILVER AWARD
Magazine Less Than a Page
B/W or Color: Campaign

ART DIRECTOR
Paul Laffy

WRITER
Brian Hayes

PHOTOGRAPHER
Dan Nourie

CLIENT
American Heritage Dictionary

AGENCY
Mullen, Wenham

ID 010026A

GOLD, SILVER, BRONZE

BRONZE AWARD
Magazine Less Than a Page
B/W or Color: Campaign

ART DIRECTORS
Eric King
Andy Azula

WRITERS
Harold Einstein
Jim Haven
Michael McKay

PHOTOGRAPHER
Hunter Freeman

CLIENT
Wall Street Journal

AGENCY
Goodby Silverstein & Partners/San Francisco

ID 010027A

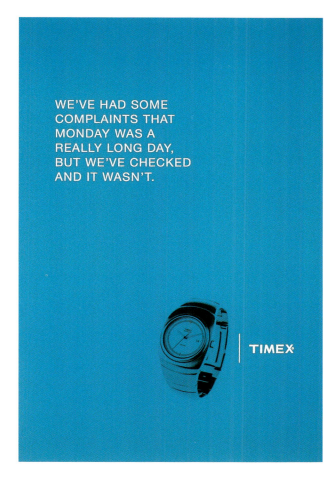

GOLD, SILVER, BRONZE

GOLD AWARD
Outdoor: Single

ART DIRECTOR
Richard Flintham

WRITER
Andy McLeod

PHOTOGRAPHER
Coppi Barbieri

CLIENT
UK Time-Timex

AGENCY
Fallon/London

ID 010028A

SILVER AWARD
Outdoor: Single

ART DIRECTOR
Dave Dye

WRITER
Sean Doyle

CLIENT
The Economist

AGENCY
Abbott Mead Vickers.BBDO/London

ID 010029A

GOLD, SILVER, BRONZE

BRONZE AWARD
Outdoor: Single

ART DIRECTOR
Alvaro Zunini

WRITERS
Carlos Betancourt
Saul Escobar
Rigoberto Gines
Alex Vazquez

PHOTOGRAPHERS
Marco Esperon
Abelardo Martin
Miguel Flores

CLIENT
Nike Mexico

AGENCY
J. Walter Thompson de Mexico/Mexico City

ID 010030A

GOLD, SILVER, BRONZE

SILVER AWARD
Outdoor: Campaign

ART DIRECTORS
Markus Bjurman
Kim Gehrig

WRITERS
Cecilia Dufils
Mark Waites
Joe De Souza

CLIENT
Britart.com

AGENCY
Mother Ltd./London

ID 010031A

GOLD, SILVER, BRONZE

GOLD AWARD
Guerilla Advertising

ART DIRECTORS
Billy McQueen
Quentin Pfiszter

WRITERS
Chris Schofield
Warwick Delmonte

PHOTOGRAPHER
Jacko Van Deventer

AGENCY PRODUCER
Ali Vernon

CLIENT
Television 3

AGENCY
Colenso BBDO/Auckland

ID 010032A

This concept utilized the disabled parking bays found next to the entrances of shopping malls. The bays were "doctored" before and during special visits by the 2000 South African Paralympic team of disabled athletes to meet their fans. An illustrator added the blur to the existing disabled icon and stenciled the Nike swoosh and the copy below it.

Non-permanent ink was used in all the executions. Complimentary press advertisements detailed the times and dates of the visits. Full permission for the executions was granted by the shopping centers' management and the National Paralympic Committee of South Africa.

GOLD, SILVER, BRONZE

SILVER AWARD
Guerilla

ART DIRECTOR
Colin Jones

WRITER
Michael Campbell

CLIENT
Coronet Books

AGENCY
Saatchi & Saatchi/London

ID 010033A

BRONZE AWARD
Guerilla

ART DIRECTOR
Michael Bond

WRITERS
Bernard Hunter
Leon Van Huyssteen

ILLUSTRATOR
Julian Dell

PHOTOGRAPHER
David Prior

CLIENT
Nike

AGENCY
The Jupiter Drawing Room
(South Africa)/Johannesburg

ID 010034A

GOLD, SILVER, BRONZE

SILVER AWARD
Trade B/W Full Page or Spread: Single

ART DIRECTORS
Jens Frank
Joerg Schrod
Thomas Hofbeck

WRITERS
Joerg Schrod
Jens Frank
Dr. Stephan Vogel

CLIENT
Ogilvy & Mather/Frankfurt

AGENCY
Ogilvy & Mather/Frankfurt

ID 010035A

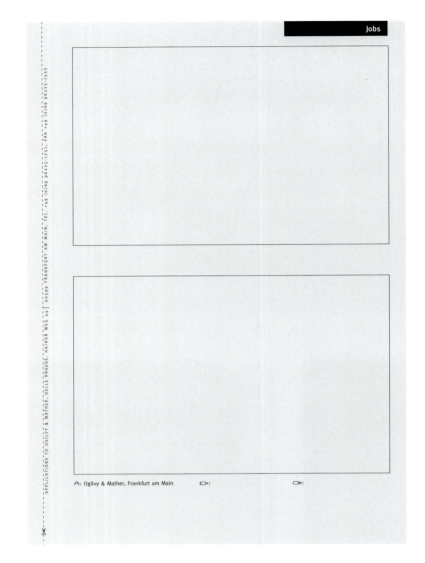

SILVER AWARD
Trade Color Full Page or Spread: Single

ART DIRECTOR
Steve Driggs

WRITER
Greg Hahn

PHOTOGRAPHER
Al Tielemans

CLIENT
Sports Illustrated

AGENCY
Fallon/Minneapolis

ID 010036A

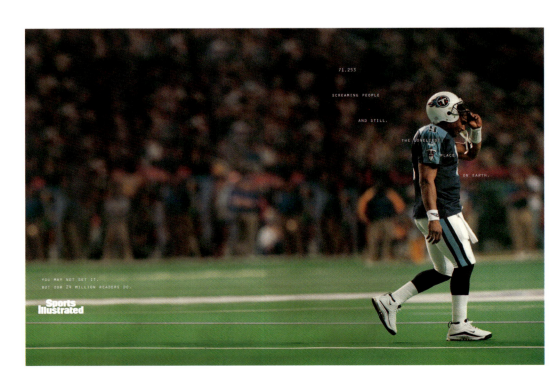

26

GOLD, SILVER, BRONZE

BRONZE AWARD
Trade Color Full Page
or Spread: Single

ART DIRECTOR
Faul Foulkes

WRITER
Tyler Hampton

ILLUSTRATOR
Greg Beauchamp

PHOTOGRAPHER
Stock

CLIENT
Advertising Club of
Los Angeles

AGENCY
Ground Zero/Los Angeles

ID 010037A

SILVER AWARD
Trade Less Than a Page B/W
or Color: Single

ART DIRECTOR
Jon Wyville

WRITER
Ken Erke

CLIENT
Checkered Past Records

AGENCY
Young & Rubicam/Chicago

ID 010038A

GOLD, SILVER, BRONZE

BRONZE AWARD
Trade Less Than a Page B/W or Color: Single

ART DIRECTOR
Jon Wyville

WRITER
Ken Erke

CLIENT
Checkered Past Records

AGENCY
Young & Rubicam/Chicago

ID 010039A

Also won:

MERIT AWARD
Collateral: Posters

---

teenage mom in food line CHRISTINA FUNK
homeless woman with sick dog LEENA WOO
homeless man with no leg JOE DESCH
single mom hooker JEANNE SHIELDS
blind man without cane ROBERT VANDENHOVEN
man with broken wheelchair NATE MILLER
alcoholic ambulance driver ADAM D'ANGELO
glass half empty guy GUY LEWELLEN

soundtrack available on
CHECKERED PAST RECORDS

GOT A REALLY BLEAK FILM THAT NEEDS SOME REALLY BLEAK MUSIC? CALL CHECKERED PAST RECORDS AT 773.404.8414 OR VISIT CHECKEREDPAST.COM FOR A FREE CD SAMPLER.

Dolby

GOLD, SILVER, BRONZE

SILVER AWARD
Trade B/W or Color Any
Size: Campaign

ART DIRECTORS
Tom Scharpf
Richard Mirabelli

WRITERS
Scott Cooney
Peter McHugh

PHOTOGRAPHER
Lorne Bridgman

CLIENT
Louder Music &
Sound Design

AGENCY
McHugh Worldwide/Edina

ID 010040A

GOLD, SILVER, BRONZE

SILVER AWARD
Trade B/W or Color
Any Size: Campaign

ART DIRECTOR
Sam Walker

WRITERS
Joe De Souza
James Jakob

ILLUSTRATOR
John Lucas

CLIENT
Premier Brands

AGENCY
Mother Ltd./London

ID 010041A

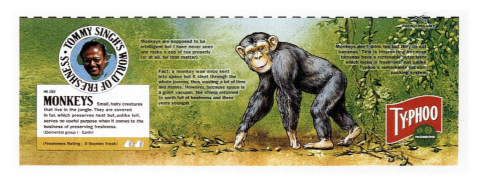

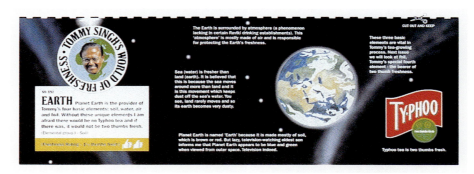

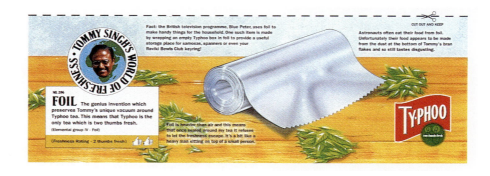

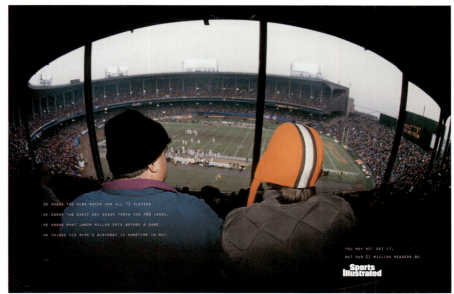

GOLD, SILVER, BRONZE

BRONZE AWARD
Trade B/W or Color
Any Size: Campaign

ART DIRECTOR
Steve Driggs

WRITER
Greg Hahn

PHOTOGRAPHERS
Al Tielemans
David Liamkyle
Robert Beck

CLIENT
Sports Illustrated

AGENCY
Fallon/Minneapolis

ID 010042A

GOLD, SILVER, BRONZE

SILVER AWARD
Collateral: Point of Purchase and In-Store

ART DIRECTOR
Bill Whitney

WRITER
Scott Jorgensen

ILLUSTRATOR
George Peters

CLIENT
Fuji Ya

AGENCY
Kruskopf Olson Advertising/Minneapolis

ID 010043A

BRONZE AWARD
Collateral: Point of Purchase and In-Store

ART DIRECTOR
Bill Whitney

WRITER
Scott Jorgensen

ILLUSTRATOR
George Peters

CLIENT
Fuji Ya

AGENCY
Kruskopf Olson Advertising/Minneapolis

ID 010044A

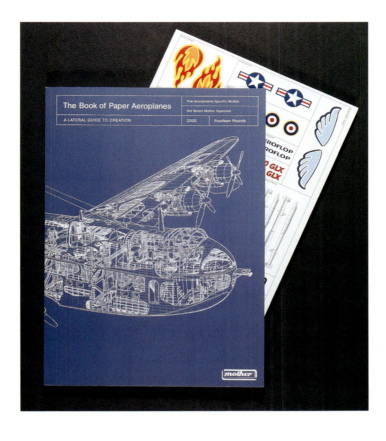

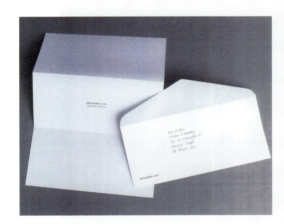

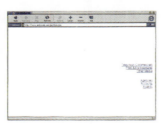

To get a job interview from several prominent Creative Directors, I bought their Internet domain names. E.g. danwieden.com, jeffgoodby.com, daviddroga.com, etc

I then sent them a direct mailer indicating that their personal Internet site is already online. They were each given a secret access password. This was to assure them that I didn't treat their domain name lightly. (The password shown in the above sample is bogus and for award presentation purposes only.)

When they logged in, they were redirected to my web site, andrewlok.com, where I offered to give them back their domain name in exchange for a job interview. They were also able to browse through my online portfolio if they wished.

GOLD, SILVER, BRONZE

SILVER AWARD
Collateral: Self-Promotion

ART DIRECTOR
Peter Vicksten

WRITER
Chad Rea

CLIENT
Mother Ltd.

AGENCY
Mother Ltd./London

ID 010045A

BRONZE AWARD
Collateral: Self-Promotion

ART DIRECTORS
Andrew Lok
Martin Loo

WRITER
Andrew Lok

CLIENT
Andrew Lok

AGENCY
onemanbrand.com/Singapore

ID 010046A

GOLD, SILVER, BRONZE

GOLD AWARD
Collateral: Posters

ART DIRECTOR
Borja Arteaga

WRITERS
Borja Arteaga
Jaume Rodriguez

ILLUSTRATOR
Borja Arteaga

PHOTOGRAPHER
Stock

CLIENT
BMW Iberia

AGENCY
* S, C, P, F/Barcelona

ID 010047A

Also won:

MERIT AWARD
Magazine Color Full Page
or Spread: Single

SILVER AWARD
Collateral: Posters

ART DIRECTOR
Paul Keister

WRITER
Ari Merkin

PHOTOGRAPHER
Brian Wilder

CLIENT
Giro Sport Design

AGENCY
Crispin Porter & Bogusky/
Miami

ID 010049A

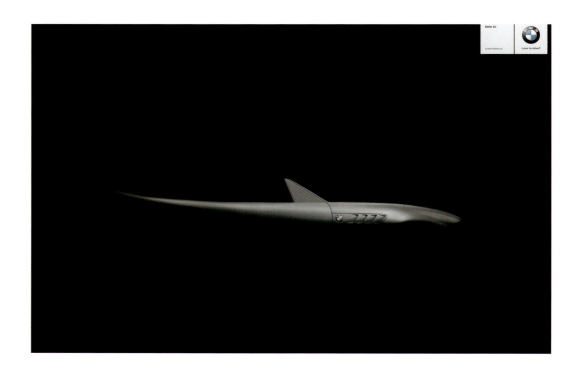

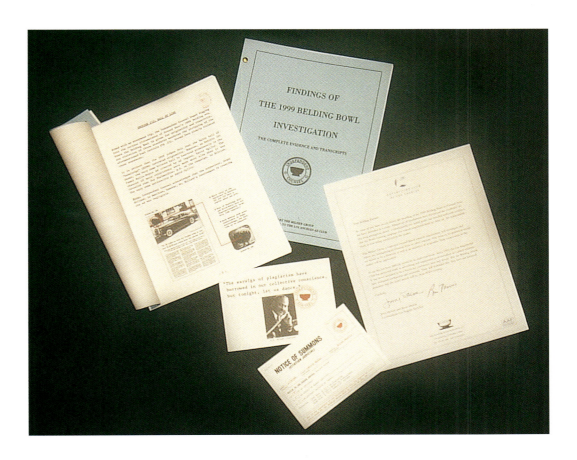

GOLD, SILVER, BRONZE

SILVER AWARD
Collateral: Posters

ART DIRECTOR
Paul Foulkes

WRITER
Tyler Hampton

ILLUSTRATOR
Greg Beauchamp

PHOTOGRAPHER
Stock

CLIENT
Advertising Club of
Los Angeles

AGENCY
Ground Zero/Los Angeles

ID 010048A

BRONZE AWARD
Collateral: Posters

ART DIRECTOR
Jack Fund

WRITER
Jack Fund

PHOTOGRAPHER
Tom Nelson

CLIENT
Gold's Gym International

AGENCY
JACK/Venice

ID 010050A

Also won:

MERIT AWARD
Magazine Color Full Page
or Spread: Single

35

GOLD, SILVER, BRONZE

GOLD AWARD
Public Service/Political
Newspaper or Magazine:
Single

ART DIRECTOR
Matt Mowat

WRITER
Chuck Meehan

PHOTOGRAPHERS
Robert Cappa
Steve Peixotto
Jackson Hill
US Army Corps

CLIENT
National D-Day Museum

AGENCY
GMO Hill Holliday/
San Francisco

ID 010051A

Also won:

MERIT AWARD
Public Service/Political
Outdoor and Posters

SILVER AWARD
Public Service/Political
Newspaper or Magazine:
Single

ART DIRECTORS
Kent Suter
Tia Doar

WRITER
Ginger Robinson

CLIENT
Willamette Week/BPN

AGENCY
Borders Perrin
Norrander/Portland

ID 010052A

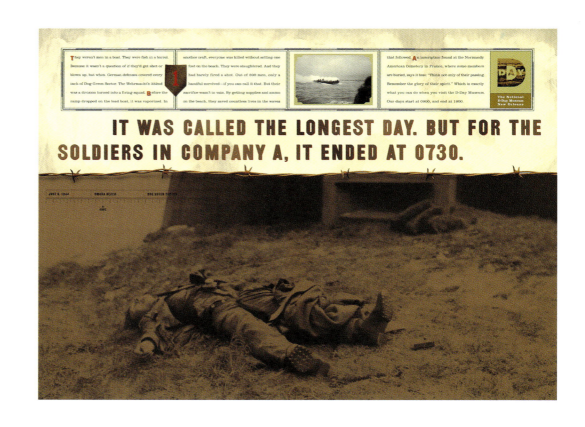

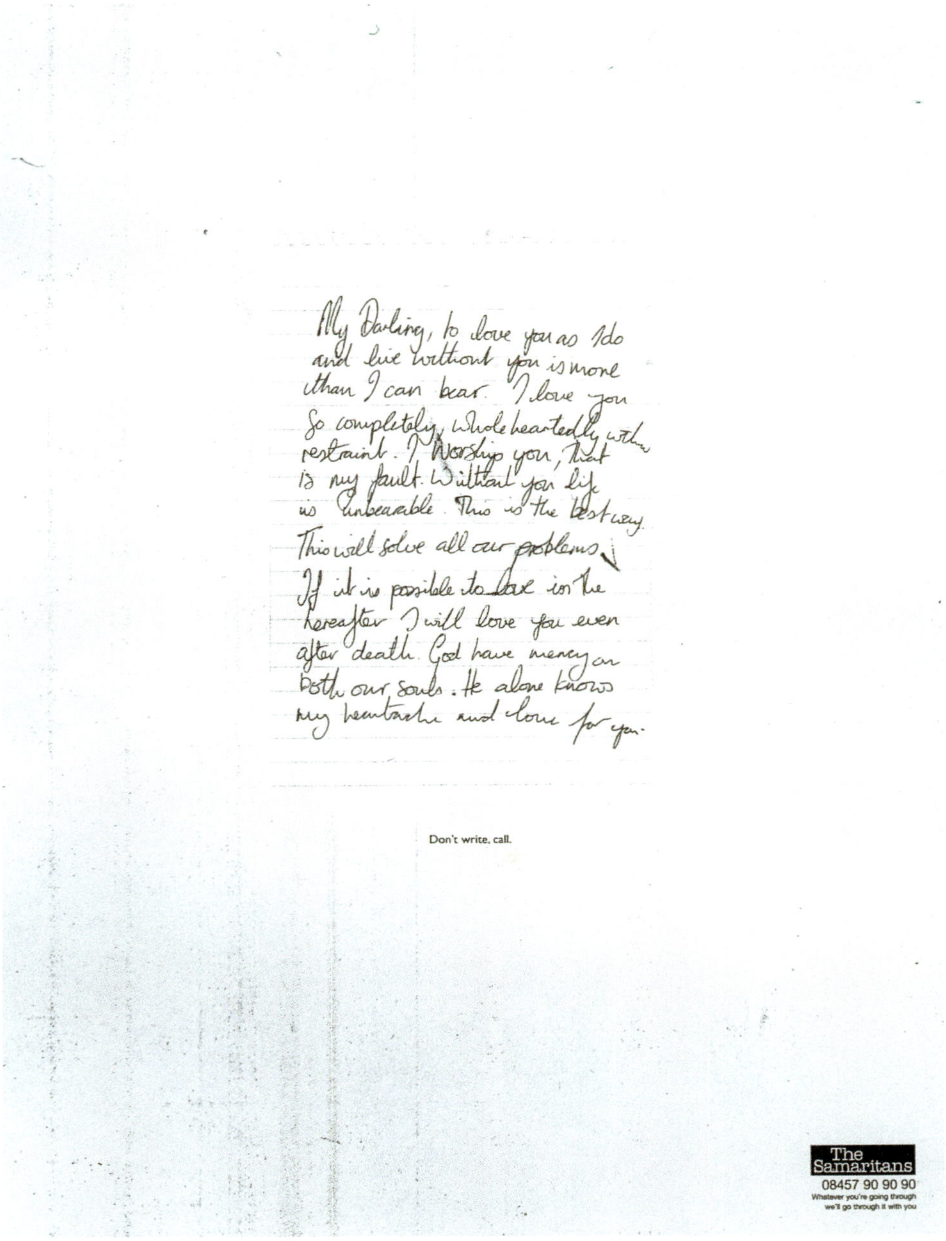

> My Darling, to love you as I do and live without you is more than I can bear. I love you so completely, wholeheartedly, without restraint. I worship you, that is my fault. Without you life is unbearable. This is the best way. This will solve all our problems. If it is possible to love in the hereafter I will love you even after death. God have mercy on both our souls. He alone knows my heartache and love for you.

Don't write, call.

The Samaritans
08457 90 90 90
Whatever you're going through
we'll go through it with you

GOLD, SILVER, BRONZE

BRONZE AWARD
Public Service/Political
Newspaper or Magazine:
Single

ART DIRECTOR
Sue Higgs

WRITER
Sue Higgs

CLIENT
The Samaritans

AGENCY
Ogilvy/London

ID 010053A

GOLD, SILVER, BRONZE

GOLD AWARD
Public Service/Political
Newspaper or Magazine:
Campaign

ART DIRECTOR
Paul Belford

WRITER
Nigel Roberts

PHOTOGRAPHER
Paul Belford

CLIENT
The Big Issue Foundation

AGENCY
TBWA/London

ID 010054A

Tonight, kids will be wandering the streets, amongst pissheads, pushers, pickpockets, never a policeman when you need one, prostitutes, perverts and pimps. They'll scavenge for food and beg for money. Then they'll try and find a doorway that someone hasn't pissed or puked in, where they can wait for the morning. And that's their idea of being safe. Safer than houses. Because their house is where they were sexually abused, and threatened with what would happen if they ever dared tell anyone about 'their little secret'. Or their house was where they were beaten, not smacked. Punched. Beaten the crap out of. They're not stupid. They know that running away is no adventure. But they will never go home. One in three of them attempts suicide. Those that fail are in and out of care until they're old enough to stay out. It's how a lot of young people end up living rough. The Big Issue Foundation knows that helping them isn't merely about getting a roof over their heads. We also have to understand what's going on in their heads. So what is it that can make someone who trusts almost no one trust us? We never push. And we're not out to reach any targets. If anyone decides to sell The Big Issue it's because they need the cash, and The Big Issue is pretty much the only legal way they can earn it. When they collect the magazines, they become aware that The Big Issue Foundation offers support for drink and drug addictions, advice and training for jobs, and of course, help with accommodation. But there's no pressure on anyone to take it. If someone does want to change their life, then they have to do it themselves, but not by themselves.

If cold, wet, hungry and scared is what thousands of kids run away to, imagine what they run away from.

Drug addict? Alcoholic? Suicidal?
Apparently, what you need is a nice cup of hot soup.

Cream of tomato, mushroom or even spicy lentil, with or without croutons, is unlikely to have ever satisfied the obsessive cravings of your average crack addict. If mulligatawny is a more effective way of blocking out the abject misery of someone's particular existence than a can or two of super strength lager, then it would probably be illegal by now, or at least a lot more expensive than that. And if leek and potato really is so comforting that it's ever given a whole new reason to carry on living to the most clinically depressed, then it's news to us. Not that we'd suggest for a moment that anyone should stop giving free soup to homeless people. They're glad of it. Anything is better than nothing. But other people's consciences can be all too easily satisfied by the knowledge that the homeless can always queue up for their nightly broth. They won't starve to death so that's enough is it? We, The Big Issue Foundation don't think so. People become homeless for any number of different reasons. Things go wrong at some point in their lives. Then they remain homeless for the simple reason that they come to accept their predicament, because they don't know how they can change it. Apart, that is, from those who start selling The Big Issue magazine. Earning money starts to rebuild their self-esteem. And when the vendors turn up to collect their magazines, they discover that we offer help with most of the root causes of homelessness: mental illness, various addictions and long-term unemployment. The Big Issue Foundation exists because we believe that every homeless person has the potential to change their life.

Litter, terrible isn't it? And dog muck.
Something really should be done about that.
Oh yes, and homeless people.

Are you worried about the homeless? Worried that they're spoiling your town or city? Worried that they might get drunk and use offensive language? Worried that they may be on drugs and planning to burgle your lovely home to fuel their filthy habit? Or do you just ignore them? Can you ignore the fact that amongst the 2500 people sleeping rough throughout Britain tonight, up to half of them will be mentally ill? There are pregnant women, children, old and infirm people. Roughly half of them are physically ill. Few of them can do anything about it because only a quarter of the country's GPs will register them. This is why their average life expectancy is just 42. How many years would that leave you? People in the UK are actually dying of homelessness. Realise and remember that these are people who've come from ordinary walks of life. Something went wrong for them. The sort of thing that can happen to any of us. You included. So who does care? There are a number of organisations who help rough sleepers by providing them with some form of accommodation. It's a start. But the homeless tend to need more than just a roof over their heads. Because charity alone does nothing for a person's self-esteem. The Big Issue Foundation helps homeless people regain the dignity of independence. Selling The Big Issue is a chance to earn. We offer help and support for addictions and mental illness, advice and training for employment, and of course, assistance in finding accommodation. Unfortunately, not enough people realise that each and every homeless person has the potential to change their life. And we think that's terrible.

How can you heroin sort your life heroin out when the heroin only thing heroin you heroin can heroin think heroin about heroin is heroin?

You're freezing your arse off in some doorway every night, you've got no job, no money, and sod all chance of any of it changing. You haven't got any answers but someone's got heroin. There's always someone who's got heroin. Risks? You haven't got anything to lose, remember. So you get off your face and you feel great. You don't have to think when you're wasted. It's a holiday for your brain. But it's only a short trip. It wears off and your life is still crap. If anything, it seems worse. But at least you've got something to look forward to now. The more you use it, the harder it gets to find the money for it, the more you value it, the more you want it, the harder it is to find the money they you owe for it, the more you need it, the harder it is to think about anything else. Alcohol's kind of the same. Give it up? Oh yeah, right. Why? Just because some dickhead in a duffel coat who's read a couple of Irvine Welsh books is telling you that they understand? Words are cheap. Nothing else is. Selling The Big Issue magazine is a way to earn a bit of cash. No strings. No self-righteousness. No law against it. When the vendors come to collect their magazines each week, they get to know about The Big Issue Foundation, that we offer support to help break addictions. We also offer help with mental illnesses, advice and training for jobs, and, of course, assistance with accommodation. It's there if they want it. But there's absolutely no pressure to take it. And that's why hundreds do, every year. The Foundation exists because we believe that homeless people all have the potential to change their lives.

There's no shortage of beds being offered to homeless young people.
But only for half an hour in the nearest cheap hotel.

How much for a blow job? Seriously, think about it. How much would you, male or female, have to be paid to give a dodgy stranger a blow job? And how much if it's without a condom? What about anal sex then? You probably can't even begin to consider an answer. But if you're young, homeless, cold, hungry, desperate and confused enough, twenty or thirty quid might cover it. maybe even just a tenner if you're craving some drugs or alcohol. And if your sexuality's already been scarred by some kind of abuse in the past, maybe it's the reason you became homeless in the first place, then selling your body to the first deviant that wants it will probably seem that bit less abhorrent. Of the two and a half thousand people who will sleep rough around Britain tonight, the youngest are the most vulnerable. While The Big Issue Foundation is doing everything it can to help homeless people re-enter society, we also have to try and stem the flow of kids dropping out of it. Education authorities, youth organisations and parents aren't doing enough to make kids aware of how easy it is to disappear from the system, and of the grim realities of homelessness. For the young people who are learning those realities from experience, selling copies of The Big Issue magazine means a safer and legal way to earn some cash. Vendors discover that we offer help and support for addictions and mental illness, advice and training for employment, and, of course, assistance in finding accommodation. The Big Issue Foundation believes that homeless people, however old, all have the potential to change their lives.

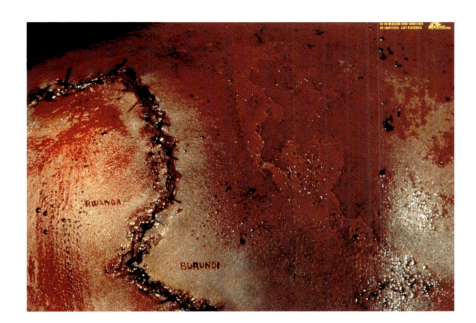
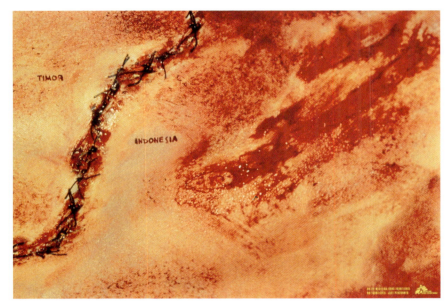
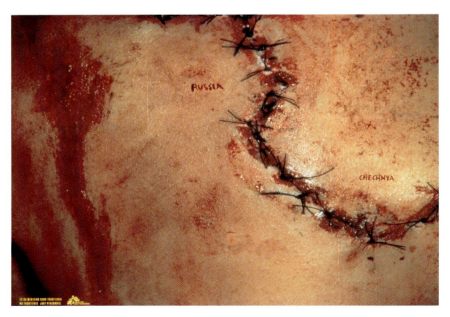

GOLD, SILVER, BRONZE

SILVER AWARD
Public Service/Political
Newspaper or Magazine:
Campaign

ART DIRECTOR
Andres Martinez

PHOTOGRAPHER
Santiago Esteban

CLIENT
Médecins Sans Frontiéres

AGENCY
McCann-Erickson/Madrid

ID 01055A

GOLD, SILVER, BRONZE

BRONZE AWARD
Public Service/Political
Newspaper or Magazine:
Campaign

ART DIRECTORS
Ted Royer
Laura Soudan

WRITER
Fernando Bellotti

ILLUSTRATOR
Mario Franco

CLIENT
Museo de la Ciudad
(Museum of the City)

AGENCY
Ogilvy & Mather Argentina/
Buenos Aires

ID 010056A

GOLD, SILVER, BRONZE

GOLD AWARD
Public Service/Political:
Outdoor and Posters

ART DIRECTORS
Sal DeVito
Greg Braun

WRITERS
Sal DeVito
Joel Tractenberg

PHOTOGRAPHER
Robert Ammirati

CLIENT
ACLU

AGENCY
DeVito/Verdi/New York

ID 010057A

GOLD, SILVER, BRONZE

SILVER AWARD
Public Service/Political:
Outdoor and Posters

ART DIRECTOR
Liz Otremba

WRITERS
Eric Husband
Dave Keepper

PHOTOGRAPHER
Curtis Johnson

CLIENT
Minneapolis League of
Women Voters

AGENCY
Colle + McVoy/Minneapolis

ID 010058A

BRONZE AWARD
Public Service/Political:
Outdoor and Posters

ART DIRECTOR
Chris Robb

WRITER
John Hage

CLIENT
Los Angeles Dance
Invitational

AGENCY
Miller Group Advertising/
Santa Monica

ID 010059A

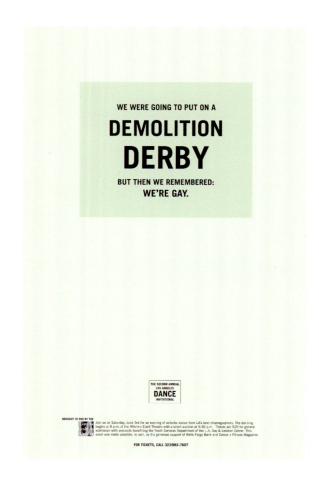

42

GOLD, SILVER, BRONZE

GOLD AWARD
Public Service/Political
Collateral: Brochures &
Direct Mail

ART DIRECTOR
Jeff DeChausse

WRITER
Jim Schmidt

CLIENT
Physicians for
Human Rights

AGENCY
Euro RSCG McConnaughy
Tatham/Chicago

ID 010060A

WWF Hotel Room Promotion.

We went to the delegates' hotel rooms. We turned the room temperature up to a maximum. We attached the cards to the air-condition regulators. This happened during the World Climate Conference, The Hague, Nov. 13-24, 2000.

BRONZE AWARD
Public Service/Political
Collateral: Brochures &
Direct Mail

ART DIRECTORS
Marco Weber
Thomas Hofbeck

WRITERS
Karolin Weisser
Dr. Stephan Vogel

CLIENT
WWF Germany

AGENCY
Ogilvy & Mather/Frankfurt

ID 010061A

GOLD, SILVER, BRONZE

GOLD AWARD
Public Service/Political Radio: Single

WRITERS
Natalie Knight
Josh Robbins
Glenn Wood

AGENCY PRODUCERS
Alesa Tong
Jen Storey

CLIENT
Youthline

AGENCY
Colenso BBDO/Auckland

ID 010062A

(In this campaign, actors posing as desperate young people cold called unsuspecting strangers in an attempt to talk about their problems. The following is a transcript of one such conversation.)

SFX:	Phone ringing.
WOMAN:	Yeah, hello.
GIRL:	Oh hello, um…you don't know me, I just needed to talk to someone.
WOMAN:	Who is…who is this?
GIRL:	It's just that my Mum, my Mum's hit me again and she hits me all the time. *(getting more upset)* And my Dad doesn't do anything about it, and I know that he knows, I know he knows, and I don't understand why he won't help me. *(The girl begins to cry.)*
WOMAN:	What phone number did you call?
GIRL:	I, I, I, didn't have anyone to talk to, I rang Youthline but the lines were all busy, I…What am I supposed to do?
WOMAN:	Did you just call a number out of the blue…?
GIRL:	Yeah, I'm so sorry. I'm not a bad person, I'm not. I'm not, I mean I know she thinks I am, but I'm not. I'm not…
WOMAN:	You're not bad and you've done the right thing calling.
GIRL:	I just can't cope anymore.
VOICEOVER:	At Youthline we only have enough phone lines to answer a third of our calls so if we can't help, who will? To make a donation call 0800 543 943 and please give generously.

SILVER AWARD
Public Service/Political Radio: Single

WRITERS
Vicente Navarro
Paco Conde

AGENCY PRODUCER
Olga Lopez

CLIENT
ILGA (International Lesbians & Gays Association)

AGENCY
Saatchi & Saatchi/Madrid

ID 010063A

ANNOUNCER 1:	Course for gays on how to appear straight. Third lesson. Repeat after me. What a great bird.
STUDENTS:	What-a-great-bird.
ANNOUNCER 1:	That blond has great airbags.
STUDENTS:	That-blond-has-great-airbags.
ANNOUNCER 1:	Yesterday I did it with Sonia.
STUDENTS:	Yesterday-I-did-it-with-Sonia.
ANNOUNCER 1:	Will you marry me?
STUDENTS:	Will-you-ma-rry-me?
ANNOUNCER 2:	If you are gay in a country like Afghanistan this could save your life. There, homosexuals are persecuted, jailed and even executed. ILGA is working so that nobody, whatever their sexual orientation, has to hide. If you want more information visit us on: ilga.org.

SFX: Busy railway station atmosphere, hustle, bustle and chatter.

(A slightly echoey tannoy announcement cuts through the noise. The voice is Liverpudlian.)

TANNOY: The next train to depart from platform five is the 13.10 to London Euston. Calling at Runcorn, Crewe, Birmingham New Street, Coventry, Rugby, Watford Junction, London Euston, homelessness, drug addiction and prostitution.

VOICEOVER: Every year 24,000 young girls arrive in London with nowhere to go. Many of them end up vulnerable and on the streets. Help Centrepoint reach them before someone else does. Call 0800 23 23 20 to make a donation.

SFX: Wind sweeping over dry land.

ANNOUNCER: In 1993 Kevin Carter was photographing a famine in Africa. As he focused on a tiny girl struggling to get to a feeding station, a vulture landed a few feet away. Carter took the picture, then chased away the bird, weeping afterward at what he'd seen. When the picture appeared, some readers were moved to send aid. Others sent hate mail to Carter for picking up the camera instead of the child, unaware that he was prohibited from doing so. He died a year later, an apparent suicide.

SFX: Music under/wind continues.

ANNOUNCER: Kevin Carter's unforgettable photo is part of *The Pulitzer Prize Photographs, Capture the Moment*, now on exhibit at the Newseum. Fifty-eight years of prize-winning photographs are on display along with the stories that describe what the photographers had to go through to get the pictures. Including wrestling their own consciences.

SFX: Music out/wind continues.

ANNOUNCER: The Pulitzer Prize Photographs, now at the Newseum in Arlington.

SFX: Wind out.

(Sound comes up on a conversation between an officer and a soldier. Throughout the commercial, you only hear the officer's voice, leaving the listener to imagine what the soldier's replies are.)

OFFICER: The only transport for 20 Ks is this 8 tonner. But the radiator's knackered. What do you think—can you fix it? *(pause where the soldier would be replying)* With a jerry can? *(to his men)* You heard him—find him one now! *(to the soldier)* How long will it take? *(pause where the soldier would be replying)* Half an hour! Mechanic, you're a miracle worker.

VOICEOVER: Right now, the Army has gaps for Vehicle Mechanics. If you think you could fill a gap, call into your local Army Careers Office.

SUPER: Army Mechanic. Be the Best.

GOLD, SILVER, BRONZE

BRONZE AWARD
Public Service/Political Radio: Single

WRITERS
Martin Gillan
Dave Lang

AGENCY PRODUCER
Ginny Wood

CLIENT
Centrepoint-Young Homelessness

AGENCY
WCRS/London

ID 010064A

SILVER AWARD
Public Service/Political Radio: Campaign

WRITER
Lisa Biskin

AGENCY PRODUCERS
Sandy Mislang
Corinne Paulsen

PRODUCTION COMPANY
Audio Master

CLIENT
Newseum

AGENCY
Adworks/Washington

ID 010065A

BRONZE AWARD
Public Service/Political Radio: Campaign

WRITERS
Mike McKenna
Greg Martin

AGENCY PRODUCERS
Jonathan Netts
Brian Jenkins

CLIENT
COI/Army

AGENCY
Saatchi & Saatchi/London

ID 010066A

GOLD, SILVER, BRONZE

GOLD AWARD
Public Service/Political
Television: Single

ART DIRECTOR
Rob Dow

WRITER
Nigel Dawson

AGENCY PRODUCER
Susie Cole

PRODUCTION COMPANY
Filmgraphics

DIRECTOR
Mat Humphrey

CLIENT
Transport Accident Commission

AGENCY
Grey Worldwide/Melbourne

ID 010067A

(The commercial moves back and forth between the scene of a car crash, a party, and a father talking about his daughter, who died in the crash.)

RUSSEL: Julie! Julie!

JULIE: Happy birthday, Dad!

AMBULANCE OFFICER: Can you hear me? Talk to me? What's your first name?

RUSSELL: Russell.

AMBULANCE OFFICER: Man she is 83.

RUSSELL: What's happened to Julie?

AMBULANCE OFFICER: Just keep looking straight ahead, Russell.

JULIE: Dad, I was not!

DAD: You were that high!

JULIE'S FATHER VOICEOVER: I'll never see her again.

RUSSEL: We should probably get going.

JULIE: Yeah.

JULIE'S FATHER VOICEOVER: Never hear her voice.

JULIE: Happy birthday, Dad.

JULIE'S FATHER: Thanks, sweetheart.

JULIE: No worries.

JULIE'S FATHER VOICEOVER: …never hear her laugh.

JULIE'S FATHER: Take care of my baby girl.

RUSSELL: I will.

JULIE'S FATHER VOICEOVER: I'll never see her get married.

JULIE (getting into car): Sure you don't want me to drive?

RUSSELL: I'm alright…I've only had a few. Besides, I've been eating your mother's food all day.

JULIE'S FATHER VOICEOVER: Cuddle her children.

JULIE'S FATHER ON LOCATION: You said she was here…where is she? Oh my god…Julie!

RUSSELL: Oh shit! No!

JULIE'S FATHER VOICEOVER: Never hear her call me Dad.

JULIE'S FATHER ON LOCATION: Russ!

JULIE'S FATHER: And I'll never forget having to choose her coffin. My beautiful baby!

SUPER: If you drink, then drive, you're a bloody idiot. TAC.

GOLD, SILVER, BRONZE

SILVER AWARD
Public Service/Political
Television: Single

ART DIRECTOR
Nick Wootton

WRITER
Jonathan John

AGENCY PRODUCER
Henrietta Curzon

PRODUCTION COMPANY
H₃O Films

DIRECTOR
Charles Hendley

CLIENT
Special Olympics

AGENCY
J. Walter Thompson/London

ID 010068A

BRONZE AWARD
Public Service/Political
Television: Single

ART DIRECTOR
Peter Souter

WRITERS
Peter Souter
Paul Weiland

AGENCY PRODUCER
Mary Francis

PRODUCTION COMPANY
Paul Weiland Film Co.

DIRECTOR
Paul Weiland

CLIENT
Timebank

AGENCY
Abbott Mead
Vickers.BBDO/London

ID 010069A

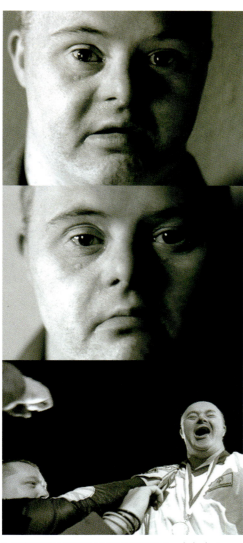

A MAN WITH DOWN'S SYNDROME: People look at you. They stare. They all stare. They shout things. They make you feel different. It's fantastic.

SFX: Enthusiastic crowd.

SUPER: Special Olympics. Be a part of it.

SFX: Music throughout.

VOICEOVER: An old lady's dogs giving up half an hour to exercise a draughtsman.

VOICEOVER: A class of seven year olds giving up an afternoon to let a stockbroker play.

VOICEOVER: A hospital vegetable garden giving up a day to help an accountant unwind.

VOICEOVER: A group of blind children giving up a morning to make a homeless person feel needed.

VOICEOVER: Young offenders giving up an hour or two to entertain a drama teacher.

VOICEOVER: A child with Down's Syndrome giving up two hours to make a computer operator smile.

SUPER: Timebank logo. www.bbc.co.uk/timebank.

VOICEOVER: Call Timebank to match your time and passions to the needs of your local community. Timebank. You get more out than you put in.

GOLD, SILVER, BRONZE

BRONZE AWARD
Public Service/Political
Television: Single

ART DIRECTOR
Alex Burnard

WRITER
Ari Merkin

AGENCY PRODUCER
Keith Dezen

PRODUCTION COMPANY
Redtree Productions

DIRECTOR
Christian Hoagland

CLIENT
American Legacy Foundation

AGENCY
Crispin Porter & Bogusky/Miami

ID 010070A

SUPER: Outside a major tobacco company.

TEENAGERS: Let's go, let's go. Go, go.

TEEN 1: Hey, excuse me! Sorry to bother you but we've got a question. Do you know how many people tobacco kills everyday? Would you say 20? Thirty? A hundred? *(pause)* You know what, we're gonna leave this here for you, so you can see what 1200 people actally look like. Keep all of them up, guys.

SUPER: truth/thetruth.com.

SFX:	Music up.
ANNOUNCER:	Bud Light presents…Real. American. Heroes.
SINGER:	Real American Heroes…
ANNOUNCER:	Today we salute you…Mr. Really Bad Toupee Wearer.
SINGER:	Mr. Really Bad Toupee Wearer.
ANNOUNCER:	More than any neon sign or exploding scoreboard ever could, your chrome-dome cover says, "Hey, guys, look at me."
SINGER:	What could you be thinkin'?
ANNOUNCER:	You think it looks natural, but it couldn't look phonier if it had a chinstrap!
SINGER:	Couldn't fool a blind man…
ANNOUNCER:	Made of space age fibers, "it" can repel anything. Rain. Wind. Snow. And especially…young women.
SINGERS:	I don't think so!
ANNOUNCER:	So crack open an ice cold Bud Light, Mr. Stud in a Rug. *(Beer pops open.)* Then crack open another for that thing on your head.
SINGERS:	I don't think it's on straight…
ANNOUNCER:	Bud Light Beer, Anheuser-Busch, St. Louis, Missouri.

GOLD, SILVER, BRONZE

GOLD AWARD
Consumer Radio: Single

WRITER
John Immesoete

AGENCY PRODUCER
Sam Pillsbury

CLIENT
Anheuser-Busch

AGENCY
DDB/Chicago

ID 010071A

SFX:	Music up.
ANNOUNCER:	Bud Light presents…Real. American. Heroes.
SINGER:	Real American Heroes…
ANNOUNCER:	Today we salute you…Mr. Pickled Pigs Feet Eater.
SINGER:	Mr. Pickled Pigs Feet Eater.
ANNOUNCER:	Ignoring all you know about pigs and where they live and what they step in, you look at their pickled paws and say, "yummy."
SINGER:	Lookin' tasty…
ANNOUNCER:	Craving only the most daring meal, you pass up the cow tongue, skate by the head cheese, dismiss the Rocky Mountain Oysters.
SINGERS:	Rocky Mountain Oysters…
ANNOUNCER:	But a pig's foot soaked in pickle juice, now that's good eatin'!
SINGER:	Save me a big one!
ANNOUNCER:	So crack open an ice cold Bud Light, Mr. Pickled Pigs Feet Eater. *(Beer pops open.)* Because it takes guts to eat those feet.
SINGER:	Thank you, Mr. Pickled Pigs Feet Eater…
ANNOUNCER:	Bud Light Beer, Anheuser-Busch, St. Louis, Missouri.

SILVER AWARD
Consumer Radio: Single

WRITER
John Immesoete

AGENCY PRODUCER
Sam Pillsbury

CLIENT
Anheuser-Busch

AGENCY
DDB/Chicago

ID 010072A

GOLD, SILVER, BRONZE

BRONZE AWARD
Consumer Radio: Single

WRITERS
Bill Cimino
Mark Gross

AGENCY PRODUCER
Sam Pillsbury

CLIENT
Anheuser-Busch

AGENCY
DDB/Chicago

ID 010073A

SINGER:	Real American Heroes…
ANNOUNCER:	Today we salute you…Mr. Chinese Food Delivery Guy. Without you we'd be forced to do the unthinkable when we wanted Chinese food—drive to a restaurant.
SINGER:	Mu-shu-gai-pan!
ANNOUNCER:	But you, sir, bring it to us in under 20.
SINGER:	Ride like the wind…
ANNOUNCER:	Armed with your rickety bike, you battle traffic, bad weather and the occasional busted elevator. And why do you do it? 'Cause somewhere a guy is waiting for his Kung-pao crab puffs and he's got $1.57 with your name on it.
SINGERS:	That's ten percent.
ANNOUNCER:	So crack open an ice cold Bud Light, *(Beer pops open.)* oh mercenary of the mandarin chicken, and know that when America is looking for a man to get the job done, you do…deliver.
SINGERS:	You deliver…
ANNOUNCER:	Bud Light Beer, Anheuser-Busch, St. Louis, Missouri.

BRONZE AWARD
Consumer Radio: Single

WRITERS
Brian Ahern
Wayne Best
Donna Foster

AGENCY PRODUCER
Erika Shufelt

CLIENT
Foodline

AGENCY
dweck!/New York

ID 010074A

PHONE GIRL:	Restaurant reservations?
FARHOD:	I need reservations, 8 o'clock Friday.
PHONE GIRL:	I'm sorry, we're fully committed.
FARHOD:	Time for plan B. You force me to name drop. Okay, then, I'm award winning actor, Mr. Nironron. Don't pretend you don't know me. I sit courtside at all the basketball matches. You saw my movies. You talking toward me, you talking towards me? You make me want a better man. No no, you you make me want to make a better men. You know what I mean. Please give me a table.
PHONE GIRL:	Look, I know you're not famous.
FARHOD:	Yes I am. You, you you can't handle my truths. Are you trying to seduce me, Mrs. Robertson?
PHONE GIRL:	Goodbye.
FARHOD:	You had me on hello? I hear dead people.
VOICEOVER:	You don't need to impersonate anyone to get a table, just log on to Foodline.com. Make online restaurant reservations, browse through reviews and more all in one place, Foodline.com. Get inside restaurants.

GOLD AWARD
Consumer Radio: Campaign

WRITER
Aaron Allen

AGENCY PRODUCER
Stacy McClain

CLIENT
OurHouse.com

AGENCY
Black Rocket/San Francisco

ID 010075A

WOMAN:	Morning. You're up early for a Saturday.
MAN:	Yeah, I'm gonna build a deck today.
WOMAN:	Is there a game on or something?
MAN:	No seriously, I'm building a deck. You don't believe me?
WOMAN:	No.
MAN:	*(pause)* It's not that hard.
WOMAN:	I'll tell you what, if you build us a deck, I'll take off all my clothes and barbecue you a steak…Stanley?…Stanley?
ANNOUNCER 1:	Tools. Advice. House calls. Sanity. Everything you need to fix up your house, or have it done for you. OurHouse.com. We're here to help. Partnered with Ace.

MAN:	Hey, honey?
WOMAN:	Hi, sweetie.
MAN:	Were you doing something to the lawn?
WOMAN:	Yeah, I put in a sprinkler system.
MAN:	What?
WOMAN:	I put in a sprinkler system.
MAN:	When did you do that?
WOMAN:	Today.
MAN:	But how…Really?
WOMAN:	Yep.
MAN:	I would've done that.
WOMAN:	Oh, that's okay. It was kind of fun.
MAN:	Does it work?
WOMAN:	What?
MAN:	Nothing. You know those trenches have to be at least ten inches deep or the pipes will freeze.
WOMAN:	Yeah, I know. They're 17.
MAN:	*(long pause)* Don't use my conditioner, okay?
WOMAN:	I'm not.
ANNOUNCER:	Tools. Materials. Advice. Sanity. OurHouse.com. We're here to help. Partnered with Ace.

HUSBAND:	Well maybe we should push into the Q4…
SFX:	Cell phone rings.
HUSBAND:	Sorry. Excuse me.
COWORKER:	No, go ahead.
HUSBAND *(whispering)*:	Hello? Hey, can I call you back…because I can't talk now…because I'm in a meeting…What do you mean the shower shocked you?…How is it my fault?…Because I wanted a dimmer switch in the bathroom….For mood…*(louder)*…For mood….Well that's your opinion…Listen, I gotta…I didn't install it upside down….I just know…I just do…I don't know, hold onto something rubber before you turn it on…Like a tennis ball…It has rubber on the inside. Listen sweetie, I can't do this now. Okay, I gotta go, Bye.
SFX:	Cell phone beeps off.
SUPER:	Tools. Advice. House calls. Sanity. Everything you need to fix up your house or have it done for you. Ourhouse.com. We're here to help. Partnered with Ace.

GOLD, SILVER, BRONZE

SILVER AWARD
Consumer Radio: Campaign

WRITERS
Rob Tarry
Joe Piccolo

AGENCY PRODUCER
Jacqueline Burgmann

CLIENT
Earl's Restaurant

AGENCY
Rethink/Vancouver

ID 010076A

ANNOUNCER: Earl's presents, the joys of eating at home…Delivery guys.
DELIVERY GUY: *(door buzzer, and lots of static throughout)* Pizza guy.
WOMAN: Come on in!
DELIVERY GUY: *(door buzzer)* Pizza guy.
WOMAN: Where are you?
DELIVERY GUY: Downstairs.
WOMAN: Well I'm buzzing you—
DELIVERY GUY: It's not working.
WOMAN: You have to pull it open when I—
DELIVERY GUY: What's that? Push?
WOMAN: No. Pull. *(door buzzer)* No, wait till I buzz—What are you doing—
DELIVERY GUY: Pizza guy.
WOMAN: Wha— *(door buzzer)*
ANNOUNCER: Earl's. You could eat at home. But why?

BRONZE AWARD
Consumer Radio: Campaign

WRITERS
Adam Chasnow
Richard Bullock
Ian Reichenthal

AGENCY PRODUCER
Leigh Fuchs

CLIENT
Hollywood Video

AGENCY
Cliff Freeman and Partners/
New York

ID 010077A

ANNOUNCER: Hollywood Video presents, *Sixty-Second Theater*, where we try (unsuccessfully) to pack all the drama and suspense of a two-hour Hollywood production into 60 seconds. Today's presentation, *The Sixth Sense*.
COLE: *(door bell, door opening. Haley Joel Osment soundalike)* Who are you?
DR: *(Bruce Willis soundalike)* I'm a child psychologist. Heard you've been having some nightmares. What's bothering you?
COLE *(whispering)*: I see dead people.
DR: You got to speak up, kid.
COLE *(whispering)*: I see dead people.
DR: What? Let's pick this up next week. *(door bell, door opening)* Hi. Last time we met you were saying…
COLE *(whispering)*: I see dead people.
DR: Oh that. Are you sure you don't have an Oedipus complex?…I'm good at those.
COLE: Nope.
DR: How about bed wetting? That's my specialty.
COLE: Just dead people. Can you help me?
DR: Sorry, time's up. *(door bell, door opening)* Sorry I'm late. Tell me more about the dead people.
COLE: They have no concept of time.
DR: What else do they do?
COLE: Ask lots of questions.
DR: They do? How come? About what?
COLE: You tell me.
DR: How would I know about dead people?
COLE: Because you're…*(whispers something unintelligible)*
DR: What did you say?
ANNOUNCER: If this doesn't satisfy your urge to see *The Sixth Sense* (and we can't say we blame you), then rent it for five days at Hollywood Video. Where we'll help you find *The Sixth Sense* or exactly the movie you're in the mood for. Celebrity voices impersonated.

ANNOUNCER: It's the boss. So what are you going to do? Let him score? What sort of man are you? Stand up to him. He'll respect you for it...But then, he is the boss. You'll make him look stupid. He'll hold it against you. You can kiss that promotion goodbye.

(A defender tackles the boss, leaving him in a heap on the floor.)

ANNOUNCER: What the...? Hey, isn't that the new kid from finance? That's what you should have done. It was a test. But wait, there's still time....

SUPER: Beware of the voices.

VOICEOVER: For career advice worth listening to and thousands of jobs, visit monster.co.uk.

GOLD, SILVER, BRONZE

GOLD AWARD
Consumer Television Over :30
Single

ART DIRECTOR
Nik Studzinski

WRITER
Gavin Kellett

AGENCY PRODUCERS
Linsey Rogers
Clare Hunter

PRODUCTION COMPANY
Harry Nash Film
Productions

DIRECTOR
Fredrik Bond

CLIENT
Monster.com

AGENCY
Saatchi & Saatchi/London

D 010078A

GOLD, SILVER, BRONZE

SILVER AWARD
Consumer Television Over :30
Single

ART DIRECTOR
Chris Lange

WRITERS
Michael Hart
Bruce Bildsten
David Lubars

AGENCY PRODUCER
Damian Stevens

PRODUCTION COMPANY
@radical.media

DIRECTOR
Errol Morris

CLIENT
Public Broadcasting System

AGENCY
Fallon/Minneapolis

ID 010079A

BRONZE AWARD
Consumer Television Over :30
Single

ART DIRECTOR
Jan Jacobs

WRITER
Clare McNally

AGENCY PRODUCER
Helena Woodfine

PRODUCTION COMPANY
Egg Productions

DIRECTOR
Kim Geldenhuys

CLIENT
BMW

AGENCY
TBWA Hunt Lascaris/Sandton

ID 010080A

(A man inside a photo booth is making very animated faces. Later, the man cuts the strips of photos.)

SFX: Opera music under.

(The man has put the pictures together so that when he fans through them, it looks as if he's singing along to the classical music.)

SUPER: Stay Curious PBS.

SFX: The sound of jet engines accelerating.

(A jet-propelled vehicle is filmed racing along at high speed. At the end of the commercial, the camera is revealed, mounted on a BMW M5.)

SUPER: The BMW M5. Fastest saloon car on the planet.

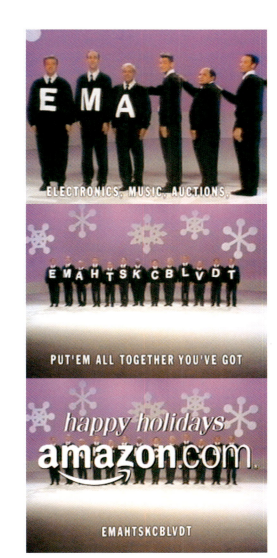

JEROME:	Man, I can't stand the Knicks, Yo.
ALAN:	Preach, Jer-Agra.
JEROME:	I would have no problem getting up for the big games in the Big Apple.
ALAN:	Hellz, no.
JEROME:	They say it's hard to play in New York… with the media scrutiny and what not…
ALAN:	Knickerbocker-please…
JEROME:	Step off…
ALAN:	To the curb, baby!
JEROME:	…as I unleash the fury with some fly Reggie Miller razzle-MA-DAMN!!!
JEROME:	Yo, Spree! You want some popcorn? 'Cause this is gonna be the best damn movie you'll ever see.
SUPER:	Live the game. Packers vs. Knicks. 7 PM Tonight. Fox Sports Net.

CHORUS:	Emahtskcblvadt? Emahtskcblvadt?
	Electronics, music, auctions, health and beauty, tools, software, kitchen, z-shops, books, lawn and patio, video, audio, dvd, toys.
	Put 'em all together you've got emahtskcblvadt and if you say, emahtskcblvadt, boy, you've said a lot there's nothin' quite like emahtskcblvadt, only Amazon's got emahtskcblvadt.

GOLD, SILVER, BRONZE

GOLD AWARD
Consumer Television :30
Single

ART DIRECTOR
Reed Collins

WRITER
Eric Silver

AGENCY PRODUCER
Kevin Diller

PRODUCTION COMPANY
Propaganda

DIRECTORS
Tom Kuntz
Mike Maguire

CLIENT
Fox Sports

AGENCY
Cliff Freeman and Partners/
New York

ID 010081A

SILVER AWARD
Consumer Television :30
Single

ART DIRECTORS
Matt Reinhardt
Ron Lim

WRITERS
Tom O'Keefe
Patrick Durkin

AGENCY PRODUCER
Jim Phox

PRODUCTION COMPANY
Headquarters

DIRECTOR
Joe Public

CLIENT
Amazon.com

AGENCY
Foote Cone & Belding/
San Francisco

ID 010082A

55

GOLD, SILVER, BRONZE

BRONZE AWARD
Consumer Television :30
Single

ART DIRECTOR
Paul Silburn

WRITER
Paul Silburn

AGENCY PRODUCER
Charlie Gatsky

PRODUCTION COMPANY
Spectre

DIRECTOR
Daniel Kleinman

CLIENT
John West

AGENCY
Leo Burnett/London

ID 010083A

GOLD AWARD
Consumer Television :30
Campaign

ART DIRECTOR
Reed Collins

WRITER
Eric Silver

AGENCY PRODUCER
Kevin Diller

PRODUCTION COMPANY
Propaganda

DIRECTORS
Tom Kuntz
Mike Maguire

CLIENT
Fox Sports

AGENCY
Cliff Freeman and Partners/
New York

ID 010084A

See Best of Show

ANNOUNCER: At the river mouth, the bears catch only the tastiest, most tender salmon. Which is what we at John West want...John West endures the worst to bring you the best.

ALAN: Yo, you know who led the league in assists last year?

JEROME: It shoulda been you, Yo.

ALAN: No doubt, Boo. No doubt...Yo, I gotta show these suckas how to play dis game!

JEROME: Let 'em know...

ALAN: None of these b-boys don't be realizin' that passing be an art, kid.

ALAN: I got the flava that ya savor...Watch my Kobe Bryant "No-Look Confusion Maker."

JEROME: Hey, Utah. Here's a little something called STYLE.

SUPER: Live the Game. Lakers vs. Jazz. 7 PM Tonight. Fox Sports Net.

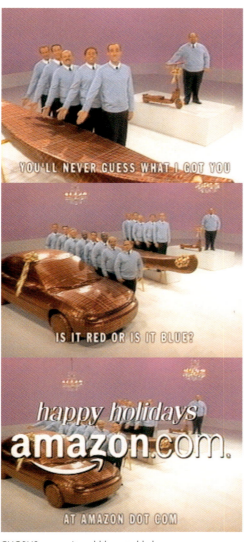

CHORUS: It could be a teddy bear,
a bike or smoke alarm.
Or possibly a new TV
or game on CD rom.

You'll never guess what I got you
at Amazon.com.

Looks like a telescope
Or a blender for the bar?
Guess again, a fountain pen?
Or teachin' tunes guitar?

You'll never guess what I got you
Is it red or is it blue?
You'll never guess what I got you
at Amazon.com.

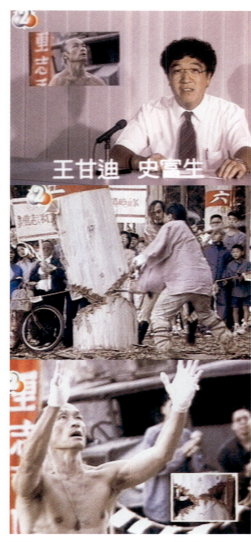

(A Chinese sports news announcer does the play-by-play as two Chinese lumberjacks chop down a large tree. An athlete then tries to catch the giant 200-foot tree falling toward him.)

SUPER: Sports news from the only region you care about. Yours. 11 PM Regional Sports Report. Fox Sports Net.

GOLD, SILVER, BRONZE

SILVER AWARD
Consumer Television :30
Campaign

ART DIRECTORS
Matt Reinhardt
Ron Lim

WRITERS
Tom O'Keefe
Patrick Durkin

AGENCY PRODUCER
Jim Phox

PRODUCTION COMPANY
Headquarters

DIRECTOR
Joe Public

CLIENT
Amazon.com

AGENCY
Foote Cone & Belding/
San Francisco

ID 010085A

BRONZE AWARD
Consumer Television :30
Campaign

ART DIRECTORS
Rossana Bardales
Taras Wayner

WRITER
Dan Morales

AGENCY PRODUCERS
Claire Grupp
Catherine Abate

PRODUCTION COMPANY
Partizan/Cape Direct

DIRECTOR
Traktor

CLIENT
Fox Sports

AGENCY
Cliff Freeman and Partners/
New York

ID 010086A

57

GOLD, SILVER, BRONZE

GOLD AWARD
Consumer Television :20 and Under: Single

ART DIRECTOR
Rick Casteel

WRITER
John Matejczyk

AGENCY PRODUCER
Lee Goldberg

PRODUCTION COMPANY
Coppos Films

DIRECTOR
Craig Gillespie

CLIENT
H & R Block

AGENCY
Young & Rubicam/Chicago

ID 01087A

SILVER AWARD
Consumer Television :20 and Under: Single

ART DIRECTOR
Rick Casteel

WRITER
John Matejczyk

AGENCY PRODUCER
Lee Goldberg

PRODUCTION COMPANY
Coppos Films

DIRECTOR
Craig Gillespie

CLIENT
H & R Block

AGENCY
Young & Rubicam/Chicago

ID 010088A

SUPER: Tax Day 6.
DAUGHTER: Hey, Dad, can I have some money?
DAD: Yup.
DAUGHTER: And the keys to the car?
DAD: You got it.
DAUGHTER: Thanks, Dad!
DAD: Love ya.
DAUGHTER: I'll be out all night!
DAD: See you in the mornin'.
SUPER: Get help. 1-800-HRBLOCK. hrblock.com. H & R BLOCK. Available at most larger Sears stores.

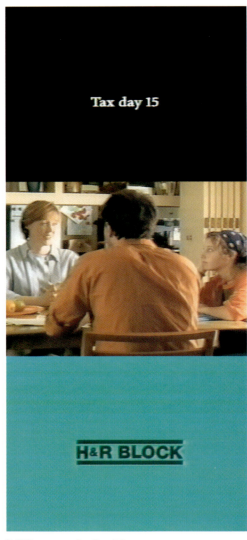

SUPER: Tax Day 15.
MOM: I've got good news for you guys... I'm pregnant.
DAUGHTER: That's great!
DAD: What? You're pregnant? Oh, honey, another baby, another deduction! Good job!
SUPER: Get help. 1-800-HRBLOCK. hrblock.com. H & R BLOCK. Available at most larger Sears stores.

SUPER: Tax Day 20.

DAD: Hey! Dad needs a quiet house, okay?!

SUPER: Get help. 1-800-HRBLOCK. hrblock.com. H & R BLOCK. Available at most larger Sears stores.

VOICEOVER: This is the amount of work an Estate Agent has to do to afford the McDonald's Quarter Pounder.

ESTATE AGENT *(opening and shutting a door quickly)*: Lounge.

VOICEOVER: The McDonald's Quarter Pounder. 99p.

GOLD, SILVER, BRONZE

GOLD AWARD
Consumer Television :20 and Under: Campaign

ART DIRECTOR
Rick Casteel

WRITER
John Matejczyk

AGENCY PRODUCER
Lee Goldberg

PRODUCTION COMPANY
Coppos Films

DIRECTOR
Craig Gillespie

CLIENT
H & R Block

AGENCY
Young & Rubicam/Chicago

ID 010089A

BRONZE AWARD
Consumer Television :20 and Under: Campaign

ART DIRECTORS
Mark Tutssel
Mark Norcutt

WRITERS
Laurence Quinn
Nick Bell

AGENCY PRODUCER
Jonathan Smith

PRODUCTION COMPANIES
Stark Films
2AM Films

DIRECTORS
Jeff Stark
Gus Filgate

CLIENT
McDonald's

AGENCY
Leo Burnett/London

ID 010090A

GOLD, SILVER, BRONZE

SILVER AWARD
Consumer Television: Varying Lengths Campaign

ART DIRECTORS
Dean Maryon
Larry Frey

WRITER
Lorenzo De Rita

AGENCY PRODUCER
Jackie Adler

PRODUCTION COMPANY
Harry Nash

DIRECTOR
Fredrik Bond

CLIENT
Adidas International

AGENCY
180/Amsterdam

ID 010091A

BRONZE AWARD
Consumer Television: Varying Lengths Campaign

ART DIRECTORS
Ewan Paterson
Rob Jack

WRITERS
Rob Jack
Ewan Paterson

AGENCY PRODUCER
Howard Spivey

PRODUCTION COMPANY
Partizan

DIRECTOR
Rocky Morton

CLIENT
Volkswagen

AGENCY
BMP DDB/London

ID 010092A

Also won:

MERIT AWARD
Consumer Television Over :30 Single

STREET WORKER: This guy throws some rubbish on the ground and just walks off as if it's not a problem.

SUPER: Cod and Chips £2.20.

2nd WORKER: Just throws it there for no reason whatsoever.

1st WORKER: And then from nowhere this guy in shorts appears.

GIRL 1: I thought, what's he doing with shorts on in this weather? He started to move it, like position it. He starts to look round the street. I thought what's he doing here?

MAN AT BUS STOP: I thought, I know what his game is, so I got sort of next to this guy, made a bit of a defensive wall, you know how you cover your…He's gonna kick it. Beautiful banana shot, looping round, swerves past my head.

1st WORKER: Smack, right into the bin.

MAN IN DOORWAY: We should all wear Adidas, keep the city safe and clean for our kids.

SUPER: Adidas makes you better. Adidas forever sport. www.adidas.com./bebetter.

MAN AT BUS STOP: The most poetic bit of rubbish I've ever seen in my life.

(A man takes his dog for a walk in the country. He doesn't want the muddy dog to mess up the interior of his pristine new Passat, so he sends him home in a cab.)

SUPER: The beautifully crafted new Passat. You'll want to keep it that way.

(Open on a stage where little girls are giving a ballet recital. The point of view is probably that of one of the girls' older brother. Death metal music plays in the background. The girls move in perfect sync with the heavy metal song.)

SUPER: CD Walkmans from R499. The Hi Fi Corp.

GIRL: It's true what Mom says? That Scamp is at a special dog ranch in the sky? Playing with other dogs?

DAD: No, no. He's right out back, buried behind the shed...In the sky, c'mon...

SFX: Tingle effects.

SUPER: NFL Preseason, ESPN.

ANNOUNCER: Football's back, make room.

GOLD, SILVER, BRONZE

SILVER AWARD
Consumer Television: Under $50,000 Budget: Single

ART DIRECTOR
Jan Jacobs

AGENCY PRODUCER
Jo Barber

PRODUCTION COMPANY
Lizard Post Production

DIRECTOR
Derek Ichilcik

CLIENT
Hi Fi Corporation

AGENCY
TBWA Hunt
Lascaris/Johannesburg

ID 010093A

Also won:

MERIT AWARD
Consumer Television :30
Single

BRONZE AWARD
Consumer Television: Under $50,000 Budget: Single

ART DIRECTOR
Paul Foulkes

WRITER
Tyler Hampton

AGENCY PRODUCER
Heidi Hawkings

PRODUCTION COMPANIES
Mindfield
Fusion Films

DIRECTOR
Marcus McCollum

CLIENT
ESPN
NFL Pre-Season

AGENCY
Ground Zero/Los Angeles

ID 010094A

GOLD, SILVER, BRONZE

BRONZE AWARD
Consumer Television: Under $50,000 Budget: Single

ART DIRECTOR
Jason Black

WRITER
Michael McCullough

AGENCY PRODUCER
Craig Potter

PRODUCTION COMPANY
Ober/Lenz Films

DIRECTOR
Tony Ober

CLIENT
Azteca Mexican Restaurants

AGENCY
WONGDOODY/Seattle

ID 010095A

GOLD AWARD
Foreign Language Television: Single

ART DIRECTOR
Vincent Pang

WRITERS
Daniel Lim
Wu Jiang Xue

AGENCY PRODUCER
Magie Tan

PRODUCTION COMPANY
Visual Impact

DIRECTOR
Lee Wei Ren

CLIENT
UNICEF

AGENCY
Saatchi & Saatchi/Hong Kong

ID 010096A

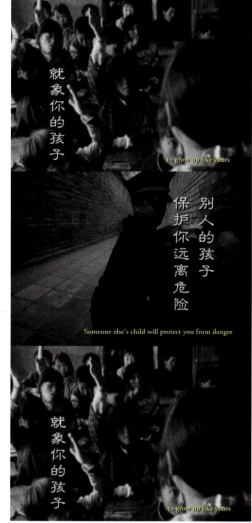

SUPER:	Azteca logo.
ANNOUNCER:	Join the Ramos Family on Azteca!
TETO:	I need the secret recipe for Mama's Molcajete!
PEPE:	Si.
TETO 2:	Hey, Pepe!
PEPE:	Ahh! Two Tetos! Which one is real?
TETO 1:	Well, I am!
TETO 2:	No, I am...
PEPE:	Uh oh!
TETO 2:	Pepe, try this.
PEPE:	Delicious! Only a Ramos could make a dish this good. Grab him.
REAL TETO:	It's Bob the Burrito King! He's been after our recipes for years.
BOB:	Next time, Pepe!
SUPER:	Azteca.
ANNOUNCER:	Azteca. Obsessed with great food.

SUPER:	Someone else's child will supply food to your family.
SUPER:	Someone else's child will pave the road you walk on.
SUPER:	Someone else's child will take you to work everyday.
SUPER:	Someone else's child will protect you from danger.
SUPER:	Someone else's child will save your life.
SUPER:	Someone else's child is even prepared to die for you.
SUPER:	All they need is a chance to grow up like yours.
SUPER:	UNICEF.

(A Golf drives through an open barrier to a parking lot, then the guard closes the barrier, which hits the back of the car's roof. We realize the car is a Golf variant.)

SUPER: Golf variant car. 15% more Golf.

SUPER: Skol brings you Skol Beer Night. The best DJs, electronic music, flirting and beer.

(An employee on a brewery quality control line removes his noise protectors and, with both hands on the conveyor belt, he does what DJs call a "skratch," as if it were a record.)

SUPER: Skol Beer Night. The best techno party on earth.

GOLD, SILVER, BRONZE

SILVER AWARD
Foreign Language Television: Single

ART DIRECTOR
Sebastien Zanini

WRITER
Pierre Marie Faussurier

AGENCY PRODUCER
Corinne Persch

PRODUCTION COMPANY
La Base

DIRECTOR
François Nemeta

CLIENT
Volkswagen France

AGENCY
DDB Advertising/Paris

ID 010097A

BRONZE AWARD
Foreign Language Television: Single

ART DIRECTOR
Eduardo Martins

WRITER
Fabio Fernandes

AGENCY PRODUCER
Daniela Andrade

PRODUCTION COMPANY
Zero Filme

DIRECTOR
Sergio Amon

CLIENT
Skol Beer

AGENCY
F/Nazca Saatchi & Saatchi/São Paulo

ID 010098A

GOLD, SILVER, BRONZE

GOLD AWARD
Multi-Media Campaign

ART DIRECTORS
Heloise Jacobs
Vanessa Norman
Micheal Bond

WRITERS
Graham Warsop
Peter Callaghan
Brendan Jack
Gavin Williams
Bernard Hunter
Leon van Huyssteen

ILLUSTRATOR
Julian Dell

PHOTOGRAPHER
David Prior

CLIENT
Nike

AGENCY
The Jupiter Drawing Room
(South Africa)/Johannesburg

ID 010099A

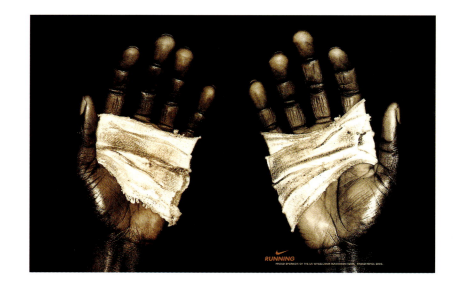

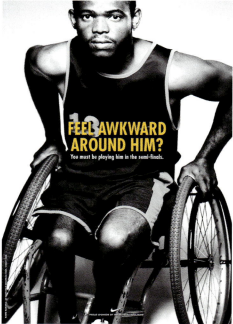

GOLD, SILVER, BRONZE

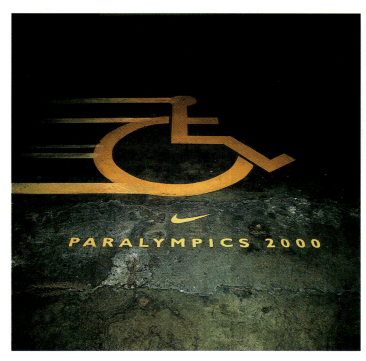

This concept utilized the disabled parking bays found next to the entrances of shopping malls. The bays were "doctored" before and during special visits by the 2000 South African Paralympic team of disabled athletes to meet their fans. An illustrator added the blur to the existing disabled icon and stenciled the Nike swoosh and the copy below it.

Non-permanent ink was used in all the executions. Complimentary press advertisements detailed the times and dates of the visits. Full permission for the executions was granted by the shopping centers' management and the National Paralympic Committee of South Africa.

SFX:	A slow heartbeat is accompanied by deep breathing. A starting gun fires, followed by rapid footsteps. The crowd cheers enthusiastically, swells to a crescendo, and then begins to fade. The footsteps come to a stop and the breathing returns to normal, accompanied by a heartbeat.
SUPER:	11,02 seconds.
SUPER:	You have just witnessed Rory Field qualify for the 2000 Paralympics.
SUPER:	Through his eyes.
SUPER:	Nike swoosh. Just Do It.

GOLD, SILVER, BRONZE

SILVER AWARD
Multi-Media Campaign

ART DIRECTOR
Moe Verbrugge
Maya Rao

WRITER
Maya Rao
Moe Verbrugge

AGENCY PRODUCER
Mila Davis

CLIENT
The Museum of Contemporary Art

AGENCY
TBWA/Chiat/Day/
Los Angeles

ID 010100A

The Demise of Culture, 2001
Glass, plastic, metal, wires
A large black box sits prominently in the living room, signifying one doesn't just arrange one's life around the box but also one's furniture.

The Demise of Culture, 2001
Glass, plastic, metal, wires
A large black box sits prominently in the living room, signifying one doesn't just arrange one's life around the box but also one's furniture.
On loan from The Museum of Contemporary Art, Los Angeles

SFX: Annoying, constant stylized beat.

SUPER: The Demise Of Culture, 2001. Glass, plastic, metal, wires. A large black box sits prominently in the living room, signifying one doesn't just arrange one's life around the box but also one's furniture.

FADE UP: On loan from The Museum of Contemporary Art, Los Angeles.

SUPER: Keep clothing away from machinery. Safety First. Winter X Games. February 2-6 Mount Snow, VT. ESPN.

GOLD, SILVER, BRONZE

BRONZE AWARD
Multi-Media Campaign

ART DIRECTOR
Kim Schoen

WRITER
Kevin Proudfoot

ILLUSTRATOR
Geoff McFetridge

AGENCY PRODUCER
Tony Stearns

PRODUCTION COMPANY
Champion Graphics

DIRECTOR
Geoff McFetridge

CLIENT
ESPN

AGENCY
Wieden + Kennedy/
New York

ID 010101A

GOLD, SILVER, BRONZE

GOLD AWARD
College Competition

ART DIRECTOR
Otis Webb

WRITER
Josh Schildkraut

SCHOOL
The Creative Circus/Atlanta

ID 010102A

ASSIGNMENT:
To promote track and field as a spectator sport.

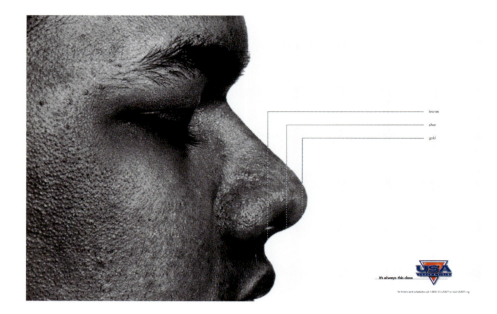

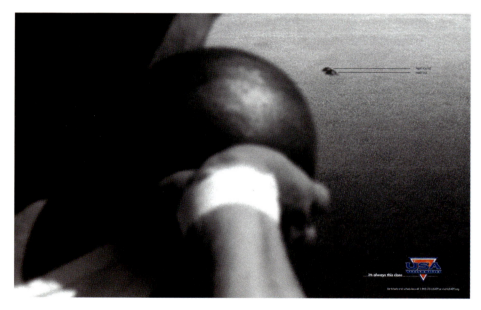

ODDS OF FINDING YOUR PASSION: 867,000 to 1
AND DOING IT BETTER THAN ANYONE: 4,680,030 to 1
WHO EVER LIVED: 9,876,354,678 to 1

PEOPLE: 6,000,000,000
WHO RUN: 562,810,398
THE 100 METERS: 729,227
IN 9.79 SECONDS: 1

CHANCES OF ASTRO DUST FORMING A PLANET: 1 in 100,000
WITH OXYGEN: 1 in 3,000,000
AND HUMAN LIFE: 1 in 4,000,000,000
THAT CAN JUMP 30 FEET: 1 in 39 BILLION

GOLD, SILVER, BRONZE

SILVER AWARD
College Competition

ART DIRECTOR
Ping Li

WRITER
Hilary Haselton

SCHOOL
VCU Adcenter/Richmond

ID 010103A

BRONZE AWARD
College Competition

ART DIRECTORS
Chris Jacobs
Jose Trujillo

WRITER
Reuben Hower

SCHOOL
University of Colorado/
Boulder

ID 010104A

69

GOLD, SILVER, BRONZE

GOLD AWARD
One Show Design

ART DIRECTOR
Chris Pinkham

WRITER
Larry Raff

CLIENT
Goodwill

AGENCY
Clarke Goward/Boston

ID 010001D

GOLD, SILVER, BRONZE

GOLD AWARD
One Show Design

DESIGNER
Dana Neibert

ART DIRECTOR
Dana Neibert

WRITERS
Dana Neibert
Ming Lai
Craig Evans

CLIENT
San Diego Ad Club

AGENCY
Di Zinno Thompson/
Coronado

ID 010002D

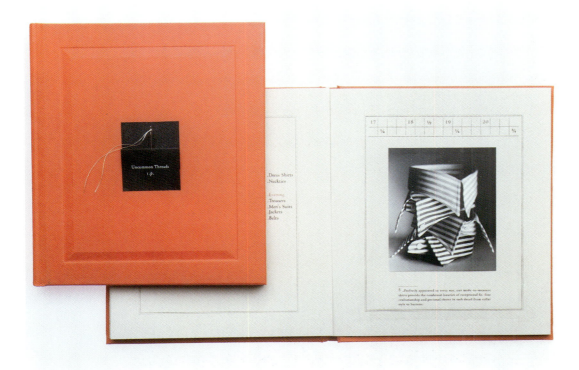

GOLD AWARD
One Show Design

DESIGNER
Jeanne Renneker

ART DIRECTOR
Marion English Powers

WRITER
Kathy Oldham

PHOTOGRAPHER
Don Harbor

CLIENT
Plain Clothes

AGENCY
Slaughter Hanson/
Birmingham, AL

ID 010003D

GOLD, SILVER, BRONZE

GOLD AWARD
One Show Design

DESIGNER
Sarah Moffet

ART DIRECTORS
David Turner
Bruce Duckworth

ILLUSTRATOR
Peter Ruane

PHOTOGRAPHER
Nick Veasey

CLIENT
Virgin Atlantic Airlines

AGENCY
Turner Duckworth/
San Francisco

ID 010004D

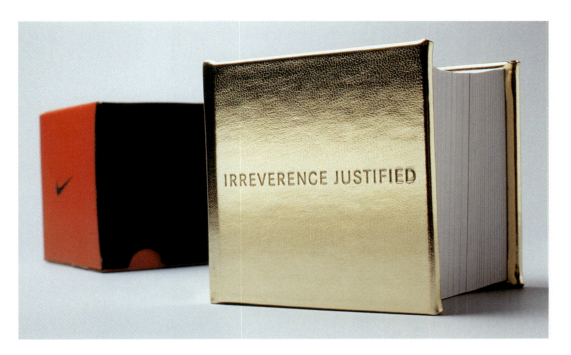

GOLD, SILVER, BRONZE

GOLD AWARD
One Show Design

DESIGNER
Robert Nakata

ART DIRECTORS
Robert Nakata
Merete Busk

WRITERS
Glenn Cole
Tim Wolfe

CLIENT
Nike

AGENCY
Wieden + Kennedy/
Amsterdam

ID 010005D

GOLD, SILVER, BRONZE

SILVER AWARD
One Show Design

DESIGNERS
Bob Dinetz
Mark Giglio
Kevin Roberson

ART DIRECTORS
Bill Cahan
Kevin Roberson
Bob Dinetz

WRITERS
Bob Dinetz
Mark Giglio
Kevin Roberson

ILLUSTRATORS
Bob Dinetz
Mark Giglio
Kevin Roberson

PHOTOGRAPHERS
Graham Macindoe
Robert Schlatter
Ken Probst
Steve McCurry
Wade Goddard
Paul Chesley
Richard Nowitz
David Turnley
Glen Allison
Peter Brown
Lars Tunbjork

CLIENT
Consolidated Papers

AGENCY
Cahan & Associates/
San Francisco

ID 010006D

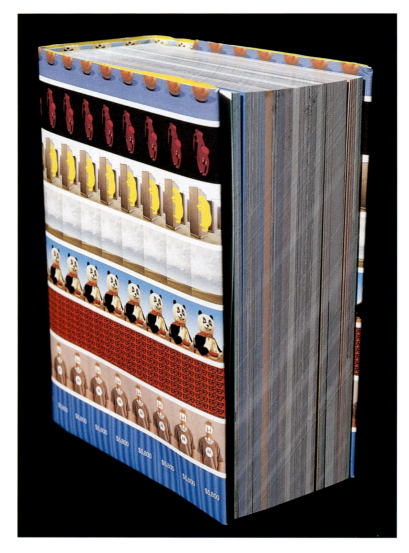

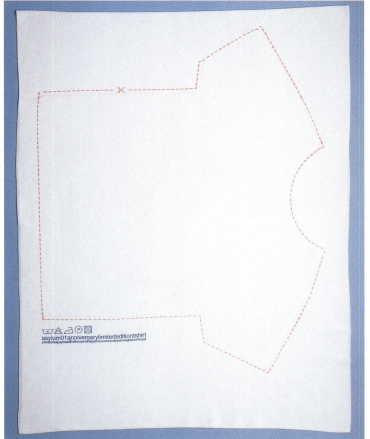

GOLD, SILVER, BRONZE

SILVER AWARD
One Show Design

ART DIRECTOR
Christopher Lee

DESIGNER
Christopher Lee

CLIENT
Design Asylum

AGENCY
Design Asylum/Singapore

ID 010007D

GOLD, SILVER, BRONZE

SILVER AWARD
One Show Design

ART DIRECTORS
Cecilia Dufils
Markus Bjurman

WRITER
Joe De Souza

ILLUSTRATOR
Markus Bjurman

CLIENT
Costa Coffee

AGENCY
Mother Ltd./London

ID 010008D

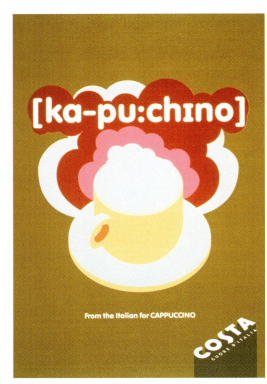

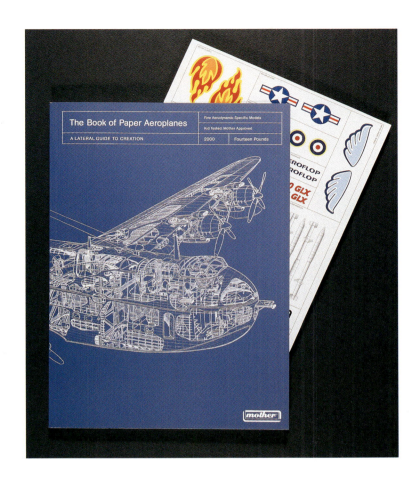

GOLD, SILVER, BRONZE

SILVER AWARD
One Show Design

ART DIRECTOR
Peter Vicksten

WRITER
Chad Rea

CLIENT
Mother Ltd.

AGENCY
Mother Ltd./London

ID 010009D

SILVER AWARD
One Show Design

ART DIRECTOR
Thomas Hilland

WRITERS
Mother Ltd.
Idle Industries

CLIENT
Mother Ltd.

AGENCY
Mother Ltd./London

ID 010010D

GOLD, SILVER, BRONZE

SILVER AWARD
One Show Design

DESIGNER
Janice Davison

ART DIRECTORS
David Turner
Bruce Duckworth

ILLUSTRATOR
Sam Hadley

CLIENT
Superdrug

AGENCY
Turner Duckworth/
San Francisco

ID 010011D

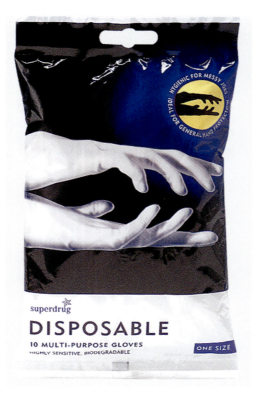

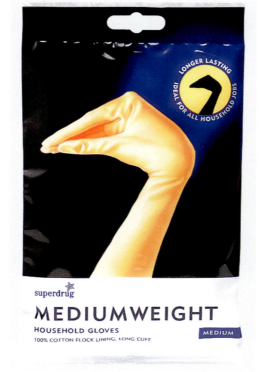

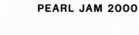
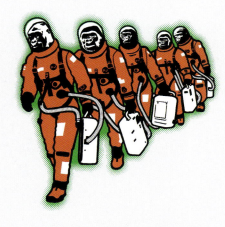

GOLD, SILVER, BRONZE

BRONZE AWARD
One Show Design

DESIGNERS
Barry Ament
Coby Schultz
Mark Atherton
George Estrada

ART DIRECTOR
Carpender Newman

ILLUSTRATORS
Barry Ament
Coby Schultz
Mark Atherton
George Estrada

CLIENT
Pearl Jam

AGENCY
Ames Design/Seattle

ID 010012D

GOLD, SILVER, BRONZE

BRONZE AWARD
One Show Design

DESIGNER
Janet Kinghorn

ART DIRECTOR
Janet Kinghorn

ILLUSTRATOR
Janet Kinghorn

CLIENT
Ruth Chowles

AGENCY
The Jupiter Drawing Room (South Africa)/Cape Town

ID 010013D

GOLD, SILVER, BRONZE

BRONZE AWARD
One Show Design

DESIGNER
Steve Sandstrom

ART DIRECTOR
Steve Sandstrom

WRITER
Steve Sandoz

CLIENT
Tazo

AGENCY
Sandstrom Design/Portland

ID 010014D

BRONZE AWARD
One Show Design

DESIGNER
Marion English Powers

ART DIRECTORS
Marion English Powers
David Webb
Jeanne Renneker

CLIENT
The Olive Room

AGENCY
Slaughter Hanson/
Birmingham, AL

ID 010015D

GOLD, SILVER, BRONZE

BRONZE AWARD
One Show Design

DESIGNERS
Geoff McFetridge
Kim Schoen
Sarah Foelske

ART DIRECTOR
Kim Schoen

WRITER
Kevin Proudfoot

ILLUSTRATOR
Geoff McFetridge

CLIENT
ESPN

AGENCY
Wieden + Kennedy/
New York

ID 010016D

Also won:

MERIT AWARD
Collateral: Posters

GOLD, SILVER, BRONZE

BRONZE AWARD
One Show Design

DESIGNERS
Geoff McFetridge
Kim Schoen
Sarah Foelske

ART DIRECTOR
Kim Schoen

WRITER
Kevin Proudfoot

ILLUSTRATOR
Geoff McFetridge

CLIENT
ESPN

AGENCY
Wieden + Kennedy/
New York

ID 010017D

Also won:

MERIT AWARDS
One Show Design

Guerilla Advertising

83

BEST OF SHOW

BEST OF SHOW

GOLD AWARD
Consumer Television :30
Campaign

ART DIRECTOR
Reed Collins

WRITER
Eric Silver

AGENCY PRODUCER
Kevin Diller

PRODUCTION COMPANY
Propaganda

DIRECTORS
Tom Kuntz
Mike Maguire

CLIENT
Fox Sports

AGENCY
Cliff Freeman and Partners/
New York

ID 010084A

Also won:

MERIT AWARDS
Consumer Television :30
Singles

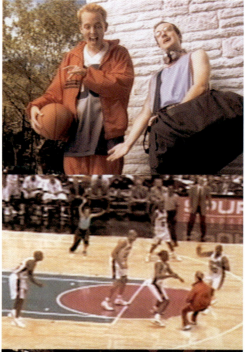

ALAN:	Yo, you know who led the league in assists last year?
JEROME:	It shoulda been you, Yo.
ALAN:	No doubt, Boo. No doubt…Yo, I gotta show these suckas how to play dis game!
JEROME:	Let 'em know…
ALAN:	None of these b-boys don't be realizin' that passing be an art, kid…I got the flava that ya savor…Watch my Kobe Bryant "No-Look Confusion Maker."
JEROME:	Hey, Utah. Here's a little something called STYLE.
SUPER:	Live the Game. Lakers vs. Jazz. 7 PM Tonight. Fox Sports Net.

JEROME:	Yo, who says you gotta be a big man to compete in the NBA?
ALAN:	Not I, Shorty.
JEROME:	That's right. Allen and Jerome…That's us! We're gonna creep on in…
ALAN:	Creepin' like a Creeper…
JEROME:	And drop some Stephon Marbury inner-city funk. I love to see the face of the fool trying to D my slammin' moves to the hole…Yo, David. You may be bigger than me, but you need to get yourself some Coppertone lotion.
ALAN:	That's right, baby.
JEROME:	…'cause you just got burned.
ALAN:	Rub that on.
JEROME:	Rub, rub, rub, rub, rub…
SUPER:	Live the Game. Nets vs. Spurs. 7PM Tonight. Fox Sports Net.

ALAN:	Yo, I swear, J, if I hear the word "Shaq" one more time…
JEROME:	Or Shaq Attack.
ALAN:	Yo, what did I just say?
JEROME:	My bad.
ALAN:	I would really show up my mad dribbling skills on this much-over-hyped team.
JEROME:	Yo. They okay.
ALAN:	Yeah, they okay. But they ain't got the Allen Iverson grace. You know if I was playin' them, I would be punishin' them. Punishin' them for thinking they could stop this. You cannot stop this! I'm fresh like a can of picante. And I'm deeper than Dante in the circles of hell…
SUPER:	Live the game. Sixers vs. Lakers. 7PM Tonight. Fox Sports Net.

JUDGES' CHOICE

JUDGES' CHOICE

CLIENT
Asia Pacific Breweries

AGENCY
Ogilvy & Mather/Singapore

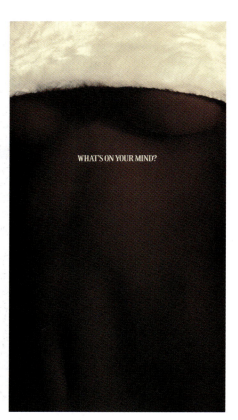

As I told my wife—the mother of my three children—the only thing on my mind when I saw these ads was a Guinness. A rich, creamy, thick, delicious Guinness. Swear. How I arrived at that without the aid of a logo, product shot or the product name appearing anywhere in the ads is why I like them so much. Such confidence. If only everybody wanted to build their brand like that. Also the art direction is really on. These things look like a Guinness tastes. Nice.

Sean Ehringer

JUDGES' CHOICE

CLIENT
Olympus Optical

AGENCY
Lowe Lintas/London

The print ads I chose for my personal Best of Show are not sardonic, ironic, sarcastic, cynical, or funny in any way.

Instead, they are deep, intelligent and brilliantly written.

They are ingenious in the way that they connect the product, the manually operated Olympus professional camera, to the user. The idea is simple: Taking a meaningful photograph is a thoughtful process. It is not automatic. The manually operated Olympus is the camera for photographers who engage their hearts and minds in their work.

Each ad features a smallish black and white photograph of an event somewhere in the world. One shows a photograph of farmers looking at a stack of corpses in El Salvador. Another, war orphans in Lebanon. The last ad is a photograph of a starving child in Uganda.

The hand-written copy is stream of consciousness, the thoughts that would go through a photographer's mind as he or she takes that photograph. In the ad for El Salvador, the copy is made up of simple, beautiful language, like: "In El Salvador, the morning harvest is stained with blood....But are you there to capture this for posterity, or just another vulture?...Are you using the right lens, is there enough film, is the lighting too harsh? Should you be using corpses to get a great composition anyway? Should their misery end up as your award-winning photograph?"

Each ad ends with "The Manual OM3TI. Taking a picture should be anything but automatic."

Joyce King Thomas

JUDGES' CHOICE

CLIENT
Britart.com

AGENCY
Mother Ltd./London

A strange thing happened on my journey back from judging in Barcelona. I forgot almost every ad I'd seen. Beyond several great television campaigns, only one poster campaign remained top of mind. I wish I'd done it. I wish someone in my agency had done it. I wish someone I knew had done it. The Britart work. It's incredibly relevant and so painfully simple.

David Droga

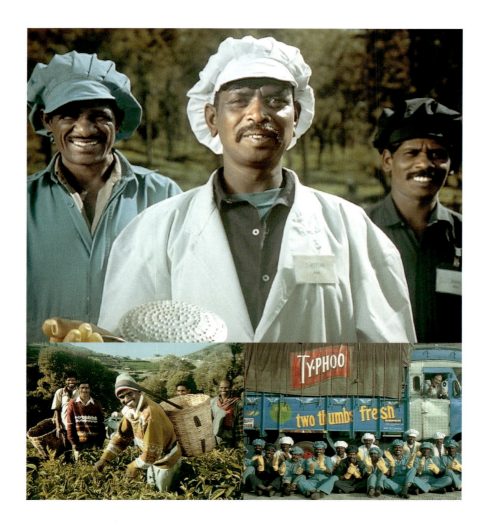

It was really nice to stay in Barcelona to judge for a week with all these great and famous creatives, but the experience was also a bit surreal to me. The organization of the One Show was perfect, almost too perfect. What I mean to say is that I felt we lost touch with reality.

We stayed at the luxurious Ritz Hotel, where we had exclusive breakfasts, lunches, champagne, cocktails, little salmon-egg-snacks, and we were treated like famous rock stars. We looked at 239,303 ads in big ballrooms with golden chandeliers and saw reels in expensive suites where room service came in with special nuts from Hungary, while outside the normal life in Barcelona went on.

Somehow I felt that a lot of the work fit that description as well: out of touch with reality. Of course, let's be clear: There was a lot of beautiful work, you'll find it all here in this book, but there was a considerable amount of stuff that had nothing to do with real life. Like it was made on a completely different planet or a long, long time ago.

Lots of ads that were full of stereotypes, sexist, insulting, sometimes even racist and addressed people as if they were babies. Maybe it's better not to mention them at all, but it scares me to see how slowly sensible advertising develops. I like advertising that is human, and I like advertisers that don't take themselves too seriously. That's why one of my favorites was the English Typhoo Tea spots. Luckily, we managed to hire the two Swedes that did them. Thank you again One Show for having me, but next time let's go to a sleazy budget hotel, somewhere in Kansas City, where life is real....

Johan Kramer

CLIENT
Premier Brands

AGENCY
Mother Ltd./London

JUDGES' CHOICE

JUDGES' CHOICE

CLIENT
Physicians for Human Rights

AGENCY
Euro RSCG McConnaughy Tatham/Chicago

On one of the tables of work I came across a small cardboard box. Inside I found a very beat up, worn shoe, with a card attached. The card explained that the owner of the shoe no longer needed it due to the fact that their entire foot and a good portion of their leg were blown off by a land mine. I've seen many horrible graphic war photos of victims, but none were as powerful as this. It's almost like I've become desensitized to those images, because I see so much of it. This ad took the violence and put it in my hand. A person's shoe seems common and everyday, but it is also a very intimate object; this personalized the violence. It was a great, relevant device to get someone's attention and deliver something meaningful. It was the most inventive and impactful ad I've seen in this category.

Matt Vescovo

I have a simple rule of thumb when judging ads. I have to think, "I wish I'd done that."

Quite a few pieces of work passed this test for me, and none more so than the mailshot for the Physicians for Human Rights.

A shoe box containing a single, used shoe, with a label attached saying something along the lines of "You are holding a shoe that belonged to a landmine victim."

A great idea for a great cause. It stopped me in my tracks.

Richard Foster

One campaign I liked in particular: the print stuff for discovery.com. They were smart, they were arresting, and they were nothing if not timely. Just very well done and very clever. Other stuff that comes to mind: the Adidas print, all the Fox TV work, the H & R Block TV spots, and, but of course, the monkey on the boat.

Janet Champ

JUDGES' CHOICE

CLIENT
Discovery.com

AGENCY
Publicis & Hal Riney/
San Francisco

JUDGES' CHOICE

CLIENT
Fox Sports

AGENCY
Cliff Freeman and Partners/
New York

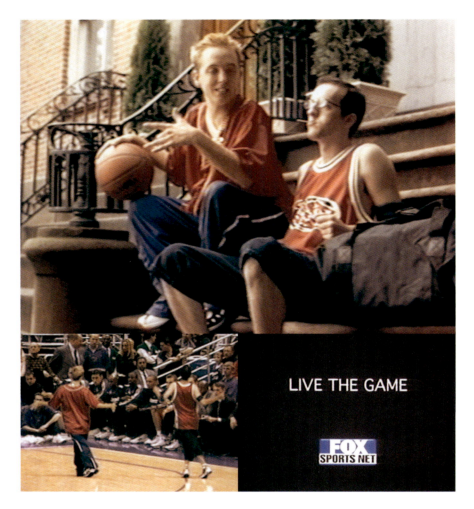

The campaign that really stood out for me was the Fox basketball TV campaign. It was fresh, funny—and I think it hit a chord with every less-than-tall white guy like me who ever hankered to dribble down court and slam dunk against anybody in the NBA. You wanted to do what they were doing. Plus the kids were just damn plain funny.

And it was either that or the monkey on the boat.

Rick McQuiston

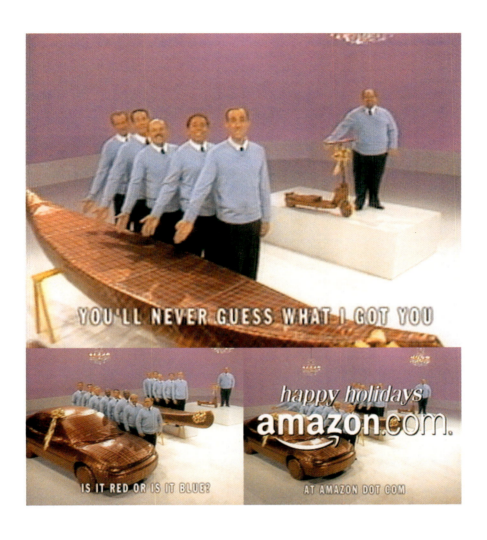

JUDGES' CHOICE

CLIENT
Amazon.com

AGENCY
Foote Cone & Belding/
San Francisco

At least 98% of the TV this year seemed to fall into one of the following executions: a) the fakeumentary or mockumentary. These need no explanation since we all have at least one on our reels; b) the gratuitously violent execution where a body part is severed, someone is set on fire, people are electrocuted, etc. Most often, B is combined with A to form the gratuitously violent mockumentary; and c) the "passion" execution where employees who make a product or provide a service or the people who use a product/service love it so much, it's become a seamless part of their real lives. Again, C is often combined with A and B to form a mockumentary where people are so passionate about something, they'll give their right arm for it.

The amazon.com campaign really stood out for its originality. It was intelligent, fun to watch, shot with imagination, relevant to the brand and everything else we want commercials to be. A rare campaign that didn't feel like it was created at a frat house. Thumbs up to the creative team for looking at the brief and not going directly to A, B or C but EMAHTSKCBLVT.

Joe Alexander

JUDGES' CHOICE

CLIENT
Molson Canada

AGENCY
TAXI/Toronto

Two things that I feel deserve special mention: The H & R Block campaign was cool, funny, and worked for a client that (I could be wrong here) is none of the above. There was also an anti-drunk driving spot from Canada with a kid trying out wheelchairs at a store that sells hospital supplies. The salesman pitches him on all the great qualities of the wheelchair and asks him why he's looking for one. The kid tells him he's going to a party that night and plans on getting hammered and driving himself home afterward. It was a great way to address a subject without the usual tear jerking.

Kara Goodrich

CLIENT
H & R Block

AGENCY
Young & Rubicam/Chicago

I was impressed by the charming and funny H & R Block campaign. It deserves recognition not only because it's great. The campaign lived through a traditional client like H & R Block and an agency that doesn't have its entire support system built around selling award-winning creative. It's refreshing and inspiring to see a team do great work when they had every excuse not to.

Susan Traecy

JUDGES' CHOICE

CLIENT
Hi Fi Corporation

AGENCY
TBWA Hunt Lascaris/
Johannesburg

I loved this ad. I was sucked in from the first moment and totally surprised by the ending. The best part was that it never cut to a shot of the person wearing the Walkman. And for this, I applaud the team who created it. Because I can hear it now, dozens of clients and nervous agency people yapping in their ear, "Shouldn't we be absolutely sure everyone 'gets it' by showing the person wearing the thing we're selling?" Let me answer that. No. I got so much more involved with this ad because I didn't see the person or the Walkman. My mind did all the work…. I saw the little girl's teenage brother, a rebellious type, tattooed, pierced and sitting in his Megadeth t-shirt having been dragged there by his Leave-It-To-Beaver-like parents, thinking about how he was going to hook up with his head-banging friends after he escaped the insanity of his little sister's ballet recital. Nobody had to show me anything, it's more involving, and fun, when I do the work. Thank you to the team that did this ad. You all deserve a raise. At the very least you deserve a pencil.

Kevin Roddy

For me the most interesting thing about the Best of Show judging was just how different everyone's opinions were. It was kind of nice being in a room full of people who all know what it takes to create good work, trying (humbly) to sway their peers in different yet valid directions. In the end an agreement was made, but it was by no means cut and dry. That's one of the things I'll always find interesting about this business (and this world, for that matter), there's really no right way to do anything. What's great to some is boring to others.

I had a few favorites in the piles of work we saw. I don't even know if they made it in the book. But then again, I sometimes like really stupid things simply because they make me smile. In my "I-need-to-get-off-my-ass-and-act" category: I'd say the get out and vote stuff with the swastikas cut in the fields made me feel like voting right there on the spot. I'd have to say my favorite without a doubt was the retail Walkman spot from South Africa with the growly deathmetal dirge playing over the children's dance recital. So simple. I pictured myself standing there with that music blasting, grinning ear to ear. I'd buy a Walkman from those guys.

Jon Soto

JUDGES' CHOICE

CLIENT
Full Circle

AGENCY
Fallon/London

The best ad I saw in Barcelona was for Full Circle clothing, and it was created and flawlessly executed by Fallon/London.

As I am normally dripping in sarcasm, I find it difficult to describe my appreciation for the ad in a sincere fashion. But my regard for the ad, which I am told is merely one in a series, knows no bounds. I love everything about it. I kept wandering back to look at it in the judging room over and over. And I found myself lobbying for it (in vain I'm afraid), over many a delicious Barcelona lunch with my fellow judges.

It is the gold standard as far I'm concerned. Simple. Brilliant. Hilarious. And it makes me want to buy the clothes. Imagine that.

Anyway, if anyone who worked on the ad at Fallon/London is reading this, please send me a reprint. I'll pay.

Stacy Wall

CLIENT
Minneapolis League of Women Voters

AGENCY
Colle + McVoy/Minneapolis

"See, you do have an opinion."

Yes, I do. I have opinions on lots of things. Just ask anyone that's ever gone out to lunch with me. I like water with my meal. That's an opinion. I like lemon in my water. That's another opinion. I like my water with lemon, but not with ice. There, that's another.

Whether these opinions are right or wrong, or just plain annoying, there's one thing for sure: They are mine. My very own. My opinions are my voice. And what better way to get me to vote than to remind me—in such a simple and poignant way—of my voice. That I do indeed have one and that it should indeed be heard. Annoying or not.

Ellen Steinberg

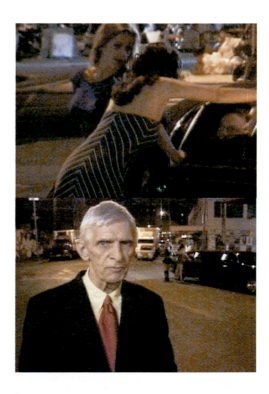

JUDGES' CHOICE

CLIENT
Volkswagen

AGENCY
BMP DDB/London

CLIENT
TDA Advertising & Design

AGENCY
TDA Advertising & Design/Boulder

My personal Best of Show was the VW spot called "Smile." It's subtle, delicate, and truthful, with the perfect small dose of arrogance. And it's not American, or Brazilian, or Spanish, English, Danish or Australian: It's universal. Just brilliant. I wish I had done it.

Fabio Fernandes

There was this TV spot for a Colorado agency, where this rather demure spokesman unflinchingly asserts that at his agency, "We never bill our prostitutes to your account." It really struck me. Because, you know, that's not how we do it at Goodby.

Paul Venables

JUDGES' CHOICE

CLIENT
Nike

AGENCY
Wieden + Kennedy/Portland

If you get the chance, check out this Nike campaign. See it on a reel, the stills don't do it justice.

Each spot is just a montage cut together from interviews with Pete Sampras and Andre Agassi, the Sampras family, the Agassi family, some Sampras fans and some Agassi fans talking about Pete and Andre. The footage is cut together like a volley at Wimbledon. Fast paced, back and forth. I think there's even a lob in there somewhere.

I really like it when a creative team comes up with an idea that travels a million miles from a strategy and somehow finds its way back to make a powerful point. But it's equally inspired when a team simply looks inside something to find an idea that has always been laying there, then crafts a powerful message about that. That's what this is. There's nothing outrageous here, no kooky ad high jinks. It's just a compelling piece of film that says something good about the two athletes, their fans, the sport and the brand.

Harry Cocciolo

CLIENT
Atomic Air Conditioning

AGENCY
Young & Rubicam/Toronto

My personal Best of Show is a print ad I call "Jesus Mittens." I saw it the first day of judging and it absolutely floored me. I talked about it for the rest of the week. Picture if you will a bedroom. On the wall is a small, plastic crucifix—the kind with Jesus still on it. On Jesus' little hands are tiny blue wool mittens. On his head is a tiny blue wool hat with a little white pom pom. And around his neck, a tiny blue and white wool scarf. The ad was for air conditioning. And it's awesome. Ever since I saw it I've been thinking about the little old Catholic lady with little knitting needles working away to keep her little Jesus warm in her nicely air conditioned apartment. "Jesus Mittens," I love you.

Gerry Graf

JUDGES' CHOICE

CLIENT
The Burke Museum

AGENCY
Foote Cone & Belding/
Seattle

Standing in the ballroom of the Ritz Hotel in Barcelona surrounded by the print campaigns entered into this year's One Show, one felt one was in the sanctum sanctorum of the world's finest advertising.

The One Show is the last bastion of copy-rich intelligent print work.

So whilst I congratulate Fox Sports as a very worthy winner of Best of Show (and there were many other excellent contenders) as a personal choice I would have taken a stand. I would have given the Best of show to a campaign that demonstrates that not only can copy ads be desirable, sometimes, they're essential. I like the Shackleton campaign very much. Each execution stopped me and there were a number: "Dead Cold Hands," "Hero," "It's Bloody Tough," "Ship," "Shackles" and "God Save The King."

If I'd seen this work and if I'd been in the same town or even in the same state, I'd have picked up the phone and booked my place at the Burke Museum in a flash.

Graham Warsop

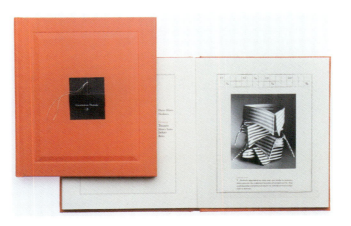

CLIENT
Plain Clothes

AGENCY
Slaughter Hanson/
Birmingham, AL

Thanks to Mary Warlick and The One Club for bringing design into this great creative competition. As the disciplines of advertising and design continue to morph into a merged form of brand building, it's only appropriate that The One Club become known for creative excellence in both.

The entries in design were on the lean side, as should be expected in the first year. Having said that, the quality of accepted winners was very good. We'll do a better job of getting the word out for next year, so both quantity and quality will improve.

My personal favorite design entry was the Slaughter Hanson book for Plain Clothes entitled Uncommon Threads. I have a thing about little hand-crafted books, and this one was one of the best I've ever seen. It's not trying to be anything more than it should be, yet all the elements, type, photography, layout, materials, etc., are just exquisite—a joy to hold as well as to see. In this "digital age," it's a refreshing reminder of the timeless power of great design.

Joe Duffy

JUDGES' CHOICE

CLIENT
Goodwill

AGENCY
Clarke Goward/Boston

It has been many weeks since the judging. I also recollect that there were nearly a thousand design entries. But the great work still stays fresh in my memory and continues to rise to the top. The Goodwill Annual Report is my favorite. The concept of printing on the brown paper bag used to package donated clothing is direct and honest. Space limitations forced text and charts to be refreshingly terse. Unlike many entries, this one could be read and recycled.

As the first One Show Design competition, a high percentage of submissions came from agencies and not design studios. Therefore, the majority of entries were ad collateral and not the anticipated design fare (i.e., annual reports and posters). Submission quality might have been improved with the participation of noteworthy and up-and-coming design firms. Future competitions will benefit from encouraging entries by category and expanding the pool of participants. The second One Show Design competition will certainly outshine the former.

Keith Helmetag

One of my favorite pieces of work in the show was the Goodwill annual report. They used a large brown recycled paper bag and printed in one color the facts and figures of the year. In the spirit of the organization you are then urged to fill the bag with used clothing and donate. A damn fine idea and a noble cause.

Graham Clifford

I also saw this catalog when judging Communications Arts. This is a small brochure for the Scifi Channel that, at first, resembles a product catalog. But the twist is what's missing. For instance, a man looking at a wrist watch that isn't there; a woman modeling a dress—without the dress.

Without knowing more about the Scifi Channel, I think their intent was to market the paranormal in a humorous and more earthly way. I wish I had this piece. It's quite brilliant and commonly overlooked. Congratulations to all who worked on it.

Jennifer Sterling

CLIENT
Scifi Channel

AGENCY
USA Networks/Scifi Channel/New York

It's been months since I judged the show. The first thing that popped into my head, and I laughed out loud when I thought about it, is Television 3's promotion for the Invisible Man. It was not well designed, maybe even ugly. But what a fantastic idea to have dogs walk around the city on leashes as if someone invisible was walking them.

Is it design, advertising, entertainment or art? Who cares. I just loved it. And I'm sure the people on the street who came across the dogs did too. (Applause).

Robert Wong

CLIENT
Television 3

AGENCY
Colenso BBDO/Auckland

GOLD ON GOLD

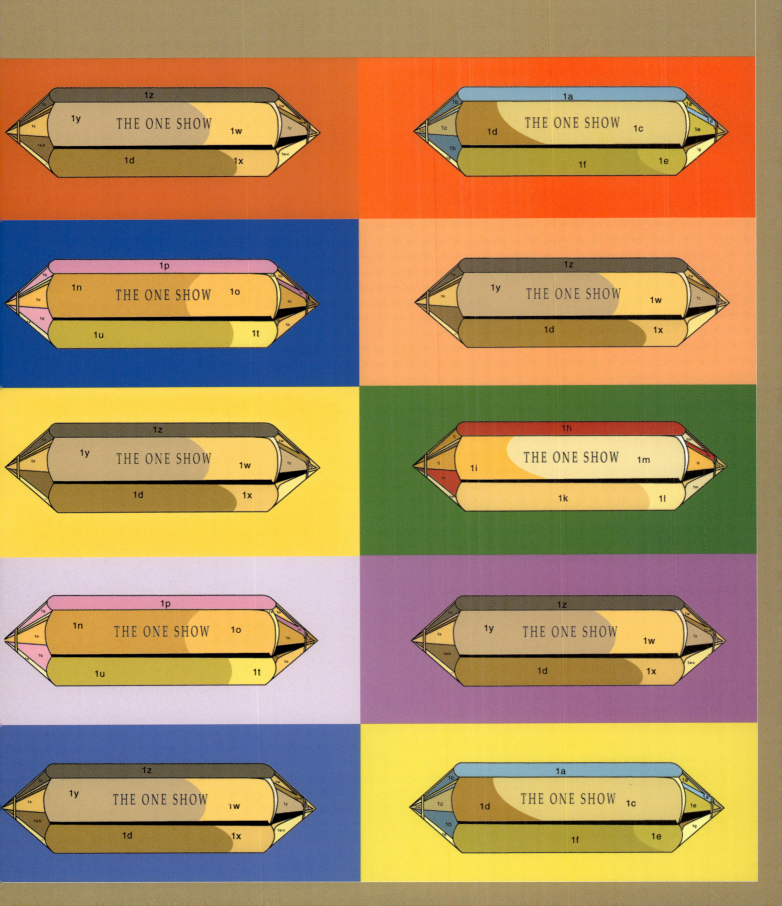

GOLD ON GOLD

GOLD AWARD
Newspaper Over 600 Lines: Campaign

CLIENT
Drinks.com

AGENCY
Mullen/Wenham

ID 010004A

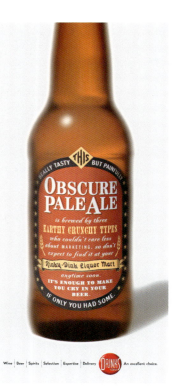

What we were trying to do in this campaign was to work in all of our favorite phrases. They are:
Suck it up
In like Flynn
Billy the stock boy
Earthy crunchy types
Dogs attacking an elk
Rinky-dink
Anonymous roadside sex

We were amazed that we got almost all of them past the client.
Thanks for the Pencil.

Ted Jendrysik
Chris Poulin
Libby DeLana

Reading the Paper, 2001
Ink on hands
Courtesy of The Museum of Contemporary Art, Los Angeles

We decided to make this assignment for The Museum of Contemporary Art, Los Angeles as hard as we possibly could on ourselves. Whether it was a billboard, a bus side, a television set, a coffee cup band or Page 2 of *The Los Angeles Times*, each concept was written for the specific location the ad would appear. 118 in all.

So here's 119:

Gold Pencil on Shelf, 2001
Metal, gold plate, 2.65 lb. Collection of Maya Rao and Moe VerBrugge

Maya Rao
Moe VerBrugge

GOLD ON GOLD

GOLD AWARD
Newspaper 600 Lines or Less: Single

CLIENT
Museum of Contemporary Art

AGENCY
TBWA/Chiat/Day/Los Angeles

ID 010007A

GOLD ON GOLD

GOLD AWARD
Magazine Color Full Page or Spread: Single

CLIENT
Volkswagen of America

AGENCY
ARNOLD Worldwide/Boston

ID 010012A

Lettuce sales up 38%

Don Shelford
Dave Weist

GOLD AWARD
Magazine Color Full Page or Spread: Campaign

CLIENT
Volkswagen of America

AGENCY
ARNOLD Worldwide/Boston

ID 010017A

This was such a great assignment. A bit scary but great. We were given one of the most recognizable things in the world to work with. And so it wasn't long before we asked ourselves, "How much can it really blend in?" Here the car had been on the road for about three years and people still seemed to wave internally or something when one drove by. That's what led us to these ads, where nothing, no matter how visually arresting, was able to up-stage the New Beetle. The line, "Hey, there's a yellow one…" or "Hey, there's a black one…" seemed to match the level of recognition people were giving it.

After we had that basic premise, we essentially added fire, bees and a woman wrapped in lettuce to illustrate our point.

Don Shelford
Dave Weist

ACCOUNT DIRECTOR JULIAN RIBEIRO: New brief coming through, guys. We'll have to do a factory visit.

CREATIVE TEAM: Jules, we feel that factory visits are a waste of time. Besides, we know how sheep dip is manufactured.

ACCOUNT DIRECTOR: Okay then. I'll go. But it's not the sheep dip brief. It's for the Seychelles.

CREATIVE TEAM: We feel that a factory visit is essential.

ACCOUNT DIRECTOR: You may be forced to sail on yachts, frolic on beaches and drink rum cocktails.

CREATIVE TEAM: Nevertheless, we feel that a factory visit is essential.

We are pleased to report that in this case, the factory visit was not a waste of time.

Wendy Moorecroft
Erik Vervroegen
Karin Barry

GOLD ON GOLD

GOLD AWARD
Magazine Color Full Page or Spread: Campaign

CLIENT
Seychelles

AGENCY
TBWA Hunt Lascaris/ Johannesburg

ID 010018A

GOLD ON GOLD

GOLD AWARD
Magazine Less Than a Page
B/W or Color: Single

CLIENT
American Heritage Dictionary

AGENCY
Mullen/Wenham

ID 010023A

We spent hours one meeting trying to convince the client that the words, "circumvolve off," didn't sound too dirty.

But in hindsight we guess it sounds just dirty enough.

Paul Laffy
Brian Hayes

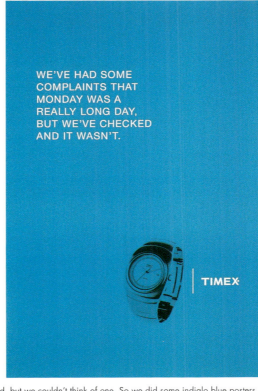

Timex initially wanted a single page black and white price promotion ad, but we couldn't think of one. So we did some indiglo blue posters instead, which luckily they really liked. Unlike most watch ads, normal people don't really think about time in terms of hundredths of seconds. Normal people think about it in terms of 'is it lunch time yet?' So we did a campaign about the measurement of time. And this is one execution in the series.

Andy McLeod
Richard Flintham

GOLD AWARD
Outdoor: Single

CLIENT
UK Time-Timex

AGENCY
Fallon/London

ID 010028A

We thought of the dog idea, and to make it easy on ourselves, and the photographer, we considered using a stuffed dog. So we phoned a few taxidermists. The first one said, "No one stuffs pets anymore mate because it's sick," and hung up. Another guy said he knew of some nice work that had been done on a mountain goat. He reckoned as long as you didn't put it near a mountain, that city folk wouldn't know the difference.

Finally we spoke to a taxidermist who thought he could help us out. He said he'd spoken to a guy the previous week who'd had a dead dog in the trunk of his car. He offered to call the guy for us and see if it was still there. At this point we thought it best to use a live one. So we used Rosie, our producer's dog and she was perfect.

Billy McQueen
Chris Schofield
Warwick Delmonte
Quentin Pfiszter

GOLD AWARD
Guerilla

CLIENT
Television 3

AGENCY
Colenso BBDO/Auckland

ID 010032A

GOLD ON GOLD

GOLD AWARD
Collateral: Posters

CLIENT
BMW Iberica

AGENCY
* S, C, P, F/Barcelona

ID 010047A

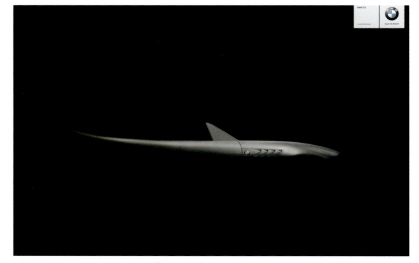

It's hard to explain with words an ad that has none. So we'll take advantage of these brief seconds of fame this book allows us to take a musical break between ads and give some space to the lyrics of one of our favorite songs:

This is the time and life that I am living
and I'll face each day with a smile
for the time that I've been given's
such a little while
and the things that I must do
consist of more than style.
(from "Forever Changes" by Love)

That's all. Love.

Borja Arteaga
Jaume Rodriguez

GOLD AWARD
Public Service/Political
Newspaper or Magazine:
Single

CLIENT
National D-Day Museum

AGENCY
GMO Hill Holliday/
San Francisco

ID 010051A

We would like to thank "The Professor"–Rob Bagot and "Slash" Noble for their peerless creative direction and Brian O'Neill for making this project a reality.

But mostly we would like to thank the men who on June 6, 1944 stepped off those boats into the teeth of an almost certain death.

When we first presented the ads to our client he requested that we not show any dead soldiers. For us it was difficult to tell the story of what happened on that day without including the sacrifice that so many men and their families made. Fortunately, common sense prevailed and our client agreed to run some very moving ads.

The generation that has been called America's greatest is dying out.

Their stories don't have to.

Matt Mowat
Chuck Meehan

GOLD ON GOLD

GOLD AWARD
Public Service/Political
Newspaper or Magazine:
Campaign

CLIENT
The Big Issue Foundation

AGENCY
TBWA/London

ID 010054A

Tonight, kids will be wandering the streets, amongst pissheads, pushers, pickpockets, never a policeman when you need one, prostitutes, perverts and pimps. They'll scavenge for food and beg for money. Then they'll try and find a doorway that someone hasn't pissed or puked in, where they can wait for the morning. And that's their idea of being safe. Safer than houses. Because their house is where they were sexually abused, and threatened with what would happen if they ever dared tell anyone about 'their little secret'. Or their house was where they were beaten, not smacked. Punched. Beaten the crap out of. They're not stupid. They know that running away is no adventure. But they will never go home. One in three of them attempts suicide. Those that fail are in and out of care until they're old enough to stay out. It's how a lot of young people end up living rough. The Big Issue Foundation knows that helping them isn't merely about getting a roof over their heads. We also have to understand what's going on in their heads. So what is it that can make someone who trusts almost no one trust us? We never push. And we're not out to reach any targets. If anyone decides to sell The Big Issue it's because they need the cash, and The Big Issue is pretty much the only legal way they can earn it. When they collect the magazines, they become aware that The Big Issue Foundation offers support for drink and drug addictions, advice and training for jobs, and of course, help with accommodation. But there's no pressure on anyone to take it. If someone does want to change their life, then they have to do it themselves, but not by themselves.

If cold, wet, hungry and scared is what thousands of kids run away to, imagine what they run away from.

Drug addict? Alcoholic? Suicidal? Apparently, what you need is a nice cup of hot soup.

Litter, terrible isn't it? And dog muck. Something really should be done about that. Oh yes, and homeless people.

There are thousands of homeless people begging in Britain. They're ignored because they're pissed and stoned. Or are they pissed and stoned because they're ignored? John Bird, who set up the Big Issue, told us about a homeless girl who used to sit on the floor outside a London burger bar, hand outstretched, asking passersby for their spare change. A man walking past felt sorry for her and decided that he would give her something more worthwhile than a few coins. So he gave her a 20 pound note and continued on his way, no doubt feeling good about himself and his most magnanimous gesture. She spent the 20 pound on the best way she knew of making herself feel good. Heroin. Cheap, badly cut heroin. Enough cheap, badly cut heroin to overdose and die.

So what should people do? They should stop the next time some flea-bitten drop-out waves a copy of the Big Issue magazine at them and buy one. But they don't. Well, some people do, but not enough. That's why we produced the campaign. We wanted people to understand what homeless people are going through, as well as what they might have gone through to become homeless in the first place.

But there are hundreds of charity campaigns about, all trying to shock themselves into the reader's conscience. Shocking imagery is the charity norm. And has become a way to help people instantly recognize and dismiss yet another plea for their hard-earned. So we decided that, rather than poke the readers in the eye, we would talk to them. No doe-eyed youngsters in rags. No dead bodies on doorsteps. No logo. No logo? We persuaded the client that the ads didn't need one. And judging by the response they've had, they didn't.

It was good to get the chance to help a great organization. It was a change to not be told that nobody reads the body copy. And it's great to give a home to a One Show Gold.

Nigel Roberts
Paul Belford

GOLD ON GOLD

GOLD AWARD
Public Service/Political:
Outdoor and Posters

CLIENT
ACLU

AGENCY
DeVito/Verdi/New York

ID 010057A

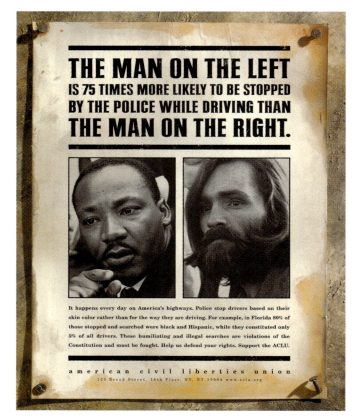

Alternatives for the man on the right could have been Jeffrey Dahmer, David Berkowitz, Adolf Hitler, or Timothy McVeigh.

Alternatives for the man on the left could have been Colin Powell, Muhammad Ali, Nelson Mandela, or Sgt. David Smith, an African-American police officer who was pulled over while driving an unmarked car in the city of Carmel, Indiana. Sgt. Smith was wearing a full uniform at the time, but was not wearing a hat which would have identified him as a police officer.

The trooper who stopped Smith appeared to be "shocked and surprised" when Sgt. Smith got out of the car. The trooper explained that he had stopped Smith because he had three antennas on the rear of his car. The trooper quickly left the scene.

Sal DeVito
Joel Tractenberg
Greg Braun

GOLD AWARD
Public Service/Political
Collateral: Brochures &
Direct Mail

CLIENT
Physicians for
Human Rights

AGENCY
Euro RSCG McConnaughy
Tatham/Chicago

ID 010060A

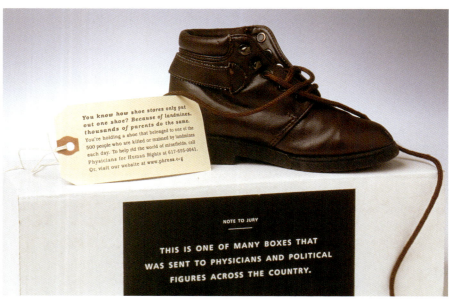

You usually hope to come up with an idea that can go on forever. That wasn't the case this time.

Jim Schmidt

116

(In this campaign, actors posing as desperate young people cold called unsuspecting strangers in an attempt to talk about their problems. The following is a transcript of one such conversation.)

SFX:	Phone ringing.
WOMAN:	Yeah, hello.
GIRL:	Oh hello, um…you don't know me, I just needed to talk to someone.
WOMAN:	Who is…who is this?
GIRL:	It's just that my Mum, my Mum's hit me again and she hits me all the time. *(getting more upset)* And my Dad doesn't do anything about it, and I know that he knows, I know he knows, and I don't understand why he won't help me. *(The girl begins to cry.)*
WOMAN:	What phone number did you call?
GIRL:	I, I, I, didn't have anyone to talk to, I rang Youthline but the lines were all busy, I…What am I supposed to do?
WOMAN:	Did you just call a number out of the blue…?
GIRL:	Yeah, I'm so sorry. I'm not a bad person, I'm not. I'm not, I mean I know she thinks I am, but I'm not. I'm not…
WOMAN:	You're not bad and you've done the right thing calling.
GIRL:	I just can't cope anymore.
VOICEOVER:	At Youthline we only have enough phone lines to answer a third of our calls so if we can't help, who will? To make a donation call 0800 543 943 and please give generously.

The key to this brief was that Youthline, a telephone counseling service for troubled youth, only had enough phone lines to take one-third of its calls. This begged the question, 'Who are they going to talk to if they can't get through to Youthline?' Would they in desperation just pick a number out of the phone book and call it? And how would the average person cope with such a call? It was an intriguing idea. To make the radio commercials as powerful as possible we knew the calls had to be made for real. But who was going to receive them? No one in the production team wanted to inflict such a disturbing event on anyone we knew and eventually the decision was made to call a compassionate girl who worked in the agency. She had no idea that the call was coming so we were convinced we'd achieve the realism we were striving for. This was helped considerably by our choice of actress who had just finished playing the role of an abuse victim in a recent theatre production. Perfect. The call was placed and as it progressed we quickly realized how powerful the commercials would be. All the hairs on our necks stood on end and the emotion in the room was so palpable we couldn't breathe or talk. It was the most harrowing recording session we had ever been in. But worth it for such effective commercials. Thanks to everyone involved, especially Mike and Wendy.

Glenn Wood
Natalie Knight
Josh Robbins

GOLD ON GOLD

GOLD AWARD
Public Service/Political
Radio: Single

CLIENT
Youthline

AGENCY
Colenso BBDO/Auckland

ID 010062A

This is the 73rd commercial created for the Transport Accident Commission in the State of Victoria. Once again it has provided a bonus for the manufacturers of tissues.

When the concept was presented there was a sniffle or two from the other side of the table.

During research (and believe us, this is one campaign that has benefited immeasurably from research) there were long pauses and a couple of surreptitious eye-wipes. One guy's spontaneous reaction was, "It would ruin my night."

During the shoot the floodgates opened amongst the crew as the father dissected his emotions. He gave a remarkable performance.

Since release, the commercial has silenced rooms whenever shown.

This is all very well, but it amounts to naught if the reaction is not reflected in behavior on the roads. While it is problematic to draw a direct relationship between advertising and road trauma, the fact is that the Victorian road toll in December 2000, when this commercial was launched, was the lowest December total since 1952.

But 29 people still died.

As we said in these pages two years ago, we have a long way to go.

Nigel Dawson
Rob Dow

GOLD AWARD
Public Service/Political
Television: Single

CLIENT
Transport Accident
Commission

AGENCY
Grey Worldwide/Melbourne

ID 010067A

GOLD ON GOLD

GOLD AWARD
Consumer Radio: Single

CLIENT
Anheuser-Busch

AGENCY
DDB/Chicago

ID 010071A

SFX:	Music up.
ANNOUNCER:	Bud Light presents…Real. American. Heroes.
SINGER:	Real American Heroes…
ANNOUNCER:	Today we salute you…Mr. Really Bad Toupee Wearer.
SINGER:	Mr. Really Bad Toupee Wearer.
ANNOUNCER:	More than any neon sign or exploding scoreboard ever could, your chrome-dome cover says, "Hey, guys, look at me."
SINGER:	What could you be thinkin'?
ANNOUNCER:	You think it looks natural, but it couldn't look phonier if it had a chinstrap!
SINGER:	Couldn't fool a blind man…
ANNOUNCER:	Made of space age fibers, "it" can repel anything. Rain. Wind. Snow. And especially…young women.
SINGERS:	I don't think so!
ANNOUNCER:	So crack open an ice cold Bud Light, Mr. Stud in a Rug. *(Beer pops open.)* Then crack open another for that thing on your head.
SINGERS:	I don't think it's on straight…
ANNOUNCER:	Bud Light Beer, Anheuser-Busch, St. Louis, Missouri.

One time, when I was a little kid, I saw a guy at the fair who painted his hair on with shoe polish.

I had a Geometry teacher in high school who favored lime green leisure suits and a huge, curly "Mr. Kotter" style toupee. He assured me that "wisenheimers" like me "would never amount to nothing."

There was a guy I worked with who was as bald as a door knob on Friday, then had a full head of hair (hairline about a half inch over his eyebrows) on Monday.

In each of these instances I was forced to hold my tongue.

Now, many years later, there is an outside chance that acknowledging these fine gentlemen will sell more beer.

I finally get to say something, I get to work with the guy from "Survivor," and I get an award from Mr. One Show Pencil Giver-Outer. I no longer feel like I amount to nothing.

John Immesoete

GOLD AWARD
Consumer Radio: Campaign

CLIENT
OurHouse.com

AGENCY
Black Rocket/San Francisco

ID 010075A

(Real room sounds. We hear a man reading a newspaper and sipping coffee. We hear a woman walk into the room.)

MAN:	Morning.
WOMAN:	Morning. You're up early for a Saturday.
MAN:	Yeah, I'm gonna build a deck today.
WOMAN:	Is there a game on or something?
MAN:	No seriously, I'm building a deck.
WOMAN:	*(pause)* Whatever.
MAN:	You don't believe me?
WOMAN:	No.
MAN:	*(pause)* It's not that hard.
WOMAN:	Pass me the sugar.
MAN:	You just wait.
WOMAN:	I'll tell you what, if you build us a deck, I'll take off all my clothes and barbecue you a steak.

(We hear the man get up, and walk out of the room.)

WOMAN:	Stanley?…Stanley?
ANNOUNCER 1:	Tools. Advice. House calls. Sanity. Everything you need to fix up your house, or have it done for you. OurHouse.com. We're here to help.
ANNOUNCER 2:	Partnered with Ace.

The idea behind the campaign was to highlight couples' relationship with home improvement. Everyone has gone through it at some point, and everyone has had problems or issues or arguments or even fights about it. There was a lot of good material there. But the tone is really what made these spots so successful. We wanted you to feel like you were really listening in on a couple's conversation. This was much harder to achieve than we thought. The production was key. We spent a lot of time throwing away voice over casting tapes until we decided to use a combination of real people (like our producer) and former television actors, basically people who had never done a radio spot before.

The next challenge was convincing radio engineers that we had to record outside the studio. Never let them tell you that they can make a documentary-sounding spot in the studio just by adding the appropriate room tone. It doesn't work. So we recorded in people's houses. This is what gave it the realistic feeling we wanted. We even had one of our actresses actually get in the shower to record (method radio acting). The hardest part of the process was ignoring everyone that kept saying "you can't do it that way" or "that won't work." By the end I would get nervous if no one told us we were doing it wrong. The spots don't work too well in script form, but when you hear them on the radio they stand out because of their subtlety and voyeuristic nature, which is pretty rare in radio.

Aaron Allen

Oh no.
It's The One Club.
And they want you to write about your monster.com ad.
So what are you going to do?
Rattle off some amusing stories about the shoot?
Share a few 'Oh so witty' anecdotes that make you look cool and interesting?
Sure, you could do that.
But it would take time.
And effort.
Those sort of things don't write themselves.
You'd have to think about it.
A lot.
And then get your secretary to type it.
Well forget that.
Just quickly knock out any old rubbish, but do it in the style of a monster.com ad.
Yes, they'll like that.
All you have to do is pretend there's a voice in your head, telling you what to write.
And everyone wins.
They get their pound of flesh.
And you get back to playing pool and watching MTV.

Gavin Kellett
Nik Studzinski

GOLD ON GOLD

GOLD AWARD
Consumer Television Over :30
Single

ART DIRECTOR
Nik Studzinski

CLIENT
Monster.com

AGENCY
Saatchi & Saatchi/London

ID 010078A

Firstly, it is amazing to win these awards. A big group hug is in order for everyone involved. Very early on Eric said to me, "Let's do something that won't win anything." I frowned and mumbled "...Alrighty then." After that we forgot about what the judges would say and worried about what our friends and like-minded NBA fans would say. That, I guess, is the trick. So here's to next year's "non-award winning" campaign.

Reed Collins
Eric Silver

GOLD AWARD
Consumer Television :30
Single

CLIENT
Fox Sports

AGENCY
Cliff Freeman and Partners/
New York

ID 010081A

This business has a lot to do with luck. You hope you stumble upon and extricate a decent idea. Then you need to luck into a great editor (Gavin Cutler), a special effects guru (Johnnie at Quiet Man) and a client who is truly a partner (Neal Tiles). The only real skill comes into play after winning a prestigious One Show pencil and having to come up with a clever Gold on Gold....I got nothin'.

Eric Silver

GOLD AWARD
Consumer Television :30
Campaign

CLIENT
Fox Sports

AGENCY
Cliff Freeman and Partners/
New York

ID 010084A

GOLD ON GOLD

GOLD AWARD
Consumer Television :20 and Under: Single

CLIENT
H & R Block

AGENCY
Young & Rubicam/Chicago

ID 010087A

Before we started shooting this scene, the script supervisor came running over, frazzled: "I don't have a script for this scene!" We told her we hadn't written it yet. We had all noticed this pre-teen's amazing talent and Craig wanted to try some stuff to make better use of her. We knew we had to get it in 11 seconds for it to work. The first try came in at 25. Craig never turned off the camera and we kept reworking the idea down until we got it in time. Craig cut and we gave the crew about five minutes to get all the laughs out of their system before we moved on.

Rick Casteel
John Matejczyk

GOLD AWARD
Consumer Television :20 and Under: Campaign

CLIENT
H & R Block

AGENCY
Young & Rubicam/Chicago

ID 010089A

There was a lot more suspense than there is room to tell it, but basically:

We went into production on seven spots. Two of them were for tax services, the client's bread and butter. The other five were for other stuff.

To make a long story short, one tax spot got killed the day before pre-pro. We locked ourselves into a hotel room, chain smoking (we're not smokers). Having already cast and scouted, we said to ourselves: "We've got a mom, dad, daughter, a house to shoot them in, and a director to shoot it. What are we going to shoot?"

We wove a loose idea of a man melting down over his attempt to do his own taxes. In callbacks we worked out a :30 script with our director, Craig Gillespie. We called it "Worried About Bill."

Halfway through the pre-pro meeting, we got a call that the other tax spot was killed, too. We called a time-out, went outside, and decided we could milk a couple spots out of the psychodrama idea. The client bought it.

We headed into production throwing out vignette ideas and shooting them as we went—some from us, some from Craig. The shoot was one of those rare cases in this business when you're actually painting with the paintbrush in your hand.

In post, we realized the vignettes for the :30s worked better as single :15s. Seven spots became 19.

If that sounds like fun, it's only in retrospect. At the time, when John's wife called from Chicago, he broke down crying because someone was nice to him. Rick canceled his trip to see his family for Christmas out of pure exhaustion. Our producer, Lee, just yelled at us a lot, but we got him to cry once, too.

John Matejczyk
Rick Casteel

DANIEL LIM
VINCENT PANG
WU JIANG XUE

同志們：
對所有中國人來說，這是具有曆史意義的一刻，我們極其之自豪——中國的電視廣告第一次贏得了 One Show 的金鉛筆大獎。它証明來自語言、文化和思想的隔閡都是可以消除的：因為人類是以人牲的真實而非地域來界定的。我們希望你們——中國未來的一代創意人，會因此而獲得激勵。

This is the first time that a Chinese commercial has won a Gold Pencil at the One Show and we're very excited about it. A One Show Pencil is a symbol of creative excellence in the English-speaking world. We have written our commentary in Chinese in the hopes that we will also reach an audience of Chinese-speaking creatives in China. Our commentary translates roughly to:

"Dear Comrades,
This is a historical moment for all of us in China. It is the first time a Chinese commercial has ever won a Gold Pencil at the One Show and we are all very honored by it. This award proves that barriers in language, culture and thinking can be dissolved: It is human truths that define us, not geographical borders. We hope that you, the future generation of Chinese creatives, are as inspired by this moment as we are."

Daniel Lim
Wu Jiang Xue

GOLD ON GOLD

GOLD AWARD
Foreign Language Television:
Single

CLIENT
UNICEF

AGENCY
Saatchi & Saatchi/Hong Kong

ID 010096A

GOLD ON GOLD

GOLD AWARD
Multi-Media Campaign

CLIENT
Nike

AGENCY
The Jupiter Drawing Room
(South Africa)/Johannesburg

ID 010099A

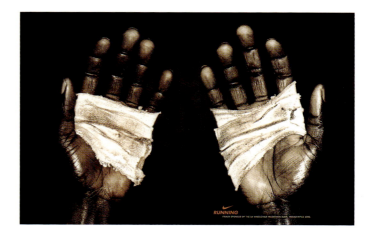

The South African Paralympic team brought home 28 medals from Atlanta in 1996. Their aim was to better this achievement in Sydney 2000. As an official sponsor of the team, Nike wanted to encourage the public to support this gifted group of athletes in their endeavor.

So, what to do?

Following our agency motto "Rem tene verba sequentur"—"Grasp the subject and the words will follow"—we went out and met the members of the Paralympic team hoping we might be inspired.

We were.

Every athlete demonstrates the irony of the word "disabled." Take, for example, a blind runner named Rory Field. He has the ability to sprint 100m in a shade over 11 seconds. If you don't think that's impressive, try it. With your eyes open.

We realized no one personifies the Nike spirit more aptly than the Paralympic team. It's not what's wrong, but what's right. It's about what you can do, never what you can't.

Showing the work to Nike was not the hard part, it was showing it to the athletes that was intimidating, as some of it was quite hard-hitting, some of it light-hearted. We overheard one athlete say, "It's good to see ads without the Boo-Hoo-Hoo factor." We knew we were on to a good thing.

The 2000 South African Paralympic team headed off for Sydney as heroes and that's how they returned. They proudly boast 38 medals.

And one Gold Pencil.

Graham Warsop
Peter Callaghan

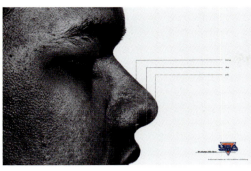 

DATE: Sometime in April

TIME: 10:58 AM
OTIS *(thick Southern accent—a bit groggy)*: Hello?
JOSH *(thick Long Island accent—not as groggy)*: Otis, you sleeping?
OTIS: Huh?
JOSH: Hey, I just got a call from school. We won a Pencil.
OTIS: Where?
JOSH: That's pretty cool, right?
OTIS: Yes, a pretty pool.
JOSH: Hung over?
OTIS: Where are the crackers?
JOSH: Should I call back later?
OTIS: Why are you yelling at me?
JOSH: Talk to you later.
OTIS: Who is this?

A special thanks to Norm, Carol, MJK, Mike and Kelly Lear and everyone at The Creative Circus for their help.

Josh Schildkraut
Otis Webb

The life of an annual report looks something like this.

You send it to some member of the board of directors. They look to find their name in print. Check to make sure the institution is still solvent. Maybe read the mission statement for the upcoming year and inevitably throw the whole thing in the trash. A first lieutenant in Vietnam probably had a longer life span than the average annual report.

Well, knowing the report we designed was eventually going to find it's way into a dumpster anyway, we figured, "Why not make sure it finds it's way into the RIGHT dumpster?"

For anyone who has ever moved, broken up with someone or simply cleaned out a closet, the big, blue Goodwill collection box is a familiar sight. With that in mind, we wanted to create an annual report that would not only serve its purpose as an informational piece, but would help further the mission of the charity as well.

Now, coming up with the idea, an annual report that doubled as a donation bag, really wasn't that difficult. Producing it was quite a different story.

The first thing you'll notice when working with a paper bag is that it's really an oblong cylinder. Creating a multi-dimensional piece on this type of medium is like designing a layout on a paper dress pattern and then praying to God that it still makes sense after the printer glues it together (on a side note, we'd like to point out bag venders rarely do annual reports).

We realized early on the design had to be flexible. It had to look good no matter how botched the printing came out. So we embraced that and used it to our advantage and tried to design something that looked better the more botched the printing was.

In the end we still feel we got lucky. Lord knows, had it not worked out, they could have all ended up in the WRONG dumpster.

Chris Pinkham
Larry Raff

GOLD ON GOLD

GOLD AWARD
College Competition

SCHOOL
The Creative Circus/Atlanta

ID 010102A

CLIENT
Goodwill

AGENCY
Clarke Goward/Boston

ID 010001D

GOLD ON GOLD

CLIENT
San Diego Ad Club

AGENCY
Di Zinno Thompson/
Coronado

ID 010002D

After utilizing the agency's educational support program to get his GED, Ming decided to enroll in the local junior college. Not satisfied with just being an advertising copywriter, his real desire was to become a professor of textiles of the Ohio River Valley. Much to his chagrin, he discovered he would have to take the SAT first.

Being good partners, Dana and I obliged Ming by helping him study for it. We even bought him some flash cards and an SAT practice book. In the midst of this academic quest, we got saddled with a San Diego Creative Show call for entries.

Inadvertently, one of the SAT practice tests ended up in the Creative Show job bag. Through a grievous error, it got sent to the client and approved before we knew what had happened.

It's too bad because our original idea for the Creative Show had a cool picture of a bowl of corn chips and cheese sauce with this headline that Ming had written: This is nacho ordinary award show.

Oh well.

**Craig Evans
Ming Lai
Dana Neibert**

CLIENT
Plain Clothes

AGENCY
Slaughter Hanson/
Birmingham, AL

ID 010003D

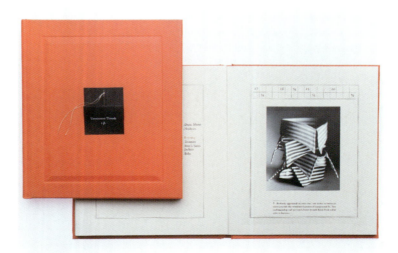

Since "Uncommon Threads" is a piece that introduces the idea of made-to-measure clothing to Plain Clothes clients, we used custom necktie patterns as backgrounds to many of the pages in this brochure. However, many of these patterns are quite complex and we needed to represent them in their simplest form, so we had to experiment quite a bit. We started hanging these so-called experiments on every bit of available wall space for days, and then weeks, until we were satisfied with the results. But, after a while you simply couldn't look at them. When you stared at all these different patterns in all these different configurations...well, it made you absolutely crazy. I'm convinced the other designer was hypnotized during the remainder of the project. We get a good laugh whenever we relive this piece–and quite glad that we are not textile designers.

**Marion English Powers
Kathy Oldham
Jeanne Renneker**

GOLD ON GOLD

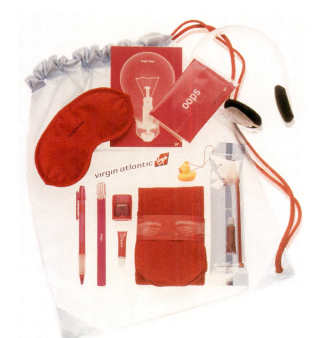

CLIENT
Virgin Atlantic

AGENCY
Turner Duckworth/
San Francisco

ID 010004D

Virgin Atlantic wanted to relieve the tedium of a long haul flight in economy class with an amenity kit that goes beyond the expected. The solution had to express the Virgin brand values (modern, style, attention to detail, human and wit) whilst providing practical creature comforts for the duration of the flight. The packs had to be light in weight, compact and economical to produce. Loosely based on airport security x-rays, the vibrantly colored translucent packages are stuffed with handy goodies from 'Pardon?' earplugs to 'oops' wipes and a wash kit complete with a tiny rubber duck called Lewis to take to the tiny bathroom. The chatty approach to the descriptions was in sympathy with those bored on board the monotonous transatlantic journeys. The bag size was increased to a useful backpack format, which amply accommodates all the extra in-flight clutter and has a functional life after the flight is over.

Sarah Moffat
Bruce Duckworth
David Turner

CLIENT
Nike

AGENCY
Wieden + Kennedy/
Amsterdam

ID 010005D

This is a limited edition book (2,000 printed) chronicling Nike's heritage from the first waffle trainer to the last Air Jordan of the 20th century. It's peppered with famous Nike slogans and athlete quotes and bound in the same material used for Michael Johnson's gold track spikes in which he broke the 200 meter world record at the Atlanta Olympics.

Our client wanted a calendar.

Glenn Cole
Robert Nakata
Tim Wolfe
Merete Busk

PRINT MERIT

MERIT AWARD
Newspaper Over 600 Lines: Single

ART DIRECTOR
Dave Dye

WRITER
Sean Doyle

CLIENT
The Economist

AGENCY
Abbott Mead Vickers.BBDO/London

010105A

MERIT AWARD
Newspaper Over 600 Lines: Single

ART DIRECTOR
Amanda Berger

WRITER
Greg Christensen

CLIENT
Loyola University Health System

AGENCY
Arian Lowe & Travis/Chicago

010106A

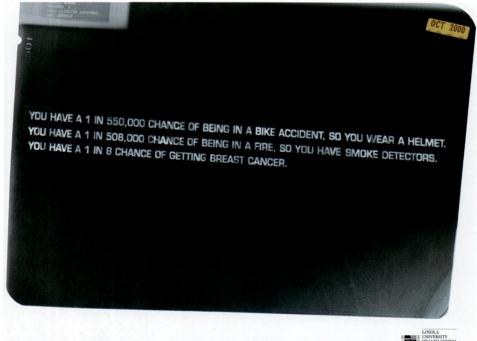

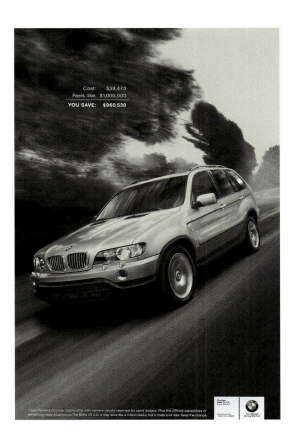

PRINT MERIT

MERIT AWARD
Newspaper Over 600 Lines:
Single

ART DIRECTOR
Andy Jex

WRITER
Rob Potts

PHOTOGRAPHER
Coppi Barbieri

CLIENT
UK Time-Timex

AGENCY
Fallon/London

010109A

MERIT AWARD
Newspaper Over 600 Lines:
Single

ART DIRECTOR
Andy Jex

WRITER
Rob Potts

PHOTOGRAPHER
Coppi Barbieri

CLIENT
UK Time-Timex

AGENCY
Fallon/London

010110A

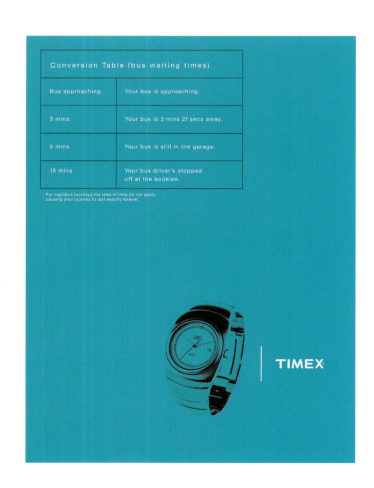

Peanuts

A moment of silence for Charles M. Schulz, 1922–2000.

Star Tribune
It's where you live.

MOST PEOPLE

I have a dream that I won the lottery.
I have a dream that I own a big house and a big car.
I have a dream that I'm a movie star.

MARTIN LUTHER KING, JR.

I have a dream that one day this nation will rise up and live out the true meaning of its creed: "We hold these truths to be self-evident, that all men are created equal." I have a dream that one day on the red hills of Georgia, the sons of former slaves and the sons of former slave owners will be able to sit down together at the table of brotherhood. I have a dream that one day even the state of Mississippi, a state sweltering with the heat of injustice, sweltering with the heat of oppression, will be transformed into an oasis of freedom and justice. I have a dream that my four little children will one day live in a nation where they will not be judged by the color of their skin but by the content of their character. I have a dream today. I have a dream that one day, down in Alabama, with its vicious racists, with its governor having his lips dripping with the words of "interposition" and "nullification," one day right there in Alabama, little black boys and black girls will be able to join hands with little white boys and white girls as sisters and brothers. I have a dream today. I have a dream that one day "every valley shall be exalted, every hill and mountain shall be made low, the rough places will be made plain, and the crooked places will be made straight, and the glory of the Lord shall be revealed, and all flesh shall see it together." This is our hope. This is the faith that I go back to the South with. With this faith, we will be able to hew out of the mountain of despair a stone of hope. With this faith, we will be able to transform the jangling discords of our nation into a beautiful symphony of brotherhood. With this faith, we will be able to work together, to pray together, to struggle together, to go to jail together, to stand up for freedom together, knowing that we will be free one day. This will be the day. This will be the day when all of God's children will be able to sing with new meaning: "My country, 'tis of thee, sweet land of liberty, of thee I sing. Land where my fathers died, land of the pilgrims' pride, from every mountainside, let freedom ring." And if America is to be a great nation, this must become true. So let freedom ring from the prodigious hilltops of New Hampshire. Let freedom ring from the mighty mountains of New York. Let freedom ring from the heightening Alleghenies of Pennsylvania! Let freedom ring from the snowcapped Rockies of Colorado! Let freedom ring from the curvaceous slopes of California! But not only that, let freedom ring from Stone Mountain of Georgia! Let freedom ring from Lookout Mountain of Tennessee! Let freedom ring from every hill and molehill of Mississippi. From every mountainside, let freedom ring. And when this happens, when we allow freedom to ring, when we let it ring from every village and every hamlet, from every state and every city, we will be able to speed up that day when all of God's children, black men and white men, Jews and Gentiles, Protestants and Catholics, will be able to join hands and sing in the words of the old Negro spiritual: "Free at last! Free at last! Thank God almighty, we are free at last!"

He dreamed of a country that was unblinded by racial hatred.
On this, the date of his birth, we honor Dr. Martin Luther King, Jr.

The Boston Globe

PRINT MERIT

MERIT AWARD
Newspaper Over 600 Lines:
Single

ART DIRECTOR
Hal Tench

WRITER
Raymond McKinney

PHOTOGRAPHERS
Corbis Sygmal
Karl Steinbrenner

CLIENT
Carfax

AGENCY
The Martin Agency/
Richmond

010113A

MERIT AWARD
Newspaper Over 600 Lines:
Single

ART DIRECTORS
Chris Poulin
Libby DeLana

WRITER
Ted Jendrysik

PHOTOGRAPHER
Ulf Skogsberg

CLIENT
Drinks.com

AGENCY
Muller/Wenham

010114A

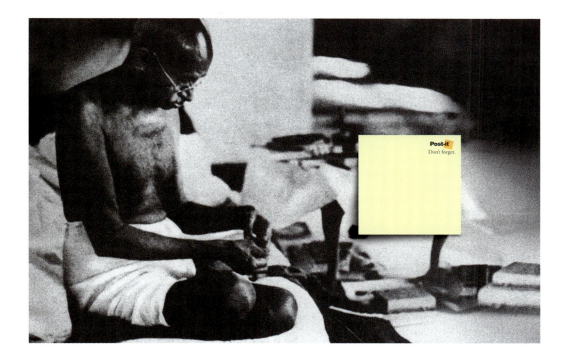

PRINT MERIT

MERIT AWARD
Newspaper Over 600 Lines: Single

ART DIRECTOR
Haridas B.

WRITERS
Haridas B.
Vidur Vohra

CLIENT
3M

AGENCY
Ogilvy & Mather/Bangalore

010115A

MERIT AWARD
Newspaper Over 600 Lines: Single

ART DIRECTOR
Craig Smith

WRITER
Andy Greenaway

ILLUSTRATOR
Yau Wai Kin

PHOTOGRAPHER
Roy Zhang

CLIENT
Asia Pacific Breweries

AGENCY
Ogilvy & Mather/Singapore

010116A

Also won:

MERIT AWARDS
Magazine Color Full Page or Spread: Single

Outdoor: Single

133

PRINT MERIT

MERIT AWARD
Newspaper Over 600 Lines: Single

ART DIRECTOR
Craig Smith

WRITER
Andy Greenaway

ILLUSTRATOR
Yau Wai Kin

PHOTOGRAPHER
Roy Zhang

CLIENT
Asia Pacific Breweries

AGENCY
Ogilvy & Mather/Singapore

010117A

Also won:

MERIT AWARD
Magazine Color Full Page or Spread: Single

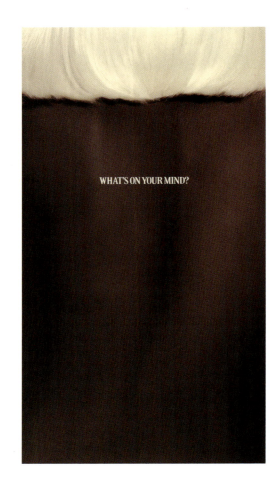

MERIT AWARD
Newspaper Over 600 Lines: Single

ART DIRECTOR
Tham Khai Meng

WRITER
Neil French

CLIENT
Borders Bookstore

AGENCY
Ogilvy & Mather/Singapore

010118A

THE BORDERS OF SANITY

The Prince[1] had found the last tycoon[2] in "The Raven"[3], drinking cider with Rosie.[4] He was…well, if not actually disgruntled, he was far from gruntled.

"It requires a surgical operation to get a joke well into a Scotch understanding,"[5] he grouched. "Journalism is basically people who can't write, interviewing people who can't talk, for people who can't read.[6] The editorial board is a parliament of whores."[7]

"Not staying on,[8] then?" ventured the little Prince.[9]

"An idea that is not dangerous is not worthy of being called an idea at all!"[10] he yelled, slamming the door behind him.

The silence hung in the air like a housebrick doesn't.[11]

"Assassination is the extreme form of censorship,"[12] she said. "Maybe the board should have tried that?"

"He's a modest little man, with a lot to be modest about,"[13] he replied. "Standards are always out of date. That's what makes them standards."[14]

He stood up.

"Ah, yes, Virginia, such is life."[15] He gathered his papers.[16] "All animals are equal, but some animals are more equal than others.[17] It's been a funny old year; a winter of discontent,[18] a silent spring,[19] a dangerous summer,[20] and now, the fall of the House of Usher."[21]

"Actually, I'm Rosie, not Virginia," she said. "Fancy a walk in the woods?"[22]

"A dance might be better?"

So over the blue remembered hills,[23] and far away, they danced to the music of time.[25]

THE END

"There are twenty-five clues to the authors of books, poems, or merely quotations on this page. The clues can be titles, well-known lines or passages…or even just 'clues'! The Borders store, on the corner of Orchard and Scotts Roads opens at nine in the morning. Next Friday, the first ten customers who give us a list of these authors can choose as many free books from our stock as they got correct answers. In other words, get three authors correct; get three free books. Up to the maximum of twenty-five books per customer. Good luck.

[129]

THE BORDERS OF SANITY

"So let us go, then, you and I,"[1] answered the ruined maid.[2] "To the far side of the world,[3] to a big hard-boiled city with no more personality than a paper cup.[4] Let's go see."

And so it was, that later,[5] when he first saw the green light at the end of Daisy's dock,[6] he realised that it is only shallow people who do not judge by appearances.[7]

He sighed, sadly, and then straightened his back. It is never difficult to distinguish between a Scotsman with a grievance and a ray of sunshine,[8] but there are few more impressive sights in the world than a Scotsman on the make.[9]

"I've had a few holidays in hell,"[10] he mused, "but *ugh!* To be in England, now that April's there.[11] A cold coming we had of it,[12] but I took the road less travelled-by.[13] The finest sight a Scotsman ever sees is the high-road that leads to England."[14]

A fellow of infinite jest,[15] he was nevertheless down and out in London,[16] which was, to his mind, more a confederacy of dunces[17] than a city of joy.[18] And he'd all but forgotten the art of eating.[19]

"Have you got a bit of cheese?"[20]

He looked down at what appeared to be a pointy hat with wee furry feet. The hat continued, "Poets have been mysteriously silent on the subject of cheese,"[21] it said, and stuck out a hand.

"Call me Ishmael,"[22] said the Hobbit,[23] (for it was such). "I'll go no more a roving by the light of the moon,[24] but since it's time for a little something,[25] and there's nothing like messing-about in boats,[26] hop in." He indicated a tiny pea-green boat.[27] "But tread softly, because you tread on my[28] fish paste and watercress

There are twenty-eight clues to the authors of books, poems, or merely quotations on this page. The clues can be titles, well-known lines or passages... or even just 'clues'! The Borders store, on the corner of Orchard and Scotts Roads opens at nine in the morning Next Thursday, the first ten customers who give us a list of these authors can choose as many free books from our stock as they got correct answers. In other words, get three authors correct; get three free books. Up to the maximum of twenty-five books per customer. Good luck.

[29]

THE BORDERS OF SANITY

The ugly American,[1] the French lieutenant's woman,[2] and one fat Englishman[3] had taken breakfast at Tiffany's.[4]

Privately, they regarded one another with fear and loathing,[5] and would have preferred a hundred years of solitude.[6] But for auld lang syne[7] (whatever that might have been), they had put away childish things,[8] and shared an omelette and a glass of wine.[9]

The thin man[10] leant back from the table. He'd been in a feeding frenzy[11] since the dawn's early light.[12]

"As God is my witness", he sighed, "I'll never be hungry again".[13] He stood, and reached for his tool. "It's time I slipped the surly bonds[14] of this fatal shore[15] and got on with managing my life.[16] I take the way to freedom!"[17]

With that, he was gone, striding across the river and into the trees.[18]

"Where's father going with that axe?"[19] enquired Lolita.[20] (Being both beautiful and damned,[21] she had learnt never to trust a man with a small black moustache).[22]

Atlas shrugged.[23] "To kill a mockingbird,"[24] he said. "Listen; can you keep your head while all about you are losing theirs?"[25]

"Yes I said I will yes" she gabbled.[26]

Making a mental note to spank her later, for misuse of punctuation, he continued. "Well, he hates birdsong;[27] that's the heart of the matter.[28] And so, down these mean streets a man must go[29] who is neither here nor there.[30]

There was a silence, while the creature, not too bright or good,[31] tried to work this out. At length, she brightened up. "I think only dull people are brilliant at breakfast",[32] she announced. Looking around, she spotted the surgeon's mate.[33]

"Hey, Whipple; squeeze this!"[34] she shouted.

Whipple did so.

There was, shall we say, a drawing-down of blinds.[35]

And so, to bed.[36]

And to all, a good night.[37]

There are thirty-seven clues to the authors of books, poems, or merely quotations on this page. The clues can be titles, well-known lines or passages... or even just 'clues'! The Borders store, on the corner of Orchard and Scotts Roads opens at nine in the morning. Next Friday, the first ten customers who give us a list of these authors can choose as many free books from our stock as they got correct answers. In other words, get three authors correct; get three free books. Up to the maximum of thirty-seven books per customer. Good luck.

[37]

PRINT MERIT

MERIT AWARD
Newspaper Over 600 Lines: Single

ART DIRECTOR
Tham Khai Meng

WRITER
Neil French

CLIENT
Borders Bookstore

AGENCY
Ogilvy & Mather/Singapore

010119A

MERIT AWARD
Newspaper Over 600 Lines: Single

ART DIRECTOR
Tham Khai Meng

WRITER
Neil French

CLIENT
Borders Bookstore

AGENCY
Ogilvy & Mather/Singapore

010120A

PRINT MERIT

MERIT AWARD
Newspaper Over 600 Lines:
Single

ART DIRECTOR
Tham Khai Meng

WRITER
Neil French

CLIENT
Borders Bookstore

AGENCY
Ogilvy & Mather/Singapore

010121A

CHAPTER TWO

Trailing clouds of glory,[1] Captain Vimes[2] shimmered into the room.[3] "Gaul is divided into three parts,"[4] he announced. "And for the really alert, and more literary among us, there were three clues in that first sentence, and four altogether, so far. Stay awake, please; for today we have naming of parts!"[5]

The dormouse fell into the teapot.[6]

The soldier glared at the offending rodent with a look that could warp walnut.[7] "Shut up," he explained.[8]

"The riddle of the sands[9] is written on the subway walls.[10] But this entire ad is a riddle, got up to look like a page from a book. Within this page are twenty-one clues, hidden references by title, quotation, or well-known passage, to famous literary figures of all sorts.

Next Tuesday morning, when Borders opens its doors, on the corner of Scotts and Orchard Roads, the first ten people to turn-up with a correct, (even if incomplete) list of these names will get as many free books of their choice as they have correct answers. In other words, get three names right, and choose three free books... up to a maximum of twenty-one." He sat down.

Suddenly, in walked a blonde. A blonde to make a bishop kick a hole in a stained-glass window.[11] She walked in beauty, like the night.[12]

"What contemptible scoundrel stole the cork from my lunch?"[13] she mumbled, and joined the dormouse in the crockery.

"Certain women should be struck regularly, like gongs,"[14] said the highwayman[15] to his coy mistress.[16] "I must arise, and go now;[17] I must go down to the seas again, the lonely sea and the sky.[18] A year in Provence,[19] down under,[20] or merely on the road,[21] will suffice."

[1]

MERIT AWARD
Newspaper Over 600 Lines:
Single

ART DIRECTOR
Craig Smith

WRITERS
Justin Lim
Eugene Cheong
Andy Greenaway

ILLUSTRATOR
Procolor

PHOTOGRAPHER
Roy Zhang

CLIENT
Do Asia

AGENCY
Ogilvy & Mather/Singapore

010122A

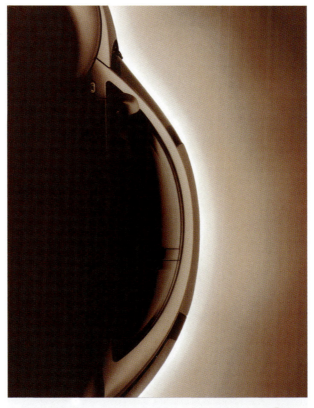

PRINT MERIT

MERIT AWARD
Newspaper Over 600 Lines:
Single

ART DIRECTOR
Craig Smith

WRITERS
Justin Lim
Eugene Cheong
Andy Greenaway

ILLUSTRATOR
Procolor

PHOTOGRAPHER
Roy Zhang

CLIENT
Do Asia

AGENCY
Ogilvy & Mather/Singapore

010123A

MERIT AWARD
Newspaper Over 600 Lines:
Single

ART DIRECTOR
Gavin Wood

WRITER
Mark Fisher

PHOTOGRAPHER
Stock

CLIENT
Volkswagen South Africa

AGENCY
Ogilvy & Mather/Cape Town

010124A

PRINT MERIT

MERIT AWARD
Newspaper Over 600 Lines: Single

ART DIRECTOR
Martin Kann

WRITER
Andy Linardatos

ILLUSTRATOR
Martin Kann

PHOTOGRAPHER
Hans Sipma

CLIENT
Richmond Savings

AGENCY
Rethink/Vancouver

010125A

MERIT AWARD
Newspaper Over 600 Lines: Single

ART DIRECTOR
Miles Turpin

WRITER
Steve Landrum

PHOTOGRAPHER
Kevin Necessary

CLIENT
Allied Model Trains

AGENCY
Saatchi & Saatchi/Torrance

010126A

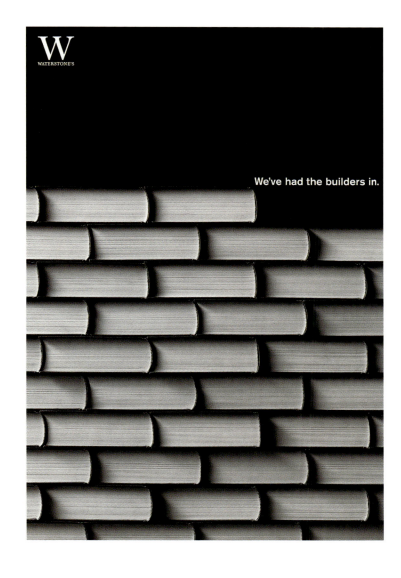

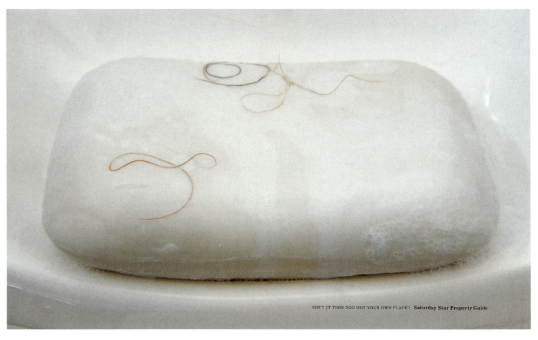

PRINT MERIT

MERIT AWARD
Newspaper Over 600 Lines:
Single

ART DIRECTOR
Carl Broadhurst

WRITER
Peter Reid

PHOTOGRAPHER
Laurie Haskell

CLIENT
Waterstone's Booksellers

AGENCY
TBWA/London

010127A

MERIT AWARD
Newspaper Over 600 Lines:
Single

ART DIRECTORS
Mariana O'Kelly
Frances Luckin

WRITERS
Frances Luckin
Mariana O'Kelly

PHOTOGRAPHER
Jakob Doman

CLIENT
Saturday Star
Property Guide

AGENCY
TBWA Hunt Lascaris/
Johannesburg

010128A

139

PRINT MERIT

MERIT AWARD
Newspaper Over 600 Lines: Single

ART DIRECTORS
Erik Vervroegen
Karin Barry

WRITER
Wendy Moorcroft

PHOTOGRAPHER
Mike Lewis

CLIENT
Seychelles

AGENCY
TBWA Hunt Lascaris/
Johannesburg

010129A

Also won:

MERIT AWARD
Magazine Color Full Page or Spread: Single

MERIT AWARD
Newspaper Over 600 Lines: Single

ART DIRECTOR
Duncan Milner

WRITER
Rob Schwartz

CLIENT
Apple

AGENCY
TBWA/Chiat/Day/
Los Angeles

010130A

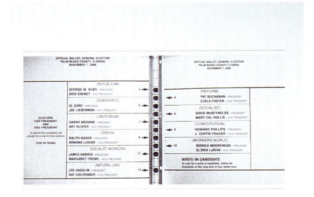

Never underestimate the power of design.

Good design isn't a luxury.
We've been making the premier tools for graphic designers
since President Carter was in the White House.

Think different.

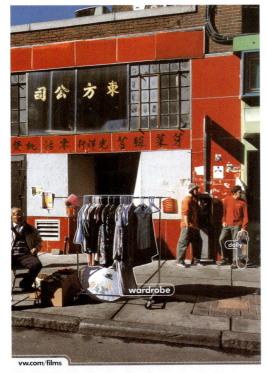

PRINT MERIT

MERIT AWARD
Newspaper Over 600 Lines:
Campaign

ART DIRECTOR
Melanie Lloyd

WRITER
Tim Brunelle

PHOTOGRAPHER
Russ Quackenbush

CLIENT
Volkswagen of America

AGENCY
ARNOLD Worldwide/Boston

01C131A

141

PRINT MERIT

MERIT AWARD
Newspaper Over 600 Lines: Campaign

ART DIRECTORS
Chris Turner
Scott Kaplan

WRITERS
Scott Kaplan
Chris Turner

CLIENT
TheStreet.com

AGENCY
DeVito/Verdi/New York

C10132A

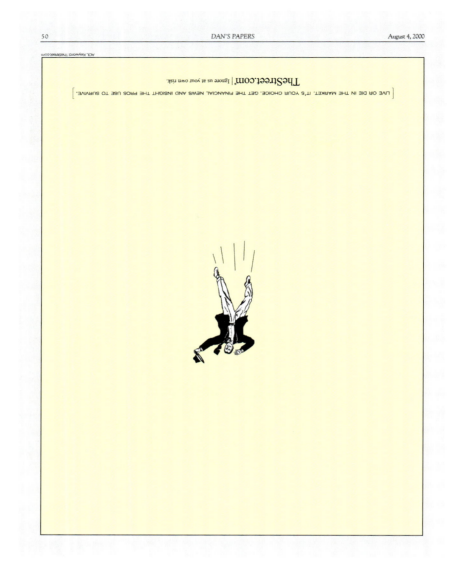

This campaign ran upside down, as shown.

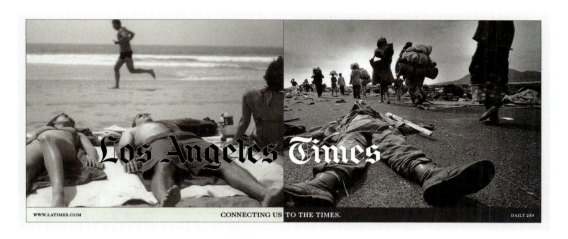

PRINT MERIT

MERIT AWARD
Newspaper Over 600 Lines:
Campaign

ART DIRECTOR
Shawn Brown

WRITER
Kristina Slade

PHOTOGRAPHERS
James Minchin
Anthony Cook
Stock

CLIENT
Los Angeles Times

AGENCY
Ground Zero/Los Angeles

010133A

143

PRINT MERIT

MERIT AWARD
Newspaper Over 600 Lines: Campaign

ART DIRECTORS
Zainal Yaacop
Saad Hussein

WRITER
Mikael Teo

ILLUSTRATOR
Kirby Ho
D. I. Joe

PHOTOGRAPHER
Teo Chai Guan

CLIENT
Sony Singapore

AGENCY
icecream!/Singapore

010134A

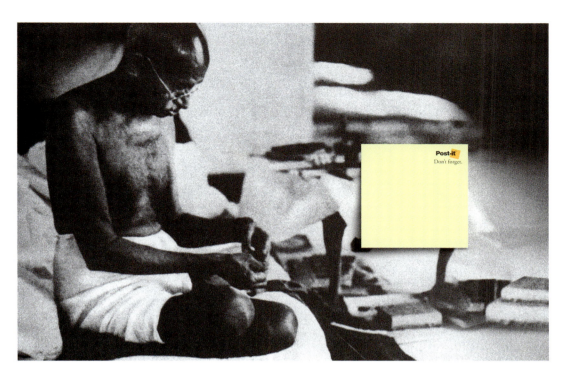

PRINT MERIT

MERIT AWARD
Newspaper Over 600 Lines:
Campaign

ART DIRECTOR
Haridas B.

WRITERS
Haridas B.
Vidur Vohra

CLIENT
3M

AGENCY
Ogilvy & Mather/Bangalore

01D135A

145

PRINT MERIT

MERIT AWARD
Newspaper Over 600 Lines:
Campaign

ART DIRECTOR
Tham Khai Meng

WRITER
Neil French

CLIENT
Borders Bookstore

AGENCY
Ogilvy & Mather/Singapore

010136A

CHAPTER TWO

Trailing clouds of glory, Captain Vimes shimmered into the room. "Gaul is divided into three parts," he announced. "And for the really alert, and more literary among us, there were three clues in that first sentence, and four altogether, so far. Stay awake, please; for today we have naming of parts!"

The dormouse fell into the teapot.

The soldier glared at the offending rodent with a look that could warp walnut. "Shut up," he explained.

"The riddle of the sands is written on the subway walls. But this entire ad is a riddle, got up to look like a page from a book. Within this page are twenty-one clues, hidden references by title, quotation, or well-known passage, to famous literary figures of all sorts.

Next Tuesday morning, when Borders opens its doors, on the corner of Scotts and Orchard Roads, the first ten people to turn-up with a correct, (even if incomplete) list of these names will get as many free books of their choice as they have correct answers. In other words, get three names right, and choose three free books... up to a maximum of twenty-one." He sat down.

Suddenly, in walked a blonde. A blonde to make a bishop kick a hole in a stained-glass window. She walked in beauty, like the night.

"What contemptible scoundrel stole the cork from my lunch?" she mumbled, and joined the dormouse in the crockery.

"Certain women should be struck regularly, like gongs," said the highwayman to his coy mistress. "I must arise, and go now; I must go down to the seas again, the lonely sea and the sky. A year in Provence, down under, or merely on the road, will suffice."

[1]

THE BORDERS OF SANITY

The ugly American, the French lieutenant's woman, and one fat Englishman had taken breakfast at Tiffany's.

Privately, they regarded one another with fear and loathing, and would have preferred a hundred years of solitude. But for auld lang syne (whatever that might have been), they had put away childish things, and shared an omelette and a glass of wine.

The thin man leant back from the table. He'd been in a feeding frenzy since the dawn's early light.

"As God is my witness", he sighed, "I'll never be hungry again." He stood, and reached for his tool. "It's time I slipped the surly bonds of this fatal shore and got on with managing my life. I take the way to freedom!"

With that, he was gone, striding across the river and into the trees.

"Where's father going with that axe?" enquired Lolita. (Being both beautiful and damned, she had learnt never to trust a man with a small black moustache.)

Atlas shrugged. "To kill a mockingbird," he said. "Listen; can you keep your head while all about you are losing theirs?"

"Yes I said I will yes" she gabbled.

Making a mental note to spank her later, for misuse of punctuation, he continued. "Well, he hates birdsong; that's the heart of the matter. And so, down these mean streets a man must go who is neither here nor there."

There was a silence, while the creature, not too bright or good, tried to work this out. At length, she brightened up. "I think only dull people are brilliant at breakfast," she announced. Looking around, she spotted the surgeon's mate.

"Hey, Whipple; squeeze this!" she shouted.

Whipple did so.

There was, shall we say, a drawing-down of blinds.

And so, to bed.

And to all, a good night.

*There are thirty-seven clues to the authors of books, poems, or merely quotations on this page. The clues can be titles, well-known lines or passages...or even just 'clues'! The Borders store, on the corner of Orchard and Scotts Roads opens at nine in the morning. Next Friday, the first ten customers who give us a list of these authors can choose as many free books from our stock as they got correct answers. In other words, get three authors correct; get three free books. Up to the maximum of thirty-seven books per customer. Good luck.

[37]

THE BORDERS OF SANITY

"So let us go, then, you and I," answered the ruined maid. "To the far side of the world, to a big hard-boiled city with no more personality than a paper cup. Let's go see."

And so it was, that later, when he first saw the green light at the end of Daisy's dock, he realised that it is only shallow people who do not judge by appearances.

He sighed, sadly, and then straightened his back. It is never difficult to distinguish between a Scotsman with a grievance and a ray of sunshine, but there are few more impressive sights in the world than a Scotsman on the make.

"I've had a few holidays in hell," he mused, "but *ugh!* To be in England, now that April's there. A cold coming we had of it, but I took the road less travelled-by. The finest sight a Scotsman ever sees is the high-road that leads to England."

A fellow of infinite jest, he was nevertheless down and out in London, which was, to his mind, more a confederacy of dunces than a city of joy. And he'd all but forgotten the art of eating.

"Have you got a bit of cheese?"

He looked down at what appeared to be a pointy hat with wee furry feet. The hat continued, "Poets have been mysteriously silent on the subject of cheese," it said, and stuck out a hand.

"Call me Ishmael," said the Hobbit, (for it was such). "I'll go no more a roving by the light of the moon, but since it's time for a little something, and there's nothing like messing-about in boats, hop in." He indicated a tiny pea-green boat. "But tread softly, because you tread on my fish paste and watercress."

*There are twenty-eight clues to the authors of books, poems, or merely quotations on this page. The clues can be titles, well-known lines or passages...or even just 'clues'! The Borders store, on the corner of Orchard and Scotts Roads opens at nine in the morning. Next Thursday, the first ten customers who give us a list of these authors can choose as many free books from our stock as they got correct answers. In other words, get three authors correct; get three free books. Up to the maximum of twenty-five books per customer. Good luck.

[29]

THE BORDERS OF SANITY

The Prince had found the last tycoon in "The Raven", drinking cider with Rosie. He was... well, if not actually disgruntled, he was far from gruntled.

"It requires a surgical operation to get a joke well into a Scotch understanding," he grouched. "Journalism is basically people who can't write, interviewing people who can't talk, for people who can't read. The editorial board is a parliament of whores."

"Not staying on, then?" ventured the little Prince.

"An idea that is not dangerous is not worthy of being called an idea at all!" he yelled, slamming the door behind him.

The silence hung in the air like a housebrick doesn't.

"Assassination is the extreme form of censorship," she said. "Maybe the board should have tried that?"

"He's a modest little man, with a lot to be modest about," he replied. "Standards are always out of date. That's what makes them standards."

He stood up.

"Ah, yes, Virginia, such is life." He gathered his papers. "All animals are equal, but some animals are more equal than others. It's been a funny old year; a winter of discontent, a silent spring, a dangerous summer, and now, the fall of the House of Usher."

"Actually, I'm Rosie, not Virginia," she said. "Fancy a walk in the woods?"

"A dance might be better?"

So over the blue remembered hills, and far away, they danced to the music of time.

THE END

*There are twenty-five clues to the authors of books, poems, or merely quotations on this page. The clues can be titles, well-known lines or passages...or even just 'clues'! The Borders store, on the corner of Orchard and Scotts Roads opens at nine in the morning. Next Friday, the first ten customers who give us a list of these authors can choose as many free books from our stock as they got correct answers. In other words, get three authors correct; get three free books. Up to the maximum of twenty-five books per customer. Good luck.

[129]

PRINT MERIT

MERIT AWARD
Newspaper Over 600 Lines:
Campaign

ART DIRECTORS
Mani Jayram
Deeksha

WRITER
Ashish Khazanchi

PHOTOGRAPHER
Bharat Sikka

CLIENT
TELCO

AGENCY
Ogilvy & Mather/New Delhi

010137A

147

PRINT MERIT

MERIT AWARD
Newspaper Over 600 Lines: Campaign

ART DIRECTOR
Simon Yeo

WRITER
M. Srinath

ILLUSTRATOR
Phenomenon

PHOTOGRAPHERS
Edward Loh
Sam Tam

CLIENT
PruLink Realty

AGENCY
Saatchi & Saatchi/Singapore

010138A

A ^(meteor / virus / serial killer / bad-ass alien) is about to destroy the world.

^(Bruce Willis / Kevin Costner / Mel Gibson / Arnold Schwarzenegger) tries to save mankind,

but he's stopped by ^(a corrupt senator / the CIA / the FBI / the Mafia).

Fighting against ^(the trauma of Vietnam / alcoholism / technology / the corrupt senator's seductive secretary),

he's able, after blowing up ^(the mother ship / the comet / the whole neighborhood / the corrupt senator's car),

to save the world.

And, at the end, he gets a ^(kiss from Julia Roberts / kiss from Meg Ryan / kiss from Sandra Bullock / hug from the President of the USA).

Cult
Hey, see an original movie.

BUY ONE, GET EVERYTHING FREE.

Model. 3957H | TELESCOPIC BATON | **THE SPY STORE** | 1804 WEST BROADWAY

PRINT MERIT

MERIT AWARD
Newspaper 600 Lines or Less: Single

ART DIRECTOR
Jose Carlos Lollo

WRITER
Cassio Zanatta

CLIENT
Cult Films

AGENCY
Almap/BBDO Comunicacoes/
São Paulo

010139A

MERIT AWARD
Newspaper 600 Lines or Less: Single

ART DIRECTOR
Lisa Francilia

WRITER
Dan Scherk

PHOTOGRAPHER
Leon Behar

CLIENT
The Spy Store

AGENCY
Bryant Fulton & Shee/
Vancouver

010140A

PRINT MERIT

MERIT AWARD
Newspaper 600 Lines or Less:
Single

ART DIRECTOR
Jim Amadeo

WRITER
Lawson Clarke

PHOTOGRAPHER
Steve Ganem

CLIENT
Ragged Mountain

AGENCY
Clarke Goward/Boston

010141A

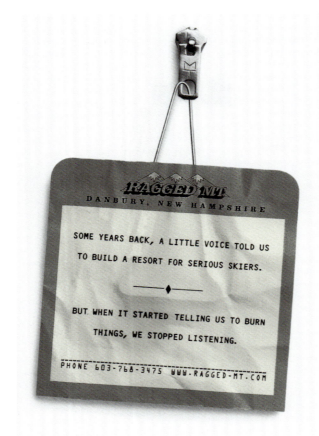

MERIT AWARD
Newspaper 600 Lines or Less:
Single

ART DIRECTOR
Jim Amadeo

WRITER
Chris DeCarlo

PHOTOGRAPHER
Steve Ganem

CLIENT
Ragged Mountain

AGENCY
Clarke Goward/Boston

010142A

PRINT MERIT

MERIT AWARD
Newspaper 600 Lines or Less:
Single

ART DIRECTOR
Bill Whitney

WRITER
Scott Jorgensen

ILLUSTRATOR
George Peters

CLIENT
Fuji Ya

AGENCY
Kruskopf Olson Advertising/
Minneapolis

010143A

MERIT AWARD
Newspaper 600 Lines or Less:
Single

ART DIRECTOR
Julian Pugsley

WRITER
Jim Garaventi

PHOTOGRAPHER
William Huber

DIRECTOR
Jonathon Bekemeier

CLIENT
Cozone.com

AGENCY
Mullen/Wenham

010144A

PRINT MERIT

MERIT AWARD
Newspaper 600 Lines or Less: Single

ART DIRECTORS
Moe Verbrugge
Maya Rao

WRITERS
Maya Rao
Moe Verbrugge

CLIENT
The Museum of Contemporary Art

AGENCY
TBWA/Chiat/Day/
Los Angeles

010145A

MERIT AWARD
Newspaper 600 Lines or Less: Single

ART DIRECTORS
Moe Verbrugge
Maya Rao

WRITERS
Maya Rao
Moe Verbrugge

CLIENT
The Museum of Contemporary Art

AGENCY
TBWA/Chiat/Day/
Los Angeles

010146A

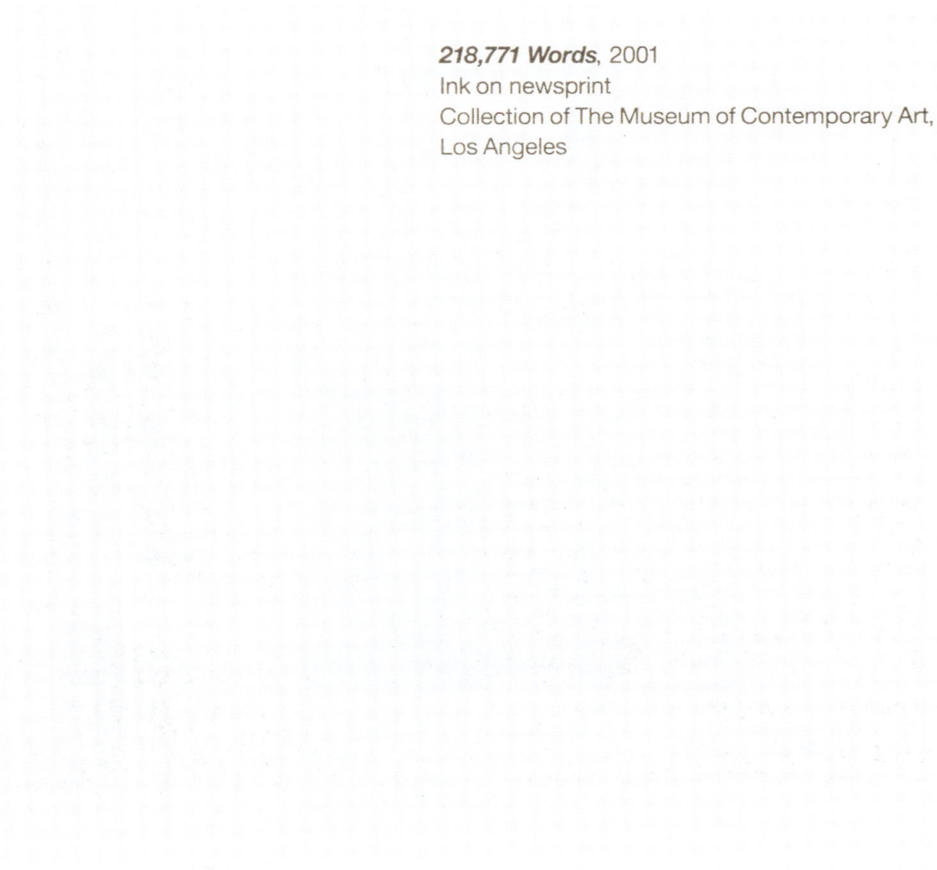

War, Peace, TV Listings, 2001
Ink on newsprint
Courtesy of The Museum of Contemporary Art,
Los Angeles

218,771 Words, 2001
Ink on newsprint
Collection of The Museum of Contemporary Art,
Los Angeles

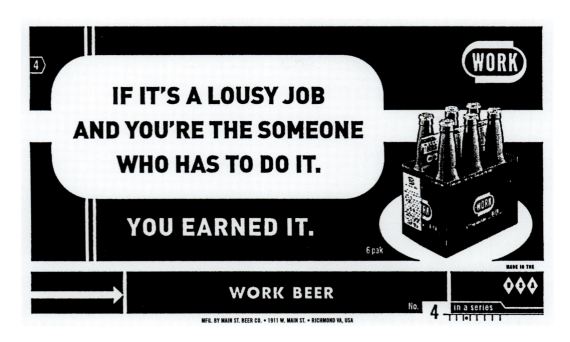

PRINT MERIT

MERIT AWARD
Newspaper 600 Lines or Less: Single

ART DIRECTORS
Cabell Harris
Paul Howalt

WRITER
Steve Covert

CLIENT
WORK Beer

AGENCY
WORK/Richmond

010147A

MERIT AWARD
Newspaper 600 Lines or Less: Single

ART DIRECTORS
Cabell Harris
Paul Howalt

WRITER
Steve Covert

CLIENT
WORK Beer

AGENCY
WORK/Richmond

010148A

PRINT MERIT

MERIT AWARD
Newspaper 600 Lines or Less: Campaign

ART DIRECTOR
Jim Amadeo

WRITERS
Lawson Clarke
Tom Kelly
Chris DeCarlo

PHOTOGRAPHER
Steve Ganem

CLIENT
Ragged Mountain

AGENCY
Clarke Goward/Boston

010149A

PRINT MERIT

MERIT AWARD
Newspaper 600 Lines or Less:
Campaign

ART DIRECTOR
Pat Wittich

WRITER
Bob Meagher

PHOTOGRAPHER
Kip Dawkins
Joe Mikos
Stock

CLIENT
TV Land

AGENCY
The Martin Agency/
Richmond

010150A

PRINT MERIT

MERIT AWARD
Newspaper 600 Lines or Less: Campaign

ART DIRECTOR
Ralph Watson

WRITER
Ken Marcus

ILLUSTRATOR
Ralph Watson

CLIENT
North Carolina Songwriters Cooperative

AGENCY
McKinney & Silver/Raleigh

010151A

MORE SPACE, NOW IN NEW YORK.
Two-room suites in the heart of downtown. Call 1-800-EMBASSY. EMBASSY SUITES HOTEL NEW YORK CITY

MORE SPACE, NOW IN NEW YORK.
Two-room suites in the heart of downtown. Call 1-800-EMBASSY. EMBASSY SUITES HOTEL NEW YORK CITY

MORE SPACE, NOW IN NEW YORK.
Two-room suites in the heart of downtown. Call 1-800-EMBASSY. EMBASSY SUITES HOTEL NEW YORK CITY

PRINT MERIT

MERIT AWARD
Newspaper 600 Lines or Less: Campaign

ART DIRECTOR
Andrew Golomb

WRITER
Lynn Braneckey

CLIENT
Embassy Suites Hotels

AGENCY
TBWA/Chiat/Day/
New York

0_0152A

157

PRINT MERIT

MERIT AWARD
Newspaper 600 Lines or Less: Campaign

ART DIRECTORS
Cabell Harris
Paul Howalt

WRITER
Steve Covert
Tim Lisko

CLIENT
WORK Beer

AGENCY
WORK/Richmond

010153A

PRINT MERIT

MERIT AWARD
Magazine B/W Full Page or Spread: Single

ART DIRECTOR
Kevin Daley

WRITER
Tim Cawley

PHOTOGRAPHER
Yelad Nivek

CLIENT
Performer

AGENCY
Pagano Schenck and Kay/
Boston

010154A

MERIT AWARD
Magazine Color Full Page or Spread: Single

ART DIRECTOR
Luciano Lincoln

WRITERS
Marcelo Nogueira
Jose Luiz Martins

PHOTOGRAPHER
Luis Otavio Moretti

CLIENT
Cia das Letras

AGENCY
Almap/BBDO Comunicacoes/
São Paulo

010156A

159

PRINT MERIT

MERIT AWARD
Magazine Color Full Page or Spread: Single

ART DIRECTORS
Luiz Sanches
Valdir Bianchi

WRITER
Roberto Pereira

PHOTOGRAPHER
Manolo Moran

CLIENT
Effem

AGENCY
Almap/BBDO
Comunicacoes/São Paulo

010157A

MERIT AWARD
Magazine Color Full Page or Spread: Single

ART DIRECTORS
Luiz Sanches
Valdir Bianchi

WRITER
Roberto Pereira

PHOTOGRAPHER
Manolo Moran

CLIENT
Effem

AGENCY
Almap/BBDO
Comunicacoes/São Paulo

010583A

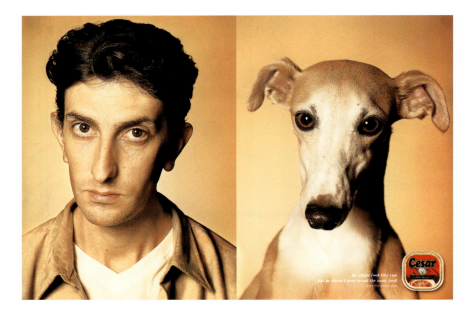

PRINT MERIT

MERIT AWARD
Magazine Color Full Page or Spread: Single

ART DIRECTORS
Luiz Sanches
Valdir Bianchi

WRITER
Roberto Pereira

PHOTOGRAPHER
Manolo Moran

CLIENT
Effem

AGENCY
Almap/BBDO
Comunicacoes/São Paulo

010584A

MERIT AWARD
Magazine Color Full Page or Spread: Single

ART DIRECTORS
Luiz Sanches
Valdir Bianchi

WRITER
Roberto Pereira

PHOTOGRAPHER
Manolo Moran

CLIENT
Effem

AGENCY
Almap/BBDO
Comunicacoes/São Paulo

010585A

MERIT AWARD
Magazine Color Full Page or Spread: Single

ART DIRECTOR
Wade Devers

WRITER
John Simpson

ILLUSTRATOR
Michael Schwab

PHOTOGRAPHERS
Clint Clemmens
Jack Richmond

CLIENT
Royal Caribbean

AGENCY
ARNOLD Worldwide/Boston

010158A

PRINT MERIT

MERIT AWARD
Magazine Color Full Page or Spread: Single

ART DIRECTOR
Don Shelford

WRITER
Dave Weist

PHOTOGRAPHERS
Stock
Bill Cash

CLIENT
Volkswagen of America

AGENCY
ARNOLD Worldwide/Boston

010159A

MERIT AWARD
Magazine Color Full Page or Spread: Single

ART DIRECTOR
Don Shelford

WRITER
Dave Weist

PHOTOGRAPHERS
Stock
Bill Cash

CLIENT
Volkswagen of America

AGENCY
ARNOLD Worldwide/Boston

010160A

PRINT MERIT

MERIT AWARD
Magazine Color Full Page or Spread: Single

ART DIRECTOR
Don Shelford

WRITER
Dave Weist

PHOTOGRAPHERS
Stock
Bill Cash

CLIENT
Volkswagen of America

AGENCY
ARNOLD Worldwide/Boston

010161A

MERIT AWARD
Magazine Color Full Page or Spread: Single

ART DIRECTOR
Adele Ellis

WRITER
Tim Gillingham

PHOTOGRAPHER
Stuart Hall

CLIENT
Volkswagen of America

AGENCY
ARNOLD Worldwide/Boston

010162A

MERIT AWARD
Magazine Color Full Page or Spread: Single

ART DIRECTOR
Adele Ellis

WRITER
Tim Gillingham

PHOTOGRAPHER
Stuart Hall

CLIENT
Volkswagen of America

AGENCY
ARNOLD Worldwide/Boston

010163A

PRINT MERIT

MERIT AWARD
Magazine Color Full Page or Spread: Single

ART DIRECTOR
Adele Ellis

WRITER
Tim Gillingham

PHOTOGRAPHER
Smari

CLIENT
Volkswagen of America

AGENCY
ARNOLD Worldwide/Boston

010164A

MERIT AWARD
Magazine Color Full Page or Spread: Single

ART DIRECTOR
Dan Shelford

WRITER
Dave Weist

PHOTOGRAPHERS
Stock
Bill Cash

CLIENT
Volkswagen of America

AGENCY
ARNOLD Worldwide/Boston

010165A

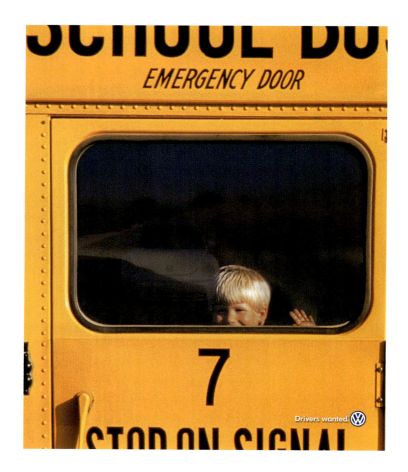

The rather spacious Golf Estate.

The new Beetle. Fun on the outside, serious underneath.

PRINT MERIT

MERIT AWARD
Magazine Color Full Page or Spread: Single

ART DIRECTOR
Ed Morris

WRITER
James Sinclair

PHOTOGRAPHER
Dave Stewart

CLIENT
Pharmacia + Upjohn

AGENCY
BMP DDB/London

010167A

Also won:

MERIT AWARD
Outdoor: Single

MERIT AWARD
Magazine Color Full Page or Spread: Single

ART DIRECTOR
Ed Morris

WRITER
James Sinclair

PHOTOGRAPHER
Kiran Master

CLIENT
Volkswagen Group

AGENCY
BMP DDB/London

010168A

MERIT AWARD
Magazine Color Full Page or Spread: Single

ART DIRECTOR
Justin Tindall

WRITER
Adam Tucker

PHOTOGRAPHER
James Day

CLIENT
Volkswagen Group

AGENCY
BMP DDB/London

010169A

165

PRINT MERIT

MERIT AWARD
Magazine Color Full Page or Spread: Single

ART DIRECTOR
Justin Tindall

WRITER
Adam Tucker

ILLUSTRATOR
Steve Dell

PHOTOGRAPHER
James Day

CLIENT
Volkswagen Group

AGENCY
BMP DDB/London

010170A

MERIT AWARD
Magazine Color Full Page or Spread: Single

ART DIRECTOR
Justin Tindall

WRITER
Adam Tucker

PHOTOGRAPHER
James Day

CLIENT
Volkswagen Group

AGENCY
BMP DDB/London

010171A

PRINT MERIT

MERIT AWARD
Magazine Color Full Page or Spread: Single

ART DIRECTOR
Rob Carducci

WRITER
Adam Chasnow

PHOTOGRAPHER
Shawn Michienzi

CLIENT
Quixi

AGENCY
Cliff Freeman and Partners/
New York

010172A

MERIT AWARD
Magazine Color Full Page or Spread: Single

ART DIRECTOR
Paul Keister

WRITER
Ari Merkin

PHOTOGRAPHER
Brian Wilder

CLIENT
Giro Sport Design

AGENCY
Crispin Porter & Bogusky/
Miami

010173A

167

PRINT MERIT

MERIT AWARD
Magazine Color Full Page or Spread: Single

ART DIRECTORS
Alex Burnard
Markham Cronin

WRITER
Ari Merkin

PHOTOGRAPHER
Alex Burnard

CLIENT
GT Bicycles

AGENCY
Crispin Porter & Bogusky/Miami

010174A

MERIT AWARD
Magazine Color Full Page or Spread: Single

ART DIRECTOR
Roger Baldacci

WRITER
Bruce Bildsten

PHOTOGRAPHER
Shawn Michienzi

CLIENT
BMW

AGENCY
Fallon/Minneapolis

010175A

PRINT MERIT

MERIT AWARD
Magazine Color Full Page or Spread: Single

ART DIRECTOR
Richard Flintham

WRITER
Andy McLeod

ILLUSTRATOR
Saddington Baynes

PHOTOGRAPHER
Spiros Politis

CLIENT
Full Circle

AGENCY
Fallon/London

010176A

MERIT AWARD
Magazine Color Full Page or Spread: Single

ART DIRECTOR
Richard Flintham

WRITER
Andy McLeod

PHOTOGRAPHER
Blinkk

CLIENT
Skoda UK

AGENCY
Fallon/London

010177A

PRINT MERIT

MERIT AWARD
Magazine Color Full Page or Spread: Single

ART DIRECTORS
Sean Farrell
Phil Covitz

WRITER
Maya Rao

PHOTOGRAPHER
William Huber

CLIENT
Nike

AGENCY
Goodby Silverstein & Partners/San Francisco

010178A

MERIT AWARD
Magazine Color Full Page or Spread: Single

ART DIRECTOR
Sean Farrell

WRITER
Maya Rao

PHOTOGRAPHER
William Huber

CLIENT
Nike

AGENCY
Goodby Silverstein & Partners/San Francisco

010179A

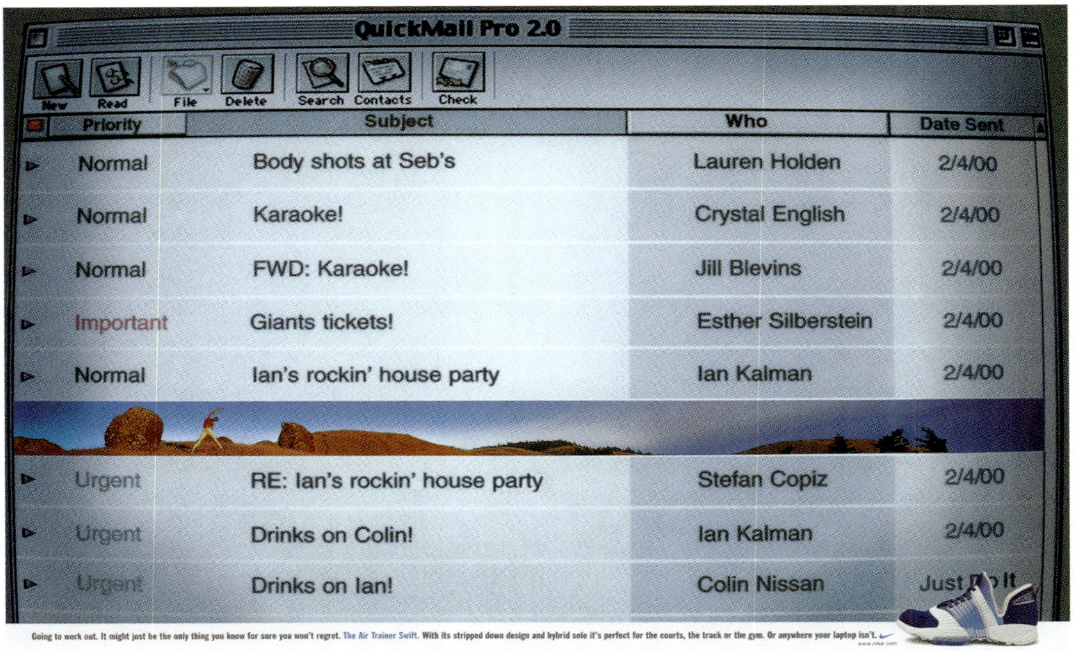

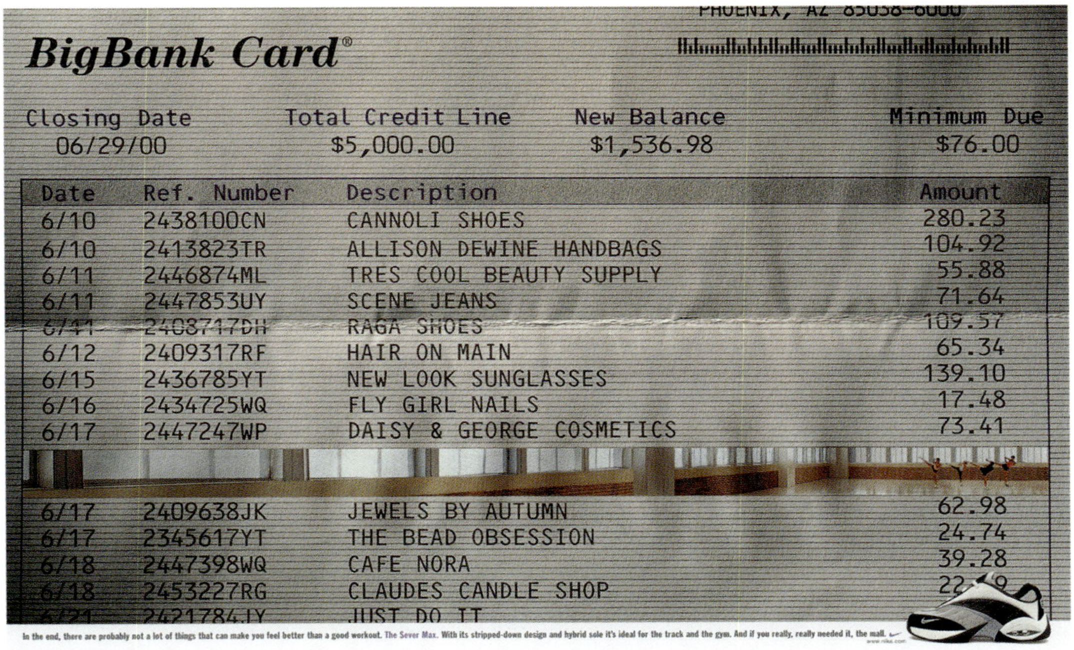

PRINT MERIT

MERIT AWARD
Magazine Color Full Page or Spread: Single

ART DIRECTOR
Sean Farrell

WRITER
Maya Rao

PHOTOGRAPHER
William Huber

CLIENT
Nike

AGENCY
Goodby Silverstein & Partners/San Francisco

010180A

MERIT AWARD
Magazine Color Full Page or Spread: Single

ART DIRECTORS
Sean Farrell
Phil Covitz

WRITER
Maya Rao

PHOTOGRAPHER
William Huber

CLIENT
Nike

AGENCY
Goodby Silverstein & Partners/San Francisco

010181A

171

PRINT MERIT

MERIT AWARD
Magazine Color Full Page or Spread: Single

ART DIRECTOR
Paul Hirsch

WRITER
Josh Denberg

PHOTOGRAPHERS
Graham Watson
Stock

CLIENT
Specialized

AGENCY
Goodby Silverstein & Partners/San Francisco

010182A

EAT THEIR BRIE. DRINK THEIR WINE. BUTCHER THEIR LANGUAGE.

MERIT AWARD
Magazine Color Full Page or Spread: Single

ART DIRECTOR
Vanessa Norman

WRITER
Peter Callaghan

PHOTOGRAPHER
David Prior

CLIENT
Nike

AGENCY
The Jupiter Drawing Room (South Africa)/Johannesburg

010184A

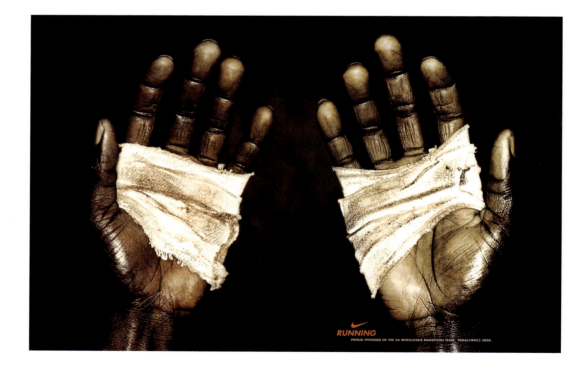

MERIT AWARD
Magazine Color Full Page or Spread: Single

ART DIRECTOR
Josh Kilmer-Purcell

WRITER
Tom Christmann

CLIENT
FreeAgent.com

AGENCY
Kirshenbaum Bond & Partners/New York

010185A

MERIT AWARD
Magazine Color Full Page or Spread: Single

ART DIRECTOR
Josh Kilmer-Purcell

WRITER
Tom Christmann

CLIENT
FreeAgent.com

AGENCY
Kirshenbaum Bond & Partners/New York

010186A

PRINT MERIT

MERIT AWARD
Magazine Color Full Page or Spread: Single

ART DIRECTOR
Mike Hahn

WRITER
Ryan Blank

PHOTOGRAPHER
Karina Taira

CLIENT
Target

AGENCY
Kirshenbaum Bond & Partners/New York

010187A

MERIT AWARD
Magazine Color Full Page or Spread: Single

ART DIRECTORS
Bradley Wood
Sean Ehringer

WRITER
Steve Morris

ILLUSTRATOR
Sean Ehringer

PHOTOGRAPHER
Mike Borthwick

CLIENT
Adidas

AGENCY
Leagas Delaney/
San Francisco

010188A

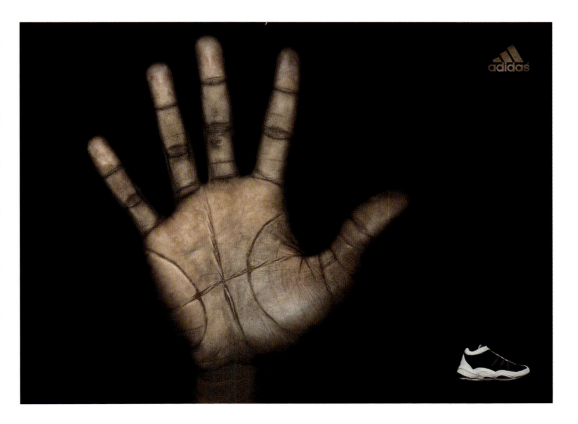

PRINT MERIT

MERIT AWARD
Magazine Color Full Page or Spread: Single

ART DIRECTORS
Bradley Wood
Sean Ehringer

WRITER
Steve Morris

ILLUSTRATOR
Tim Caton

PHOTOGRAPHER
Mike Borthwick

CLIENT
Adidas

AGENCY
Leagas Delaney/
San Francisco

010189A

MERIT AWARD
Magazine Color Full Page or Spread: Single

ART DIRECTOR
Roger Camp

WRITER
Matt Elhardt

PHOTOGRAPHERS
Clang
Cameron Barnum

CLIENT
Adidas

AGENCY
Leagas Delaney/
San Francisco

010190A

175

PRINT MERIT

MERIT AWARD
Magazine Color Full Page or Spread: Single

ART DIRECTOR
Roger Camp

WRITER
Matt Elhardt

PHOTOGRAPHERS
Clang
Cameron Barnum

CLIENT
Adidas

AGENCY
Leagas Delaney/
San Francisco

010191A

MERIT AWARD
Magazine Color Full Page or Spread: Single

ART DIRECTOR
Roger Camp

WRITER
Matt Elhardt

PHOTOGRAPHERS
Clang
Cameron Barnum

CLIENT
Adidas

AGENCY
Leagas Delaney/
San Francisco

010192A

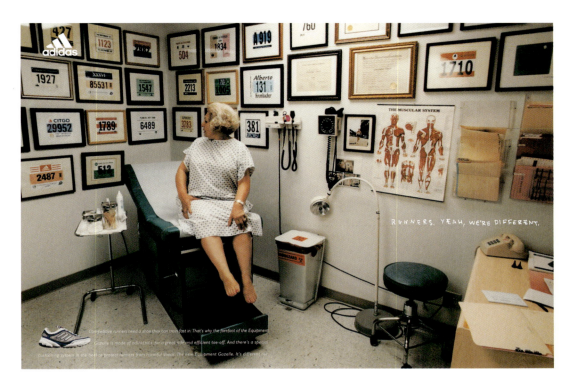

PRINT MERIT

MERIT AWARD
Magazine Color Full Page or Spread: Single

ART DIRECTOR
Christopher Toland

WRITERS
Scott Wild
Steve Morris

PHOTOGRAPHER
Will Van Overbeek

CLIENT
Adidas

AGENCY
Leagas Delaney/
San Francisco

010193A

MERIT AWARD
Magazine Color Full Page or Spread: Single

ART DIRECTOR
Christopher Toland

WRITERS
Scott Wild
Steve Morris

PHOTOGRAPHER
Will Van Overbeek

CLIENT
Adidas

AGENCY
Leagas Delaney/
San Francisco

010194A

177

PRINT MERIT

MERIT AWARD
Magazine Color Full Page or Spread: Single

ART DIRECTOR
Steve Mapp

WRITER
Matt Rivitz

ILLUSTRATORS
Haydaen Foell
Barbara Ambler

PHOTOGRAPHER
Stock

CLIENT
Salomon

AGENCY
Leagas Delaney/
San Francisco

010195A

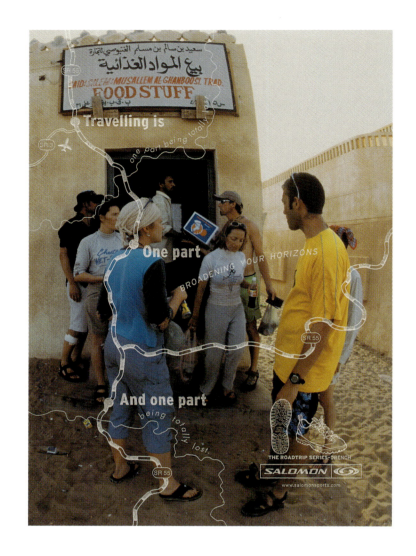

MERIT AWARD
Magazine Color Full Page or Spread: Single

ART DIRECTOR
Steve Mapp

WRITER
Matt Rivitz

ILLUSTRATORS
Hayden Foell
Barbara Ambler

PHOTOGRAPHER
Stock

CLIENT
Salomon

AGENCY
Leagas Delaney/
San Francisco

010196A

PRINT MERIT

MERIT AWARD
Magazine Color Full Page or Spread: Single

ART DIRECTORS
Sean Riley
Michael Wright

WRITER
Jeff Ross

PHOTOGRAPHER
Jim Erickson

CLIENT
The Timberland Company

AGENCY
The Martin Agency/
Richmond

010197A

MERIT AWARD
Magazine Color Full Page or Spread: Single

ART DIRECTORS
Cecilia Dufils
Markus Bjurman

WRITERS
Cecilia Dufils
Markus Bjurman

PHOTOGRAPHER
Johan Fowelin

CLIENT
Harvey Nichols

AGENCY
Mother Ltd./London

010198A

PRINT MERIT

MERIT AWARD
Magazine Color Full Page or Spread: Single

ART DIRECTOR
Craig Smith

WRITER
Andy Greenaway

ILLUSTRATOR
Yau Wai Kin

PHOTOGRAPHER
Roy Zhang

CLIENT
Asia Pacific Breweries

AGENCY
Ogilvy & Mather/Singapore

010199A

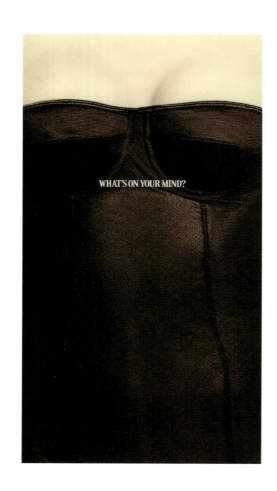

MERIT AWARD
Magazine Color Full Page or Spread: Single

ART DIRECTOR
Craig Smith

WRITER
Andy Greenaway

ILLUSTRATOR
Yau Wai Kin

PHOTOGRAPHER
Roy Zhang

CLIENT
Asia Pacific Breweries

AGENCY
Ogilvy & Mather/Singapore

010201A

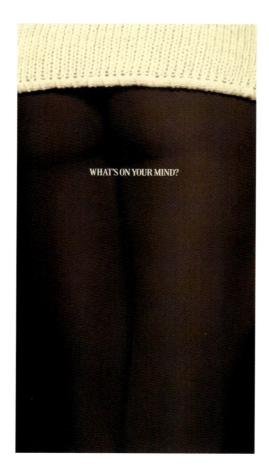

PRINT MERIT

MERIT AWARD
Magazine Color Full Page or Spread: Single

ART DIRECTOR
Troy McGuinness

WRITER
David Ross

PHOTOGRAPHER
Tom Feiler

CLIENT
CKF, Royal Chinet

AGENCY
Ogilvy & Mather/Toronto

010203A

MERIT AWARD
Magazine Color Full Page or Spread: Single

ART DIRECTORS
Roger Camp
Mike McCommon

WRITERS
Mike McCommon
Roger Camp

PHOTOGRAPHER
Lauren Greenfield

CLIENT
Discovery.com

AGENCY
Publicis & Hal Riney/
San Francisco

010204A

181

PRINT MERIT

MERIT AWARD
Magazine Color Full Page or Spread: Single

ART DIRECTORS
Roger Camp
Mike McCommon

WRITERS
Roger Camp
Mike McCommon

PHOTOGRAPHER
Stefan Ruiz

CLIENT
Discovery.com

AGENCY
Publicis & Hal Riney/
San Francisco

010205A

MERIT AWARD
Magazine Color Full Page or Spread: Single

ART DIRECTORS
Roger Camp
Mike McCommon

WRITERS
Mike McCommon
Roger Camp

PHOTOGRAPHER
Stefan Ruiz

CLIENT
Discovery.com

AGENCY
Publicis & Hal Riney/
San Francisco

010206A

PRINT MERIT

MERIT AWARD
Magazine Color Full Page or Spread: Single

ART DIRECTOR
Maximo Vazquez

WRITER
Augusto Sola

ILLUSTRATOR
Hugo Horita

CLIENT
Nike SA

AGENCY
RATTO/BBDO SA/
Buenos Aires

010207A

MERIT AWARD
Magazine Color Full Page or Spread: Single

ART DIRECTOR
Erik Vervroegen

WRITER
Wendy Moorcroft

PHOTOGRAPHER
Mike Lewis

CLIENT
Seychelles

AGENCY
TBWA Hunt Lascaris/
Johannesburg

010209A

183

PRINT MERIT

MERIT AWARD
Magazine Color Full Page or Spread: Single

ART DIRECTOR
Erik Vervroegen

WRITER
Wendy Moorcroft

PHOTOGRAPHER
Mike Lewis

CLIENT
Seychelles

AGENCY
TBWA Hunt Lascaris/Johannesburg

010210A

MERIT AWARD
Magazine Color Full Page or Spread: Single

ART DIRECTOR
Erik Vervroegen

WRITER
Wendy Moorcroft

PHOTOGRAPHER
Mike Lewis

CLIENT
Seychelles

AGENCY
TBWA Hunt Lascaris/Johannesburg

010211A

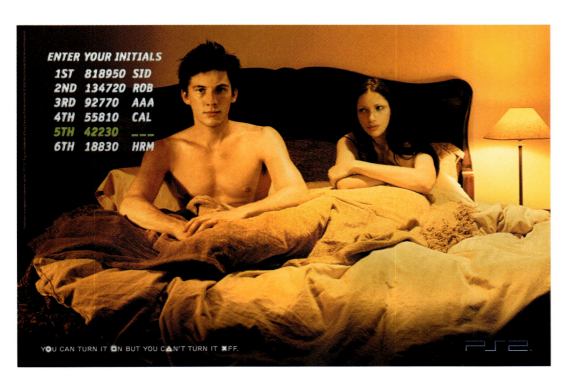

PRINT MERIT

MERIT AWARD
Magazine Color Full Page or Spread: Single

ART DIRECTORS
Lew Willig
Eric King

WRITERS
Scott Duchon
Scott Wild

PHOTOGRAPHER
Tom Stoddart

CLIENT
PlayStation

AGENCY
TBWA/Chiat/Day/
San Francisco

010212A

MERIT AWARD
Magazine Color Full Page or Spread: Single

ART DIRECTOR
Mark Chila

WRITER
John Robertson

PHOTOGRAPHER
Michael Eastman

CLIENT
Taylor Guitars

AGENCY
VITROROBERTSON/
San Diego

010213A

PRINT MERIT

MERIT AWARD
Magazine Color Full Page or Spread: Single

ART DIRECTOR
Kim Schoen

WRITER
Ilicia Winokur

ILLUSTRATOR
Leah Singer

CLIENT
Nike

AGENCY
Wieden + Kennedy/
New York

010214A

PRINT MERIT

MERIT AWARD
Magazine Color Full Page or Spread: Single

ART DIRECTOR
Kim Schoen

WRITER
Ilicia Winokur

ILLUSTRATOR
Dylan Stone

PHOTOGRAPHER
Dylan Stone

CLIENT
Nike

AGENCY
Wieden + Kennedy/
New York

010215A

PRINT MERIT

MERIT AWARD
Magazine Color Full Page or Spread: Single

ART DIRECTORS
Jon Wyville
Chuck Taylor

WRITER
Tohru Oyasu

PHOTOGRAPHER
Heimo

CLIENT
Nascar

AGENCY
Young & Rubicam/Chicago

010216A

MERIT AWARD
Magazine Color Full Page or Spread: Single

ART DIRECTOR
Demian Veleda

WRITER
Barbara Esses

PHOTOGRAPHER
Daniel Ackerman

CLIENT
Pirelli

AGENCY
Young & Rubicam/
Buenos Aires

010217A

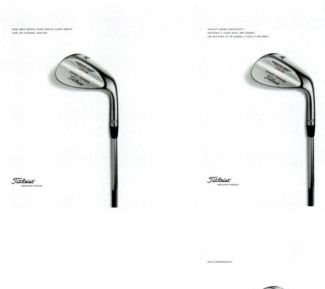

PRINT MERIT

MERIT AWARD
Magazine Color Full Page or Spread: Campaign

ART DIRECTOR
Steve Pratt

WRITER
Al Jackson

PHOTOGRAPHER
Jim Hubrigste

CLIENT
Acushnet/FootJoy/Titleist/Pinacle/Cobra

AGENCY
ARNOLD Worldwide/Boston

010218A

PRINT MERIT

MERIT AWARD
Magazine Color Full Page or Spread: Campaign

ART DIRECTOR
Adele Ellis

WRITER
Tim Gillingham

PHOTOGRAPHERS
Stuart Hall
Smari

CLIENT
Volkswagen of America

AGENCY
ARNOLD Worldwide/Boston

010219A

PRINT MERIT

MERIT AWARD
Magazine Color Full Page or Spread: Campaign

ART DIRECTOR
David Szabo

WRITER
David Szabo

ILLUSTRATOR
Samson Leung

PHOTOGRAPHERS
Lester Lee
Po Fun
Himson Leung
Jen Halim

CLIENT
Glenoak Foods

AGENCY
Beast/Hong Kong

010220A

191

PRINT MERIT

MERIT AWARD
Magazine Color Full Page or Spread: Campaign

ART DIRECTOR
Mark Reddy

WRITER
Dean Webb

PHOTOGRAPHER
Telegraph Colour Library & Corbis Images

CLIENT
Anheuser-Busch

AGENCY
BMP DDB/London

010221A

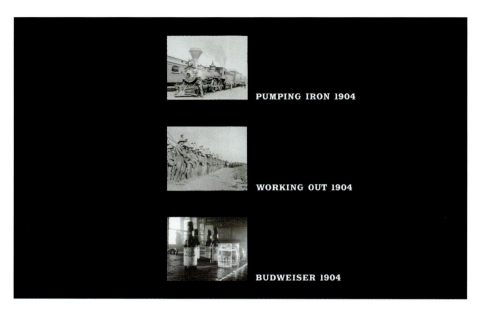

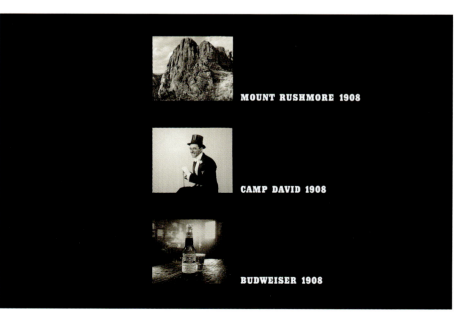

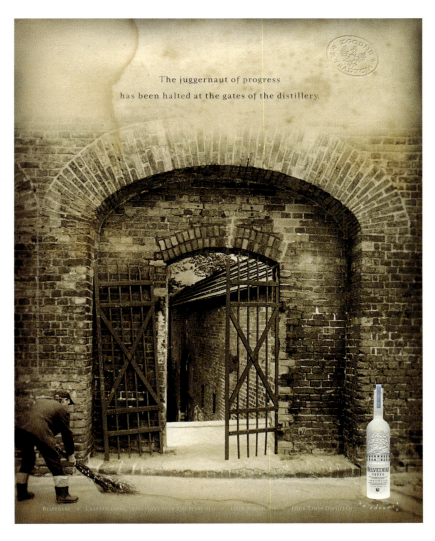

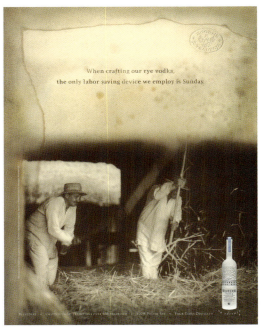

PRINT MERIT

MERIT AWARD
Magazine Color Full Page or Spread: Campaign

ART DIRECTOR
Jac Coverdale

WRITERS
Jerry Fury
Kelly Trewartha

PHOTOGRAPHERS
Raymond Meeks
Jac Coverdale

CLIENT
Belvedere Vodka

AGENCY
Clarity Coverdale Fury/
Minneapolis

010222A

PRINT MERIT

MERIT AWARD
Magazine Color Full Page or Spread: Campaign

ART DIRECTOR
Rob Carducci

WRITER
Adam Chasnow

PHOTOGRAPHER
Shawn Michienzi

CLIENT
Quixi

AGENCY
Cliff Freeman and Partners/
New York

010223A

PRINT MERIT

MERIT AWARD
Magazine Color Full Page or Spread: Campaign

ART DIRECTOR
Tony Calcao

WRITER
Rob Strasberg

PHOTOGRAPHER
Mark Laita

CLIENT
Giro Sport Design

AGENCY
Crispin Porter & Bogusky/
Miami

010224A

PRINT MERIT

MERIT AWARD
Magazine Color Full Page or Spread: Campaign

ART DIRECTORS
Alex Burnard
Markham Cronin

WRITER
Ari Merkin

PHOTOGRAPHERS
Heimo
Alex Burnard
Sebastian Gray

CLIENT
GT Bicycles

AGENCY
Crispin Porter & Bogusky/
Miami

010225A

PEUGEOT 206 GTi. ABNORMAL POWER.
0-60mph in 7.1 sec. 'The greatest GTi of all time' (Auto Express).

PEUGEOT 206 GTi. ABNORMAL POWER.
0-60mph in 7.1 sec. 'The greatest GTi of all time' (Auto Express).

PEUGEOT 206 GTi. ABNORMAL POWER.
0-60mph in 7.1 sec. 'The greatest GTi of all time' (Auto Express).

PRINT MERIT

MERIT AWARD
Magazine Color Full Page or Spread Campaign

ART DIRECTOR
Oliver Caporn

WRITER
Dom Gettins

PHOTOGRAPHER
Jenny Van Sommers

CLIENT
Peugeot UK

AGENCY
Euro RSCG Wnek Gosper/ London

010226A

PRINT MERIT

MERIT AWARD
Magazine Color Full Page or Spread: Campaign

ART DIRECTOR
Steve Sage

WRITERS
Michael Hart
Mike Gibbs
Roger Baldacci

PHOTOGRAPHERS
Clint Clemmons
Shawn Michienzi

CLIENT
BMW

AGENCY
Fallon/Minneapolis

010227A

PRINT MERIT

MERIT AWARD
Magazine Color Full Page or Spread: Campaign

ART DIRECTORS
Paul Hirsch
Josh Denberg
Claude Shade

WRITERS
Josh Denberg
Paul Hirsch

PHOTOGRAPHER
Kenji Toma

CLIENT
Nike

AGENCY
Goodby Silverstein & Partners/San Francisco

010228A

PRINT MERIT

MERIT AWARD
Magazine Color Full Page or Spread: Campaign

ART DIRECTOR
Paul Hirsch

WRITER
Josh Denberg

PHOTOGRAPHERS
Graham Watson
Stock

CLIENT
Specialized

AGENCY
Goodby Silverstein & Partners/San Francisco

010229A

The Specialized Vegas T.J.

Arise.

specialized.com

dirt jumping specific geometry   no-weld headtube   48 spoke wheels

The Specialized 415 Pro.

Grind.

specialized.com

flush mount peg system   pro level frame improvements   asphalt street tires

When held up to the light, the bicyclist on the back of each ad can be seen through the page, interacting with the scenes on the front.

PRINT MERIT

MERIT AWARD
Magazine Color Full Page or Spread: Campaign

ART DIRECTOR
Andy Azula

WRITER
Aaron Stern

PHOTOGRAPHER
Claude Shade

CLIENT
Specialized

AGENCY
Goodby Silverstein & Partners/San Francisco

010230A

201

PRINT MERIT

MERIT AWARD
Magazine Color Full Page or Spread: Campaign

ART DIRECTORS
Eric King
Andy Azula
Crystal English

WRITERS
Jim Haven
Harold Einstein

PHOTOGRAPHER
Keith Brauneis

CLIENT
Wall Street Journal

AGENCY
Goodby Silverstein & Partners/San Francisco

010231A

PRINT MERIT

MERIT AWARD
Magazine Color Full Page or Spread: Campaign

ART DIRECTOR
Grant Richards

WRITER
Scott Aal

PHOTOGRAPHER
Daniel Proctor

CLIENT
Bell Helmets

AGENCY
Grant Scott & Hurley/ San Francisco

010232A

PRINT MERIT

MERIT AWARD
Magazine Color Full Page or Spread: Campaign

ART DIRECTOR
Thomas Hoffman

PHOTOGRAPHER
Claus Sonne

CLIENT
Bianco Shoes

AGENCY
Grey/Copenhagen

010233A

PRINT MERIT

MERIT AWARD
Magazine Color Full Page or Spread: Campaign

ART DIRECTOR
Josh Kilmer-Purcell

WRITER
Tom Christmann

CLIENT
FreeAgent.com

AGENCY
Kirshenbaum Bond & Partners/New York

010234A

PRINT MERIT

MERIT AWARD
Magazine Color Full Page or Spread: Campaign

ART DIRECTOR
Roger Camp

WRITER
Matt Elhardt

PHOTOGRAPHERS
Clang
Cameron Barnum

CLIENT
Adidas

AGENCY
Leagas Delaney/
San Francisco

010235A

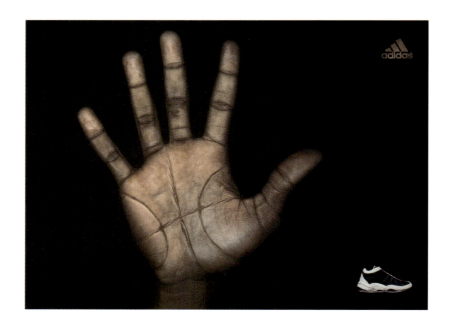

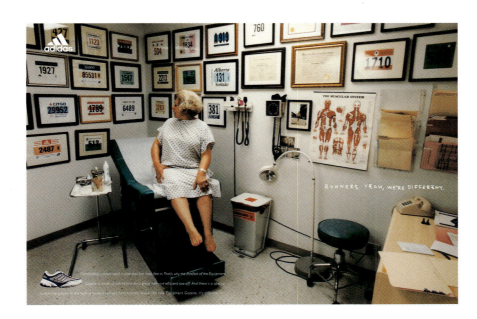

PRINT MERIT

MERIT AWARD
Magazine Color Full Page or Spread: Campaign

ART DIRECTOR
Christopher Toland

WRITERS
Scott Wild
Steve Morris

PHOTOGRAPHER
Will Van Overbeek

CLIENT
Adidas

AGENCY
Leagas Delaney/
San Francisco

010236A

207

PRINT MERIT

MERIT AWARD
Magazine Color Full Page or Spread: Campaign

ART DIRECTOR
Steve Mapp

WRITER
Matt Rivitz

ILLUSTRATORS
Hayden Foell
Barbara Ambler

PHOTOGRAPHERS
Stock
Laura Crosta

CLIENT
Salomon

AGENCY
Leagas Delaney/
San Francisco

010237A

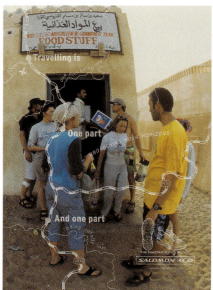

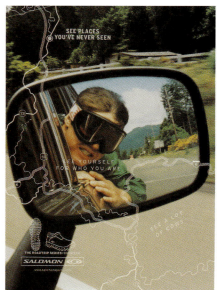

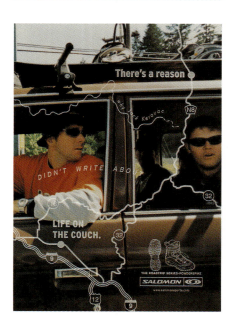

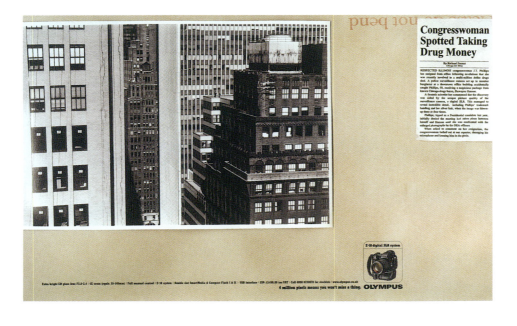

PRINT MERIT

MERIT AWARD
Magazine Color Full Page or Spread: Campaign

ART DIRECTOR
Steve Williams

WRITER
Adrian Lim

PHOTOGRAPHER
David Preutz

CLIENT
Olympus Optical Co.

AGENCY
Lowe Lintas/London

010238A

PRINT MERIT

MERIT AWARD
Magazine Color Full Page or Spread: Campaign

ART DIRECTORS
Sean Riley
Michael Wright

WRITER
Jeff Ross

PHOTOGRAPHER
Jim Erickson

CLIENT
The Timberland Company

AGENCY
The Martin Agency/
Richmond

010239A

PRINT MERIT

MERIT AWARD
Magazine Color Full Page or Spread: Campaign

ART DIRECTORS
Cecilia Dufils
Markus Bjurman

WRITERS
Cecilia Dufils
Markus Bjurman

PHOTOGRAPHER
Johan Fowelin

CLIENT
Harvey Nichols

AGENCY
Mother Ltd./London

010240A

PRINT MERIT

MERIT AWARD
Magazine Color Full Page or Spread: Campaign

ART DIRECTOR
Mary Rich

WRITER
Stephen Mietelski

PHOTOGRAPHER
Craig Orsini

CLIENT
Boeri

AGENCY
Mullen/Wenham

010241A

PRINT MERIT

MERIT AWARD
Magazine Color Full Page or Spread: Campaign

ART DIRECTOR
Graeme Jenner

WRITER
Brad Reilly

PHOTOGRAPHER
David Prior

CLIENT
Virgin Atlantic

AGENCY
Net#work BBDO/Benmore

010242A

PRINT MERIT

MERIT AWARD
Magazine Color Full Page or Spread: Campaign

ART DIRECTOR
Grover Tham

WRITER
Grover Tham

ILLUSTRATOR
Henry Chan
Fusion

PHOTOGRAPHER
Roy Lee

CLIENT
Crown Motors-Lexus

AGENCY
Saatchi & Saatchi/Hong Kong

010243A

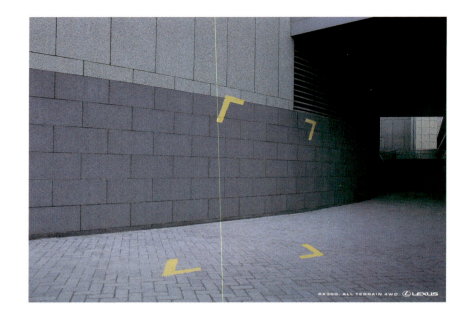

PRINT MERIT

MERIT AWARD
Magazine Color Full Page or Spread: Campaign

ART DIRECTOR
Amabel Minchan

WRITER
Jose Luis Alberola

PHOTOGRAPHER
Luis Enrique Gonzalez

CLIENT
Sony España, SA

AGENCY
Saatchi & Saatchi/Madrid

010244A

PRINT MERIT

MERIT AWARD
Magazine Color Full Page or Spread: Campaign

ART DIRECTOR
Guilherme Jahara

WRITER
Rodolfo Sampaio

PHOTOGRAPHER
Opcao Fotoarquivo

CLIENT
Brazilian Post Service

AGENCY
Salles D'Arcy Publicidade/
São Paulo

010245A

39.3 seconds was the total time needed by Louise Cunningham to fall in love with her Taylor. And that included **4.3 seconds** to look at the price tag and wince.

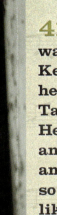

41.8 seconds was all it took for Kelly Gilhooly to decide he had to have the Taylor guitar. He just stood around and played for another **25 minutes** so he wouldn't look like some kind of trust fund baby or something.

29 seconds. Sometimes that's all it takes to know you want a Taylor guitar. Jeff Payne went to 15 stores over 9 months and played 47 guitars, but it all pretty much got decided in 29 seconds.

PRINT MERIT

MERIT AWARD
Magazine Color Ful Page or Spread: Campaign

ART DIRECTOR
Mark Chila

WRITER
John Robertson

PHOTOGRAPHER
Michael Eastman

CLIENT
Taylor Guitars

AGENCY
VITROROBERTSON/
San Diego

010246A

PRINT MERIT

MERIT AWARD
Magazine Color Full Page or Spread: Campaign

ART DIRECTOR
Matt Stein

WRITER
Jon Goldberg

PHOTOGRAPHERS
Matt Jones
Graham MacIndoe

CLIENT
ESPN

AGENCY
Wieden + Kennedy/
New York

010248A

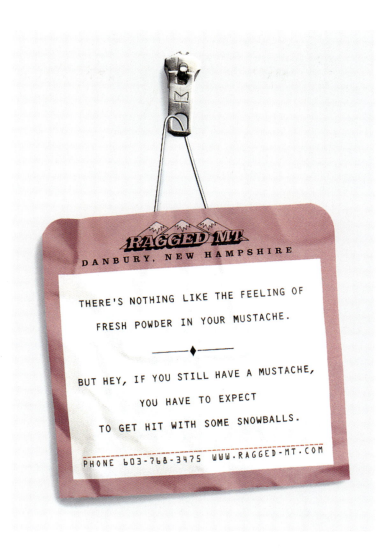

PRINT MERIT

MERIT AWARD
Magazine Less Than a Page
B/W or Color: Single

ART DIRECTOR
Jim Amadeo

WRITER
Tom Kelly

PHOTOGRAPHER
Steve Ganem

CLIENT
Ragged Mountain

AGENCY
Clarke Goward/Boston

010249A

MERIT AWARD
Magazine Less Than a Page
B/W or Color: Single

ART DIRECTOR
Bill Whitney

WRITER
Scott Jorgensen

ILLUSTRATOR
George Peters

CLIENT
Fuji Ya

AGENCY
Kruskopf Olson
Advertising/Minneapolis

010250A

PRINT MERIT

MERIT AWARD
Magazine Less Than a Page
B/W or Color: Single

ART DIRECTOR
Paul Laffy

WRITER
Brian Hayes

PHOTOGRAPHER
Dan Nourie

CLIENT
American Heritage Dictionary

AGENCY
Mullen/Wenham

010251A

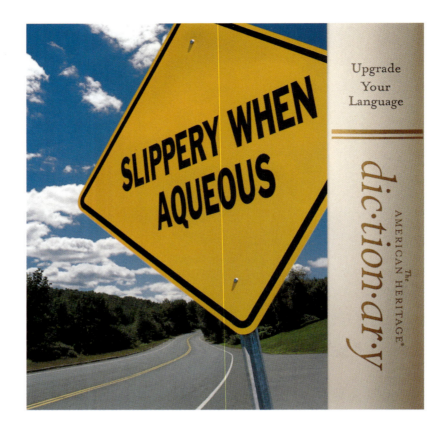

MERIT AWARD
Magazine Less Than a Page
B/W or Color: Single

ART DIRECTOR
Gerard Caputo

WRITER
Susan Ebling

PHOTOGRAPHER
William Huber

CLIENT
L. L. Bean

AGENCY
Mullen/Wenham

010252A

Prepositions are <u>not</u> words to end sentences with.

Prepositions look clumsy when placed at the end of a sentence. However, instances where they appear perfectly acceptable are not entirely unheard of.

This tip was brought to you by the British Council's Advanced Writing course. To enrol, please call us on 473-1111.

 The British Council

Foreign words and phrases are not *apropos*.

Like technical jargon, foreign words and phrases can often confuse your communication. Unless, of course, you have *bona fide* reasons to use them. This tip was brought to you by the British Council's Advanced Writing course. To enrol, call us on 473-1111.

 The British Council

Use exclamation marks sparingly!!!

"Rubbish!" some might scream. But, because of their sensational nature, exclamation marks are best reserved for use (one only, please) with direct quotations. This tip was brought to you by the British Council's Advanced Writing course. To enrol, call 473-1111.

 The British Council

One-word sentences? Eliminate.

One-word. Sentences. Such. As. These. Should. Be. Used. Sparingly. If. At. All. But. Some. Writers. Will. Occasionally. Use. Them. Just. To. Make. A. Point. This tip was brought to you by the British Council's Advanced Writing course. To enrol, call us on 473-1111.

 The British Council

Understatement is *always* best.

Keep your communication simple, unless you're exaggerating for effect. If we had a penny for every time we've said this, we'd be billionaires. This tip was brought to you by the British Council's Advanced Writing course. To enrol, call us on 473-1111.

 The British Council

PRINT MERIT

MERIT AWARD
Magazine Less Than a Page
B/W or Color: Campaign

ART DIRECTOR
Bill Whitney

WRITER
Scott Jorgensen

ILLUSTRATOR
George Peters

CLIENT
Fuji Ya

AGENCY
Kruskopf Olson Advertising/
Minneapolis

010254A

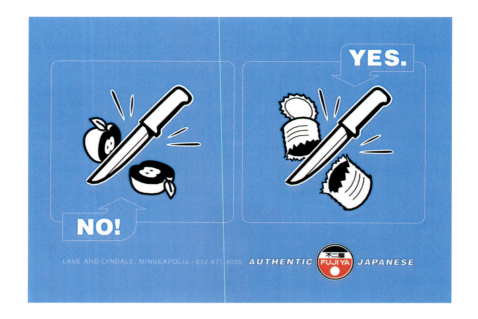

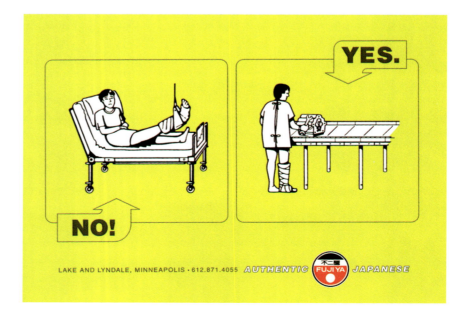

We have Irish malt whisky
We have darts.
For heaven's sake, please enjoy them separately.

Irish men like pale women with loads of freckles.
Maybe you should be drinking what they're drinking.

Nightly entertainment. Over and above the Irishmen who've been drinking at the bar since noon.

PRINT MERIT

MERIT AWARD
Magazine Less Than a Page
B/W or Color: Campaign

ART DIRECTOR
Kevin Daley

WRITER
Kim Cawley

CLIENT
The Times

AGENCY
Pagano Schenck and Kay/
Boston

010255A

PRINT MERIT

MERIT AWARD
Magazine Less Than a Page
B/W or Color: Campaign

ART DIRECTOR
Dean Lee

WRITER
Randy Stein

PHOTOGRAPHER
Dean Lee

CLIENT
McDonald's

AGENCY
Palmer Jarvis DDB/
Vancouver

010256A

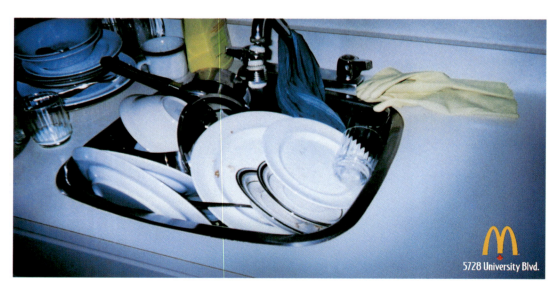

PRINT MERIT

MERIT AWARD
Outdoor: Single

ART DIRECTOR
Adele Ellis

WRITER
Tim Gillingham

PHOTOGRAPHER
Stuart Hall

CLIENT
Volkswagen of America

AGENCY
ARNOLD Worldwide/Boston

010257A

MERIT AWARD
Outdoor: Single

ART DIRECTOR
Adele Ellis

WRITER
Tim Gillingham

PHOTOGRAPHER
Smari

CLIENT
Volkswagen of America

AGENCY
ARNOLD Worldwide/Boston

010258A

PRINT MERIT

MERIT AWARD
Outdoor: Single

ART DIRECTOR
Lavin Kwan

WRITER
Ronnie Yeung

PHOTOGRAPHER
Jen Halim

CLIENT
Pharmacia + UpJohn/
Regaine

AGENCY
Bates/Hong Kong

010259A

MERIT AWARD
Outdoor: Single

ART DIRECTOR
Fishcakes

WRITER
Thomas Patten

PHOTOGRAPHER
Morgan Henry

CLIENT
Nike Retail

AGENCY
Cole and Weber/
Red Cell/Portland

010261A

PRINT MERIT

MERIT AWARD
Outdoor: Single

ART DIRECTOR
Fishcakes

WRITER
Thomas Patten

PHOTOGRAPHER
Morgan Henry

CLIENT
Nike Retail

AGENCY
Cole and Weber/
Red Cell/Portland

010262A

MERIT AWARD
Outdoor: Single

ART DIRECTOR
Steve Cochran

WRITERS
Steve Cochran
Leon Wilson
Lucien Law

PHOTOGRAPHER
Jacko van Deventer

CLIENT
Monaco

AGENCY
Colenso BBDO/Auckland

010263A

PRINT MERIT

MERIT AWARD
Outdoor: Single

ART DIRECTOR
Steve Cochran

WRITERS
Steve Cochran
Leon Wilson
Lucien Law

PHOTOGRAPHER
Jacko van Deventer

CLIENT
Monaco

AGENCY
Colenso BBDO/Auckland

010264A

MERIT AWARD
Outdoor: Single

ART DIRECTOR
Eric King
Andy Azula

WRITERS
Jim Haven
Harold Einstein

PHOTOGRAPHER
Hunter Freeman

CLIENT
Wall Street Journal

AGENCY
Goodby Silverstein & Partners/San Francisco

010265A

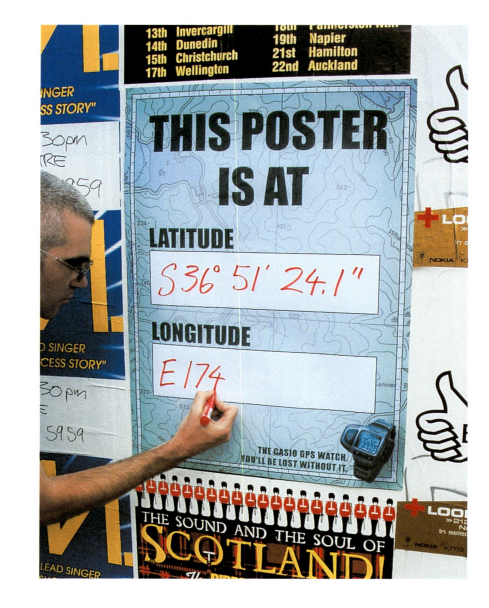

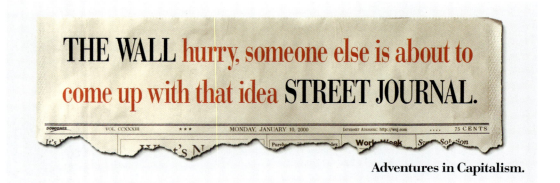

PRINT MERIT

MERIT AWARD
Outdoor: Single

ART DIRECTOR
Tobias Rosenberg

WRITER
Thomas Asbek

CLIENT
Kansas Workwear

AGENCY
Grey/Copenhagen

010266A

MERIT AWARD
Outdoor: Single

ART DIRECTOR
Richard Conner

WRITER
Julie Adams

PHOTOGRAPHER
Andy Roberts

CLIENT
John West

AGENCY
Leo Burnett/London

010267A

PRINT MERIT

MERIT AWARD
Outdoor: Single

ART DIRECTOR
Annie Wong

WRITERS
Simon Handford
Troy Sullivan

CLIENT
The Economist

AGENCY
Ogilvy & Mather/Hong Kong

010269A

MERIT AWARD
Outdoor: Single

ART DIRECTORS
Jackie End
Bill Montgomery

WRITERS
Jackie End
Bill Montgomery

CLIENT
The Absolut Company

AGENCY
TBWA/Chiat/Day/New York

010270A

PRINT MERIT

MERIT AWARD
Outdoor: Single

ART DIRECTORS
Moe Verbrugge
Maya Rao

WRITERS
Maya Rao
Moe Verbrugge

CLIENT
The Museum of
Contemporary Art

AGENCY
TBWA/Chiat/Day/
Los Angeles

010271A

MERIT AWARD
Outdoor: Single

ART DIRECTORS
Moe Verbrugge
Maya Rao

WRITERS
Maya Rao
Moe Verbrugge

CLIENT
The Museum of
Contemporary Art

AGENCY
TBWA/Chiat/Day/
Los Angeles

010272A

231

PRINT MERIT

MERIT AWARD
Outdoor: Campaign

ART DIRECTORS
Robert Oliver
Dave Dye
Mike Durban

WRITERS
Tim Riley
Sean Doyle
Tony Strong

CLIENT
The Economist

AGENCY
Abbott Mead
Vickers.BBDO/London

010273A

Ever go blank at the crucial... thingy?

The Economist

Having potential is great, if you're 12.

The Economist

A poster should contain no more than eight words, which is the maximum the average reader can take in at a single glance. This, however, is a poster for Economist readers.

"Can I phone an Economist reader please Chris?"

Lose the ability to slip out of meetings unnoticed.

The Economist

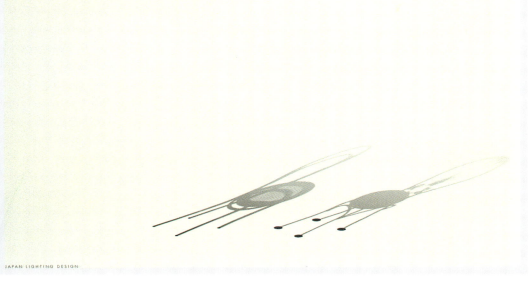

PRINT MERIT

MERIT AWARD
Outdoor: Campaign

ART DIRECTOR
Yuji Tokuda

PHOTOGRAPHER
Takashi Seo

CLIENT
Japan Lighting Design

AGENCY
Dentsu/Tokyo

010274A

PRINT MERIT

MERIT AWARD
Outdoor: Campaign

ART DIRECTOR
Eric King
Andy Azula

WRITERS
Jim Haven
Harold Einstein

PHOTOGRAPHER
Hunter Freeman

CLIENT
Wall Street Journal

AGENCY
Goodby Silverstein &
Partners/San Francisco

010275A

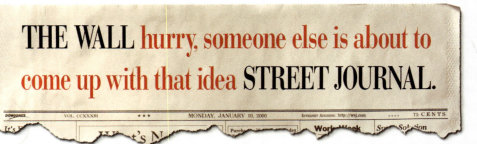

PRINT MERIT

MERIT AWARD
Outdoor: Campaign

ART DIRECTOR
Shawn Brown

WRITER
Kristina Slade

PHOTOGRAPHERS
James Minchin
Stock

CLIENT
Los Angeles Times

AGENCY
Ground Zero/Los Angeles

010276A

PRINT MERIT

MERIT AWARD
Outdoor: Campaign

ART DIRECTOR
Rashid Salleh

WRITER
Peter Moyse

PHOTOGRAPHERS
One Twenty One
Charles Chua

CLIENT
Lotto News Plus

AGENCY
Octagon/Singapore

010277A

PRINT MERIT

MERIT AWARD
Outdoor: Campaign

ART DIRECTORS
Andrew Tinning
Andy Blood

WRITERS
Andrew Tinning
Andy Blood

ILLUSTRATORS
Ingrid Berzins
Ali Teo

CLIENT
Auckland Regional Council

AGENCY
Saatchi & Saatchi
New Zealand/Auckland

010279A

PRINT MERIT

MERIT AWARD
Outdoor: Campaign

ART DIRECTORS
Moe Verbrugge
Maya Rao

WRITERS
Maya Rao
Moe Verbrugge

CLIENT
The Museum of Contemporary Art

AGENCY
TBWA/Chiat/Day/
Los Angeles

010280A

PRINT MERIT

MERIT AWARD
Guerilla Advertising

ART DIRECTOR
Mark Sorensen

WRITER
Mark Sorensen

CLIENT
Radio K

AGENCY
Clarity Coverdale Fury/
Minneapolis

010281A

MERIT AWARD
Guerilla Advertising

ART DIRECTOR
Sweta Pathak

WRITER
Parveez Shaikh

CLIENT
Parke-Davis

AGENCY
Contract Advertising/
Mumbai

010282A

PRINT MERIT

MERIT AWARD
Guerilla Advertising

ART DIRECTOR
Kenny Choo

WRITERS
Alvin Wong
Andrew Lok

PHOTOGRAPHER
Edward Loh

CLIENT
Singapore Cancer Society

AGENCY
Dentsu Young & Rubicam/
Singapore

010283A

MERIT AWARD
Guerilla Advertising

ART DIRECTOR
Joe Fago

WRITER
Joe Fago

PHOTOGRAPHER
Joe Vaughn

CLIENT
White Castle Restaurants

AGENCY
J. Walter Thompson/Detroit

010284A

PRINT MERIT

MERIT AWARD
Guerilla Advertising

ART DIRECTOR
David Cohen

WRITER
Ian Graham

ILLUSTRATOR
David Cohen

PHOTOGRAPHER
Joe Jacobs

CLIENT
He'Brew (Shmaltz Brewery)

AGENCY
Kirshenbaum Bond & Partners West/San Francisco

010285A

MERIT AWARD
Guerilla Advertising

ART DIRECTOR
David Cohen

WRITER
Ian Graham

ILLUSTRATOR
David Cohen

PHOTOGRAPHER
Joe Jacobs

CLIENT
He'Brew (Shmaltz Brewery)

AGENCY
Kirshenbaum Bond & Partners West/San Francisco

010286A

PRINT MERIT

MERIT AWARD
Guerilla Advertising

ART DIRECTOR
Rob Nielsen

WRITER
Jack Stephens

CLIENT
Heinz Salad Cream

AGENCY
Leo Burnett/London

010287A

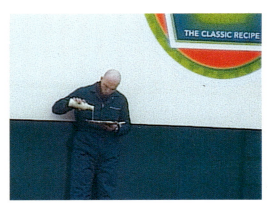

Over a two week period, with the help of Heinz Salad Cream, one man actually ate this poster.

MERIT AWARD
Guerilla Advertising

ART DIRECTOR
Vancelee Teng

WRITERS
Vancelee Teng
Sirirut Angkasupornkul

PHOTOGRAPHER
Tawatchai Plienpairojana

CLIENT
SSL Healthcare

AGENCY
Lowe Lintas & Partners/
Bangkok

010288A

MERIT AWARD
Guerilla Advertising

ART DIRECTOR
Rui Alves

WRITER
John Davenport

ILLUSTRATOR
Debbie Nina

CLIENT
Virgin Atlantic

AGENCY
Net#work BBDO/Benmore

010289A

PRINT MERIT

MERIT AWARD
Guerilla Advertising

ART DIRECTOR
Mark Fairbanks

WRITER
Mark Fairbanks

PHOTOGRAPHER
Steve Nicholls

CLIENT
Ford of Britain

AGENCY
Ogilvy/London

010290A

MERIT AWARD
Guerilla Advertising

ART DIRECTORS
Rob Messeter
Mike Crowe

WRITERS
Rob Messeter
Mike Crowe

PHOTOGRAPHERS
Kitty McCorry
Sam Mahayni

CLIENT
Mattell/Scrabble

AGENCY
Ogilvy/London

010291A

PRINT MERIT

MERIT AWARD
Guerilla Advertising

ART DIRECTORS
Rob Messeter
Mike Crowe

WRITERS
Rob Messeter
Mike Crowe

PHOTOGRAPHERS
Sam Mahayni
Kitty McCorry

CLIENT
Mattell/Scrabble

AGENCY
Ogilvy/London

010292A

PRINT MERIT

MERIT AWARD
Guerilla Advertising

ART DIRECTOR
David Malan

WRITER
Gordon Ray

CLIENT
BP/Sanccob

AGENCY
Ogilvy & Mather/Cape Town

010293A

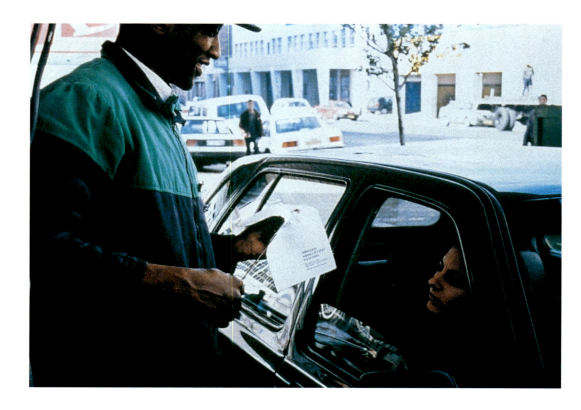

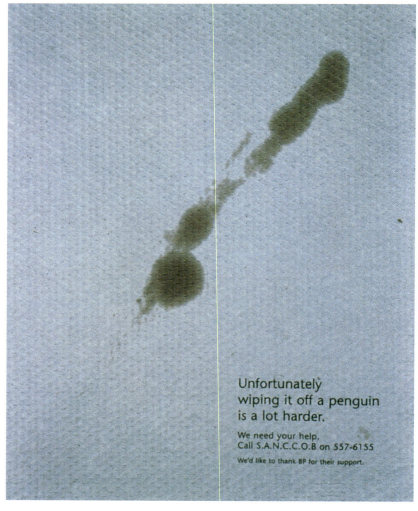

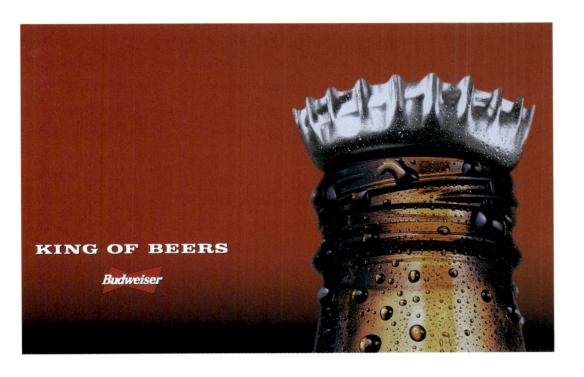

PRINT MERIT

MERIT AWARD
Guerilla Advertising

ART DIRECTOR
Debra Clausen

WRITER
Neil Gardiner

CLIENT
Capetalk

AGENCY
Ogilvy & Mather/Cape Town

010294A

MERIT AWARD
Guerilla Advertising

ART DIRECTOR
Dan Pawych

WRITER
David Daga

ILLUSTRATOR
Keystone Studios

PHOTOGRAPHER
Tom Szuba

CLIENT
Labatt Breweries of Canada

AGENCY
Palmer Jarvis DDB
Downtown/Toronto

010295A

PRINT MERIT

MERIT AWARD
Guerilla Advertising

ART DIRECTORS
Mark Mason
Slade Gill

WRITERS
Slade Gill
Mark Mason

CLIENT
Allan Beacham

AGENCY
Saatchi & Saatchi/
Cape Town

010296A

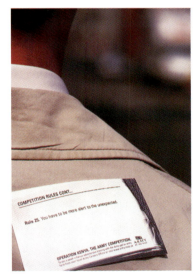

PRINT MERIT

MERIT AWARD
Guerilla Advertising

ART DIRECTOR
Dave Hobbs

WRITER
Richard Stoney

CLIENT
COI/The Army

AGENCY
Saatchi & Saatchi/London

010297A

PRINT MERIT

MERIT AWARD
Trade B/W Full Page or Spread: Single

ART DIRECTOR
Simon McQueen

WRITER
Antonia Clayton

PHOTOGRAPHER
Jenny Van Sommers

CLIENT
Business Pages

AGENCY
Abbott Mead Vickers.BBDO/London

010300A

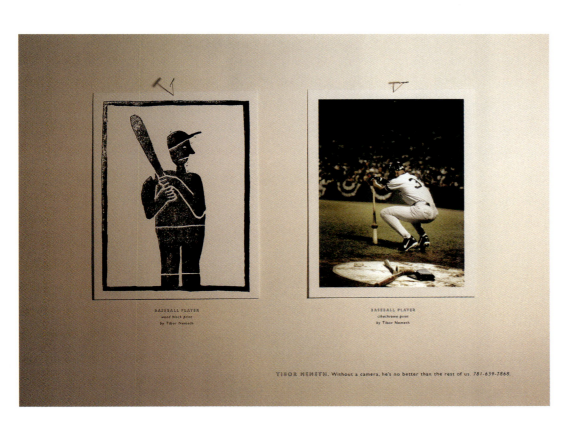

PRINT MERIT

MERIT AWARD
Trade B/W Full Page or Spread: Single

ART DIRECTOR
Wade Devers

WRITER
John Simpson

ILLUSTRATOR
Tibor Nemeth

PHOTOGRAPHER
Tibor Nemeth

CLIENT
Tibor Nemeth Photography

AGENCY
ARNOLD Worldwide/Boston

010310A

PRINT MERIT

MERIT AWARD
Trade B/W Full Page or Spread: Single

ART DIRECTOR
Richard Flintham

WRITER
Andy McLeod

CLIENT
Fallon

AGENCY
Fallon/London

010301A

MERIT AWARD
Trade B/W Full Page or Spread: Single

ART DIRECTOR
Steve Driggs

WRITER
Greg Hahn

PHOTOGRAPHER
John Biever

CLIENT
Sports Illustrated

AGENCY
Fallon/Minneapolis

010302A

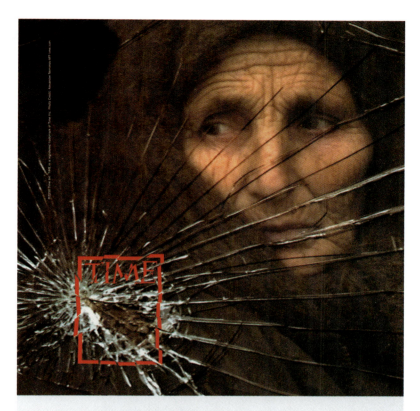

Insightful war correspondents.

Regrettably, still reporting.

The world's most interesting magazine.

THE CORRECT TECHNIQUE
FOR LIFTING HEAVY OBJECTS.

Fig.1 Before lifting, stand upright and bend backwards half a dozen times. This is especially important when a single heavy lift is being attempted.

Fig.2 Position yourself close to the load and keep a firm footing, with your feet wide apart.

Fig.3 Bend your knees, straighten your back and get a secure grip on the load.

Fig.4 Keeping your back straight, pick up the load, holding it as close to your body as possible.

Fig.5 Lean back slightly to keep your balance and lift the load by straightening your knees.

Fig.6 Finally, once upright, turn your body by moving your feet and avoid twisting your lower back.

NEXT WEEK: Opening the wrapper.

PRINT MERIT

MERIT AWARD
Trade B/W Full Page or Spread: Single

ART DIRECTOR
Koh Hwee Peng

WRITER
Priti Kapur

ILLUSTRATOR
Pro Color

PHOTOGRAPHER
Alex Kaikeong Studio

CLIENT
Republic of Singapore Air Force

AGENCY
Leo Burnett/Singapore

010305A

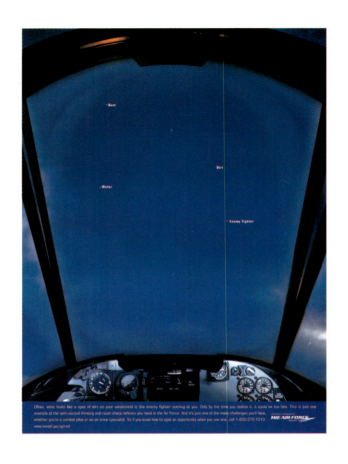

MERIT AWARD
Trade B/W Full Page or Spread: Single

ART DIRECTORS
Tom Scharpf
Richard Mirabelli

WRITERS
Scott Cooney
Peter McHugh

PHOTOGRAPHER
Lorne Bridgman

CLIENT
Louder Music & Sound Design

AGENCY
McHugh Worldwide/Edina

010306A

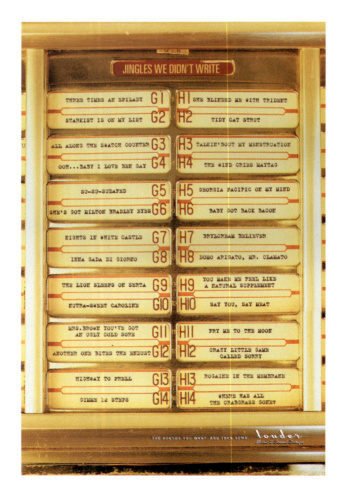

PRINT MERIT

MERIT AWARD
Trade B/W Full Page or Spread: Single

ART DIRECTORS
Guillermo Caro
German Paino
Ted Royer

WRITERS
Javier Campopiano
Daniel Comar

PHOTOGRAPHER
Millennium

CLIENT
Afrodita TV

AGENCY
Ogilvy & Mather Argentina/
Buenos Aires

010307A

MERIT AWARD
Trade B/W Full Page or Spread: Single

ART DIRECTOR
Jason Evans

WRITER
Jason Evans

PHOTOGRAPHER
Greg Blue

CLIENT
Palmer Jarvis DDB

AGENCY
Palmer Jarvis DDB/
Vancouver

010299A

PRINT MERIT

MERIT AWARD
Trade B/W Full Page or Spread: Single

ART DIRECTOR
Maurice Wee

WRITER
Renee Lim

PHOTOGRAPHER
Nicholas Leong

CLIENT
Discovery Asia

AGENCY
Saatchi & Saatchi/ Singapore

010308A

MERIT AWARD
Trade B/W Full Page or Spread: Single

ART DIRECTOR
Maurice Wee

WRITER
Renee Lim

PHOTOGRAPHER
Nicholas Leong

CLIENT
Discovery Asia

AGENCY
Saatchi & Saatchi/ Singapore

010309A

PRINT MERIT

MERIT AWARD
Trade B/W Full Page or Spread: Single

ART DIRECTORS
Vikram Gaikwad
Raj Kamble

ILLUSTRATOR
Mahesh Kubal

PHOTOGRAPHER
Prasad Naik

CLIENT
Gufic Healthcare

AGENCY
SSC&B Lintas/Mumbai

010311A

MERIT AWARD
Trade B/W Full Page or Spread: Single

ART DIRECTOR
Will Roth

WRITER
John Robertson

PHOTOGRAPHER
Mika Manninen

CLIENT
Taylor Guitars

AGENCY
VITROROBERTSON/
San Diego

010312A

257

PRINT MERIT

MERIT AWARD
Trade Less Than a Page B/W
or Color: Single

ART DIRECTOR
Andy Jex

WRITER
Rob Potts

PHOTOGRAPHER
Coppi Barbieri

CLIENT
UK Time-Timex

AGENCY
Fallon/London

010314A

MERIT AWARD
Trade Less Than a Page B/W
or Color: Single

ART DIRECTOR
Bob Barrie

WRITER
Dean Buckhorn

PHOTOGRAPHER
Stock

CLIENT
UJA Federation

AGENCY
Fallon/Minneapolis

010313A

Conversion Table (police response times)	
Burglary	3 mins 18 secs
Armed Robbery Armed Robbery via donut shop	2 mins 56 secs 32 mins 56 secs
Leggy blonde with lost bus pass	0.012 secs
The Great Train Robbery	4 hrs 11 mins*

*Delayed at Newport Pagnell.

TIMEX

Generosity: ☐ ✓
Integrity: ☐ ✓
50-yard dash: ☐ ✓
Hair: ☐ ✓

Maurice Lévy. Hands down our favorite global leader. **Fallon**

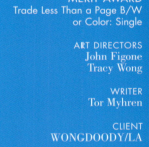

WHEN I'M ON THE
CRAPPER,
MY BEST FRIEND IS THE:

- **A** SPORTS PAGE
- **B** BUSINESS PAGE
- **C** DISCOUNT OFFICE SUPPLY CATALOG

OFFICIAL MASCOT

If you answered (C), you're sick *and* in luck. WONGDOODY/LA is looking for an experienced office manager who knows their way around an Office Max like nobody's business. Fax resume to Amy at 310.858.4041.

OFFICIAL LOGO

PRINT MERIT

MERIT AWARD
Trade Less Than a Page B/W or Color: Single

ART DIRECTOR
Andy Minisman

WRITER
David Johnson

PHOTOGRAPHER
Stock

CLIENT
Fila

AGENCY
Merkley Newman Harty/ New York

010315A

MERIT AWARD
Trade Less Than a Page B/W or Color: Single

ART DIRECTORS
John Figone
Tracy Wong

WRITER
Tor Myhren

CLIENT
WONGDOODY/LA

AGENCY
WONGDOODY/Seattle

010316A

PRINT MERIT

MERIT AWARD
Trade Less Than a Page B/W
or Color: Single

ART DIRECTOR
Jon Wyville

WRITER
Ken Erke

CLIENT
Checkered Past Records

AGENCY
Young & Rubicam/Chicago

010317A

MERIT AWARD
Trade Less Than a Page B/W
or Color: Single

ART DIRECTOR
Jon Wyville

WRITER
Ken Erke

CLIENT
Checkered Past Records

AGENCY
Young & Rubicam/Chicago

010318A

Also won:

MERIT AWARD
Collateral: Posters

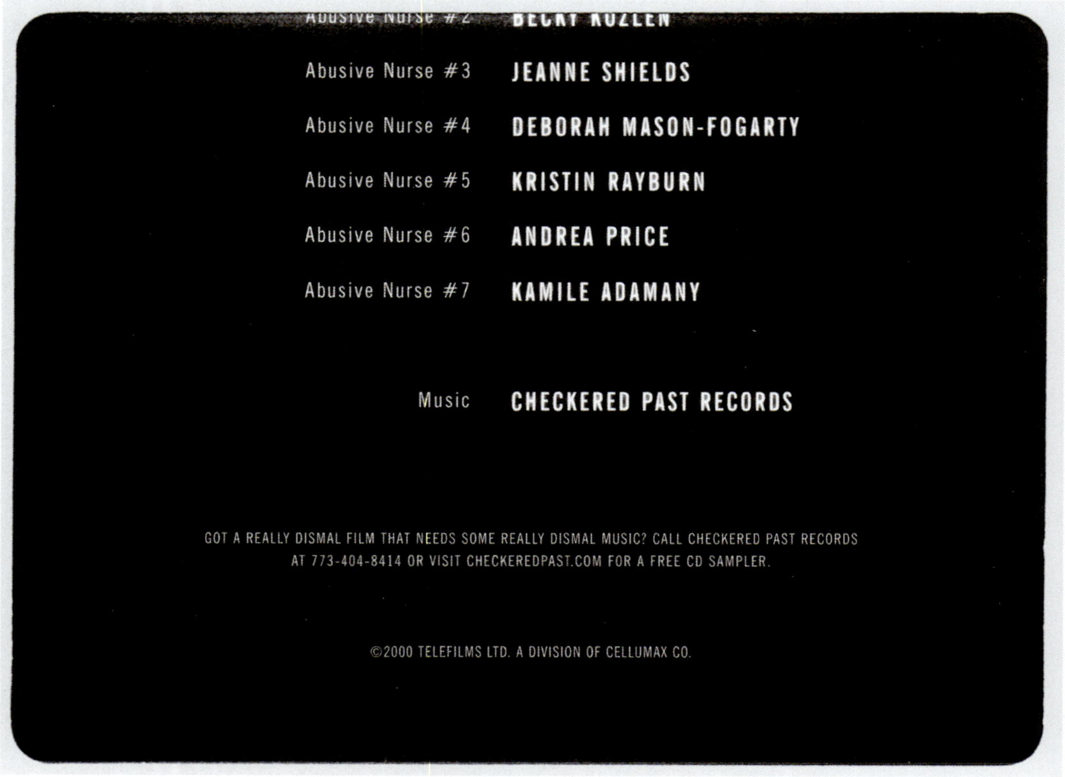

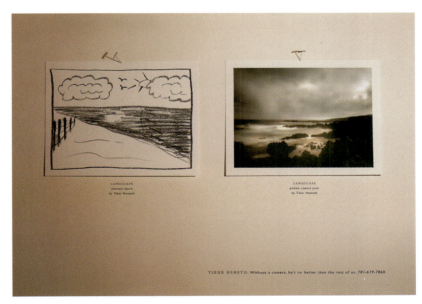
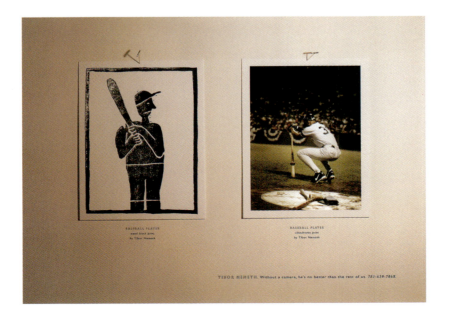

PRINT MERIT

MERIT AWARD
Trade B/W cr Color Any
Size: Campaign

ART DIRECTOR
Wade Devers

WRITER
John Simpson

ILLUSTRATOR
Tibor Nemeth

PHOTOGRAPHER
Tibor Nemeth

CLIENT
Tibor Nemeth Photography

AGENCY
ARNOLD Worldwide/Boston

010327A

PRINT MERIT

MERIT AWARD
Trade B/W or Color Any Size: Campaign

ART DIRECTOR
Sonya Grewal

WRITER
Christine Montaquila

PHOTOGRAPHER
William Huber

CLIENT
Sauder

AGENCY
Cramer-Krasselt/Chicago

010319A

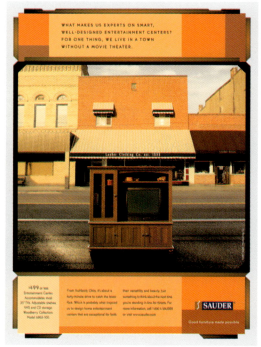

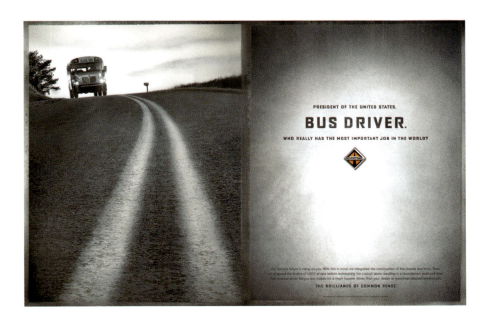

PRINT MERIT

MERIT AWARD
Trade B/W or Color Any
Size: Campaign

ART DIRECTOR
Dan Bryant

WRITERS
Roger Baldacci
Franklin Tipton

PHOTOGRAPHER
R. J. Muna

CLIENT
International

AGENCY
Fallon/Minneapolis

010320A

PRINT MERIT

MERIT AWARD
Trade B/W or Color Any
Size: Campaign

ART DIRECTOR
Steve Driggs

WRITER
Greg Hahn

PHOTOGRAPHERS
Manny Millan
John Biever
Robert Beck

CLIENT
Sports Illustrated

AGENCY
Fallon/Minneapolis

010321A

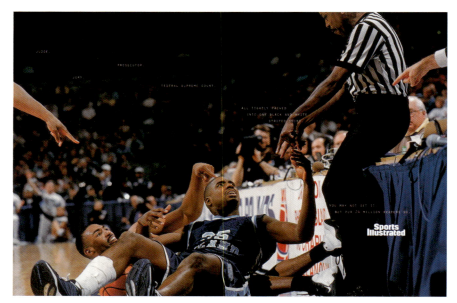

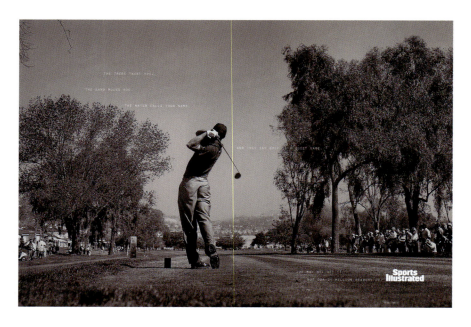

264

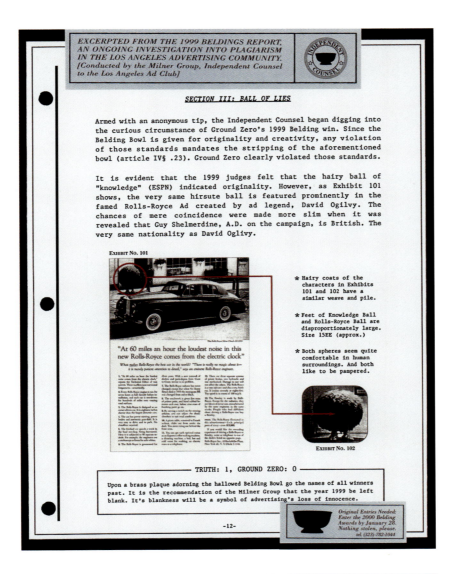
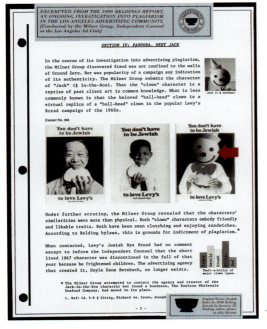
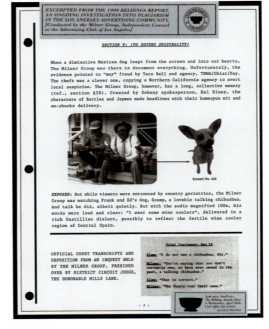

PRINT MERIT

MERIT AWARD
Trade B/W cr Color Any
Size: Campaign

ART DIRECTOR
Paul Foulkes

WRITER
Tyler Hampton

ILLUSTRATOR
Greg Beauchamp

PHOTOGRAPHER
Stock

CLIENT
Advertising Club of
Los Angeles

AGENCY
Ground Zero/Los Angeles

010322A

PRINT MERIT

MERIT AWARD
Trade B/W or Color Any
Size: Campaign

ART DIRECTORS
Myrtle
Tomato

WRITERS
Myrtle
Squid

CLIENT
AAR

AGENCY
Myrtle/London

010323A

PRINT MERIT

MERIT AWARD
Trade B/W or Color Any
Size: Campaign

ART DIRECTORS
Guillermo Caro
German Paino
Ted Royer

WRITERS
Javier Campopiano
Daniel Comar

PHOTOGRAPHER
Millennium

CLIENT
Afrodita TV

AGENCY
Ogilvy & Mather Argentina/
Buenos Aires

010324A

PRINT MERIT

MERIT AWARD
Trade B/W or Color Any
Size: Campaign

ART DIRECTOR
Maurice Wee

WRITER
Renee Lim

PHOTOGRAPHER
Nicholas Leong

CLIENT
Discovery Asia

AGENCY
Saatchi & Saatchi/
Singapore

010325A

PRINT MERIT

MERIT AWARD
Trade B/W or Color Any Size: Campaign

ART DIRECTOR
Will Roth

WRITER
John Robertson

PHOTOGRAPHER
Mika Manninen

CLIENT
Taylor Guitars

AGENCY
VITROROBERTSON/
San Diego

010328A

PRINT MERIT

MERIT AWARD
Trade B/W or Color Any
Size: Campaign

ART DIRECTOR
Yu Kung

WRITER
Dominic Corp

ILLUSTRATOR
Jasper Goodall

CLIENT
BMW

AGENCY
WCRS/London

010329A

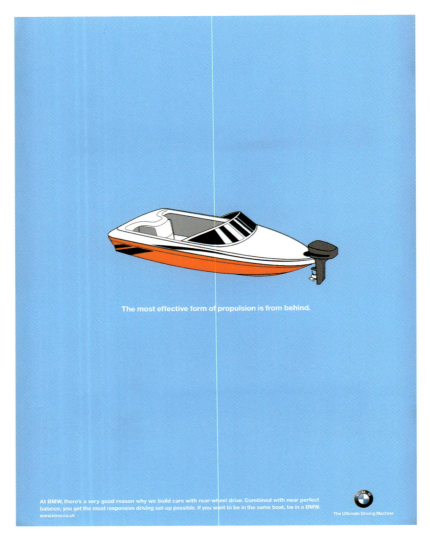

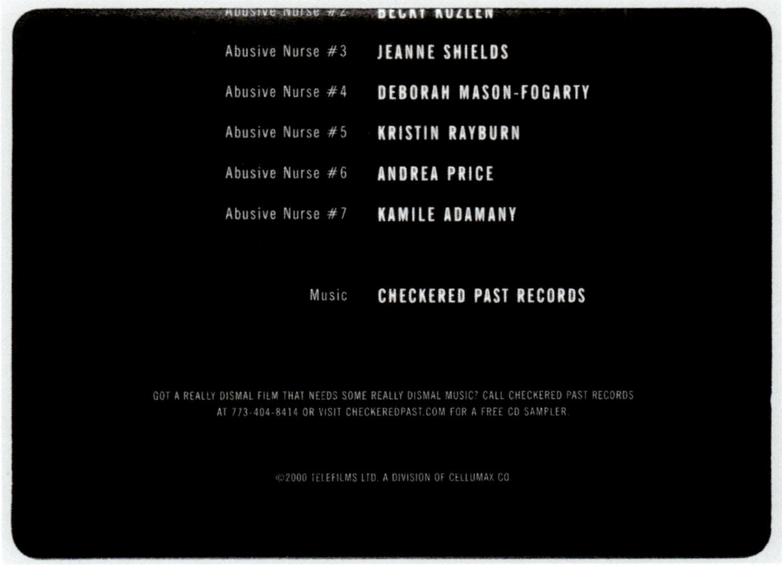

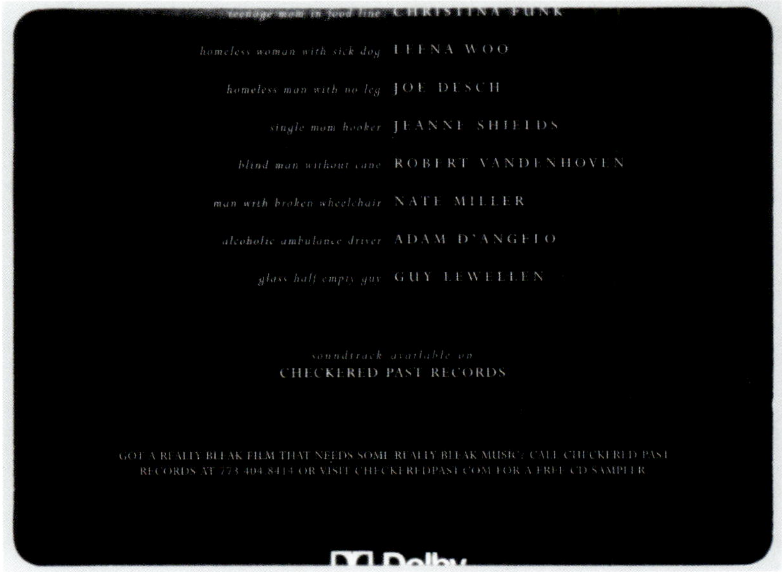

PRINT MERIT

MERIT AWARD
Trade B/W or Color Any
Size: Campaign

ART DIRECTOR
Jon Wyville

WRITER
Ken Erke

CLIENT
Checkered Past Records

AGENCY
Young & Rubicam/Chicago

010330A

PRINT MERIT

MERIT AWARD
Trade B/W or Color Any
Size: Campaign

ART DIRECTOR
Denis Kakazu

WRITER
Heitor Dhalia

PHOTOGRAPHER
Joao Avila

CLIENT
About Magazine

AGENCY
Young & Rubicam Brasil/
São Paulo

010331A

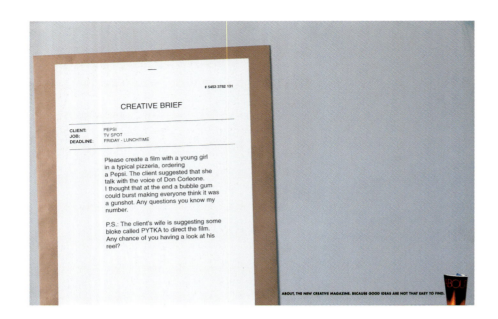
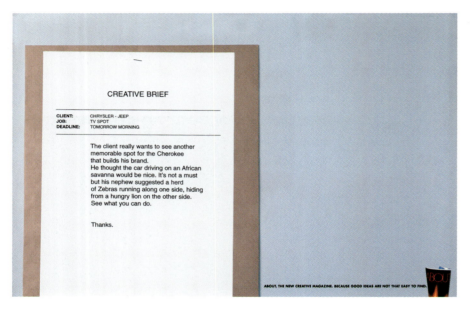
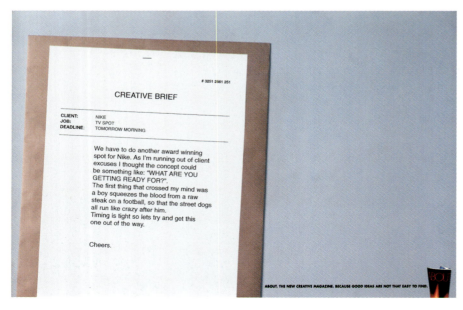

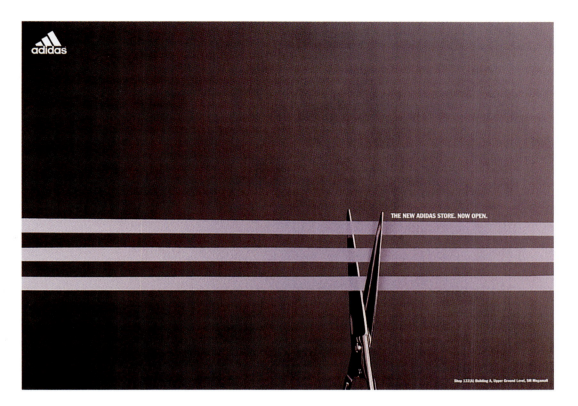

PRINT MERIT

MERIT AWARD
Collateral: Point of Purchase and In-Store

ART DIRECTOR
David Ferrer

WRITER
Dino Ocampo

PHOTOGRAPHER
Caloy Legaspi

CLIENT
Adidas Philippines

AGENCY
BBDO/Guerrero Ortega/
Makati City

010332A

MERIT AWARD
Collateral: Point of Purchase and In-Store

ART DIRECTOR
Lisa Francilia

WRITER
Dan Scherk

PHOTOGRAPHER
Leon Behar

CLIENT
The Spy Store

AGENCY
Bryant Fulton & Shee/
Vancouver

010333A

273

PRINT MERIT

MERIT AWARD
Collateral: Point of Purchase and In-Store

ART DIRECTOR
Jerome Marucci

WRITER
Crockett Jeffers

CLIENT
Wiffle Ball

AGENCY
Butler Shine & Stern/
Sausalito

010334A

MERIT AWARD
Collateral: Point of Purchase and In-Store

ART DIRECTOR
Jerome Marucci

WRITER
Crockett Jeffers

CLIENT
Wiffle Ball

AGENCY
Butler Shine & Stern/
Sausalito

010335A

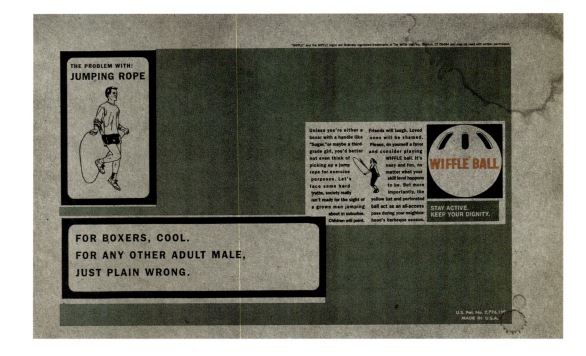

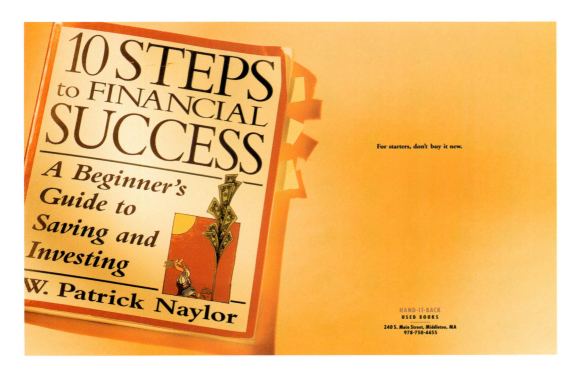

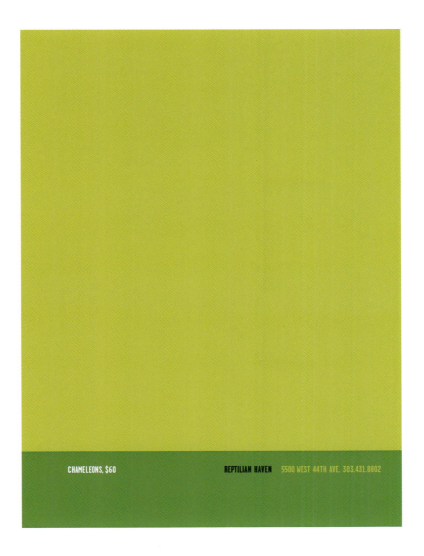

PRINT MERIT

MERIT AWARD
Collateral: Point of Purchase and In-Store

ART DIRECTOR
Adam Pierno

WRITER
Eivind Ueland

PHOTOGRAPHER
Christopher Harting

CLIENT
Hand-It-Back Bookstore

AGENCY
Hill Holliday Connors Cosmopulos/Boston

010336A

MERIT AWARD
Collateral: Point of Purchase and In-Store

ART DIRECTOR
Dan Kiefer

WRITER
Jay Roth

CLIENT
Reptilian Haven

AGENCY
The Integer Group/Lakewood

010337A

PRINT MERIT

MERIT AWARD
Collateral: Point of Purchase and In-Store

ART DIRECTORS
Jana Benjafield
Mick Colliss

WRITERS
Mick Colliss
Jana Benjafield
Ron Samuel

CLIENT
Adventure World

AGENCY
JDA/Perth

010338A

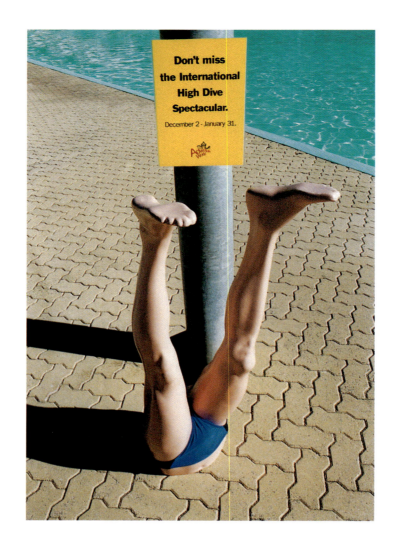

MERIT AWARD
Collateral: Point of Purchase and In-Store

ART DIRECTOR
Paul Soady

WRITER
Andy Stern

PHOTOGRAPHER
Kovar

CLIENT
Jack in the Box

AGENCY
Kowloon Wholesale Seafood Co./Santa Monica

010339A

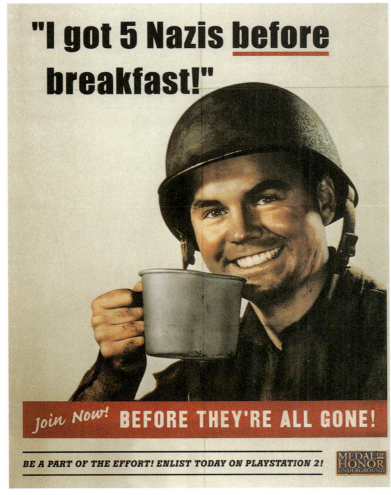

PRINT MERIT

MERIT AWARD
Collateral: Point of Purchase and In-Store

ART DIRECTOR
Mark Taylor

WRITER
Tony Stern

PHOTOGRAPHER
Stock

CLIENT
Electronic Arts

AGENCY
Odiorne Wilde Narraway & Partners/San Francisco

010340A

MERIT AWARD
Collateral: Point of Purchase and In-Store

ART DIRECTOR
Addy Khaotong

WRITER
Troy Lim

ILLUSTRATORS
Procolor
Lim Seng Niah

PHOTOGRAPHER
One Twenty One

CLIENT
Sony Asia Pacific

AGENCY
Saatchi & Saatchi/Singapore

010341A

277

PRINT MERIT

MERIT AWARD
Collateral: Point of Purchase and In-Store

ART DIRECTOR
Kevin Thoem

WRITER
Al Jackson

CLIENT
Brunswick Lanes

AGENCY
Sawyer Riley Compton/ Atlanta

010342A

MERIT AWARD
Collateral: Point of Purchase and In-Store

ART DIRECTOR
Kim Schoen

WRITER
Kevin Proudfoot

ILLUSTRATOR
Geoff McFetridge

CLIENT
ESPN

AGENCY
Wieden + Kennedy/ New York

010343A

Also won:

MERIT AWARD
One Show Design

PRINT MERIT

MERIT AWARD
Collateral: Point of Purchase and In-Store

ART DIRECTOR
Kim Schoen

WRITER
Kevin Proudfoot

ILLUSTRATOR
Geoff McFetridge

CLIENT
ESPN

AGENCY
Wieden – Kennedy/New York

010344A

Also won:

MERIT AWARD
One Show Design

MERIT AWARD
Collateral: Point of Purchase and In-Store

ART DIRECTOR
Mark Watson

WRITER
Cal McAllister

PHOTOGRAPHER
Sonic Stock Photography

CLIENT
Seattle SuperSonics

AGENCY
WONGDOODY/Seattle

010346A

279

PRINT MERIT

MERIT AWARD
Collateral: Point of Purchase and In-Store

ART DIRECTORS
Paul Howalt
Cabell Harris

WRITER
Steve Covert

CLIENT
WORK Beer

AGENCY
WORK/Richmond

010347A

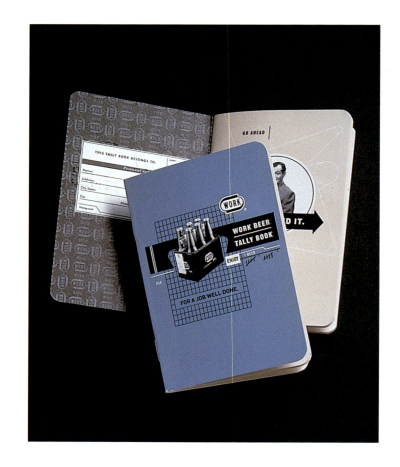

MERIT AWARD
Collateral: Self-Promotion

ART DIRECTOR
Jerry Underwood

WRITER
Alex Grossman

ILLUSTRATOR
Steven Stankiewicz

PHOTOGRAPHER
Brian Mahany

CLIENT
Steven Stankiewicz

AGENCY
Butler Shine & Stern/Sausalito

010348A

PRINT MERIT

MERIT AWARD
Collateral: Self-Promotion

ART DIRECTOR
Jerry Underwood

WRITER
Alex Grossman

ILLUSTRATOR
Steven Stankiewicz

PHOTOGRAPHER
Brian Mahany

CLIENT
Steven Stankiewicz

AGENCY
Butler Shine & Stern/
Sausalito

010349A

MERIT AWARD
Collateral: Self-Promotion

ART DIRECTOR
Nick Cohen

WRITERS
Nick Cohen
Deacon Webster

CLIENT
Mad Dogs & Englishmen

AGENCY
Mad Dogs & Englishmen/
San Francisco

010350A

PRINT MERIT

MERIT AWARD
Collateral: Self-Promotion

ART DIRECTOR
Michel Edens

WRITER
Deacon Webster

ILLUSTRATOR
Michel Edens

CLIENT
Mad Dogs & Englishmen

AGENCY
Mad Dogs & Englishmen/
San Francisco

010351A

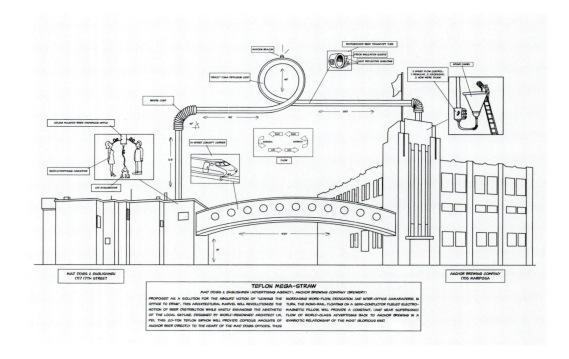

MERIT AWARD
Collateral: Self-Promotion

ART DIRECTORS
Kevin Reid
Patrick Murray
Jeff Hopfer
Ryan Turner
Rachel Migliore
Matt Dalin
Tom Nynas
Ashley Coursey Bull

WRITERS
Charles Stephenson
Bill Chochran
Mike Renfro
Brian Pierce
Kevin Swisher
Erik Fahrenkopf
Chris Smith
Chip Thompson

CLIENT
The Richards Group

AGENCY
The Richards Group/Dallas

010352A

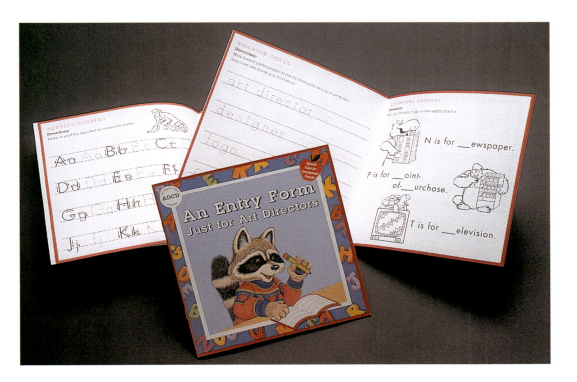

PRINT MERIT

MERIT AWARD
Collateral: Self-Promotion

ART DIRECTOR
Rich Rodgers

WRITER
Eric Liebhauser

ILLUSTRATOR
Sherry Neideigh

CLIENT
Art Director's Club
of Denver

AGENCY
TDA Advertising &
Design/Boulder

010354A

MERIT AWARD
Collateral: Self-Promotion

WRITER
Tom O'Connor

CLIENT
Tom O'Connor

AGENCY
Tom O'Connor Worldwide/
Roswell

010355A

Tom O'Connor
Copywriter
1210 Martin Ridge Road
Roswell, GA 30076
(678) 596-9016
rolltoc@yahoo.com

EXPERIENCE

Tom O'Connor, 1975 - present

PRINT MERIT

MERIT AWARD
Collateral: Posters

ART DIRECTOR
Aaron Alden

WRITER
Tom Van Ness

ILLUSTRATOR
Aaron Alden

PHOTOGRAPHER
Vikki Kerr

CLIENT
B-Line Snowboards

AGENCY
Barnhart/CMI/Denver

010356A

MERIT AWARD
Collateral: Posters

ART DIRECTOR
Aaron Alden

WRITER
Tom Van Ness

ILLUSTRATOR
Aaron Alden

PHOTOGRAPHER
Vicki Kerr

CLIENT
B-Line Snowboards

AGENCY
Barnhart/CMI/Denver

010357A

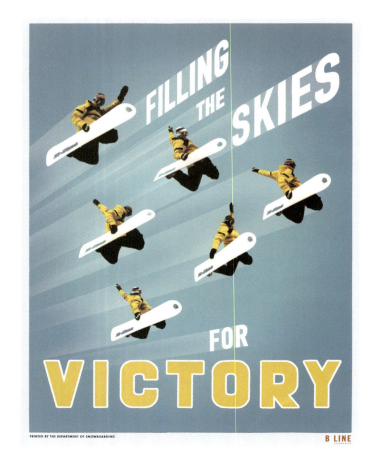

PRINT MERIT

MERIT AWARD
Collateral: Posters

ART DIRECTORS
Michael Cohen
Mark Cohen

WRITERS
Michael Cohen
Mark Cohen

PHOTOGRAPHER
Jim Fiscus

CLIENT
ESPN Tour de France

AGENCY
Bayless Cronin/Atlanta

010358A

MERIT AWARD
Collateral: Posters

ART DIRECTOR
Shelley Stout

WRITER
Mike Ward

PHOTOGRAPHER
Sam Walsh

CLIENT
Columbia Sportswear

AGENCY
Borders Perrin Norrander/
Portland

010359A

PRINT MERIT

MERIT AWARD
Collateral: Posters

ART DIRECTOR
Mike Lyons

WRITER
Don Dunbar

PHOTOGRAPHER
Stock

CLIENT
Joe Jackson Society

AGENCY
Cramer-Krasselt/Chicago

010360A

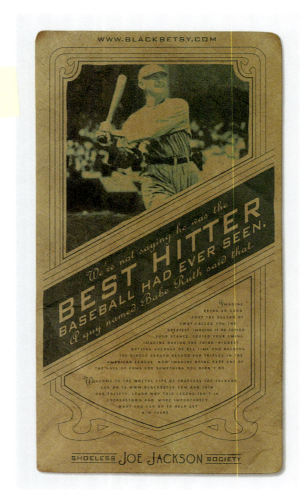

MERIT AWARD
Collateral: Posters

ART DIRECTOR
Tony Calcao

WRITER
Rob Strasberg

PHOTOGRAPHER
Mark Laita

CLIENT
Giro Sport Design

AGENCY
Crispin Porter & Bogusky/Miami

010361A

PRINT MERIT

MERIT AWARD
Collateral: Posters

ART DIRECTOR
Tony Calcao

WRITER
Rob Strasberg

PHOTOGRAPHER
Mark Laita

CLIENT
Giro Sport Design

AGENCY
Crispin Porter & Bogusky/
Miami

010362A

MERIT AWARD
Collateral: Posters

ART DIRECTOR
Tony Calcao

WRITER
Rob Strasberg

PHOTOGRAPHER
Mark Laita

CLIENT
Giro Sport Design

AGENCY
Crispin Porter & Bogusky/
Miami

010363A

287

PRINT MERIT

MERIT AWARD
Collateral: Posters

ART DIRECTOR
Joseph McGlennon

WRITER
Anand Arumugam Vathiyar

PHOTOGRAPHER
Stock

CLIENT
Nike

AGENCY
Dentsu Young & Rubicam/
Singapore

010364A

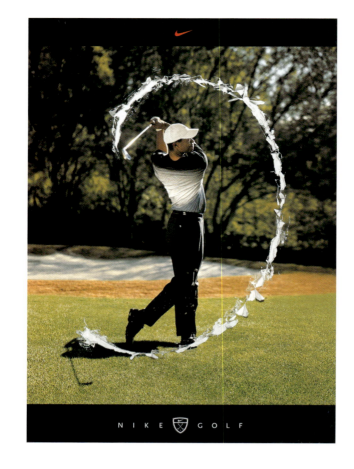

MERIT AWARD
Collateral: Posters

ART DIRECTOR
Jesus Felix

WRITER
Delores Stark

PHOTOGRAPHERS
Bill Debold
Gary Russ

CLIENT
Harry Knowles

AGENCY
GSD&M/Austin

010365A

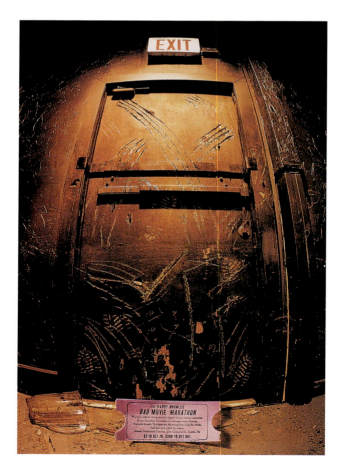

PRINT MERIT

MERIT AWARD
Collateral: Posters

ART DIRECTOR
Doug Pedersen

WRITER
Curtis Smith

PHOTOGRAPHERS
Steve Murray
Pat Staub

CLIENT
North Carolina
Travel & Tourism

AGENCY
Loeffler Ketchum Mountjoy/
Charlotte

010366A

MERIT AWARD
Collateral: Posters

ART DIRECTOR
Matt Lockett

WRITER
Anne Macomber

PHOTOGRAPHER
Matt Lockett

CLIENT
Mutual UFO Network
Museum

AGENCY
McClain Finlon Advertising/
Denver

010367A

PRINT MERIT

MERIT AWARD
Collateral: Posters

ART DIRECTORS
Hans-Friedrich Schoenhoff
Marco Weber

WRITER
Hans-Friedrich Schoenhoff

CLIENT
Landeszentrale F. Gesundheitsförderung/IBM

AGENCY
Ogilvy & Mather/Frankfurt

010369A

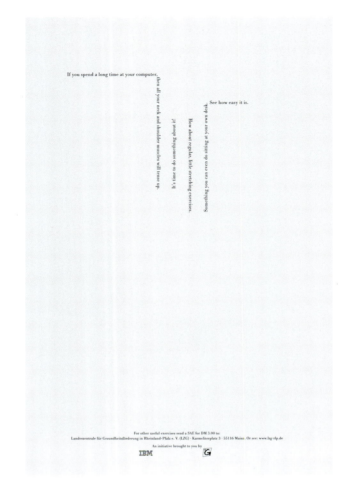

MERIT AWARD
Collateral: Posters

ART DIRECTOR
Haven Simmons

WRITER
Mike Zulawinski

PHOTOGRAPHER
Gary M. Jensen

CLIENT
Professional Bull Riders

AGENCY
R & R Partners/Las Vegas

010370A

PRINT MERIT

MERIT AWARD
Collateral: Posters

ART DIRECTORS
Greg Nations
Joe Baran

WRITER
Vinny Warren

PHOTOGRAPHERS
Carol King
Vinny Warren

CLIENT
Pub Tours of Ireland

AGENCY
rain/Elmhurst

010371A

MERIT AWARD
Collateral: Posters

ART DIRECTOR
Thomas Dooley

WRITER
Jonathan Schoenberg

PHOTOGRAPHER
Brooks Freehill

CLIENT
Cannondale

AGENCY
TDA Advertising & Design/Boulder

010372A

PRINT MERIT

MERIT AWARD
Collateral: Posters

ART DIRECTOR
Thomas Dooley

WRITER
Jonathan Schoenberg

PHOTOGRAPHER
Brooks Freehill

CLIENT
Cannondale

AGENCY
TDA Advertising & Design/
Boulder

010373A

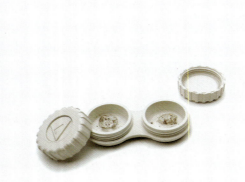

MERIT AWARD
Collateral: Posters

ART DIRECTOR
Thomas Dooley

WRITER
Jonathan Schoenberg

PHOTOGRAPHER
Brooks Freehill

CLIENT
Cannondale

AGENCY
TDA Advertising & Design/
Boulder

010374A

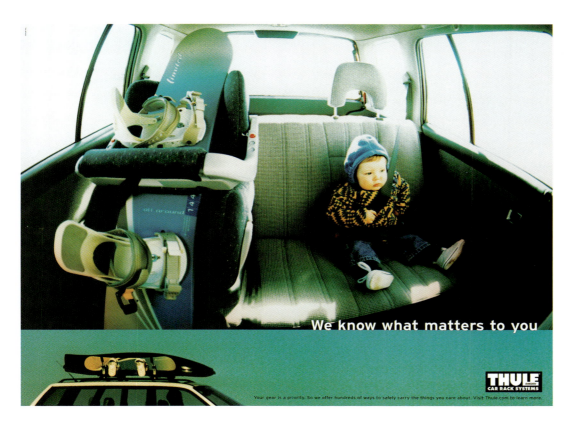

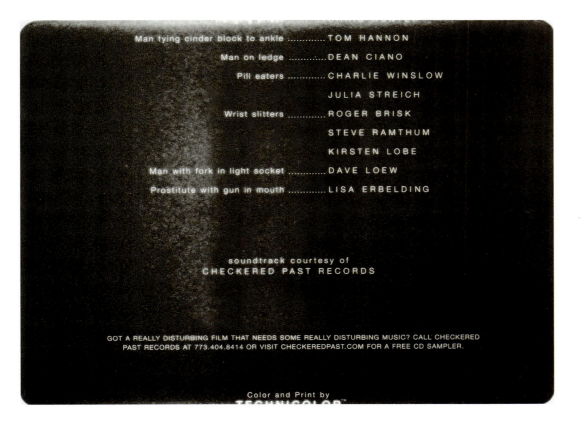

PRINT MERIT

MERIT AWARD
Collateral: Posters

ART DIRECTOR
Dan Richardson

WRITERS
Eric Liebhauser
Jonathan Schoenberg

PHOTOGRAPHER
Brooks Freehill

CLIENT
Thule

AGENCY
TDA Advertising & Design/Boulder

010375A

MERIT AWARD
Collateral: Posters

ART DIRECTOR
Jon Wyville

WRITER
Ken Erke

CLIENT
Checkered Past Records

AGENCY
Young & Rubicam/Chicago

010378A

PRINT MERIT

MERIT AWARD
Multi-Media Campaign

ART DIRECTOR
Pat Wittich

WRITER
Bob Meagher

PHOTOGRAPHERS
Kip Dawkins
Karl Steinbrenner

ILLUSTRATOR
David Boisineau

AGENCY PRODUCER
Jenny Kennedy

CLIENT
TV Land

AGENCY
The Martin Agency/
Richmond

010581A

TIMES CHANGE. Great TV Doesn't.

ANDY GRIFFITH: Mmm, mmm. Octypus, yellow tail, seaweed with wasabi on it.

AUNT BEA: More California Roll, Andy?

ANDY GRIFFITH: Mmm, mmm.

(Opie runs out of the room.)

AUNT BEA: That's funny, I thought he liked sushi.

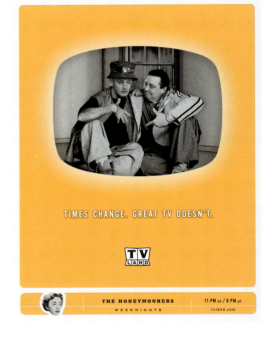

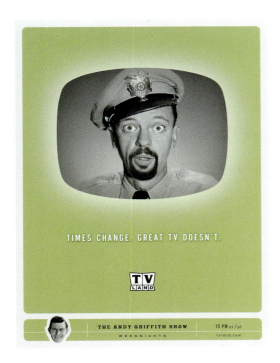
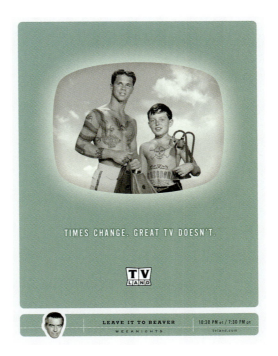

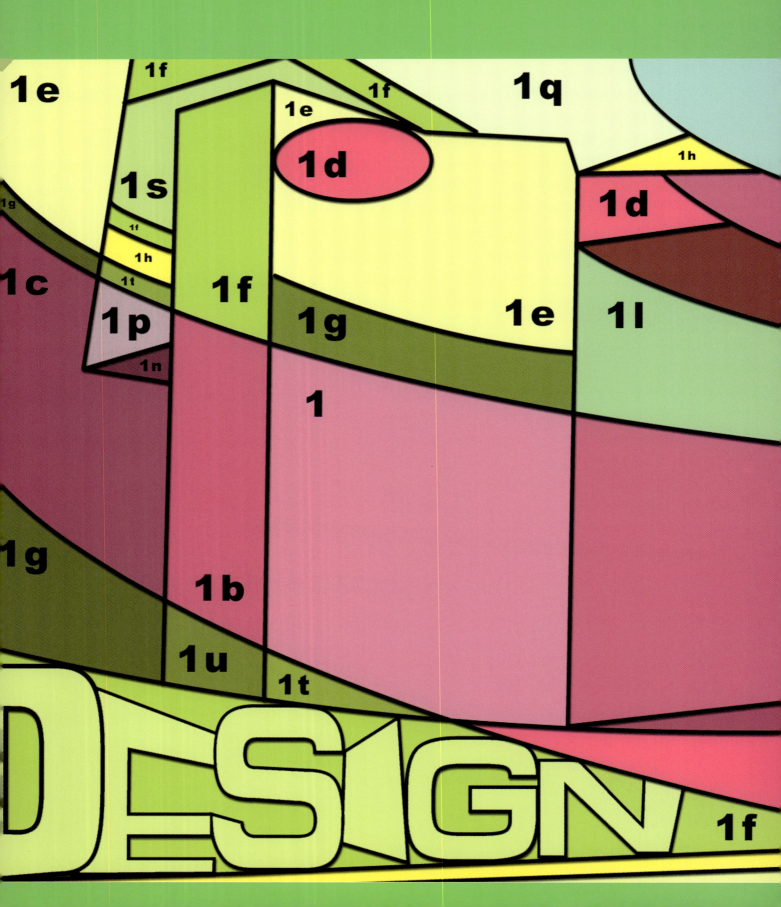

DESIGN

DESIGN MERIT

MERIT AWARD
One Show Design

DESIGNER
Dean Maryon

ART DIRECTOR
Dean Maryon

WRITER
Larry Frey

CLIENT
180

AGENCY
180/Amsterdam

010018D

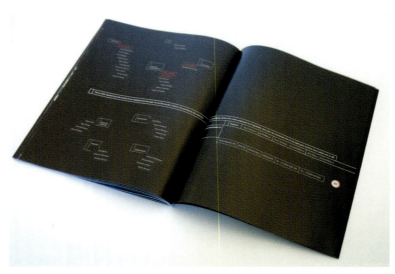

DESIGN MERIT

MERIT AWARD
One Show Design

DESIGNER
Tomas Lorente

ART DIRECTOR
Tomas Lorente

WRITER
Carlos Domingos

PHOTOGRAPHERS
Alexandre Catan
Andreas Heiniger
Arnaldo Pappalardo
Cassio Vasconcellos
Claudio Elisabetsky
Cristiano Mascaro
João Henrique Neto
Klaus Mitteldorf
Luis Crispino
Mauricio Nahas
Miro
Paulo Vainer
Pedro Martinelli
Ricardo Barcellos
Roberto Donaire
Willy Biondani

CLIENT
Burti Graphics

AGENCY
Age./São Paulo

010019D

MERIT AWARD
One Show Design

DESIGNER
Scott Arrowood

ART DIRECTOR
Douglas Dearden

CLIENT
iArchives

AGENCY
AND/Salt Lake City

010020D

299

DESIGN MERIT

MERIT AWARD
One Show Design

DESIGNER
Brian McDonough

ART DIRECTORS
Douglas Dearden
Scott Arrowood

WRITERS
Amy Cohen
Christy Anderson

ILLUSTRATOR
Wayne Coe

CLIENT
Sumus Interactive

AGENCY
AND/Salt Lake City

010021D

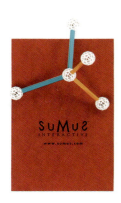
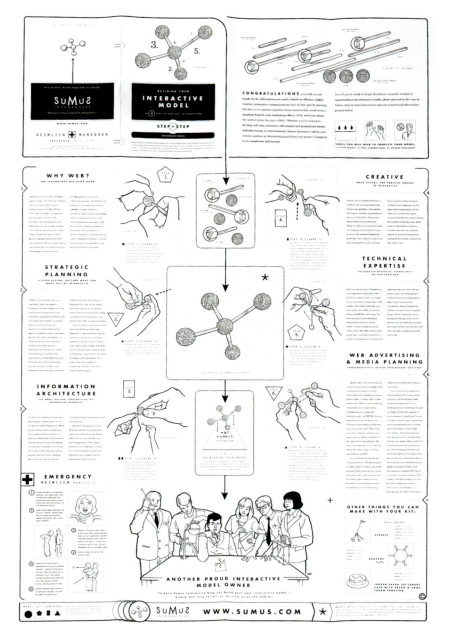

DESIGN MERIT

MERIT AWARD
One Show Design

DESIGNERS
Randall Myers
Clint! Runge

ART DIRECTORS
Randall Myers
Clint! Runge

ILLUSTRATOR
Randall Myers
Clint! Runge

CLIENT
Nebraska Wesleyan University

AGENCY
Archriva/Lincoln

010022D

MERIT AWARD
One Show Design

DESIGNERS
Steve Yaffe
Clif Wong

ART DIRECTORS
Steve Yaffe
Julian Newman
Clif Wong

WRITER
Eitan Chitayat

ILLUSTRATOR
Julian Newman

PHOTOGRAPHER
Bill Cash

CLIENT
Volkswagen of America

AGENCY
ARNOLD Worldwide/Boston

010023D

DESIGN MERIT

MERIT AWARD
One Show Design

DESIGNER
Julian Newman

ART DIRECTOR
Julian Newman

WRITER
Eitan Chitayat

ILLUSTRATOR
Julian Newman

PHOTOGRAPHER
Bill Cash

CLIENT
Volkswagen of America

AGENCY
ARNOLD Worldwide/Boston

010024D

MERIT AWARD
One Show Design

DESIGNER
Clif Wong

ART DIRECTORS
Clif Wong
Julian Newman

WRITER
Eitan Chitayat

ILLUSTRATOR
Julian Newman

PHOTOGRAPHER
Bill Cash

CLIENT
Volkswagen of America

AGENCY
ARNOLD Worldwide/Boston

010025D

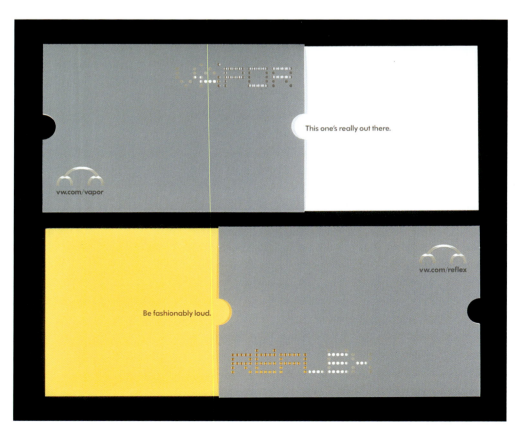

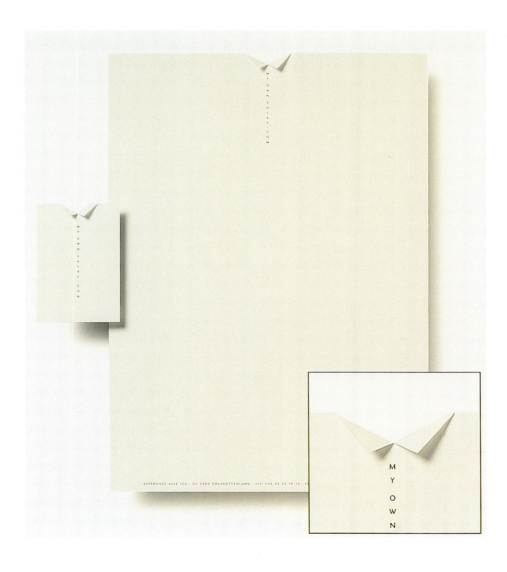

DESIGN MERIT

MERIT AWARD
One Show Design

ART DIRECTORS
Brian Fink
Branden Scharr

WRITERS
Courtney Hipp
Patrick McLean

PHOTOGRAPHERS
David Neff
Aaron Stevenson

CLIENT
Transamerica

AGENCY
Axiom Creative Group/
Charlotte

010026D

MERIT AWARD
One Show Design

DESIGNER
Lars Hartmann

ART DIRECTOR
Lars Hartmann

CLIENT
Myownshirt.com

AGENCY
BBDO Denmark/
Copenhagen

010027D

DESIGN MERIT

MERIT AWARD
One Show Design

DESIGNER
Willis Wong

ART DIRECTOR
Willis Wong

WRITERS
K. C. Tsang
Paul Chan

ILLUSTRATOR
Willis Wong

PHOTOGRAPHERS
Almond Chu
Lars Cheng
Lawrence Ching
Nelson Cheung
Willis Wong
Paul Chan

CLIENT
SCMP Book Publishing

AGENCY
BBDO/Hong Kong

010028D

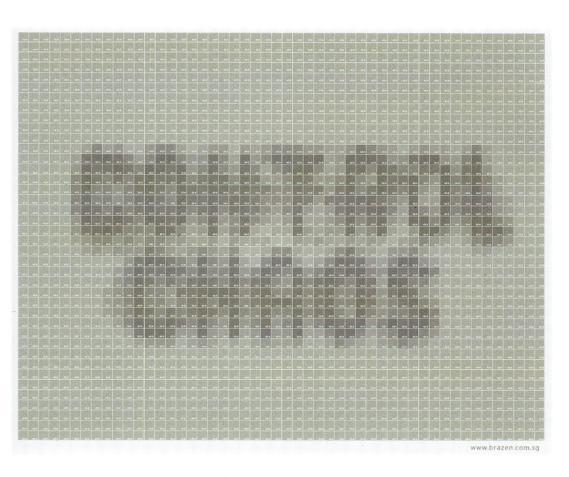

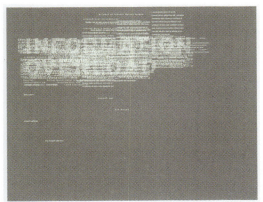

DESIGN MERIT

MERIT AWARD
One Show Design

ART DIRECTORS
Jackson Tan
Alvin Tan
Melvin Chee

WRITER
Jackson Tan

CLIENT
Brazen Communications

AGENCY
Brazen Communications/
Singapore

010029D

DESIGN MERIT

MERIT AWARD
One Show Design

ART DIRECTOR
Jason Skinner

WRITER
Kerry Graham

CLIENT
Cumberland Science Museum

AGENCY
The Buntin Group/Nashville

010030D

DESIGN MERIT

MERIT AWARD
One Show Design

ART DIRECTOR
Sharon Harms

WRITER
Kerry Graham

PHOTOGRAPHER
John Guider

CLIENT
Tennessee
Repertory Theatre

AGENCY
The Buntin Group/Nashville

010031D

DESIGN MERIT

MERIT AWARD
One Show Design

DESIGNER
Kevin Roberson

ART DIRECTOR
Bill Cahan

WRITER
Tony Leighton

ILLUSTRATOR
Steve Hussey

PHOTOGRAPHERS
Lars Tunbjork
Steven Ahlgren
Catherine Ledner

CLIENT
Gartner Group

AGENCY
Cahan & Associates/
San Francisco

010032D

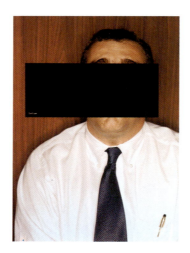

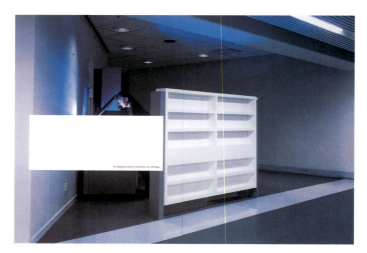

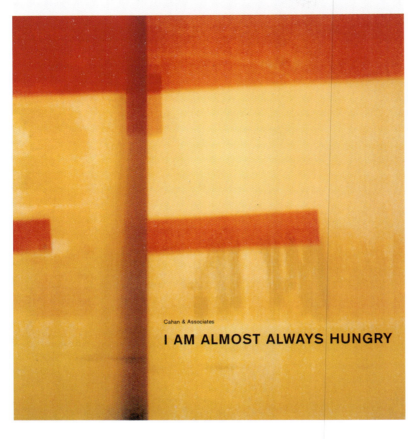

DESIGN MERIT

MERIT AWARD
One Show Design

DESIGNER
Bob Dinetz

ART DIRECTOR
Bill Cahan

WRITERS
Bob Dinetz
Kevin Roberson
Sharon Lichtenfeld
Bill Cahan
Thom Elkjer
Ken Coupland
Chris Harges
JoAnna di Paulo
Marty Neumeier
Glen Helfand
Tom Vanderbilt

ILLUSTRATOR
Carol Fabricatore

PHOTOGRAPHERS
Tony Stromberg
William Mercer McLeod
Robert Schlatter
William Howard
Bob Dinetz

CLIENT
Princeton
Architectural Press

AGENCY
Cahan & Associates/
San Francisco

010033D

DESIGN MERIT

MERIT AWARD
One Show Design

DESIGNER
David Schrimpf

CLIENT
A. T. Cross Pens

AGENCY
Carmichael Lynch/
Minneapolis

010034D

MERIT AWARD
One Show Design

DESIGNER
a'Tony Lindvall

WRITER
Katie Franson

PHOTOGRAPHER
Sara Jorde

CLIENT
Potlatch

AGENCY
Carmichael Lynch/
Minneapolis

010035D

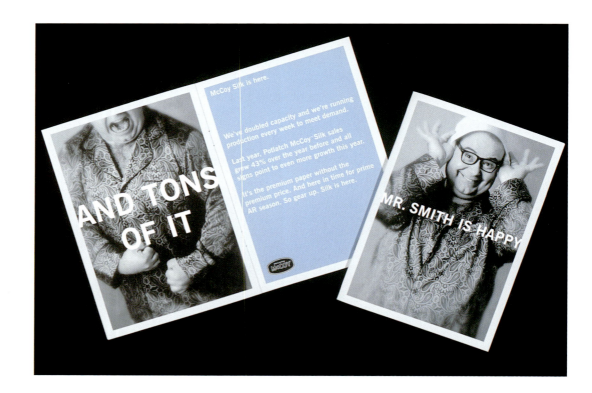

DESIGN MERIT

MERIT AWARD
One Show Design

DESIGNER
David Schrimpf

WRITER
Joan Abrahamson

CLIENT
Wabedo

AGENCY
Carmichael Lynch/Minneapolis

010036D

MERIT AWARD
One Show Design

DESIGNERS
Matt Crouch
Kevin Fitzgerald
Jacob Escobedo
Bob Fisher

ART DIRECTOR
Gary Albright

WRITERS
Jennifer Titus
Eric Bone
Merril Hagan

CLIENT
Cartoon Network

AGENCY
Cartoon Network/Atlanta

010037D

311

DESIGN MERIT

MERIT AWARD
One Show Design

DESIGNERS
Bob Fisher
Jacob Escobedo

ART DIRECTOR
Gary Albright

WRITER
Jimmy Hamiter

CLIENT
Cartoon Network

AGENCY
Cartoon Network/Atlanta

010038D

MERIT AWARD
One Show Design

ART DIRECTOR
Alyssa D'Arienzo Toro

WRITER
Steve Connelly

PHOTOGRAPHER
Craig Orsini

CLIENT
Kryptonite

AGENCY
Connelly Partners/Boston

010039D

DESIGN MERIT

MERIT AWARD
One Show Design

DESIGNERS
Cara Ang
Christopher Lee
Larry Peh
Kai
Liew Weiping
Michelle Tan

ART DIRECTOR
Christopher Lee

WRITER
Evelyn Tan

ILLUSTRATORS
Cara Ang
Christopher Lee
Liew Weiping

PHOTOGRAPHERS
Christopher Lee
Larry Peh
Kai

CLIENT
Design Asylum

AGENCY
Design Asylum/Singapore

010040D

313

DESIGN MERIT

MERIT AWARD
One Show Design

DESIGNER
Kai

ART DIRECTORS
Christopher Lee
Kai

CLIENT
Pierside Kitchen & Bar

AGENCY
Design Asylum/Singapore

010041D

MERIT AWARD
One Show Design

DESIGNER
Conan Wang

ART DIRECTORS
Jonathan Brown
Conan Wang

CLIENT
Orange County Ad Club

AGENCY
DGWB/Santa Ana

010042D

DESIGN MERIT

MERIT AWARD
One Show Design

DESIGNER
Tom Riddle

ART DIRECTOR
Tom Riddle

ILLUSTRATOR
Tom Riddle

PHOTOGRAPHER
Chris Sheenan

CLIENT
International Truck & Engine Corp.

AGENCY
Duffy/Minneapolis

010047D

DESIGN MERIT

MERIT AWARD
One Show Design

DESIGNERS
Kobe Suvongse
Joe Monnens

ART DIRECTOR
Kobe Suvongse

WRITERS
Mark Wirt
Scott Barger

PHOTOGRAPHER
Deborah Jones

CLIENT
Iowa Beef Producers

AGENCY
Duffy/Minneapolis

010048D

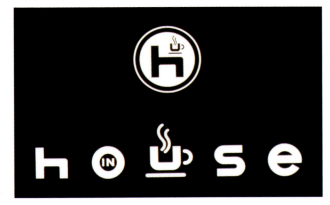

DESIGN MERIT

MERIT AWARD
One Show Design

DESIGNERS
Alan Colvin
Ken Sakurai
Craig Duffney

ART DIRECTOR
Alan Colvin

ILLUSTRATORS
Alan Colvin
Ken Sakurai
Craig Duffney

PHOTOGRAPHER
Richard Klein

CLIENT
Nordstrom

AGENCY
Duffy/Minneapolis

010049D

DESIGN MERIT

MERIT AWARD
One Show Design

DESIGNER
Genevieve Gorder

ART DIRECTOR
Jon Rosen

WRITER
Jenna Hall

PHOTOGRAPHER
Maribel Dato

CLIENT
Advertising Women of New York (AWNY)

AGENCY
Duffy/New York

010043D

MERIT AWARD
One Show Design

DESIGNER
Genevieve Gorder

ART DIRECTOR
Jon Rosen

WRITER
Jenna Hall

PHOTOGRAPHER
Maribel Dato

CLIENT
Advertising Women of New York (AWNY)

AGENCY
Duffy/New York

010044D

DESIGN MERIT

MERIT AWARD
One Show Design

DESIGNER
Neil Powell

CLIENT
Trick Dog Cafe

AGENCY
Duffy/New York

010045D

DESIGN MERIT

MERIT AWARD
One Show Design

DESIGNER
Rory Hanrahan

ART DIRECTOR
Alan Leusink

WRITER
Bobby Pierce

ILLUSTRATOR
Alan Baker

CLIENT
Viant

AGENCY
Duffy/New York

010046D

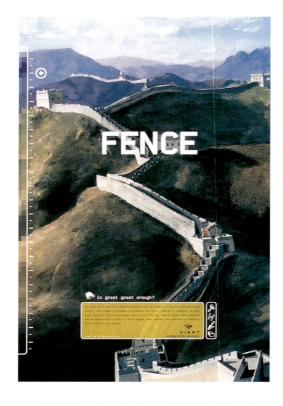
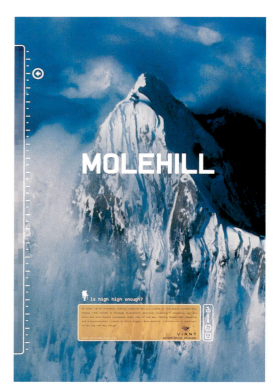
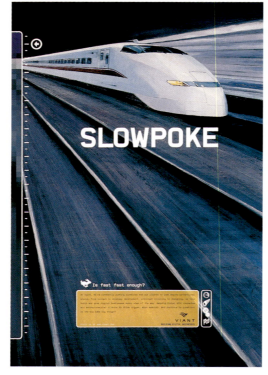

DESIGN MERIT

MERIT AWARD
One Show Design

DESIGNER
Jacquie Van Keuren

WRITER
Robert Duncan

PHOTOGRAPHER
Will Yarbrough

CLIENT
Gum Joy Records

AGENCY
Duncan Channon/
San Rafael

010050D

MERIT AWARD
One Show Design

DESIGNERS
Claudia Gamboa
André Vela

ART DIRECTOR
Ney Valle

WRITER
Ana Tavares

PHOTOGRAPHERS
Artist's Archive
Lygia Pape

CLIENT
Casa França-Brazil
Foundation

AGENCY
Dupla Design/
Rio de Janeiro

010051D

DESIGN MERIT

MERIT AWARD
One Show Design

ART DIRECTOR
Bob Lebron

WRITER
Diana Fair

ILLUSTRATOR
Erik Jastrebski

PHOTOGRAPHER
Chris Schrameck

CLIENT
AT&T

AGENCY
DVC Group/Morristown

010052D

MERIT AWARD
One Show Design

DESIGNER
Bhupal Ramnathkar

ART DIRECTOR
Bhupal Ramnathkar

WRITER
Tony Pereira

PHOTOGRAPHER
Ajay Salvi

CLIENT
Ajay Salvi

AGENCY
Enterprise Nexus Communications Private Limited/Mumbai

010053D

DESIGN MERIT

MERIT AWARD
One Show Design

ART DIRECTOR
Steve Cullen

WRITER
Steve Cullen

CLIENT
Ad Club of Greater Boston

AGENCY
Fort Franklin/Boston

010054D

MERIT AWARD
One Show Design

DESIGNER
Marc Gallucci

ART DIRECTOR
Marc Gallucci

CLIENT
Bulmers America

AGENCY
Fort Franklin/Boston

010055D

DESIGN MERIT

MERIT AWARD
One Show Design

DESIGNER
Marc Gallucci

ART DIRECTOR
Marc Gallucci

CLIENT
Bulmers America

AGENCY
Fort Franklin/Boston

010056D

MERIT AWARD
One Show Design

ART DIRECTOR
Steve Cullen

WRITER
Steve Cullen

CLIENT
New York University

AGENCY
Fort Franklin/Boston

010122D

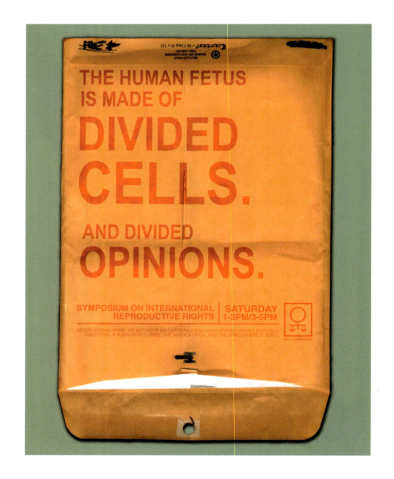

324

DESIGN MERIT

MERIT AWARD
One Show Design

DESIGNER
Graham Clifford

ART DIRECTOR
Graham Clifford

WRITER
Matt Sherring

CLIENT
Backbone NYC

AGENCY
Graham Clifford Design/
New York

010057D

DESIGN MERIT

MERIT AWARD
One Show Design

DESIGNER
Graham Clifford

ART DIRECTOR
Graham Clifford

WRITER
Matt Sherring

CLIENT
Headmint

AGENCY
Graham Clifford Design/
New York

010058D

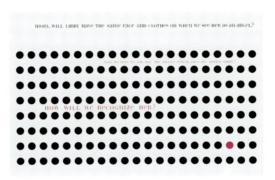

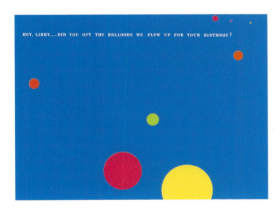
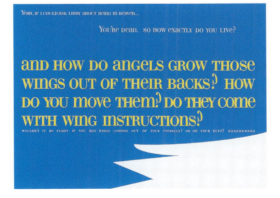

DESIGN MERIT

MERIT AWARD
One Show Design

DESIGNER
Annette Simon

ART DIRECTOR
Annette Simon

WRITER
Jack Simon

ILLUSTRATOR
Annette Simon

CLIENT
GSD&M/Idea University Press

AGENCY
GSD&M/Austin

010060D

DESIGN MERIT

MERIT AWARD
One Show Design

DESIGNER
Marty Erhart

ART DIRECTOR
Gene Brenek

PHOTOGRAPHER
Philip Esparza

CLIENT
Hill Country Ride for AIDS

AGENCY
GSD&M/Austin

010059D

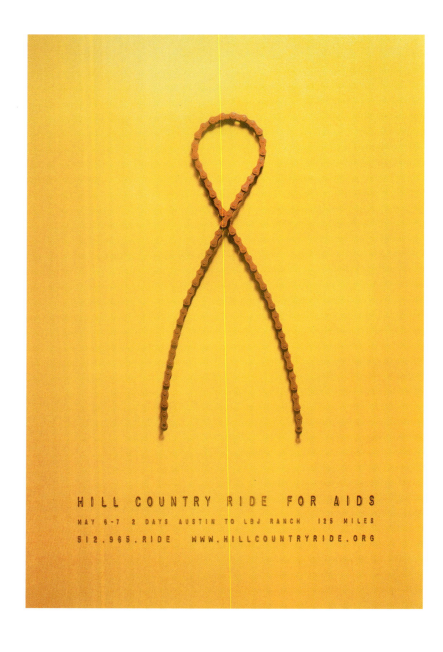

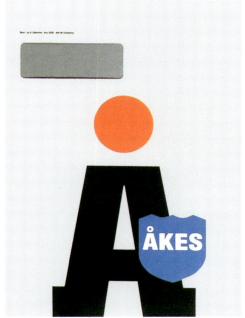

DESIGN MERIT

MERIT AWARD
One Show Design

DESIGNER
Andreas Kittel

ART DIRECTOR
Andreas Kittel

CLIENT
Åkes Locksmith & Security

AGENCY
Happy Forsman &
Bodenfors/Gothenburg

010061D

DESIGN MERIT

MERIT AWARD
One Show Design

DESIGNERS
Andreas Kittel
Helena Redman

ART DIRECTORS
Andreas Kittel
Helena Redman

WRITER
Lasse Brunnström

PHOTOGRAPHER
Ola Bergengren

CLIENT
Röhsska Museet

AGENCY
Happy Forsman &
Bodenfors/Gothenburg

010062D

DESIGN MERIT

MERIT AWARD
One Show Design

DESIGNERS
Andreas Kittel
Helena Redman

ART DIRECTORS
Andreas Kittel
Helena Redman

PHOTOGRAPHER
Ola Bergengren

CLIENT
Röhsska Museet

AGENCY
Happy Forsman &
Bodenfors/Gothenburg

010063D

DESIGN MERIT

MERIT AWARD
One Show Design

DESIGNERS
Andreas Kittel
Helena Redman

ART DIRECTORS
Andreas Kittel
Helena Redman

ILLUSTRATOR
Orcavision Digital
Art Studio

CLIENT
Röhsska Museet

AGENCY
Happy Forsman &
Bodenfors/Gothenburg

010064D

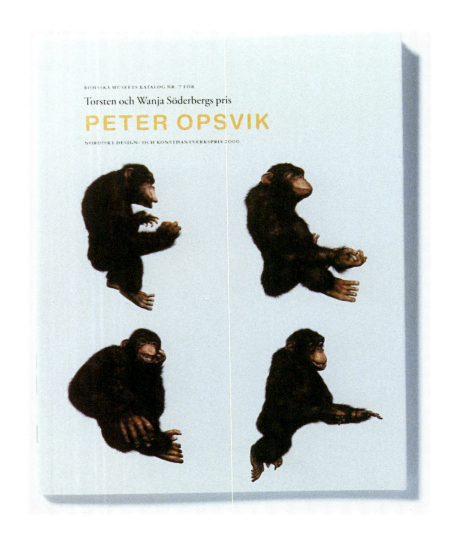

DESIGN MERIT

MERIT AWARD
One Show Design

DESIGNER
Mikael Blom

ART DIRECTORS
Anders Kornestedt
Helena Redman

ILLUSTRATOR
Fredrik Persson

CLIENT
SCA Hygiene Products

AGENCY
Happy Forsman &
Bodenfors/Gothenburg

010065D

DESIGN MERIT

MERIT AWARD
One Show Design

DESIGNERS
Andrew Smith
Gretchen Cook
Mary Hermes
Julie Lock
Holly Craven
Elmer Dela Cruz
Belinda Bowling
Amy Fawcette

ART DIRECTOR
Jack Anderson

ILLUSTRATORS
Gretchen Cook
Andrew Smith

CLIENT
Space Needle

AGENCY
Hornall Anderson
Design Works/Seattle

010066D

DESIGN MERIT

MERIT AWARD
One Show Design

DESIGNERS
Lisa Cerveny
Bruce Branson-Meyer
Mary Chin Hutchinson
Jana Nishi
Don Stayner

ART DIRECTORS
Jack Anderson
Lisa Cerveny

WRITER
Eric LeBrecht

PHOTOGRAPHER
Anthony Mex

CLIENT
XOW!

AGENCY
Hornall Anderson
Design Works/Seattle

010067D

DESIGN MERIT

MERIT AWARD
One Show Design

DESIGNERS
Steve Mitchell
Luke Oeth
Britt Lundberg

CLIENT
Hunt Adkins

AGENCY
Hunt Adkins/Minneapolis

010068D

MERIT AWARD
One Show Design

DESIGNER
Anne Rotondo

ART DIRECTOR
Anne Rotondo

WRITER
Larry Werner

ILLUSTRATOR
Stock

CLIENT
Shell Oil

AGENCY
J. Walter Thompson/
Houston

010069D

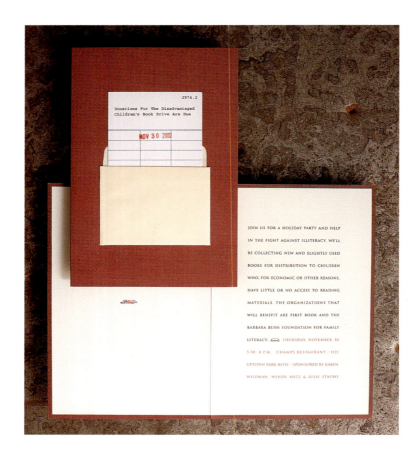

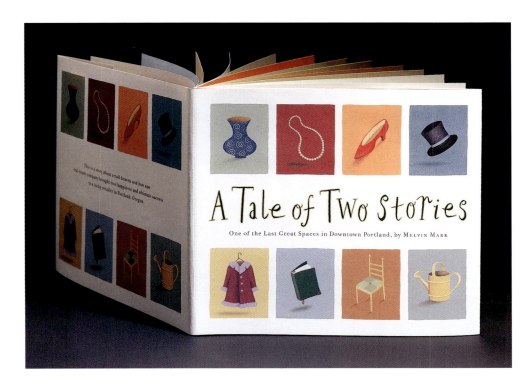

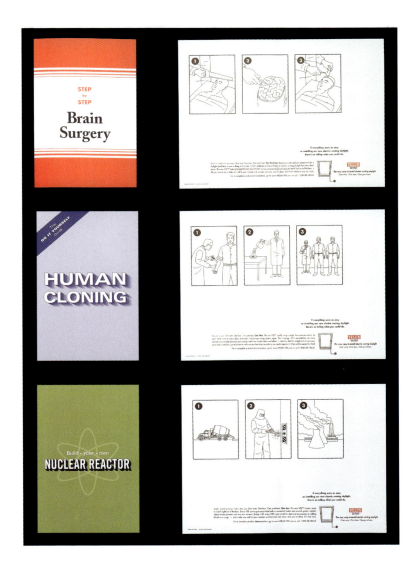

DESIGN MERIT

MERIT AWARD
One Show Design

DESIGNERS
Amy Johnson
Starlee Matz

ART DIRECTOR
Amy Johnson

WRITER
Leslee Dillon

ILLUSTRATOR
Amy Johnson

CLIENT
Melvin Mark Development

AGENCY
Lift Communications/
Portland

010070D

MERIT AWARD
One Show Design

DESIGNER
Doug Pedersen

ART DIRECTOR
Doug Pedersen

WRITER
Curtis Smith

ILLUSTRATOR
Floyd Coffey

CLIENT
Velux Skylights

AGENCY
Loeffler Ketchum
Mountjoy/Charlotte

010071D

DESIGN MERIT

MERIT AWARD
One Show Design

ART DIRECTOR
Daniel George Wan

WRITER
Daniel George Wan

ILLUSTRATOR
Procolor

PHOTOGRAPHER
Derrick Lim Photography

CLIENT
Sara Lee Singapore

AGENCY
M & C Saatchi/Singapore

010072D

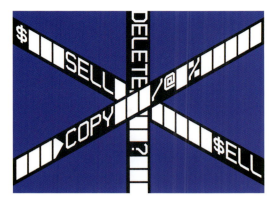
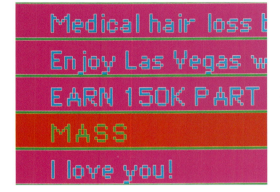
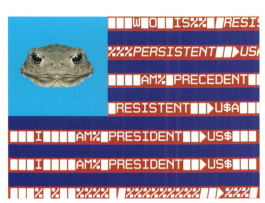
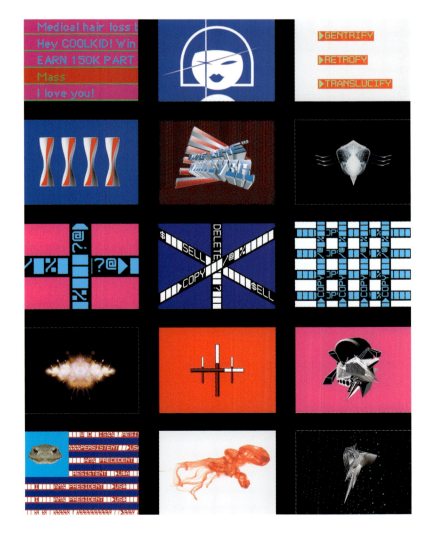

DESIGN MERIT

MERIT AWARD
One Show Design

DESIGNER
Stephan Valter

ART DIRECTOR
Stephan Valter

WRITER
Stephan Valter

CLIENT
mass.com

AGENCY
mass/New York

010073D

DESIGN MERIT

MERIT AWARD
One Show Design

DESIGNERS
Kim Gehrig
Cecilia Dufils

ART DIRECTORS
Markus Bjurman
Jamie Johnson

WRITER
Joe De Souza

PHOTOGRAPHER
Mother

CLIENT
Britart.com

AGENCY
Mother Ltd./London

010074D

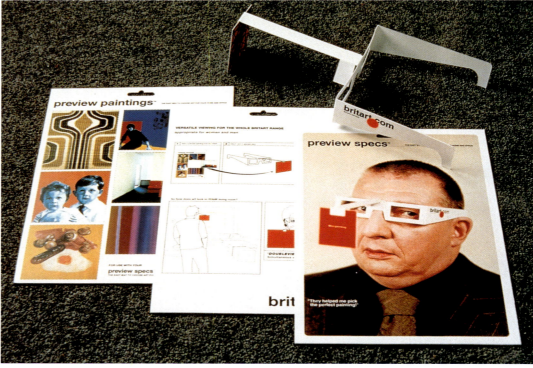

DESIGN MERIT

MERIT AWARD
One Show Design

DESIGNER
Erin Blankley

ART DIRECTORS
Russel Hicks
Patricia Russoniello

WRITERS
Deb Krassner
Dave Maciolek
Joe Bianco

ILLUSTRATORS
Sergio Cuan
Steve Crespa

PHOTOGRAPHER
Steffany Rubin

CLIENT
Nickelodeon Creative Resources

AGENCY
Nickelodeon Creative Resources/New York

010075D

MERIT AWARD
One Show Design

DESIGNER
Erin Blankely

ART DIRECTORS
Russel Hicks
Patricia Russoniello

WRITERS
Deb Krassner
Dave Maciolek
Joe Bianco

ILLUSTRATORS
Sergio Cuan
Steve Crespo

PHOTOGRAPHER
Steffany Rubin

CLIENT
Nickelodeon Creative Resources

AGENCY
Nickelodeon Creative Resources/New York

010076D

341

DESIGN MERIT

MERIT AWARD
One Show Design

DESIGNER
Marino A. Gallo

ART DIRECTOR
Marino A. Gallo

WRITER
Pio Shunker

PHOTOGRAPHER
Christian Jacobson

CLIENT
American Express

AGENCY
Ogilvy & Mather/New York

010077D

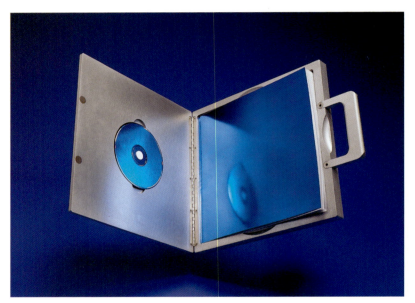

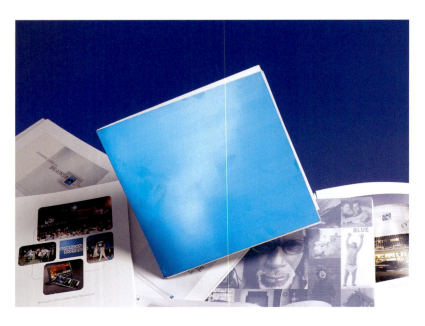

New Salon opening at 9:00 pm on August 24, at B-40, Panchsheel Enclave. You're invited.

DESIGN MERIT

MERIT AWARD
One Show Design

ART DIRECTOR
Sunil V.

WRITER
Satbir Singh

ILLUSTRATOR
Bhim Singh

CLIENT
Ambika Pillai

AGENCY
Ogilvy & Mather/New Delhi

010078D

DESIGN MERIT

MERIT AWARD
One Show Design

DESIGNER
Rodolfo Borrell

ART DIRECTOR
Rodolfo Borrell

WRITERS
Rodolfo Borrell
Carolina Guisande

CLIENT
Oscar de la Renta

AGENCY
Pages/BBDO/
Santo Domingo

010079D

DESIGN MERIT

MERIT AWARD
One Show Design

DESIGNER
Mike Joyce

ART DIRECTOR
Mike Joyce

CLIENT
J Records

AGENCY
Platinum Design/New York

010080D

MERIT AWARD
One Show Design

DESIGNERS
Eileen Elterman
Carol Thompson

ART DIRECTORS
Stacey May
Eileen Elterman

WRITER
Ray Calvo

CLIENT
Pronto Design

AGENCY
Pronto Design/New York

010081D

345

DESIGN MERIT

MERIT AWARD
One Show Design

DESIGNER
Michael Tan

ART DIRECTOR
Michael Tan

WRITER
Parag Tembulkar

PHOTOGRAPHER
Shooting Gallery

CLIENT
Mazda

AGENCY
Publicis/Singapore

010082D

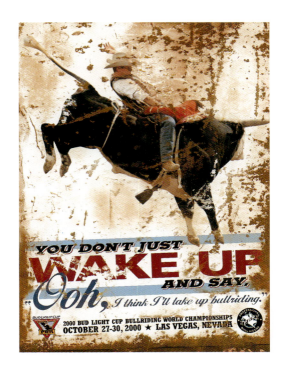
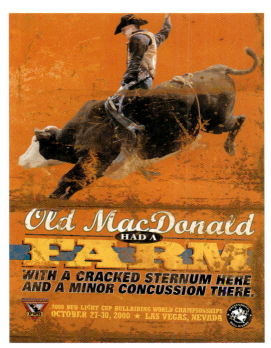
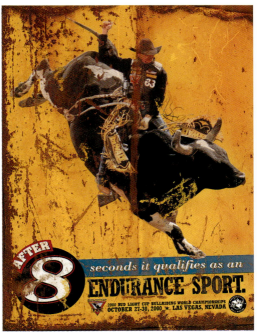

DESIGN MERIT

MERIT AWARD
One Show Design

ART DIRECTOR
Haven Simmons

WRITER
Mike Zulawinski

PHOTOGRAPHER
Gary M. Jensen

CLIENT
Professional Bull Riders

AGENCY
R & R Partners, Las Vegas

010083D

DESIGN MERIT

MERIT AWARD
One Show Design

DESIGNERS
Ian Grais
Chris Staples

ART DIRECTOR
Ian Grais

CLIENT
Rethink

AGENCY
Rethink/Vancouver

010084D

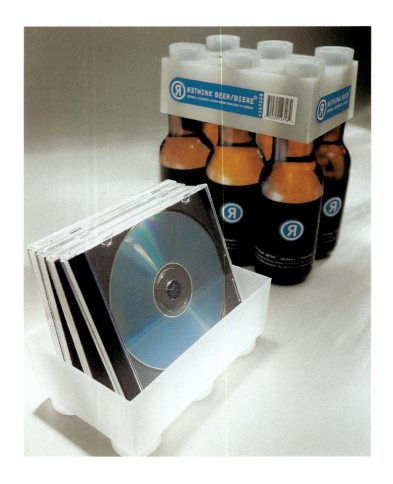

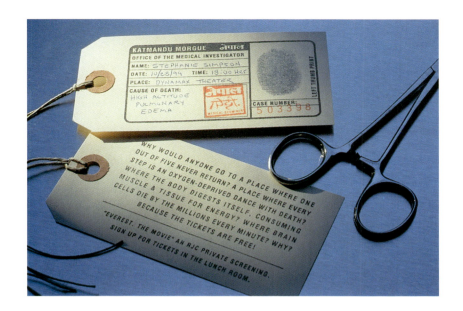

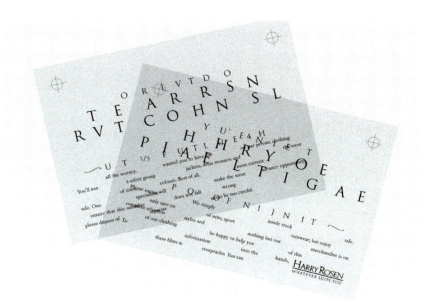

DESIGN MERIT

MERIT AWARD
One Show Design

ART DIRECTOR
Tim McGrath

WRITER
Tim Pegors

CLIENT
Rick Johnson & Company

AGENCY
Rick Johnson & Company/
Albuquerque

010085D

MERIT AWARD
One Show Design

ART DIRECTOR
Robert Kingston

WRITER
Rich Cooper

CLIENT
Harry Rosen

AGENCY
Roche Macaulay &
Partners/Toronto

010086D

DESIGN MERIT

MERIT AWARD
One Show Design

ART DIRECTORS
David Shultz
Ken Waldron

WRITERS
David Henthorne
Ron Foth, Jr.

CLIENT
Westerville North
High School

AGENCY
Ron Foth/Columbus

010087D

MERIT AWARD
One Show Design

DESIGNERS
Tanya Davis
John Bateson

ART DIRECTOR
Mark McConnachie

WRITER
Geraldine Gardner

CLIENT
Quantel

AGENCY
Roundel/London

010088D

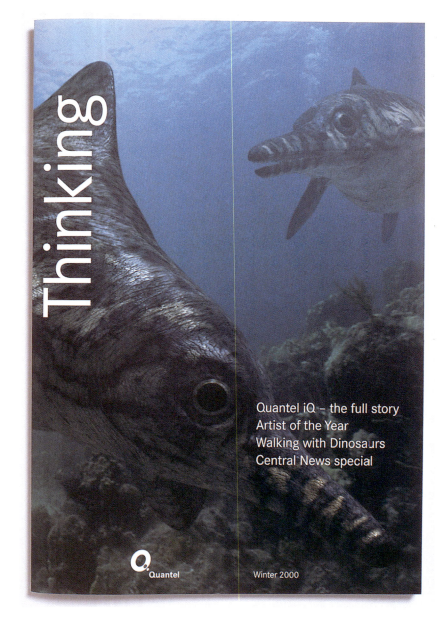

350

DESIGN MERIT

MERIT AWARD
One Show Design

DESIGNER
Paul Ingle

ART DIRECTOR
John Bateson

WRITER
Ruth Emslie

PHOTOGRAPHER
Richard Learoyd

CLIENT
Zanders Fine Papers

AGENCY
Roundel/London

010089D

DESIGN MERIT

MERIT AWARD
One Show Design

DESIGNER
David Day

WRITER
Rafiq Lehmann

ILLUSTRATOR
David Day

PHOTOGRAPHER
RSN Archives

CLIENT
Republic of Singapore Navy

AGENCY
Saatchi & Saatchi/ Singapore

010090D

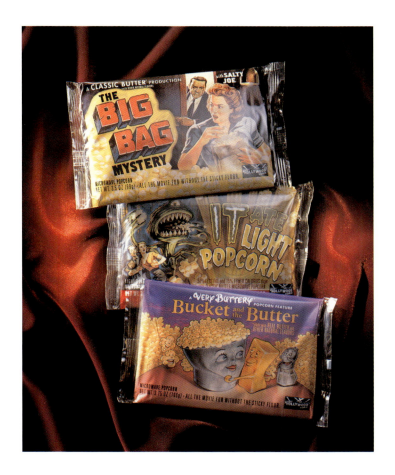

DESIGN MERIT

MERIT AWARD
One Show Design

DESIGNERS
Steve Sandstrom
Greg Parra

ART DIRECTOR
Steve Sandstrom

WRITER
Steve Sandoz

PHOTOGRAPHER
Mark Hooper

CLIENT
Graphic Arts Center

AGENCY
Sandstrom Design/Portland

010091D

MERIT AWARD
One Show Design

DESIGNERS
Jon Olsen
Andre Burgoyne

ART DIRECTOR
Jon Olsen

WRITER
Leslee Dillon

ILLUSTRATOR
Jeff Foster

CLIENT
Hollywood Video

AGENCY
Sandstrom Design/Portland

010092D

DESIGN MERIT

MERIT AWARD
One Show Design

DESIGNERS
Steve Sandstrom
Andrew Randall

ART DIRECTOR
Steve Sandstrom

WRITER
Steve Sandoz

PHOTOGRAPHER
Hiroshi Iwaya

CLIENT
Tazo

AGENCY
Sandstrom Design/Portland

010093D

DESIGN MERIT

MERIT AWARD
One Show Design

ART DIRECTOR
Kevin Thoem

WRITER
Al Jackson

PHOTOGRAPHER
Tibor Nemeth

CLIENT
Fastreader

AGENCY
Sawyer Riley
Compton/Atlanta

010094D

DESIGN MERIT

MERIT AWARD
One Show Design

DESIGNER
Marion English Powers

ART DIRECTOR
David Webb

WRITER
Kathy Oldham

ILLUSTRATOR
David Webb

PHOTOGRAPHER
Don Harbor

CLIENT
Greater Alabama Boy Scouts Council

AGENCY
Slaughter Hanson/ Birmingham, AL

010095D

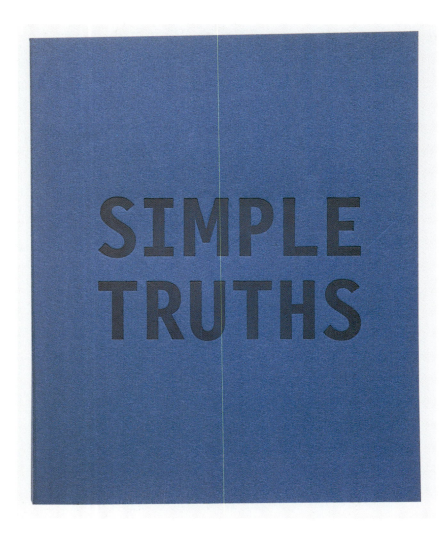

DESIGN MERIT

MERIT AWARD
One Show Design

DESIGNERS
Jennifer Tatham
Alan Henderson

ART DIRECTOR
Marion English Powers

WRITERS
Dave Smith
Dan Monroe

CLIENT
Slaughter Hanson

AGENCY
Slaughter Hanson/
Birmingham, AL

010096D

DESIGN MERIT

MERIT AWARD
One Show Design

DESIGNER
Tim Cole

ART DIRECTOR
Glenn Harrison

WRITER
McKinsey & Company

ILLUSTRATOR
Tim Cole

CLIENT
McKinsey & Company

AGENCY
Tango Design/London

010097D

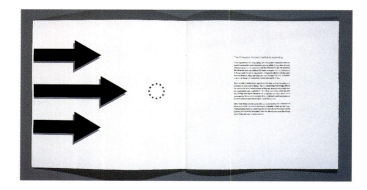

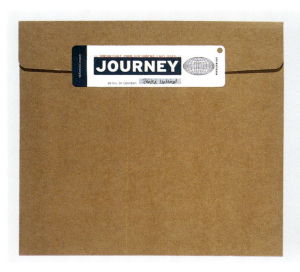
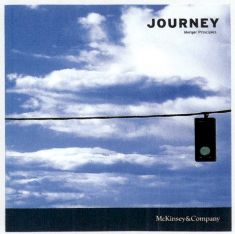

DESIGN MERIT

MERIT AWARD
One Show Design

DESIGNER
Kieron Molloy

ART DIRECTOR
Glenn Harrison

WRITER
McKinsey & Company

ILLUSTRATOR
Kieron Molloy

CLIENT
McKinsey & Company

AGENCY
Tango Design/London

010098D

DESIGN MERIT

MERIT AWARD
One Show Design

DESIGNER
Natalie Cusson

ART DIRECTOR
Jane Hope

CLIENT
Tattoo Direct & Digital

AGENCY
TAXI/Toronto

010099D

DESIGN MERIT

MERIT AWARD
One Show Design

ART DIRECTOR
Betsy Nathane

WRITER
Craig Crawford

CLIENT
Lexus

AGENCY
Team One Advertising/
El Segundo

010100D

DESIGN MERIT

MERIT AWARD
One Show Design

DESIGNER
George Rautenbach

ART DIRECTORS
Margie Backhouse
George Rautenbach

WRITER
Petra Oelofse

PHOTOGRAPHER
Mike Lewis

CLIENT
Seychelles Tourism & Marketing Authority

AGENCY
Tequila/Johannesburg

010101D

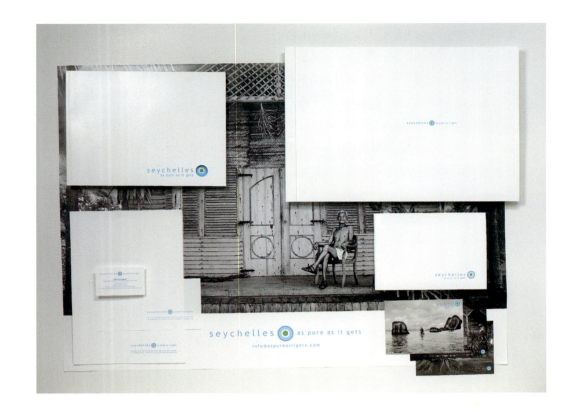

DESIGN MERIT

MERIT AWARD
One Show Design

ART DIRECTORS
Jessica Peck
Amber Brown

WRITER
Josh Weinstein

CLIENT
Tracey Edwards Company

AGENCY
The Tracey Edwards
Company/Manchester

010102D

DESIGN MERIT

MERIT AWARD
One Show Design

ART DIRECTORS
Laurent Fauchère
Antoine Tinguely
Nathalie Delagorce

CLIENT
Flix Television Networks

AGENCY
Trollback & Company/
New York

010103D

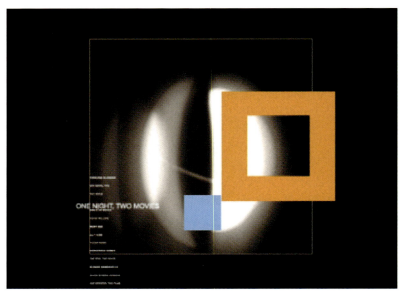

MERIT AWARD
One Show Design

DESIGNER
Antoine Tinguely

ART DIRECTOR
Antoine Tinguely

CLIENT
Logo

AGENCY
Trollback & Company/
New York

010104D

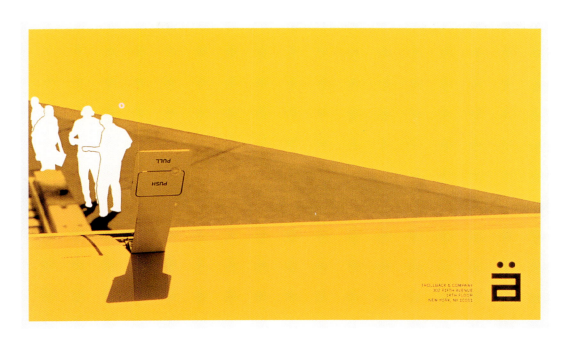

DESIGN MERIT

MERIT AWARD
One Show Design

DESIGNER
Laurent Fauchère

ART DIRECTOR
Laurent Fauchère

PHOTOGRAPHER
Antoine Tinguely

CLIENT
Trollback & Company

AGENCY
Trollback & Company/
New York

010105D

DESIGN MERIT

MERIT AWARD
One Show Design

DESIGNERS
Todd Neale
Laurent Fauchère
Antoine Tinguely
Chris Haak

ART DIRECTORS
Todd Neale
Laurent Fauchère
Antoine Tinguely
Chris Haak

CLIENT
Television National Network

AGENCY
Trollback & Company/
New York

010106D

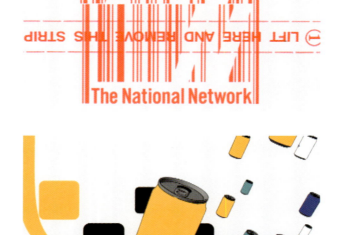

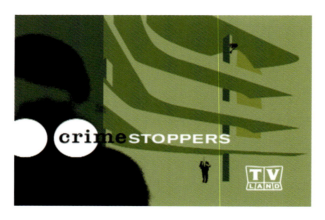

MERIT AWARD
One Show Design

DESIGNERS
Nathalie Delagorce
Antoine Tinguely
Laurent Fauchère
Chris Haak

ART DIRECTORS
Nathalie Delagorce
Antoine Tinguely
Laurent Fauchère
Chris Haak

CLIENT
TVLand Televsion Network

AGENCY
Trollback & Company/
New York

010107D

DESIGN MERIT

MERIT AWARD
One Show Design

DESIGNERS
Jeff Lubow
Calvin Chu
Paul Smith
Josh Nichols

ART DIRECTORS
Jeff Lubow
Calvin Chu
Paul Smith
Josh Nichols
Peter Gatto

WRITERS
Jeff Lubow
Geoff MacDonald

ILLUSTRATOR
Calvin Chu

PHOTOGRAPHER
Gus Butera

CLIENT
Scifi Channel

AGENCY
USA Networks/Scifi
Channel/New York

010108D

MERIT AWARD
One Show Design

DESIGNERS
Pam Purcer
Adam Levite

ART DIRECTOR
Dean Lubensky

WRITER
Traci Terril

CLIENT
VH1

AGENCY
VH1 Off Air Creative/
New York

010109D

DESIGN MERIT

MERIT AWARD
One Show Design

DESIGNER
Jason Rand

ART DIRECTORS
Dean Lubensky
Jason Rand

WRITER
Traci Terrill

CLIENT
VH1

AGENCY
VH1 Off Air Creative/
New York

010110D

MERIT AWARD
One Show Design

DESIGNERS
Pam Purser
Adam Levite

ART DIRECTOR
Dean Lubensky

WRITER
Traci Terrill

CLIENT
VH1

AGENCY
VH1 Off Air Creative/
New York

010111D

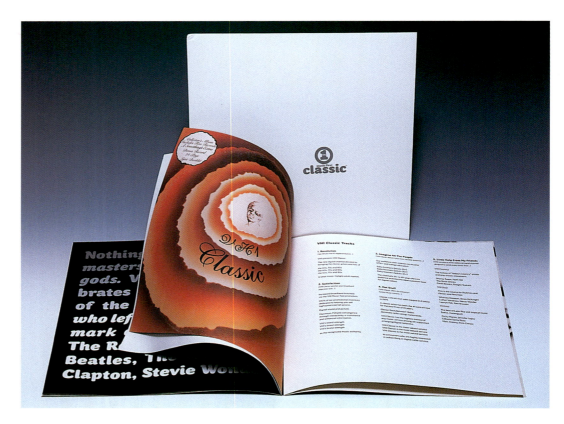

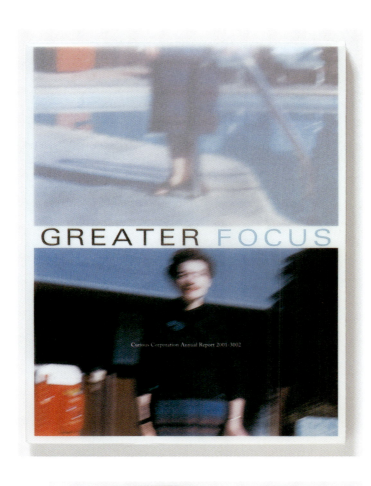
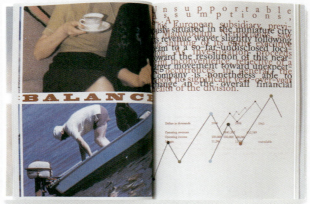
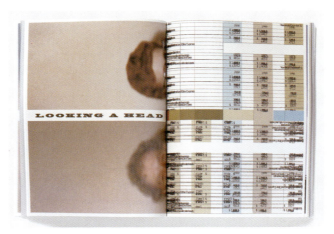

DESIGN MERIT

MERIT AWARD
One Show Design

DESIGNER
Frank Viva

ART DIRECTOR
Frank Viva

WRITERS
Doug Dolan
Frank Viva

PHOTOGRAPHER
Aldo Cipriani

CLIENT
Arjo Wiggins Fine Papers

AGENCY
Viva Dolan/Toronto

010112D

DESIGN MERIT

MERIT AWARD
One Show Design

ART DIRECTOR
Kelley Lear

WRITERS
Mike Lear
Markham Cronin

ILLUSTRATORS
Tom Fleck
Kelley Lear
Stock

CLIENT
Creative Club of Atlanta

AGENCY
WestWayne/Atlanta

010113D

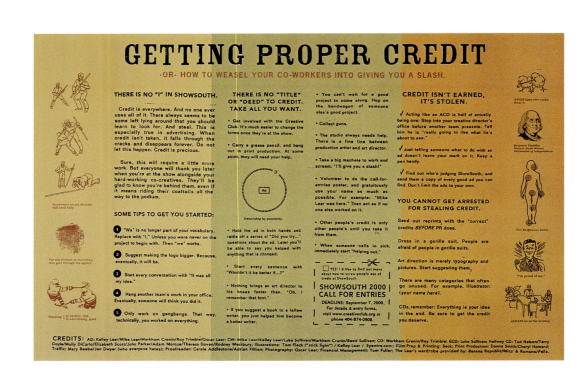

MERIT AWARD
One Show Design

DESIGNERS
Geoff McFetridge
Kim Schoen
Sarah Foelske

ART DIRECTOR
Kim Schoen

WRITER
Kevin Proudfoot

ILLUSTRATOR
Geoff McFetridge

CLIENT
ESPN

AGENCY
Wieden + Kennedy/
New York

010114D

DESIGN MERIT

MERIT AWARD
One Show Design

DESIGNER
Mark Staples

ART DIRECTOR
Lyle Owerko

WRITER
Lyle Owerko

CLIENT
Wonderlust Industries

AGENCY
Wonderlust Industries/
New York

010117D

PUBLIC SERVICE/POLITICAL

Public
SERVICE

PUBLIC SERVICE/ POLITICAL

MERIT AWARD
Public Service/Political
Newspaper or Magazine:
Single

ART DIRECTOR
Robert Oliver

WRITER
Tim Riley

PHOTOGRAPHER
Willabel Cole Mitchell

CLIENT
ICRF

AGENCY
Abbott Mead
Vickers.BBDO/London

010381A

MERIT AWARD
Public Service/Political
Newspaper or Magazine:
Single

ART DIRECTOR
Tony Calcao

WRITER
Rob Strasberg

PHOTOGRAPHER
Tony Calcao

CLIENT
American Legacy
Foundation

AGENCIES
ARNOLD Worldwide,
Crispin Porter Bogusky/
Boston

010382A

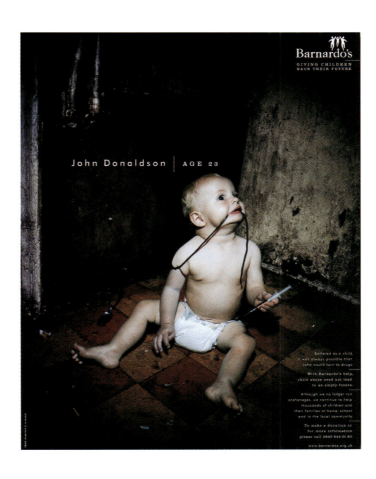

PUBLIC SERVICE/
POLITICAL

MERIT AWARD
Public Service/Political
Newspaper or Magazine:
Single

ART DIRECTOR
Adrian Rossi

WRITER
Alex Grieve

PHOTOGRAPHER
Nick Georghiou

CLIENT
Andrew Nebel/Barnardo's

AGENCY
Bartle Bogle Hegarty/
London

010383A

MERIT AWARD
Public Service/Political
Newspaper or Magazine:
Single

ART DIRECTORS
Kent Suter
Tia Doar

WRITER
Ginger Robinson

CLIENT
Williamette Week/BPN

AGENCY
Borders Perrin Norrander/
Portland

010384A

375

PUBLIC SERVICE/ POLITICAL

MERIT AWARD
Public Service/Political
Newspaper or Magazine: Single

ART DIRECTORS
Kent Suter
Tia Doar

WRITER
Ginger Robinson

PHOTOGRAPHER
Stock

CLIENT
Williamette Week/BPN

AGENCY
Borders Perrin Norrander/ Portland

010385A

MERIT AWARD
Public Service/Political
Newspaper or Magazine: Single

ART DIRECTORS
Kent Suter
Tia Doar

WRITER
Ginger Robinson

PHOTOGRAPHER
Keith Collier

CLIENT
Williamette Week/BPN

AGENCY
Borders Perrin Norrander/ Portland

010386A

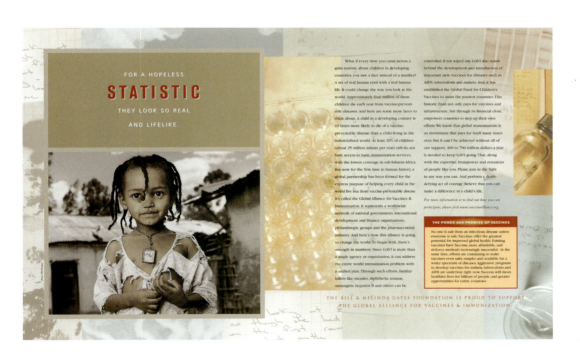

PUBLIC SERVICE/POLITICAL

MERIT AWARD
Public Service/Political
Newspaper or Magazine:
Single

ART DIRECTOR
Sidney Araujo

WRITERS
Eduardo Lima
Victor Sant'Anna

PHOTOGRAPHER
Joao Caetano

CLIENT
Fundacao SOS Mata Atlântica

AGENCY
F/Nazca Saatchi & Saatchi/
São Paulo

010390A

MERIT AWARD
Public Service/Political
Newspaper or Magazine:
Single

ART DIRECTOR
Matt Mowat

WRITER
Chuck Meehan

PHOTOGRAPHERS
Robert Cappa
Steve Peixotto
Jackson Hill
U.S. Army Corps

CLIENT
National D-Day Museum

AGENCY
GMO Hill Holliday/
San Francisco

010391A

Also won:

MERIT AWARD
Public Service/Political:
Outdoor and Posters

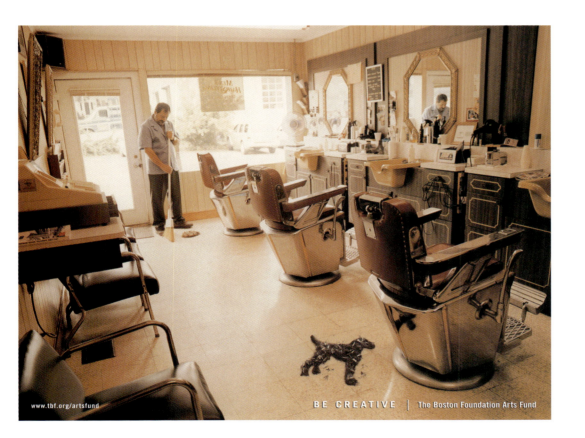

PUBLIC SERVICE/ POLITICAL

MERIT AWARD
Public Service/Political
Newspaper or Magazine:
Single

ART DIRECTOR
Matt Mowat

WRITER
Chuck Meehan

PHOTOGRAPHERS
Robert Cappa
Steve Peixotto
Jackson Hill
U.S. Army Corps

CLIENT
National D-Day Museum

AGENCY
GMO Hill Holliday/
San Francisco

010392A

MERIT AWARD
Public Service/Political
Newspaper or Magazine:
Single

ART DIRECTOR
Tom Hurd

WRITER
Eick McHugh

PHOTOGRAPHER
Russ Quakenbush

CLIENT
Boston Fund For The Arts
(BARBER)

AGENCY
Holland Mark Advertising/
Boston

010393A

379

PUBLIC SERVICE/POLITICAL

MERIT AWARD
Public Service/Political
Newspaper or Magazine:
Single

ART DIRECTOR
Cristiana Boccassini

WRITERS
Enrica Ficai Veltroni
Simon Connolly

ILLUSTRATOR
Graziano Ross

PHOTOGRAPHER
Stock

CLIENT
WWF ITALIA ONLUS

AGENCY
J. Walter Thompson Italia/Milan

010394A

MERIT AWARD
Public Service/Political
Newspaper or Magazine:
Single

ART DIRECTOR
Tay Guan Hin

WRITER
Alex Shipley

ILLUSTRATOR
Procolor

PHOTOGRAPHER
Stock

CLIENT
Survival International

AGENCY
Leo Burnett/Singapore

010395A

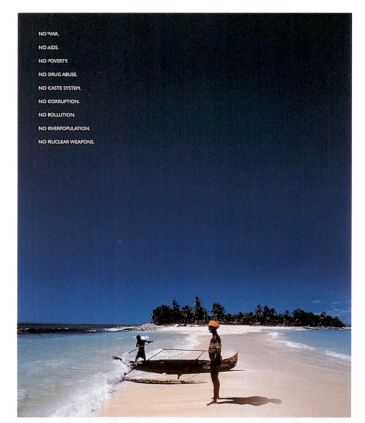

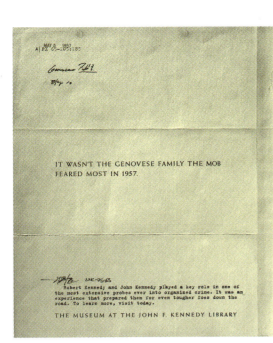

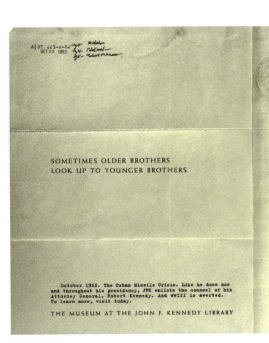

PUBLIC SERVICE/ POLITICAL

MERIT AWARD
Public Service/Political
Newspaper or Magazine: Single

ART DIRECTORS
Tom Gibson
Cliff Sorah

WRITER
Joe Alexander

PHOTOGRAPHER
Kennedy Library Archives

CLIENT
John F. Kennedy Library Foundation

AGENCY
The Martin Agency/ Richmond

010396A

MERIT AWARD
Public Service/Political
Newspaper or Magazine: Single

ART DIRECTORS
Tom Gibson
Cliff Sorah

WRITER
Joe Alexander

PHOTOGRAPHER
Kennedy Library Archives

CLIENT
John F. Kennedy Library Foundation

AGENCY
The Martin Agency/ Richmond

010397A

PUBLIC SERVICE/ POLITICAL

MERIT AWARD
Public Service/Political
Newspaper or Magazine:
Single

ART DIRECTORS
Guillermo Caro
Ted Royer

WRITERS
Daniel Comar
Dana Labaton
Javier Campopiano

ILLUSTRATOR
Mario Franco

PHOTOGRAPHER
Daniel Ackerman

CLIENT
Conin (Malnutrition Fighting Association)

AGENCY
Ogilvy & Mather Argentina/ Buenos Aires

010398A

MERIT AWARD
Public Service/Political
Newspaper or Magazine:
Single

ART DIRECTORS
Ian Grais
Mark Mizgala

WRITER
Alan Russell

PHOTOGRAPHER
Dave Robertson

CLIENT
St. John Ambulance

AGENCY
Palmer Jarvis DDB/ Vancouver

010399A

If cold, wet, hungry and scared is what thousands of kids run away to, imagine what they run away from.

Tonight, kids will be wandering the streets, amongst pissheads, pushers, pickpockets, never a policeman when you need one, prostitutes, perverts and pimps. They'll scavenge for food and beg for money. Then they'll try and find a doorway that someone hasn't pissed or puked in, where they can wait for the morning. And that's their idea of being safe. Safer than houses. Because their house is where they were sexually abused, and threatened with what would happen if they ever dared tell anyone about 'their little secret'. Or their house was where they were beaten, not smacked. Punched. Beaten the crap out of. They're not stupid. They know that running away is no adventure. But they will never go home. One in three of them attempts suicide. Those that fail are in and out of care until they're old enough to stay out. It's how a lot of young people end up living rough. The Big Issue Foundation knows that helping them isn't merely about getting a roof over their heads. We also have to understand what's going on in their heads. So what is it that can make someone who trusts almost no one trust us? We never push. And we're not out to reach any targets. If anyone decides to sell The Big Issue it's because they need the cash, and The Big Issue is pretty much the only legal way they can earn it. When they collect the magazines, they become aware that The Big Issue Foundation offers support for drink and drug addictions, advice and training for jobs, and of course, help with accommodation. But there's no pressure on anyone to take it. If someone does want to change their life, then they have to do it themselves, but not by themselves.

Drug addict? Alcoholic? Suicidal?
Apparently, what you need is a nice cup of hot soup.

Cream of tomato, mushroom or even spicy lentil, with or without croutons, is unlikely to have ever satisfied the obsessive cravings of your average crack addict. If mulligatawny is a more effective way of blocking out the abject misery of someone's particular existence than a can or two of super strength lager, then it would probably be illegal by now, or at least a lot more expensive than it is. And if leek and potato really is so comforting that it's ever given a whole new reason to carry on living to the most clinically depressed, then it's news to us. Not that we'd suggest for a moment that anyone should stop giving free soup to homeless people. They're glad of it. Anything is better than nothing. But other people's consciences can be all too easily satisfied by the knowledge that the homeless can always queue up for their nightly broth. They won't starve to death so that's enough is it? We, The Big Issue Foundation don't think so. People become homeless for any number of different reasons. Things go wrong at some point in their lives. Then they remain homeless for the simple reason that they come to accept their predicament, because they don't know how they can change it. Apart, that is, from those who start selling The Big Issue magazine. Earning money starts to rebuild their self-esteem. And when the vendors turn up to collect their magazines, they discover that we offer help with most of the root causes of homelessness: mental illness, various addictions and long-term unemployment. The Big Issue Foundation exists because we believe that every homeless person has the potential to change their life.

PUBLIC SERVICE/ POLITICAL

MERIT AWARD
Public Service/Political Newspaper or Magazine: Single

ART DIRECTOR
Paul Belford

WRITER
Nigel Roberts

PHOTOGRAPHER
Paul Belford

CLIENT
The Big Issue Foundation

AGENCY
TBWA/London

010400A

MERIT AWARD
Public Service/Political Newspaper or Magazine: Single

ART DIRECTOR
Paul Belford

WRITER
Nigel Roberts

PHOTOGRAPHER
Paul Belford

CLIENT
The Big Issue Foundation

AGENCY
TBWA/London

010401A

PUBLIC SERVICE/POLITICAL

MERIT AWARD
Public Service/Political
Newspaper or Magazine:
Single

ART DIRECTOR
Paul Belford

WRITER
Nigel Roberts

CLIENT
The Science Museum

AGENCY
TBWA/London

010402A

MERIT AWARD
Public Service/Political
Newspaper or Magazine:
Single

ART DIRECTOR
Mike Withers

WRITER
John Bollinger

PHOTOGRAPHER
Carl Posey

CLIENT
United Negro College Fund

AGENCY
Young & Rubicam/
New York

010403A

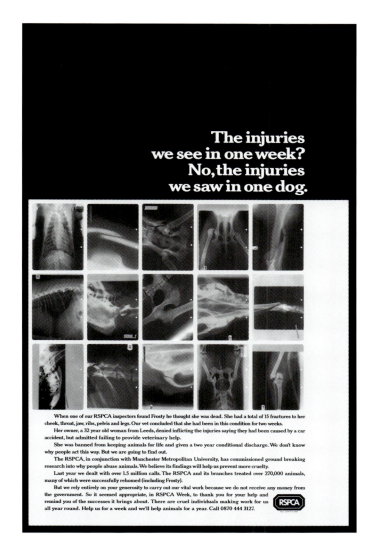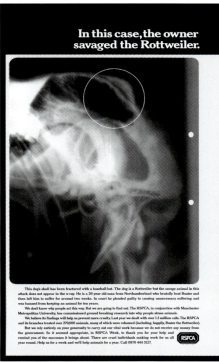

PUBLIC SERVICE/
POLITICAL

MERIT AWARD
Public Service/Political
Newspaper or Magazine:
Campaign

ART DIRECTOR
Ron Brown

WRITER
Peter Souter

PHOTOGRAPHER
Laurie Haskell

CLIENT
RSPCA

AGENCY
Abbott Mead
Vickers.BBDO/London

010404A

PUBLIC SERVICE/ POLITICAL

MERIT AWARD
Public Service/Political
Newspaper or Magazine:
Campaign

ART DIRECTOR
Steve Tom

WRITER
Stu Cooperrider

PHOTOGRAPHER
Bruce Peterson

CLIENT
Massachusetts Department
of Public Health

AGENCY
ARNOLD Worldwide/Boston

010405A

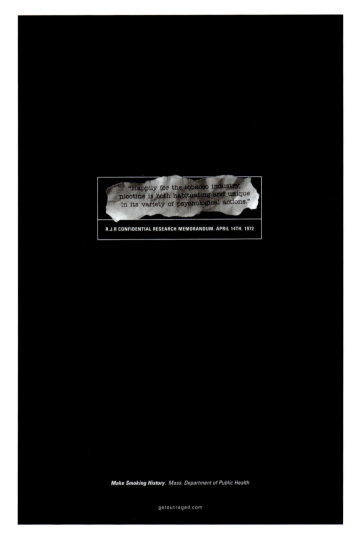
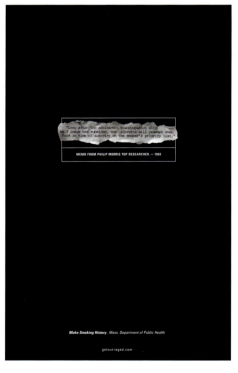
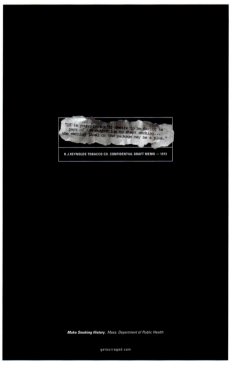

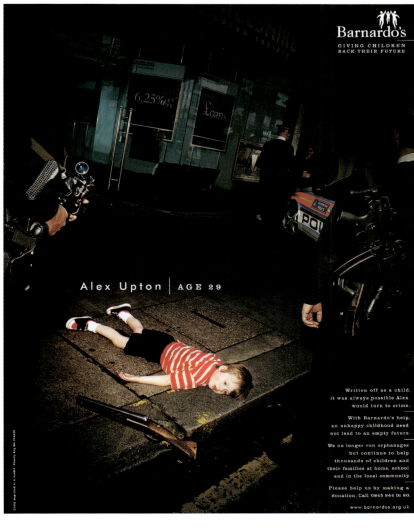

PUBLIC SERVICE/ POLITICAL

MERIT AWARD
Public Service/Political
Newspaper or Magazine:
Campaign

ART DIRECTOR
Adrian Rossi

WRITER
Alex Grieve

PHOTOGRAPHER
Nick Georghiou

CLIENT
Andrew Nebel/Barnardo's

AGENCY
Bartle Bogle Hegarty/
London

010406A

PUBLIC SERVICE/ POLITICAL

MERIT AWARD
Public Service/Political Newspaper or Magazine: Campaign

ART DIRECTORS
Kent Suter
Tia Doar

WRITER
Ginger Robinson

PHOTOGRAPHER
Keith Collier

CLIENT
Williamette Week/BPN

AGENCY
Borders Perrin Norrander/ Portland

010407A

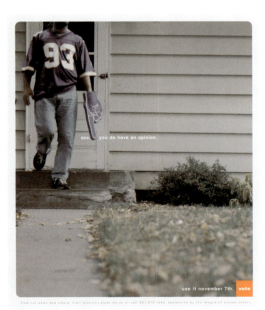

PUBLIC SERVICE/ POLITICAL

MERIT AWARD
Public Service/Political
Newspaper or Magazine:
Campaign

ART DIRECTOR
Liz Otremba

WRITERS
Eric Husband
Dave Keepper

PHOTOGRAPHER
Curtis Johnson

CLIENT
Minneapolis League of Women Voters

AGENCY
Colle + McVoy/Minneapolis

010408A

PUBLIC SERVICE/ POLITICAL

MERIT AWARD
Public Service/Political
Newspaper or Magazine:
Campaign

ART DIRECTOR
Carlos Jorge

WRITERS
Felix del Valle
Miguel Madariaga

CLIENT
Amnistia International

AGENCY
CONTRAPUNTO/Madrid

010409A

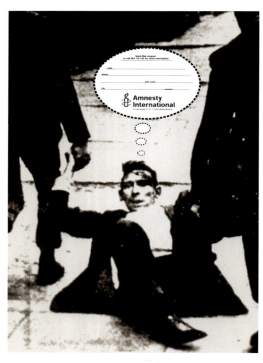
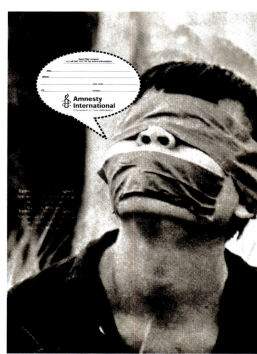

PUBLIC SERVICE/ POLITICAL

MERIT AWARD
Public Service/Political
Newspaper or Magazine:
Campaign

ART DIRECTOR
Neil Dewsbury

WRITER
Robert Tsao

PHOTOGRAPHERS
Tang Kim Yee
Picture Farm

CLIENT
Samaritans of Singapore

AGENCY
Dentsu Young & Rubicam/ Singapore

010410A

Become a maid in Singapore and become part of the family.

Imagine you're a young woman from Indonesia, Malaysia, Myanmar, the Philippines or Sri Lanka.

You've been raised in extreme poverty and squalid living conditions. Unemployment is a way of life.

Imagine that, in order to help your family survive, you work for another in Singapore.

Imagine moving to a country where the language and culture are unfamiliar. You'll have no one to confide in, to seek advice from, to protect you.

Now imagine what it's like to rise at 5am and stop working 18 hours later.

What's more, you may not get a day off because it's not included in your contract. You have no chance to relax, recharge, pray or even talk with fellow maids from your homeland.

You feel drained. Isolated. Vulnerable.

Then imagine that just as you feel completely abandoned, you're invited to become much closer to one member of the family.

It begins when the man of the house brushes your breasts every time he takes his baby from your arms.

Imagine your tormentor is so clever that he thoughtfully prepares a warm drink every night for his wife. Laced with sedatives.

You try to reason with him, but he threatens to revoke your work permit if you reject him.

You alert his wife, but she goes into deep denial, accusing you of lying to get out of your contract.

And just when you think things couldn't get any worse, imagine finding out you're pregnant.

By law, you're sent home, loaded not with cash but an extra burden.

You feel discarded. Humiliated. Unvindicated.

Now, perhaps you're imagining that this is only an extreme case of one unlucky girl.

Then he offers to pay you five times your monthly salary if you sleep with him.

For some, this could be a tempting offer. You've heard of maids hitting the jackpot, financially and romantically, with an employer.

But since day one, you've followed guidelines given by your maid agency to avoid unwanted attention.

You wear loose T-shirts and long pants. When using the bathroom, you always lock the door. You only speak to the wife, unless addressed by her husband.

Nevertheless, you're still nagged frequently to have sex. When you refuse, you're pummelled with insults.

Then one day, he tries a different tactic.

Imagine having your T-shirt and bra yanked up around your neck, so you can be 'checked' for AIDS.

Imagine being so terrified you consider leaping several stories to escape. But before you decide, you're dragged back into the bedroom and raped.

Now imagine it happening again, with a witness. He comes into your room to soothe a crying baby. When he exits, you're left sobbing.

Unfortunately, you're dreaming.

Just a few years ago, 100 cases of sexual abuse, from harassment to rape were reported to the police within a twelve-month period.

All the incidents mentioned above have appeared in print. They have been combined together from many documented offences, suffered by many different women.

Sadly, there's probably many more who remain silent, afraid to lose their livelihood.

Thankfully, the vast majority of employers always treat their maids with respect.

Indeed, for every horror story in print there's a heartwarming tale about a maid who's been adopted as an auntie.

More importantly, those that don't adopt a professional attitude are subject to suitably severe punishments, such as caning. But first, they have to be caught.

So if you suspect a maid is being sexually abused, help her to contact us. If you're certain, call the police.

Because after all's said and done, there's no reason why this kind of family affair should be kept in the family.

SAMARITANS OF SINGAPORE
1800 2214444 (24hrs)

In Singapore, some maids are forced to eat leftovers.

The reality of being a maid in Singapore is sometimes hard to swallow.

Take, for example, the two-month nightmare of one fifteen-year old maid.

By the time she found refuge at the Indonesian embassy, she was diagnosed with a broken bone in her left arm, malnutrition resulting in beriberi and anaemia, and a 8 x 12cm burn on her back, requiring a full-thickness skin graft.

Though her other injuries left no permanent trace, they are no less appalling. Or traumatic.

According to her testimony, she was hit repeatedly on the back and buttocks with a broomstick.

She was burned on the forearm with a red-hot iron. Slammed headfirst into a wall. Scalded with boiling water. Jabbed in the stomach and genitals with a steel ruler.

And, as the piece de resistance, forced to eat dog faeces. Not just once, but three times on two separate occasions.

Surely this maid must have done something to provoke this vicious behavior. In way, she did.

Once, she woke up an hour late, at 6.30am. She rushed into the kitchen, where she was greeted by a fist in the face.

Another time, the family's son came back from school and took it upon himself to judge her performance. She got into hot water, literally. Poured from a kettle over her back, chest and limbs.

Now, perhaps you're thinking that this is no more than an unfortunate, but isolated event. If only that were true.

Recently, nearly 200 cases, ranging from bullying to outright brutality, were reported to the police in one year. But, like other examples of domestic violence, countless other incidents never come to the attention of the authorities.

So why would any reasonable female from Myanmar, Malaysia, Indonesia, Sri Lanka or the Philippines want to work in Singapore?

Over 100,000 foreign women do so because of extreme poverty, appalling living conditions and skyrocketing unemployment in their home country.

And they'll risk their physical and mental well-being for a mere $250 a month, on average.

Of course, there's a great possibility that this ad may not apply to you at all. You might not employ a maid. Or if you do, she could even be a trusted member of your family. So why not throw this ad in the bin?

Because there are others who obviously have no problem treating their help like trash. The Singapore government has recently recognised the dangers that foreign maids face, and have threatened stiffer penalties for those who mistreat them.

If the government is willing to crack down on these abuses, shouldn't we? The police can't be everywhere at once. And maids shouldn't have to threaten their livelihood without knowing that the law protects them as well.

So don't turn a blind eye. Don't be deaf to the stories you hear. Don't rationalise that action on your part will only endanger them further. And most of all, don't be dumb. Pick up the phone and call the police.

Only then will maids in Singapore feel secure enough to fight for just treatment.

Because, finally, they'll know that other people give a shit.

SAMARITANS OF SINGAPORE
1800 2214444 (24hrs)

Maid in Singapore.

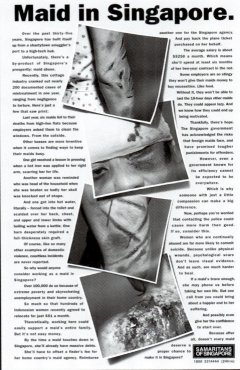

Over the past thirty-five years, Singapore has built itself up from a shantytown smuggler's port to a high-tech hub.

Unfortunately, there's a by-product of Singapore's prosperity: maid abuse.

Recently, this cottage industry cranked out nearly 200 documented cases of mistreatment in one year, ranging from negligence to torture. Here's just a few that saw print:

Last year, six maids fell to their deaths from high-rise flats because employers asked them to clean the windows. From the outside.

Other bosses are more inventive when it comes to finding ways to keep their maids busy.

One girl received a lesson in pressing when a hot iron was applied to her right arm, scarring her for life.

Another woman was reminded who was head of the household when she was beaten so badly her skull was knocked out of shape.

And one got into hot water, literally – forced into the toilet and scalded over her back, chest, and upper and lower limbs with boiling water from a kettle. One burn desperately required a full-thickness skin graft.

Of course, like so many other examples of domestic violence, countless incidents are never reported.

So why would anyone consider working as a maid in Singapore?

Over 100,000 do so because of extreme poverty and skyrocketing unemployment in their home country.

So much so that hundreds of Indonesian women recently agreed to relocate for just S$1 a month.

Theoretically, working here could easily support a maid's entire family. But it's not easy money.

By the time a maid touches down in Singapore, she'll already have massive debts. She'll have to offset a finder's fee for her home country's maid agency. Reimburse another one for the Singapore agency. And pay back the plane ticket purchased on her behalf.

The average salary is about S$250 a month. Which means she'll spend at least six months of her two-year contract in the red.

Some employers are so stingy they won't give their maids money to buy necessities. Like food.

Without it, they won't be able to last the 18-hour days other maids do. They could appear lazy. And we know how they could end up being motivated.

Thankfully, there's hope. The Singapore government has acknowledged the risks that foreign maids face, and have promised tougher punishments for offenders.

However, even a government known for its efficiency cannot be expected to be everywhere.

Which is why someone with just a little compassion can make a big difference.

Now, perhaps you're worried that contacting the police could cause more harm than good. If so, consider this.

Women who are continually abused are far more likely to commit suicide. Because unlike physical wounds, psychological scars don't leave visual evidence. And as such, are much harder to heal.

If a maid's brave enough, she may phone us before taking her own life. But one call from you could bring about a happier end to her suffering.

And possibly even give her the confidence to start over.

Because after all, doesn't every maid deserve a proper chance to make it in Singapore?

SAMARITANS OF SINGAPORE
1800 2214444 (24hrs)

PUBLIC SERVICE/POLITICAL

MERIT AWARD
Public Service/Political
Newspaper or Magazine:
Campaign

ART DIRECTORS
Barbara Eibel
Sal DeVito
Greg Braun
Eric Schutte

WRITERS
Mark Teringo
Sal DeVito
Joel Tractenberg
Lee Seidenberg

PHOTOGRAPHER
Robert Ammirati

CLIENT
ACLU

AGENCY
DeVito/Verdi/New York

010411A

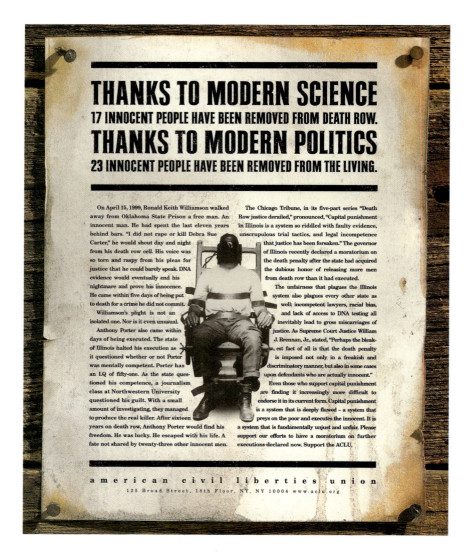

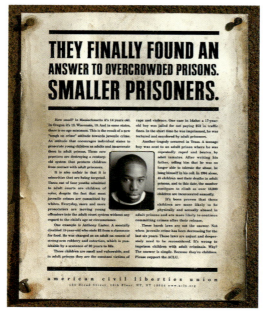

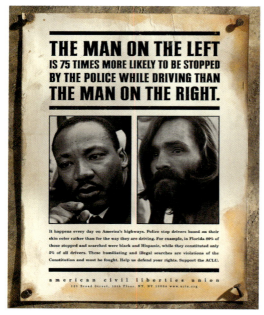

The blood pressure rises and the pulse rate increases. The central nervous system receives nerve impulses and remains in a state of alert. The heart beat is altered and the face becomes slightly red. There's no way to conceal love sickness.

Emotion is hard to explain. You have to feel it.
See Guignard at the São Paulo Museum of Art.

"The Lyrical Humanism of Guignard". One of the best painters of Brazilian Modernism.

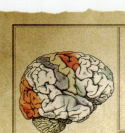

The nerve impulses initiated by a cerebral reading of a pleasant stimulus activate 14 facial muscles, dislocate the jaw, causing it to jut forward. The upper and lower lips open. That's when a smile appears on your face.

Emotion is hard to explain. You have to feel it.
See Guignard at the São Paulo Museum of Art.

"The Lyrical Humanism of Guignard". One of the best painters of Brazilian Modernism.

The eyelids close and the eyeballs curve slightly upwards. The spinal nerves send electrical impulses to the muscles in order to activate them. And then you feel that you can do anything you want.

Emotion is hard to explain. You have to feel it.
See Guignard at the São Paulo Museum of Art.

"The Lyrical Humanism of Guignard". One of the best painters of Brazilian Modernism.

PUBLIC SERVICE/ POLITICAL

MERIT AWARD
Public Service/Political
Newspaper or Magazine:
Campaign

ART DIRECTOR
Paulo Diehl

WRITER
Flavio Casarotti

ILLUSTRATOR
Archive

CLIENT
MASP-São Paulo
Art Museum

AGENCY
DM9 DDB/São Paulo

010389A

PUBLIC SERVICE/ POLITICAL

MERIT AWARD
Public Service/Political
Newspaper or Magazine:
Campaign

ART DIRECTOR
Sidney Araujo

WRITERS
Eduardo Lima
Victor Sant' Anna

PHOTOGRAPHER
Joao Caetano

CLIENT
Fundacao SOS Mata Atlântica

AGENCY
F/Nazca Saatchi & Saatchi/ São Paulo

010412A

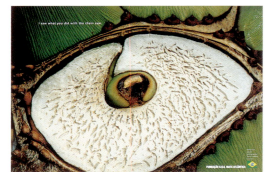

PUBLIC SERVICE/
POLITICAL

MERIT AWARD
Public Service/Political
Newspaper or Magazine:
Campaign

ART DIRECTOR
Matt Mowat

WRITER
Chuck Meehan

PHOTOGRAPHERS
Robert Cappa
Steve Peixotto
Jackson Hill
U.S. Army Corps

CLIENT
National D-Day Museum

AGENCY
GMO Hill Holliday/
San Francisco

010413A

PUBLIC SERVICE/ POLITICAL

MERIT AWARD
Public Service/Political
Newspaper or Magazine:
Campaign

ART DIRECTOR
Matt Mowat

WRITER
Chuck Meehan

PHOTOGRAPHERS
Robert Cappa
Steve Peixotto
Jackson Hill
U.S. Army Corps

CLIENT
National D-Day Museum

AGENCY
GMO Hill Holliday/
San Francisco

010414A

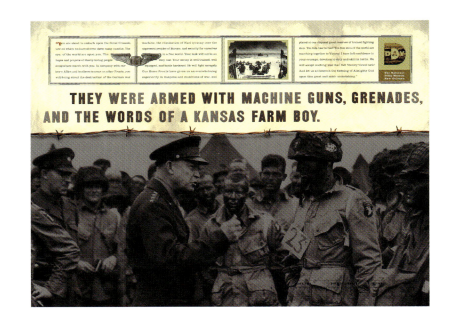

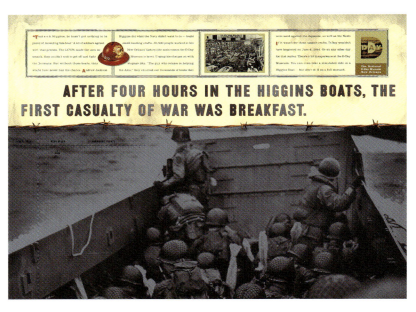

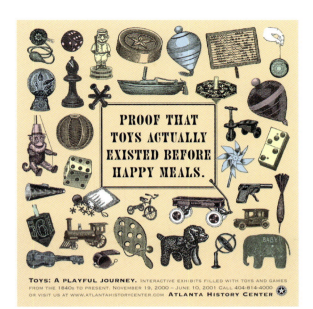
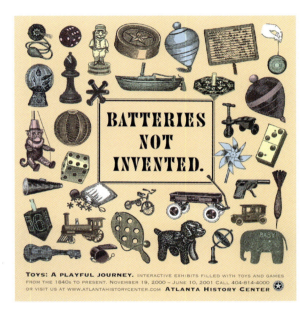
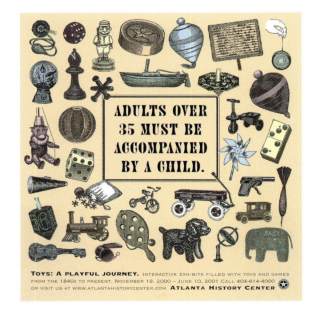

PUBLIC SERVICE/
POLITICAL

MERIT AWARD
Public Service/Political
Newspaper or Magazine:
Campaign

ART DIRECTOR
Joe Paprocki

WRITERS
Mike Lear
Paul Crawford

CLIENT
Atlanta History Center

AGENCY
Huey/Paprocki/Atlanta

010415A

PUBLIC SERVICE/POLITICAL

MERIT AWARD
Public Service/Political
Newspaper or Magazine:
Campaign

ART DIRECTOR
Luca Cinquepalmi

WRITER
Bruno Bertelli

PHOTOGRAPHER
Pierpaolo Ferrari

CLIENT
Lega Per La Lotta Contro I
Tumori (Cancer League)

AGENCY
J. Walter Thompson Italia/
Milan

010416A

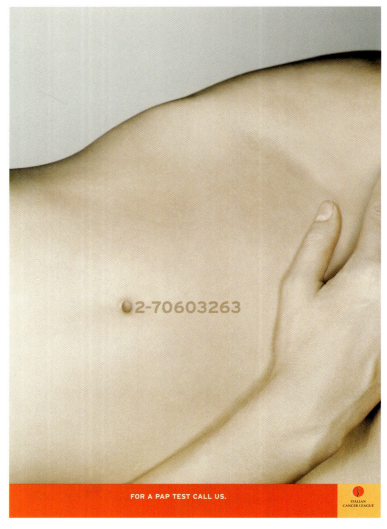

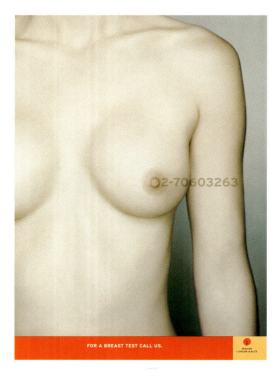

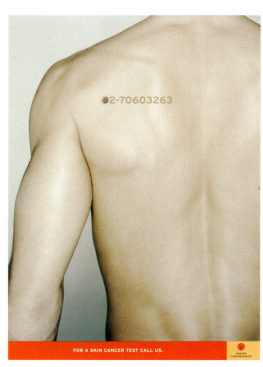

PUBLIC SERVICE/POLITICAL

MERIT AWARD
Public Service/Political
Newspaper or Magazine:
Campaign

ART DIRECTORS
Tom Gibson
Cliff Sorah

WRITER
Joe Alexander

PHOTOGRAPHER
Kennedy Library Archives

CLIENT
John F. Kennedy Library
Foundation

AGENCY
The Martin Agency/
Richmond

010417A

PUBLIC SERVICE/ POLITICAL

MERIT AWARD
Public Service/Political
Newspaper or Magazine:
Campaign

ART DIRECTOR
Tom Gibson

WRITER
Anne Marie Hite

PHOTOGRAPHER
Kennedy Library Archives

CLIENT
John F. Kennedy Library Foundation

AGENCY
The Martin Agency/ Richmond

010418A

IN HOSTILE TERRITORY, SURROUNDED BY THE ENEMY, ARMED WITH A COCONUT.

It's the kind of story directors in Hollywood dream about.

A handsome, young Navy lieutenant, son of a millionaire, Harvard graduate, stranded on a deserted island in the South Pacific. His PT boat and two of his crewmen lost at sea. The lieutenant and the ten surviving crewmen presumed dead.

For days he swims the enemy-infested waters searching for a boat that might rescue them.

He swims back to the island, determined to save his men. With no boat or radio, he makes use of his only resource, a coconut. He carves a message on its shell: NAURU ISL COMMANDER NATIVE KNOWS POSIT HE CAN PILOT 11 ALIVE NEED SMALL BOAT KENNEDY. Two island natives deliver the coconut to a coastwatcher on a nearby island. They establish a rendezvous point.

JFK and the crew of PT 109.

The natives return to escort the lieutenant. The rescue begins.

It had been a harrowing six days since the enemy destroyer rammed PT 109. But Kennedy, hidden under palm fronds so he wouldn't be spotted by enemy aircraft, was in good spirits.

Kennedy received the Navy and Marine Corps Medal for "extremely heroic conduct" which included towing a badly burned crewmember to the island. He also received the Purple Heart for injuries suffered during the sinking of PT 109.

Now through November 1, you can see these and other artifacts from Kennedy's World War II service (including the coconut shell which he kept on his desk in the Oval Office). It's part of a special exhibit that celebrates Kennedy's naval career and lifelong love of the sea. The JFK Museum is located at Columbia Point in Boston. Call (617) 929-4500.

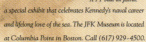
A PT boat on patrol.

VISIT THE MUSEUM AT THE JOHN F. KENNEDY LIBRARY

SUMMER 1924: JFK'S SEVENTH YEAR OF TRAINING FOR THE U.S. NAVY.

Visitors to the Hyannis Port area were often struck by the image of a seemingly empty boat sailing itself around the harbor.

Locals dismissed the familiar sight. Just one of the Kennedy children out for a sail. They were so young, their heads could barely be seen above the gunwales.

The Kennedys' boat was christened the "Tenovus" because, at the time, their family consisted of ten. When the youngest son, Edward, was born, the family acquired another boat. They named it "Onemore."

John Kennedy, best known for his humor and wit, was all business when it came to sailing. His prep school roommate crewed with Kennedy expecting a day of fun in the sun. He was shocked by the lack of congeniality on the boat and spent five hours shivering in the cold spray. But Kennedy's diligence paid off. He was a consistent winner.

JFK's love of the sea wasn't restricted to sailing. He pursued the sport of swimming with a similar passion, earning a proud position on the Harvard swim team.

When JFK joined the Navy in 1941, he quickly gained his men's respect. And for good reason. It was a job he'd spent his entire life preparing for.

In 1942, Kennedy became a lieutenant in the U.S. Navy.

As Commander-in-Chief, JFK promoted a strong naval defense.

You can learn more about Kennedy's lifelong love of the sea and see his favorite sailboat, the "Victura," at a special exhibit now through November 1. The JFK Museum is at Columbia Point in Boston. Call (617) 929-4500.

VISIT THE MUSEUM AT THE JOHN F. KENNEDY LIBRARY

THE FUTURE PRESIDENT OF THE UNITED STATES AND HIS YOUNGER BROTHER JACK.

Joseph P. Kennedy Sr. had always dreamed his son would one day become president. His son Joe, that is.

But on August 12, 1944, Joe Kennedy Jr., a lieutenant in the U.S. Navy, volunteered to fly a Navy Liberator bomber that was loaded with explosives. Its target, a German V-2 bomb base. A malfunction caused the plane to explode in midair. Joe Kennedy Jr. died, a hero.

And so, seemingly, did his father's dreams of ever having a son in the White House.

Jack Kennedy returned from the war in 1943, also a hero, and began to pursue his own dreams. Having already published a best-selling book, "Why England Slept," he took a job as a reporter with Hearst newspapers. He covered the Potsdam Conference, the San Francisco conference that established the United Nations and the British elections. But after a few months, he began to long for a more active role in government. Hesitant, but with his father's encouragement, he decided to run for the 11th District seat in the House of Representatives.

JFK's ability to win over Boston's toughest crowds was a surprise to his father. And it was perhaps an even greater surprise to JFK. He defeated nine opponents in a landslide victory. And he proved that like his father, the former ambassador to Great Britain, and his grandfather, the former mayor of Boston, politics was indeed in his blood.

In 1960, Joseph Kennedy Sr.'s dream finally came true. His son was elected president. His son Jack, that is.

Now through November 1, you can learn more about the World War II events that changed John Kennedy's life and perhaps even history. It's part of a special exhibit honoring JFK's naval career and his lifelong love of the sea and sailing. The Museum at the John F. Kennedy Library is located at Columbia Point in Boston. If you would like more information, call (617) 929-4500.

VISIT THE MUSEUM AT THE JOHN F. KENNEDY LIBRARY

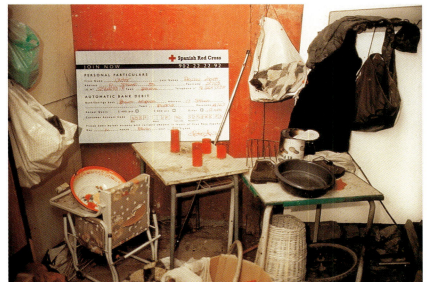

PUBLIC SERVICE/
POLITICAL

MERIT AWARD
Public Service/Political
Newspaper or Magazine:
Campaign

ART DIRECTOR
Lara Hernandez

WRITERS
Miguel Bueno
Gloria Hernandez

PHOTOGRAPHER
Marcos Gutierrez

CLIENT
Cruz Roja
(Spanish Red Cross)

AGENCY
McCann-Erickson/Madrid

010419A

401

PUBLIC SERVICE/ POLITICAL

MERIT AWARD
Public Service/Political
Newspaper or Magazine:
Campaign

ART DIRECTOR
Paul Belford

WRITER
Nigel Roberts

PHOTOGRAPHERS
Laurie Haskell
Christopher Griffith

CLIENT
Science Museum

AGENCY
TBWA/London

010420A

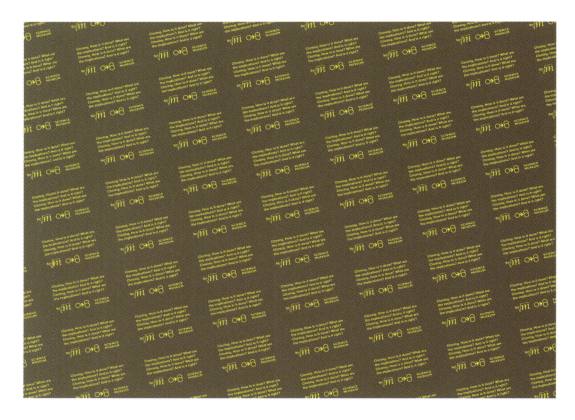

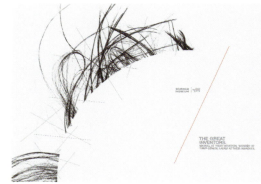

PUBLIC SERVICE/
POLITICAL

MERIT AWARD
Public Service/Political
Newspaper or Magazine:
Campaign

ART DIRECTOR
Mike Withers

WRITER
John Bollinger

PHOTOGRAPHER
Carl Posey

CLIENT
United Negro College Fund

AGENCY
Young & Rubicam/
New York

010421A

PUBLIC SERVICE/ POLITICAL

MERIT AWARD
Public Service/Political:
Outdoor and Posters

ART DIRECTORS
Kent Suter
Tia Doar

WRITER
Ginger Robinson

PHOTOGRAPHER
Stock

CLIENT
Williamette Week/BPN

AGENCY
Borders Perrin Norrander/
Portland

010422A

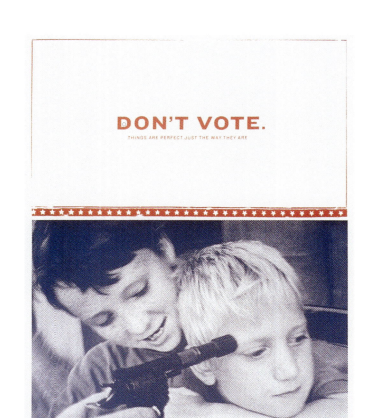

MERIT AWARD
Public Service/Political:
Outdoor and Posters

ART DIRECTORS
Paul Stechshulte
Jac Coverdale

WRITER
Michael Atkinson

PHOTOGRAPHER
Curtis Johnson

CLIENT
Alzheimers Association

AGENCY
Clarity Coverdale Fury/
Minneapolis

010423A

PUBLIC SERVICE/ POLITICAL

MERIT AWARD
Public Service/Political:
Outdoor and Posters

ART DIRECTORS
Paul Stechshulte
Jac Coverdale

WRITER
Michael Atkinson

PHOTOGRAPHER
Curtis Johnson

CLIENT
Alzheimers Association

AGENCY
Clarity Coverdale Fury/ Minneapolis

010424A

MERIT AWARD
Public Service/Political:
Outdoor and Posters

ART DIRECTOR
Liz Otremba

WRITERS
Eric Husband
Dave Keepper

PHOTOGRAPHER
Curtis Johnson

CLIENT
Minneapolis League of Women Voters

AGENCY
Colle + McVoy/Minneapolis

010425A

PUBLIC SERVICE/ POLITICAL

MERIT AWARD
Public Service/Political:
Outdoor and Posters

ART DIRECTOR
Liz Otremba

WRITERS
Eric Husband
Dave Keepper

PHOTOGRAPHER
Curtis Johnson

CLIENT
Minneapolis League of Women Voters

AGENCY
Colle + McVoy/Minneapolis

010426A

MERIT AWARD
Public Service/Political:
Outdoor and Posters

ART DIRECTOR
Eric Schutte

WRITER
Lee Seidenberg

PHOTOGRAPHER
Robert Ammirati

CLIENT
ACLU

AGENCY
DeVito/Verdi/New York

010427A

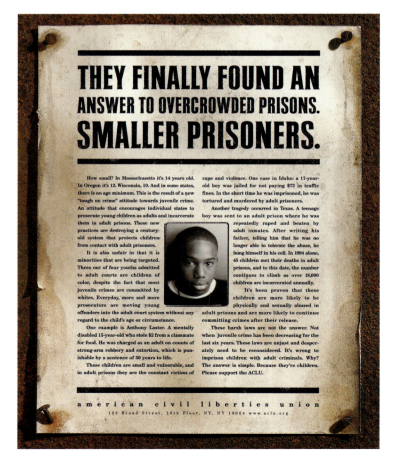

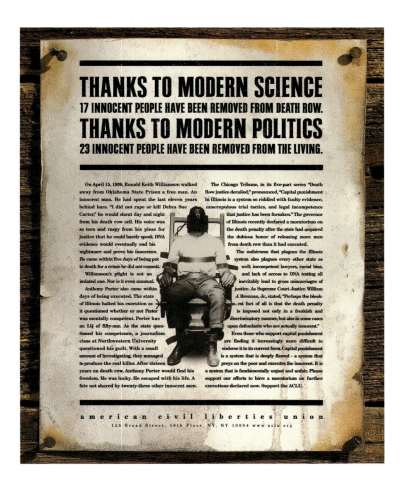

NEW YORK JEWS

SAN FRANCISCO CHINAMEN

CLEVELAND INDIANS

No race, creed or religion should endure the ridicule faced by Native Americans today. Please help us put an end to this mockery and racism, by visiting www.ncai.org or calling (202)466-7767.

NATIONAL CONGRESS OF AMERICAN INDIANS

PUBLIC SERVICE/
POLITICAL

MERIT AWARD
Public Service/Political:
Outdoor and Posters

ART DIRECTOR
Barbara Eibel

WRITER
Mark Teringo

PHOTOGRAPHER
Robert Ammirati

CLIENT
ACLU

AGENCY
DeVito/Verdi/New York

010428A

MERIT AWARD
Public Service/Political:
Outdoor and Posters

ART DIRECTOR
Susanne Macarelli

WRITER
Erhan Erdem

PHOTOGRAPHER
Robert Ammirati

CLIENT
National Congress of
American Indians

AGENCY
DeVito/Verdi/New York

010429A

407

PUBLIC SERVICE/POLITICAL

MERIT AWARD
Public Service/Political:
Outdoor and Posters

ART DIRECTOR
Ryan Dickey

WRITER
Mike Roe

ILLUSTRATOR
Mike Quirk

PHOTOGRAPHER
Don Mason

CLIENT
Burke Museum of Natural History & Culture

AGENCY
FCB/Seattle

010430A

MERIT AWARD
Public Service/Political:
Outdoor and Posters

ART DIRECTOR
Andy Nordfors

WRITER
Beth Kinney

ILLUSTRATOR
Jason Walden

PHOTOGRAPHER
Marcus Swanson

CLIENT
Burke Museum of Natural History & Culture

AGENCY
FCB/Seattle

010431A

PUBLIC SERVICE/ POLITICAL

MERIT AWARD
Public Service/Political:
Outdoor and Posters

ART DIRECTORS
Ian Grais
Mark Mizgala

WRITER
Alan Russell

PHOTOGRAPHER
Charles Peterson

CLIENT
St. John Ambulance

AGENCY
Palmer Jarvis DDB/
Vancouver

010434A

MERIT AWARD
Public Service/Political:
Outdoor and Posters

ART DIRECTORS
Ian Grais
Mark Mizgala

WRITER
Alan Russell

PHOTOGRAPHER
Stock

CLIENT
St. John Ambulance

AGENCY
Palmer Jarvis DDB/
Vancouver

010435A

PUBLIC SERVICE/
POLITICAL

MERIT AWARD
Public Service/Political:
Outdoor and Posters

ART DIRECTOR
Kevin R. Smith

WRITER
Dave Pullar

CLIENT
New Hope Democrats
For Al Gore

AGENCY
Pullar Smith/Minneapolis

010436A

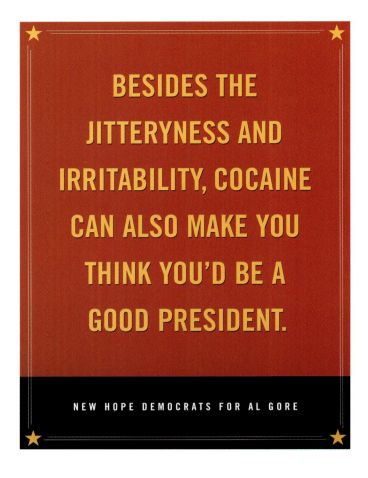

MERIT AWARD
Public Service/Political:
Outdoor and Posters

ART DIRECTOR
Kevin R. Smith

WRITER
Dave Pullar

CLIENT
New Hope Democrats
For Al Gore

AGENCY
Pullar Smith/Minneapolis

010437A

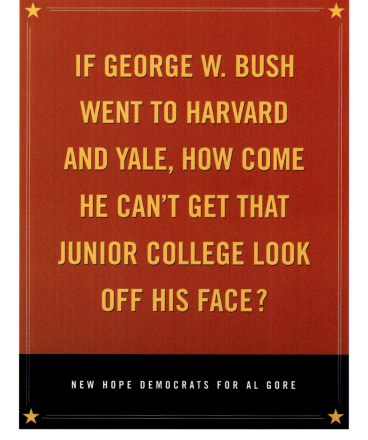

To warn smokers about the potential consequences of smoking, we designed stickers that were put into cigarette packs. The stickers were designed to look like average grocery store price stickers, but on taking a closer look, the smoker is hit with something else.

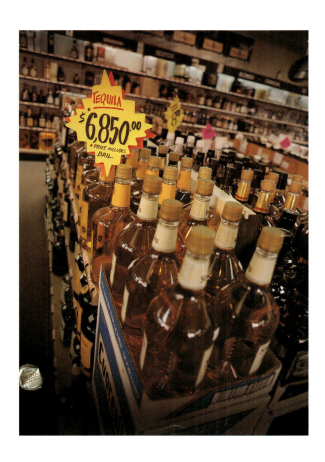

PUBLIC SERVICE/
POLITICAL

MERIT AWARD
Public Service/Political:
Outdoor and Posters

ART DIRECTOR
Simon Yeo

WRITER
M. Srinath

ILLUSTRATOR
Procolor

PHOTOGRAPHER
Eric Seow

CLIENT
Smoke Free Singapore

AGENCY
Saatchi & Saatchi/
Singapore

010438A

MERIT AWARD
Public Service/Political:
Outdoor and Posters

ART DIRECTORS
Kevin Thoem
Tammy Anderson

WRITERS
Ari Weiss
Katy Davis
Al Jackson
Brett Compton

PHOTOGRAPHER
Chris Davis

CLIENT
Georgia Tech

AGENCY
Sawyer Riley Compton/
Atlanta

010439A

411

PUBLIC SERVICE/ POLITICAL

MERIT AWARD
Public Service/Political:
Outdoor and Posters

ART DIRECTORS
Kevin Thoem
Tammy Anderson

WRITERS
Ari Weiss
Katy Davis
Al Jackson
Brett Compton

PHOTOGRAPHER
Chris Davis

CLIENT
Georgia Tech

AGENCY
Sawyer Riley Compton/
Atlanta

010440A

MERIT AWARD
Public Service/Political:
Outdoor and Posters

ART DIRECTOR
David Waraksa

WRITER
Steve Covert

PHOTOGRAPHER
Dean Hawthorne

CLIENT
Richmond Ballet

AGENCY
WORK/Richmond

010441A

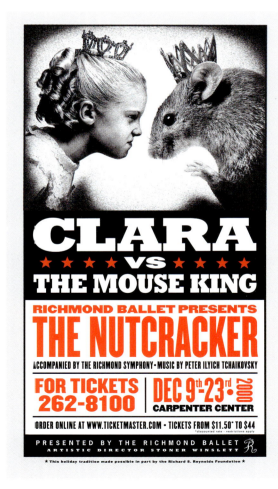

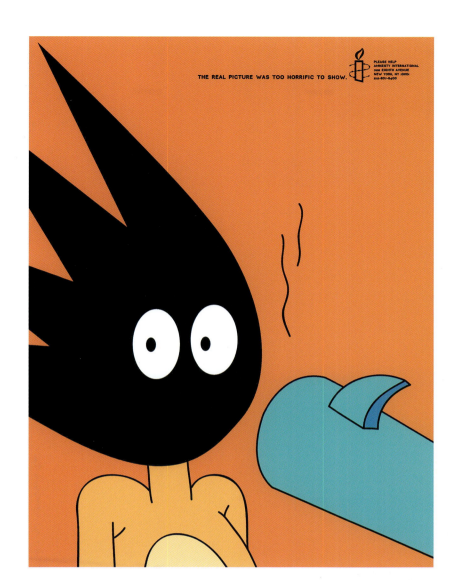

PUBLIC SERVICE/ POLITICAL

MERIT AWARD
Public Service/Political:
Outdoor and Posters

ART DIRECTOR
Denis Kakazu

WRITER
Anselmo Ramos

ILLUSTRATOR
Denis Kakazu

CLIENT
Amnesty International

AGENCY
Young & Rubicam/Miami

010442A

PUBLIC SERVICE/POLITICAL

MERIT AWARD
Public Service/Political Radio: Single

WRITER
Alan Russell

AGENCY PRODUCER
Nicolette Eus

CLIENT
Crimestoppers

AGENCY
Palmer Jarvis DDB/Vancouver

010443A

SFX:	Phone ring, answering machine pick-up. Rock music playing in background.
MAN:	Hi, this is Jason and Shawn. We're not here to answer your call at the moment. We're actually out ripping off a van, then heading over to the west side to break into some sucker's house. Hopefully end up with a good score. Gotta pay for some of those habits you know. You know what to do after the beep.
ANNOUNCER:	If only it was this easy to spot a criminal. Crime Stoppers. Call 669-TIPS.

MERIT AWARD
Public Service/Political Radio: Campaign

WRITERS
Chris Edwards
Bill Wright

AGENCY PRODUCER
Brian Sweeney

CLIENT
American Legacy Foundation

AGENCIES
ARNOLD Worldwide, Crispin Porter Bogusky/Boston

010444A

SFX:	Sounds of pages being ripped out of magazines throughout.
ETHAN:	This is for putting stuff in cigarettes that make them more addictive.
D'ANNE:	This is for making a product that kills 1200 people a day.
RYAN:	This is for sticking me with a habit that costs me 40 bucks a week.
KARA:	This is for hooking my little brother.
RANDY:	This is for taking seven years off my life.
ALEX:	This is for actually creating the need for a nicotine patch.
RYAN:	I don't know, I just like ripping stuff.
JOEL:	This is for the seven people who'll die from your product by the time this commercial is over.
LEVON:	This is for saying, "Today's teenager is tomorrow's potential regular customer."
WHITNEY:	This is for the billions of dollars you make off smoking each year.
ETHAN:	This is for the 430,000 people who die from smoking each year.
IAN:	This…is for my mother.
ALEX:	Next time you see a cigarette ad, rip it out. Who knows, maybe if there were fewer cigarette ads, there'd be fewer cigarette deaths. For more about Rip It Out check out thetruth.com.
JOEL:	This has been a "rip it out" reminder from truth.
ALEX:	Please practice safe ripping. Only rip out ads from magazines that are yours. Thank you.

STODDARD: I'm Rick Stoddard. And who am I to ask you to quit smoking? Well for one thing, I quit, so I know it can be done. For another thing, my wife Marie never quit. And I know what happened there, too. She got lung cancer. She got brain tumors. She lost the use of her arm. Then her legs. Then her hair fell out in such tangled clumps I had to cut it all off leaving her bald. Then Marie died at the ripe old age of 46. Forty-six. So, who am I to ask you to quit smoking? *(pause)* I'm the voice of experience. That's who I am.

ANNOUNCER: If you need help quitting, call 1-800-TRY TO STOP. There are a lot of ways to give up cigarettes and a lot of people willing to help. That's 1-800-TRY TO STOP. A message from the Massachusetts Department of Public Health.

VOICEOVER: I started smoking pot when I was about 13. By the time I got about 18, I started getting into amphetamine use like speed 'n ecstasy 'n that, and then I started using it through the needle. It was just sort of a natural progression to whack something else in the needle and give that a go. And then it got me by the balls 'n then I just started using it a couple of times a week and then from then on it's just, it's just a fix. It's not a good life.

PUBLIC SERVICE/
POLITICAL

MERIT AWARD
Public Service/Political Radio:
Campaign

WRITER
Bill Girouard

AGENCY PRODUCER
Danae Fogarty

CLIENT
Massachusetts Department
of Public Health

AGENCY
ARNOLD Worldwide/Boston

010445A

MERIT AWARD
Public Service/Political Radio:
Campaign

WRITER
Jon Mahney

AGENCY PRODUCER
Jon Mahney

CLIENT
Public Service

AGENCY
Clemenger Harvie Edge/
Melbourne

010446A

PUBLIC SERVICE/ POLITICAL

MERIT AWARD
Public Service/Political
Television: Single

ART DIRECTOR
Randy Gerda

WRITER
Eric Gutierrez

AGENCY PRODUCER
Deb Narine

PRODUCTION COMPANY
Spy Films/Toronto

DIRECTOR
Gord McWatters

CLIENT
Alliance to Save Energy

AGENCY
DDB/Seattle

010447A

MERIT AWARD
Public Service/Political
Television: Single

ART DIRECTOR
Brent Ladd

WRITER
Alon Shoval

AGENCY PRODUCER
Jeff Johnson

PRODUCTION COMPANY
Stiefel & Company

DIRECTOR
Peter Darley Miller

CLIENT
Peace Council

AGENCY
GSD&M/Austin

010448A

FATHER: We're at a crucial stage with energy usage. Prices are just too high. We need to cut consumption and we need alternatives. That's what drove us to attempt the first static-electricity powered home. Static cells under the carpet collect energy and transfer it as needed throughout the house. Success has been…elusive. It hasn't been everything we'd hoped. But, besides making the house itself more energy efficient, the smartest thing we did, the bright spot, if you will, is that we equipped the house with Energy Star products, which use less juice and save money. Static electricity may not be viable. But, hey, we've taken a step toward the future. Our future.

SUPER: Alliance to Save Energy. Save money, energy, the planet.

VOICEOVER: Anyone can make their home more energy efficient.

MOM VOICEOVER: Goodnight, sweetie.

CHILD VOICEOVER: Goodnight, mommy.

SFX: An "mm" sound as before a kiss. Static shock.

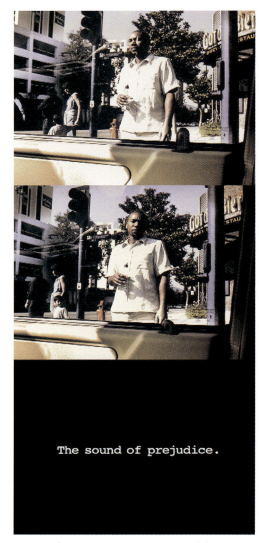

(A young African-American man waits at a stop light.)

SFX: Loud power lock.

SUPER: The sound of prejudice. Keep the peace.

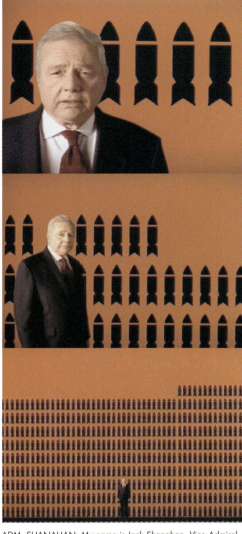

ADM. SHANAHAN: My name is Jack Shanahan, Vice Admiral, US Navy, retired. One of our nuclear bombs blows up Hiroshima 15 times over.

SFX: Military snare drum hits.

ADM. SHANAHAN: Five devastate Russia.

SFX: Five military snare drum hits.

ADM. SHANAHAN: After that, this is how many the US has left.

SFX: Military snare becomes drum roll.

ADM. SHANAHAN: I feel safe reducing nuclear weapons and investing the savings in education. Do you?

SUPER: Move our money. businessleaders.org.

(A child's voice lists several violent scenes from films as if he were counting sheep.)

ANNOUNCER: Pay attention to what your child is watching.

SUPER: What does your child count to fall asleep? SWR—Watch out what your child is watching. SWR Television.

PUBLIC SERVICE/ POLITICAL

MERIT AWARD
Public Service/Political
Television: Single

ART DIRECTOR
Dave Gardiner

WRITER
Joe Berkeley

AGENCY PRODUCER
Wendy Hudson

PRODUCTION COMPANY
Picture Park

DIRECTOR
Harry McCoy

CLIENT
Business Leaders for
Sensible Priorities

AGENCY
Hill Holliday Connors
Cosmopulos/Boston

010449A

MERIT AWARD
Public Service/Political
Television: Single

ART DIRECTOR
Patrick They

WRITER
Christian Seifert

DIRECTORS
Christian Seifert
Patrick They

CLIENT
SWR Television Station

AGENCY
Ogilvy & Mather/Frankfurt

010450A

PUBLIC SERVICE/ POLITICAL

MERIT AWARD
Public Service/Political
Television: Campaign

ART DIRECTOR
Paul Keister

WRITER
Tim Roper

AGENCY PRODUCER
David Rolfe

PRODUCTION COMPANY
Redtree Productions

DIRECTOR
Christian Hoagland

CLIENT
Florida Department of Health

AGENCY
Crispin Porter & Bogusky/ Miami

010451A

SUPER: Louisville, KY. May 2000.

BOY: We are wondering if you could help us. We wanted to deliver this to the head of marketing. We just wanted to present the Golden Fish Hook Award to the makers of Kool cigarettes.

FEMALE EXECUTIVE: Fish Hook Award? What does it mean?

BOY: To the makers of Kool with a 'K' cigarettes we present the Golden Fish Hook Award for using sex to lure scores of under-aged males into smoking.

MALE EXECUTIVE: One of the things we've found is that the reason kids smoke really doesn't have anything to do with advertising.

BOY: Well, how come you guys spent $15 million on advertising if it doesn't do anything? If I was 15 years old, I'd want to be cool. It seems that it's saying if you smoke cigarettes then you'd be cool. Right? You know a third of the people who smoke your product will eventually die.

MALE EXECUTIVE: One hundred percent of the people are eventually going to die.

BOY: All right, we gotta go. Enjoy the Golden Fish Hook Award.

SUPER: TRUTH.

PUBLIC SERVICE/
POLITICAL

MERIT AWARD
Public Service/Political
Television: Campaign

ART DIRECTOR
Pat Harris

WRITER
Steve O'Brien

AGENCY PRODUCER
Richard Farmer

PRODUCTION COMPANY
Mindfield

DIRECTOR
Marcus McCollum

CLIENT
Hunger Free America

AGENCY
Ground Zero/Los Angeles

010452A

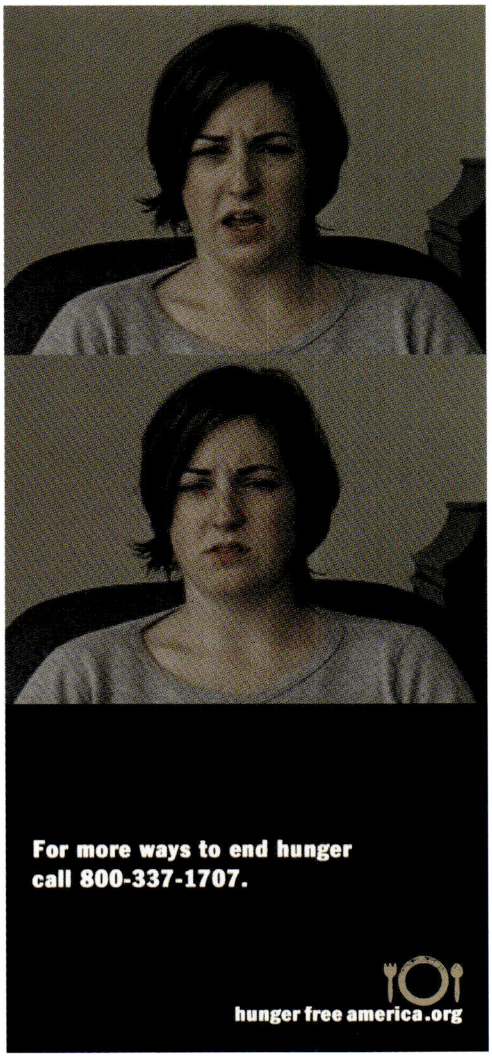

WOMAN: You can make a can of baby formula last a week just by adding water. At first, you only want to add a little bit of water, and then, as your baby's system gets used to it you can continue to add more water each time. You want to make sure that you don't add too much water, because if your baby starts crying and fusses and refuses to drink it, you'll have wasted a whole meal.

SUPER: For more ways to end hunger call 800-337-1707. hungerfreeamerica.org.

RADIO

RADIO MERIT

MERIT AWARD
Consumer Radio: Single

WRITER
Hayes Steinberg

PRODUCTION COMPANY
Pirate Radio and Television

CLIENT
Labatt Breweries of Canada

AGENCY
Ammirati Puris/Toronto

010453A

BIG HAM:	Big Ham kazoos.
CAMERON:	Hi, it's Cameron calling "Out of the Blue." Do you do singing telegrams?
BIG HAM:	Absolutely.
CAMERON:	Okay. What type of stuff do you have?
BIG HAM:	Well, is it for guys or girls for starters?
CAMERON:	I don't know, how can I put this? Well, there's this guy at work, we were, uh, originally we were going to demote him, but then we thought it may be better if we just transferred him.
BIG HAM:	So you're, you're transferring him to another area of the company?
CAMERON:	Yeah.
BIG HAM:	Okay, where are you sending him?
CAMERON:	Um, North Battleford.
BIG HAM:	No kidding, eh? Then I'd recommend sending our "Crazy Cowboy." Imagine for a minute you guys are sitting around doing your thing, and at some strategic point in runs this cowboy. And he'll zero in on our boy and say, "Hey man, you know we heard what a root tooting shoot off little country guy you were and we hot damn heard that someone was sending you out here to the Wild West," and he rides around the room going "bum da bum da bum da bum you're getting out of here, bum da bum da bum da bum you're getting out of here."
CAMERON:	Wow. What else do you have?
BIG HAM:	Um, the only thing, like, we have, "Transvestite Tina."
CAMERON:	Hey, I'm calling "Out of the Blue." You could be next. Labatt Blue.

MERIT AWARD
Consumer Radio: Single

WRITER
Aaron Allen

AGENCY PRODUCER
Stacy McClain

CLIENT
OurHouse.com

AGENCY
Black Rocket/San Francisco

010454A

MAN:	Hey, honey?
WOMAN:	Hi, sweetie.
MAN:	Were you doing something to the lawn?
WOMAN:	Yeah, I put in a sprinkler system.
MAN:	When did you do that?
WOMAN:	Today.
MAN:	But how...Really?
WOMAN:	Yep.
MAN:	I would've done that.
WOMAN:	Oh, that's okay. It was kind of fun.
MAN:	Does it work?
WOMAN:	What?
MAN:	Nothing. You know those trenches have to be at least ten inches deep or the pipes will freeze.
WOMAN:	Yeah, I know. They're 17.
MAN:	*(long pause)* Don't use my conditioner, okay?
WOMAN:	I'm not.
ANNOUNCER:	Tools. Materials. Advice. Sanity. OurHouse.com. We're here to help. Partnered with Ace.

ANNOUNCER: Hollywood Video presents, *Sixty-Second Theater*, where we try (unsuccessfully) to pack all the drama and suspense of a two-hour Hollywood production into 60 seconds. Today's presentation, *The Sixth Sense*.

COLE: *(door bell, door opening. Haley Joel Osment soundalike)* Who are you?

DR: *(Bruce Willis soundalike)* I'm a child psychologist. Heard you've been having some nightmares. What's bothering you?

COLE *(whispering)*: I see dead people.

DR: You got to speak up, kid.

COLE *(whispering)*: I see dead people.

DR: What? Let's pick this up next week. *(door bell, door opening)* Hi. Last time we met you were saying...

COLE *(whispering)*: I see dead people.

DR: Oh that. Are you sure you don't have an Oedipus complex?...I'm good at those.

COLE: Nope.

DR: How about bed wetting? That's my specialty.

COLE: Just dead people. Can you help me?

DR: Sorry, time's up. *(door bell, door opening)* Sorry I'm late. Tell me more about the dead people.

COLE: They have no concept of time.

DR: What else do they do?

COLE: Ask lots of questions.

DR: They do? How come? About what?

COLE: You tell me.

DR: How would I know about dead people?

COLE: Because you're...*(whispers something unintelligible)*

DR: What did you say?

ANNOUNCER: If this doesn't satisfy your urge to see *The Sixth Sense* (and we can't say we blame you), then rent it for five days at Hollywood Video. Where we'll help you find *The Sixth Sense* or exactly the movie you're in the mood for. Celebrity voices impersonated.

RADIO MERIT

MERIT AWARD
Consumer Radio: Single

WRITER
Adam Chasnow

AGENCY PRODUCER
Leigh Fuchs

CLIENT
Hollywood Video

AGENCY
Cliff Freeman and Partners/
New York

010455A

MERIT AWARD
Consumer Radio: Single

WRITERS
Adam Chasnow
Ian Reichenthal

AGENCY PRODUCER
Leigh Fuchs

CLIENT
Hollywood Video

AGENCY
Cliff Freeman and Partners/New York

010456A

ANNOUNCER:	Hollywood Video presents, *Sixty Second Theater*, where we try (unsuccessfully) to pack all the drama and suspense of a two-hour Hollywood production into 60 seconds. Today's presentation, *Saving Private Ryan*.
SFX:	Bombing and gunfire in the distance.
MAJOR:	Captain, your platoon made it through Normandy alive. You and your men deserve an award.
CAPTAIN:	*(Tom Hanks-soundalike)* Aw, that's not necessary.
MAJOR:	Great. Then we're sending you behind enemy lines to find Private Ryan.
CAPTAIN:	Who's Private Ryan?
MAJOR:	A soldier we can't find.
CAPTAIN:	Where should we look?
MAJOR:	We're not sure.
CAPTAIN:	What does he look like?
MAJOR:	We don't know.
CAPTAIN:	What's his favorite ice cream?
MAJOR:	What?
CAPTAIN:	That might help us find him.
MAJOR:	Just get him!
SFX:	Knock, knock. Door opens.
CAPTAIN:	Excuse me, are you Private Ryan?
SOLDIER 1:	No.
CAPTAIN:	Is anyone in this foxhole named Ryan?
MANY SOLDIERS:	No!!
CAPTAIN:	Because if your name's "Ryan," you're going home.
MANY SOLDIERS:	*(together)* I'm Ryan! That's me! I'm Ryan! My name's Ryan!
SOLDIER 4:	Captain, over here. I think we found him!
CAPTAIN:	What's your name, soldier?
RYAN:	*(Matt Damon-soundalike)* Ryan, sir.
CAPTAIN:	What's your favorite ice cream?
RYAN:	Um…Pistachio.
CAPTAIN:	It's him. Ryan, come with us, you're going home.
RYAN:	No, Captain. The fifth regiment is my family now and these men are my brothers, I could never say goodbye to them.
SFX:	Bombs.
RYAN:	Goodbye, guys!!
ANNOUNCER:	If this doesn't satisfy your urge to see *Saving Private Ryan* (and we can't say we blame you), then rent it at Hollywood Video. Welcome to Hollywood. Hollywood Video. Celebrity voices impersonated.

ANNOUNCER:	Hollywood Video presents, *Sixty-Second Theater*, where we try (unsuccessfully) to pack a two-hour Hollywood production into 60 seconds. Today's presentation, *Austin Powers: The Spy Who Shagged Me*.
BASIL:	Come in Austin Powers!
AUSTIN:	*(Mike Myers-soundalike)* Yeah, baby!
BASIL	Using this time machine, we're going to send you back to 1969.
AUSTIN:	But I've already shagged everyone in 1969!
BASIL:	Well, Dr. Evil has time traveled there to steal your mojo, and if you don't stop him, you'll never shag again.
AUSTIN:	Crikey! My mojo?!! I'm on my way!!
FELICITY:	*(Heather Graham-soundalike)* Welcome to 1969, I'm the slinky blonde American agent here to help you find your mojo.
AUSTIN:	We've gotta get my mojo back now, baby.
FELICITY:	I'll have to fly you to the moon.
AUSTIN:	Oh, behave!
SFX:	Fast countdown; rocket launch.
AUSTIN:	Dr. Evil, can I have my mojo back?
DR. EVIL:	Sure, all you have to do is escape from the jail cell, get bitten in the crotch by my 1/8th-size clone, flush him into outer space and redirect the laser aimed at Earth.
SFX:	Jail cell door clink; growl-bite-ouch; flush; screaming midget in space; laser explosion.
AUSTIN:	That was easy. Now can I have my mojo back?
DR. EVIL:	Here, catch!!!
AUSTIN:	I'll never shag again!
FELICITY:	You don't need your mojo.
AUSTIN :	You're right! In 1999, they have pills so strong, even Bob Dole is shagging again. (Although side effects include abnormal vision, acid indigestion and nasal congestion.)
ANNOUNCER:	If this doesn't satisfy your urge to see *Austin Powers: The Spy Who Shagged Me* (and we can't say we blame you), then rent it for five days at Hollywood Video. Welcome to Hollywood. Hollywood Video. Celebrity voices impersonated.

RADIO MERIT

MERIT AWARD
Consumer Radio: Single

WRITERS
Adam Chasnow
Richard Bullock

AGENCY PRODUCER
Leigh Fuchs

CLIENT
Hollywood Video

AGENCY
Cliff Freeman and Partners/
New York

010457A

RADIO MERIT

MERIT AWARD
Consumer Radio: Single

WRITERS
Tom Blandford
Kent Elliott

CLIENT
Gordo Snowboards

AGENCY
Copper/Kalamazoo

010458A

SFX: Emotional guitar.

SKI MEDIC: As a Ski Patrol Emergency medic, I've seen it all. And the thing I encounter the most, year after year, is snow down the crack. This occurs when a snowboarder is sitting in the snow trying to get in or out of their bindings. In this position, snow easily gets into the backside of their pants and in a matter of seconds, they've got snow down the crack. Often times, a victim, unable to bear the pain, will scream out, "I've got snow down my crack." It's so frustrating, because there's nothing you can do. You just have to wait it out and hope for the best. The good news is it's completely avoidable. By simply going to Gordo's Snowboard Store in the Maple Hill Mall in Kalamazoo, you can buy External High Back Step-In Bindings for only $149. So call Gordo at 349-8238 and see what he can do for you this winter. And bring an end to the senseless pain and anguish of snow down the crack.

MERIT AWARD
Consumer Radio: Single

WRITERS
Pat Burke
Bill Cimino
Mark Gross

AGENCY PRODUCER
Sam Pillsbury

CLIENT
Anheuser-Busch

AGENCY
DDB/Chicago

010459A

ANNOUNCER: Bud Light presents…Real. American. Heroes.

SINGER: Real American Heroes…

ANNOUNCER: Today we salute you…Mr. Putt Putt Golf Course Designer.

SINGER: Mr. Putt Putt Golf Course Designer.

ANNOUNCER: Through the magic of astroturf and animatronics you've taken the time-honored game of golf and made it fun again.

SINGER: Keep on strokin'!

ANNOUNCER: They said a three foot putt wasn't a challenge, so you added windmills.

SINGERS: Tiny windmills!

ANNOUNCER: While lesser men wasted time with fairways and sandtraps, you had visions of fiberglass volcanoes and giant clown heads.

SINGER: Clowns freak me out now.

ANNOUNCER: So crack open an ice cold Bud Light, Mr. Putt Putt Golf Course Designer. *(beer pops open)* Because you and I know that a round of golf should always, always include Indian teepees.

SINGER: Mr. Putt Putt Golf Course Designer.

ANNOUNCER: Bud Light Beer, Anheuser-Busch, St. Louis, Missouri.

ANNOUNCER: Bud Light presents…Real. American. Heroes.

SINGER: Real American Heroes…

ANNOUNCER: Today we salute you…Mr. Bass Plaque Maker.

SINGER: Mr. Bass Plaque Maker.

ANNOUNCER: Only a true artist like yourself can turn five pounds of dead fish into a work of art.

SINGER: No fishy smell now!

ANNOUNCER: In your capable hands we know that our trout will never look trashy, our croppy, never crappy.

SINGERS: Never crappy.

ANNOUNCER: Thanks to you we can say, "I caught this bass. What have you ever done?"

SINGER: Tell me now.

ANNOUNCER: So crack open an ice cold Bud Light, Mr. Bass Plaque Maker *(beer pops open)*, because, while a trophy wife may grow old and wrinkled, a trophy bass can now remain…forever young.

SINGERS: Forever young, forever young.

ANNOUNCER: Bud Light Beer, Anheuser-Busch, St. Louis, Missouri.

RADIO MERIT

MERIT AWARD
Consumer Radio: Single

WRITERS
Paul Speed
John Immesoete

AGENCY PRODUCER
Sam Pillsbury

CLIENT
Anheuser-Busch

AGENCY
DDB/Chicago

010460A

ANNOUNCER: Bud Light presents…Real. American. Heroes.

SINGER: Real American Heroes…

ANNOUNCER: Today we salute you…Mr. Male Football Cheerleader.

SINGER: Mr. Male Football Cheerleader.

ANNOUNCER: Real men don't just play smashmouth football. Real men turn cartwheels and somersaults on the sidelines, tucked safely away from the action.

SINGER: Don't touch me now!

ANNOUNCER: Fourth down and inches, the game's on the line, it all comes down to you. Will you call for a perky pyramid or a peppy line dance?

SINGER: Get on my shoulders…

ANNOUNCER: Knock 'em back, knock 'em back allll the way to Hackensack.

SINGERS: Rah, rah, rah, rah, sissboombah!

ANNOUNCER: So grab an ice cold Bud Light, Mr. Male Football Cheerleader. *(beer pops open)* You may never score a touchdown—but you're peppy.

SINGERS: Yay!

ANNOUNCER: That's gotta count for somethin'.

SINGER: That's gotta count for somethin'.

ANNOUNCER: Bud Light Beer, Anheuser-Busch, St. Louis, Missouri.

MERIT AWARD
Consumer Radio: Single

WRITER
John Immesoete

AGENCY PRODUCER
Sam Pillsbury

CLIENT
Anheuser-Busch

AGENCY
DDB/Chicago

010461A

MERIT AWARD
Consumer Radio: Single

WRITER
Steve Dildarian

AGENCY PRODUCER
Cindy Epps

CLIENT
Anheuser-Busch

AGENCY
Goodby Silverstein & Partners/San Francisco

010462A

SFX:	Swamp and a typewriter.
LOUIE:	"It was a day like any other, except for the haunting cry of a lone earthworm." Ooh I like that.
FRANK:	Louie.
LOUIE:	"I reached for my Budweiser longneck. Its longness lengthened my soul."
FRANK:	Louie, what are you doing?
LOUIE:	I'm writing a novel, be quiet.
FRANK:	Oh, boy.
LOUIE:	"A voice called to me, ask not for whom the swamp tolls, Louie, it tolls for thee, and it's tolling big time, baby."
FRANK:	Louie, stop writing, please. I can't take it.
LOUIE:	Oh, Frankie, I was in the zone.
FRANK:	Just stick to the comedy.
LOUIE:	Frank, there is more to me than comedy.
FRANK:	Like what?
LOUIE:	Like a tortured artist.
FRANK:	If anyone's tortured, it's me.
LOUIE:	Alas, Frank.
FRANK:	Alas?
LOUIE:	How can you say these things? I'm spilling my guts unto the page.
FRANK:	Yeah, well, I'm gonna spill my lunch unto the page.
LOUIE:	You do not appreciate the arts.
FRANK:	Louie face it, you're writing a novel so women will think you're cool.
LOUIE:	Crossed my mind.
FRANK:	You're pathetic.
LOUIE:	Quiet, Frank, I must write. "It was a day like any other, except that Frank could not stop yapping..."
FRANK:	It's gonna be a long summer.
LOUIE:	"'Yap on', he said. 'Yap on,' quoth the raven."
ANNOUNCER:	Anheuser-Busch, St. Louis, Missouri.

ANNOUNCER: *(in the style of the Hindenburg announcer)* And it's gliding into the Land Rover Centre, a beautiful, permanent four-wheel-drive machine, the Land Rover. It's starting to rain here again, and I imagine the people inside are looking down out of their windows at all the people below, enjoying their ride in this amazing contraption from across the Atlantic and—it's up on the lift! Ohmigod, they're changing the oil and it's not costing them anything! Oh, there are men underneath it. They're checking all the fluids and topping them off! They're checking and checking...I've never seen anything like this before, and all the people agree it's wonderful. It's absolutely wonderful. It's five or six feet in the air and it's coming down and...oh, the savings for all the passengers on routine maintenance! Oh, the savings! I can't believe it. I just can't believe it. I can't talk, ladies and gentlemen. I'm going to have to stop. This is just the most terrific thing I've ever seen.

VOICEOVER: Now when you buy a new Land Rover Discovery Series II or Range Rover by August 31, scheduled maintenance is included for four years or 50,000 miles. Come see what a Land Rover is made of. Land Rover. Courage.

SFX: Phone ringing, then picking up.

OPERATOR: Welcome to Phonsino, the telephone casino. It's a little bit of Vegas, over the phone.

MAN: Oh, yeah...

OPERATOR: Okay, let's play slots! To spin the reels, press pound on your touch-tone phone.

SFX: Beep, sound of reels spinning.

MAN: C'mon, baby!

OPERATOR: Here they come...cherry...cherry...plum. Oooooh so close.

MAN: Aarrrrgh...

OPERATOR: Okay, let's play Blackjack. Here, I've dealt you a six of hearts and an eight of clubs. That's 14. I've dealt myself 20. To hit, press one. To stay, press two.

MAN: Hit me!

SFX: Beep.

OPERATOR: It's a nine of spades. Oooh, you busted. I win again.

MAN: Doh!

ANNOUNCER: Want real Vegas excitement? Come to Viejas Casino for the thrill of real coin slots. Vegas Blackjack and Poker. Plus the best buffet in California. Viejas Casino. Play for real. Slot tumblers, Viejas!

OPERATOR: Okay, put on your poker face...oooh, that's a good one.

RADIO MERIT

MERIT AWARD
Consumer Radio: Single

WRITER
Michael Buss

AGENCY PRODUCER
Dan Brown

CLIENT
Land Rover North America

AGENCY
GSD&M/Austin

010463A

MERIT AWARD
Consumer Radio: Single

WRITER
Patrick Emerick

AGENCY PRODUCERS
Amy Krause
Cat Sautter

CLIENT
Viejas Casino

AGENCY
matthews/mark/San Diego

010464A

RADIO MERIT

MERIT AWARD
Consumer Radio: Single

WRITER
Alex Loomis

AGENCY PRODUCER
Molly Anderson

PRODUCTION COMPANY
One Union Recording

CLIENT
Open Table

AGENCY
Odiorne Wilde Narraway & Partners/San Francisco

010465A

HOSTESS: Chez Chez, how can I help you?

MAN: I'd like a reservation for two.

HOSTESS: And when did you want to dine with us?

MAN: I want that reservation you've got at eight o'clock tonight.

HOSTESS: Okay, we could sit you at 7:15 or 9:45. Would that work for you?

MAN: How about I just take the one at eight?

HOSTESS: The closest I could give you is 7:15.

MAN: Liar.

HOSTESS: I'm sorry?

MAN: You lied.

HOSTESS: I wouldn't lie, sir.

MAN: I can see your reservations online at OpenTable.com.

HOSTESS: Oh, there it is–eight o'clock. I must have overlooked it.

MAN: That's a load.

ANNOUNCER: OpenTable.com lets you view and book reservations online.

HOSTESS: What name can I put with your reservation, sir?

MAN: How about Hugh Lie?

HOSTESS: Hugh…Lie. Table for two at eight o'clock. I hope you enjoy your evening.

MAN: Liar.

ANNOUNCER: OpenTable.com–Restaurant reservations. Right this way. Look for it at AOL under keyword OpenTable.

MERIT AWARD
Consumer Radio: Single

WRITERS
David Chiavegato
Rich Pryce-Jones

AGENCY PRODUCER
Johnny Chambers

CLIENT
Labatt Breweries of Canada

AGENCY
Palmer Jarvis DDB
Downtown/Toronto

010466A

ANNOUNCER: At Bud Light, we believe the more we can help guys deal with life's problems the more time they'll have to enjoy themselves with their friends. That's why Bud Light has started the gritty, inspirational beer voice guy advice hotline. Hello, caller?

CALLER 1: Yeah. My boss is a real jerk. What should I do?

BEER GUY: You work hard for a living. You're not always appreciated. But you don't care. You're your own man. And at the end of a hard day you like to kick back and have a cold Bud Light.

CALLER 1: You're right! I am my own man…just like you said.

ANNOUNCER: Next caller.

CALLER 2: My accountant says that I've maxed out on my capital gains exemption but he's counting the appreciation on inherited property that's still held by a trust. Is he right?

BEER GUY: You are a complex man with complex, uh, problems. You take that exemption thing and, uh, give it your all. Dig deep into your tax gains and, uh, stand strong and proud.

CALLER 2: What the hell is that supposed to mean?

ANNOUNCER: That's about all the time we have. Remember. Good advice leads to good times. Now this calls for a Bud Light.

ANNOUNCER: Earl's presents, the joys of eating at home…Ambiance.

SFX: Awful, stifling room ambiance. Clinking forks. Clock ticking.

MAN: How's your pork chop?

SFX: *(long awkward pause)*…tick…tick…tick…

WOMAN: I'm leaving you.

SFX *(long awkward pause)*…tick…tick…tick…

MAN: Mine's pretty good.

SFX: …tick…tick…

ANNOUNCER: Earl's. You could eat at home. But why?

ANNOUNCER: Earl's presents, the joys of eating at home…Delivery guys.

DELIVERY GUY: *(door buzzer, and lots of static throughout)* Pizza guy.

WOMAN: Come on in!

DELIVERY GUY: *(door buzzer)* Pizza guy.

WOMAN: Where are you?

DELIVERY GUY: Downstairs.

WOMAN: Well I'm buzzing you—

DELIVERY GUY: It's not working.

WOMAN: You have to pull it open when I—

DELIVERY GUY: What's that? Push?

WOMAN: No. Pull. *(door buzzer)* No, wait till I buzz—What are you doing—

DELIVERY GUY: Pizza guy.

WOMAN: Wha— *(door buzzer)*

ANNOUNCER: Earl's. You could eat at home. But why?

ANNOUNCER: Hey, kids! Wassup? Are you down with the new rides at Playland? Hell's Gate! The Revelation! The Hellevator! But don't let the names scare you! They're wholesome fun for the wh—

SFX: Reeerch! Ad plays backward.

EVIL BACKWARD VOICE: Playland is evil. The nightmare is here. Evil rides…evil rides…

SFX: Reeerch!

ANNOUNCER: —only at Playland!

RADIO MERIT

MERIT AWARD
Consumer Radio: Single

WRITERS
Rob Tarry
Joe Piccolo

AGENCY PRODUCER
Jacqueline Burgmann

CLIENT
Earl's Restaurant

AGENCY
Rethink/Vancouver

010467A

MERIT AWARD
Consumer Radio: Single

WRITERS
Rob Tarry
Joe Piccolo

AGENCY PRODUCER
Jacqueline Burgmann

CLIENT
Earl's Restaurant

AGENCY
Rethink/Vancouver

010468A

MERIT AWARD
Consumer Radio: Single

ART DIRECTOR
Ian Grais

WRITER
Rob Tarry

AGENCY PRODUCER
Christina Tan

CLIENT
Playland

AGENCY
Rethink/Vancouver

010469A

RADIO MERIT

MERIT AWARD
Consumer Radio: Single

WRITERS
Michael Whitney
Tom Whitney

AGENCY PRODUCER
Michael Whitney

CLIENT
St. Paul Pioneer Press

AGENCY
Whitney Morse/Minneapolis

010470A

SFX: Record scratch. Then brief sample of the intro guitar riff to Smoke on the Water, the easiest riff in rock. Someone stops the record, then tries to mimic it, practicing the riff over and over again on guitar. But the guitarist just can't get it.

ANNOUNCER: Let it go. Pioneer Press classifieds. 651-222-1111. For those times when it just ain't gonna happen.

MERIT AWARD
Consumer Radio: Single

WRITERS
Dean Saling

AGENCY PRODUCER
Craig Potter

CLIENT
Seattle SuperSonics

AGENCY
WONGDOODY/Seattle

010471A

IRS GUY: Hello, Mr. Watson. Come on in and have a seat. Let's go ahead and get started with your audit. I've been looking through your records and there seem to be some discrepancies…

SFX: Air horn blasts. It's incredibly loud.

IRS GUY: Er, for example, these receipts for quote unquote entertainment…

SFX: Air horn blasts.

MAN: Brick!

IRS GUY: What is that?…That noise. Anyway, I see here you've expensed scotch and cigars…

SFX: Air horn blasts.

MAN: Choke!

IRS GUY: What are you doing?

MAN: What?

IRS GUY: Is that an air horn?

MAN: I don't hear anything.

IRS GUY: Mr. Potter, you're not going to distract me…

SFX: Air horn blasts.

MAN: AI-I-I-R BAL-L-L! What?

ANNOUNCER: Being a Sonics fan is better in the Key. Single game tickets are now available.

IRS GUY: So, it looks like you owe the IRS a total of…

SFX: Air horn blasts.

MAN: I'm sorry, I didn't catch that.

ANNOUNCER: Sonics Basketball. It's better in the Key.

SFX:	Phone rings.
ABSOLOCKLY:	Morning. Absolock.
CAMERON:	Hi, it's Cameron calling "Out of the Blue." You're a locksmith, right? I was wondering if you could help me out?
ABSOLOCKLY:	What do you need?
CAMERON:	Well, I've got a bit of a situation here, uh. I have a lock that I can't really…I lost the key.
ABSOLOCKLY:	To what? A car lock? Door lock?
CAMERON:	Well, it's kind of, it's totally embarrassing.
ABSOLOCKLY:	Well, tell me. You know, you have the problem. You know, tell me and I'll solve the problem for you, right?
CAMERON:	Okay. I, um, I'm, uh, I'm, I'm handcuffed to my bed and I need you to unlock it.
ABSOLOCKLY:	What was that again?
CAMERON:	I'm handcuffed to my bed, and I need you to unlock it.
ABSOLOCKLY:	Oh, boy. How long have you been in that position?
CAMERON:	A couple of hours.
ABSOLOCKLY:	So there is no way you could get, duh, duh, the person who put the cuff on to come back and unlock it for you?
CAMERON:	She's not too happy with me right now.
ABSOLOCKLY:	Uh, huh. Whereabouts are you? In a house?
CAMERON:	Yeah.
ABSOLOCKLY:	Who's gonna open the door?
CAMERON:	Well, you'll have to open the door.
ABSOLOCKLY:	How can we unlock it?
CAMERON:	You're a locksmith, right?
ABSOLOCKLY:	Uh huh.
CAMERON:	Hey, I'm calling "Out of the Blue." You could be next. Labatt Blue.

RADIO MERIT

MERIT AWARD
Consumer Radio: Campaign

WRITER
Hayes Steinberg

PRODUCTION COMPANY
Pirate Radio and Television

CLIENT
Labatt Breweries of Canada

AGENCY
Ammirati Puris/Toronto

010472A

RADIO MERIT

MERIT AWARD
Consumer Radio: Campaign

WRITERS
Aaron Allen
Paul Charney
Bob Kerstetter

AGENCY PRODUCERS
Stacy McClain
Hannah Murray

CLIENT
OurHouse.com

AGENCY
Black Rocket/San Francisco

010473A

WOMAN:	Hi, honey.
MAN:	Monkey cakes.
WOMAN:	What's that smell?
MAN:	I'm redoing the floors.
WOMAN:	You're redoing the floors?
MAN:	Yep. With shellac. Shellaca-dack-adoo.
WOMAN:	Oh come on, honey. Jeez open a window. Bob, you're drooling.
MAN:	I like it. Drooling.
WOMAN:	Were you shellacking all day?
MAN:	Heeeeeeeee.
WOMAN:	Oh my god.
MAN:	Hoooooo.
WOMAN:	Bob, sweetie, look at me. I'm right over here.
MAN:	Mommy….mmm.
WOMAN:	That's it. I'm calling Dr. Levine.
ANNOUNCER:	Tools. Advice. Housecalls. Sanity. Everything you need to fix up your house, or have it done for you. Ourhouse.com. We're here to help. Partnered with Ace.

MERIT AWARD
Consumer Radio: Campaign
WRITER: Chuck Meehan
AGENCY PRODUCER: Suzanne Clarke
CLIENT: Ameristar Casinos
AGENCY: GMO Hill Holliday/San Francisco
010611A

FEMALE PROSECUTER:	Now Mr. Moyer, how do you respond to the charge of sexual harassment?
MOYER:	These are vicious lies made by a frustrated employee who obviously needs help.
PROSECUTER:	But isn't it true that you made sexual advances toward my client on a number of occasions?
MOYER:	No it is not. By the way, that's a gorgeous dress you're wearing.
PROSECUTER:	Mr. Moyer, on the night of September third, didn't you tell my client to meet you in your hotel room?
MOYER:	No I did not! You work out a lot, don't you?
PROSECUTER:	Mr. Moyer, did you or did you not promise to promote my client if she'd have sex with you?
MOYER:	For the last time, no! I'm innocent!...Listen, you wanna get a drink after this?
SFX:	Thud.
ANOUNCER:	No Chance.
SFX:	Coins hitting metal tray.
VOICEOVER:	Welcome to Ameristar Casino.
ANNOUNCER:	Chance. Here's your chance to get the highest payouts possible. Just wrestle our one arm bandits until they cry "uncle." Ameristar Casino. Your best chance.

MERIT AWARD
Consumer Radio: Campaign
WRITER: Chuck Meehan
AGENCY PRODUCERS: Karena Dacker, Susanne Carek
CLIENT: Ameristar Casinos
AGENCY: GMO Hill Holliday/San Francisco
010612A

SFX:	Play button hit on cassette player. Tape starts.
VOICEOVER 1:	The Japanese language is a rich and beautiful one. When learning Japanese, it is important to use inflection and tone in the right places. Here's how you say, "Hello, how are you?" Hirosh Ke one gash e mass ahio gasiamasu ogenky de ska. Now repeat.
SFX:	Tape rewinding.
VOICEOVER 1:	Hirosh Ke one gash e mass ahio gasiamasu ogenky de ska. Now repeat.
SFX:	Tape rewinding.
GUY:	Haroshkouno gosh ohio guys say day kinky day wash.
SFX:	Thud.
ANNOUNCER:	No chance.
SFX:	Coins hitting metal tray.
VOICEOVER 2:	Welcome to Ameristar Casino.
ANNOUNCER:	Chance. Now's your chance to play the loosest slots in town. With over 500 machines, there are plenty of spots to get lucky. Ameristar Casino. Your best chance.

RADIO MERIT

MERIT AWARD
Consumer Radio: Campaign

WRITERS
Mark Ray
Laura McCarley

AGENCY PRODUCER
Susan Clark Lazarus

CLIENT
US Weekly

AGENCY
GSD&M/Austin

010474A

ANNOUNCER 1: What's up this week in US Weekly magazine? In our cover story, Julia Roberts talks to US about her life, her new movie and her new love Benjamin Bratt-packer Demi Moore cares for the kids while Bruce Willis and his girlfriend suck-faced with more charges, Puff Daddy is worried and laying very low-cut tops are the rage as we show how to get big cleavage without big Tipper Gore gives US a peek inside Al's presidential campaignful accusations fly about why Halle Berry fled after hitting another Carson Daly talks with Marc Anthony, the hottest salsa star in the country singers Vince Gill and Amy Grant tie the not Bryant Gumbel, whose wife has thrown away the welcome Matt Damon describes the thrill of holding an Oscar statuesque singer Bijou Phillips sounds a bit like Fiona Apple Cider House Rules star Tobey McGuire chills with his buddy Leonardo DiCameron Diaz stars in the new Charlie's Angels with Drew Barrymore and more features, photos, fashion and music, it's all the freshest news you'll ever read.

ANNOUNCER 2: US Weekly. A lot can happen in a week. Pick up the premiere issue of US Weekly on sale now. Look for the cover with Julia Roberts.

MERIT AWARD
Consumer Radio: Campaign

WRITERS
Dick Sittig
Rob Goldenberg
Dave Gassman
Barney Goldberg

AGENCY PRODUCERS
Fiona Forsyth
Sue Collister

CLIENT
Jack in the Box

AGENCY
Kowloon Wholesale
Seafood Co./Santa Monica

010475A

JACK: Hi, this is Jack, founder of Jack in the Box. Let's go to Paul Schultz on line seven.

PAUL: Mr. Box, with all due respect, sir, I don't think I can be a cashier for you anymore.

JACK: I'm sorry to hear that, can I ask why?

PAUL: You guys want me to say a naughty word.

JACK: Which is...?

PAUL: I don't want to say.

JACK: It's okay, Paul, you can tell me.

PAUL: Breast. Hee hee.

JACK: As in chicken breast?

PAUL: Yeah, hee hee. I can't say that in public.

JACK: Paul, people need to know my Spicy Chicken Sandwich is made from real chicken breast, then seasoned with just the right amount of spice and served hot because we don't make it 'til you order it...

PAUL: So it's okay to say it?

JACK: Absolutely. And let me just say it's refreshing to have such a well-mannered young man working for me.

PAUL: Gee, thanks, Mr. Box, I'm...

SFX: Clicking of phone line picking up.

MOM: Paul, honey, your pancakes are ready.

PAUL: Shut up, Mom, I'm talking to my (beep) boss.

SFX: Phone clicking.

PAUL: Sorry, Jack, what did you say?

JACK: We're going to miss you, Paul. And now here's Stephanie T., a real live, sane crewmember from Bakersfield.

JIB EMPLOYEE: Come on in for Jack's Spicy Chicken Sandwich. It's made with real chicken breast, just the right amount of spice, and always served hot and tasty because we don't make it 'til you order it.

WOMAN *(reading from a book)*: He stepped backward from the barrier before he turned to his cot, and lying on it, became as remote from her as a stone crusader lying in a tomb. After a long, pregnant pause, the doctor replied…

ANTHONY HOPKINS: I ate his liver with some fava beans and a nice Chianti…

WOMAN: Oooh!

SFX: Dramatic music; up and under.

ANNOUNCER: You've read our books. Now see our movies. Silence of the Lambs. Just one of 10,000 movies now at a Chapters store near you.

RADIO MERIT

MERIT AWARD
Consumer Radio: Campaign

WRITER
Zak Mroueh

AGENCY PRODUCER
Louise Blouin

PRODUCTION COMPANY
Pirate Radio and Television

CLIENT
Chapters

AGENCY
TAXI/Toronto

010476A

TELEVISION

TELEVISION MERIT

MERIT AWARD
Consumer Television Over :30
Single

ART DIRECTORS
Dean Maryon
Larry Frey

WRITER
Lorenzo De Rita

AGENCY PRODUCER
Jackie Adler

PRODUCTION COMPANY
Harry Nash

DIRECTOR
Fredrik Bond

CLIENT
Adidas International BV

AGENCY
180/Amsterdam

010477A

MERIT AWARD
Consumer Television Over :30
Single

ART DIRECTOR
Paul Brazier

WRITER
Nick Worthington

AGENCY PRODUCER
Frank Lieberman

PRODUCTION COMPANY
Academy

DIRECTOR
Jonathan Glazer

CLIENT
Wrangler

AGENCY
Abbott Mead Vickers.BBDO/London

010478A

SFX: Music.

SUPER: Kiki Square, 23m above sea level.

WOMAN IN PINK DRESS: The poor fish, it just looked as though it was screaming for water.

WOMAN IN CAR: It was dying, it was lying there dying and nobody was helping it.

WOMAN IN PINK DRESS: Until this big man came along, picked up the fish under his arm and he just shot off down the road.

WOMAN IN CAR: He jumped up onto the bonnet of our car and I thought he was going to come through the windscreen.

WOMAN IN PINK DRESS: All his muscles were bulging and he was just holding this fish just so tight.

ATTENDANT: Of course it was Jonah Lomu, he bursts through the car wash, bang. By jingos, he was moving.

OLD DIVER: It was just on his last gasp and he threw the fish into the water and it saved its life. Wearing Adidas makes you more caring about fish and alligators and cats and elephants and even people.

SUPER: Adidas makes you better. Adidas forever sport. www.adidas.com/be better.

(The spot features the travels of a character crossing the states from east to west. He is a Jack Kerouac figure, jumping freight trains, riding buses, hitch hiking. Throughout the spot are scenes from his travels.)

SFX: Yellow Brick Road from the Wizard of Oz throughout.

SUPER: Whatever you ride. Wrangler.

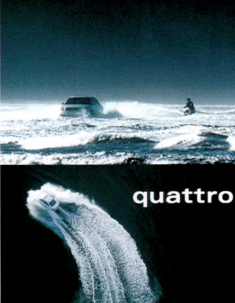

(A wake-boarder goes through a breathtaking repertoire of tricks—spinning, skiing backwards, performing somersaults. We reveal that the skier is in being towed by a silver Audi A6 4.2 Quattro.)

SUPER: Quattro. Audi logo.

(A teenager passes his driving test. His father, the owner of a new Passat, is distraught at the thought of his son driving the Passat and tries to persuade the examiner to reverse his decision.)

SUPER: The beautifully crafted new Passat. You'll want to keep it that way.

TELEVISION MERIT

MERIT AWARD
Consumer Television Over :30
Single

ART DIRECTOR
Alasdair Welsh

WRITER
Nick O'Bryan-Tear

AGENCY PRODUCER
Andy Gulliman

PRODUCTION COMPANY
Spectre

DIRECTOR
Daniel Kleinman

CLIENT
Audi/Rawdon Glover

AGENCY
Bartle Bogle Hegarty/
London

010479A

MERIT AWARD
Consumer Television Over :30
Single

ART DIRECTORS
Ewan Paterson
Rob Jack

WRITERS
Rob Jack
Ewan Paterson

AGENCY PRODUCER
Howard Spivey

PRODUCTION COMPANY
Partizan

DIRECTOR
Rocky Morton

CLIENT
Volkswagen Group

AGENCY
BMP DDB/London

010481A

TELEVISION MERIT

MERIT AWARD
Consumer Television Over :30
Single

ART DIRECTOR
No Wenley

WRITER
Jeremy Craigen

AGENCY PRODUCER
Howard Spivey

PRODUCTION COMPANY
Blink Productions

DIRECTOR
Ivan Zacharias

CLIENT
Volkswagen Group

AGENCY
BMP DDB/London

010482A

MERIT AWARD
Consumer Television Over :30
Single

ART DIRECTOR
Dean Hanson

WRITER
Greg Hahn

AGENCY PRODUCERS
Marty Wetherall
Judy Brink

PRODUCTION COMPANY
hungry man

DIRECTOR
John O'Hagan

CLIENT
Electronic Data Systems

AGENCY
Fallon/Minneapolis

010483A

(A car journey. As seen from a VW Beetle.)

SFX: Epic western music under. Meows.

COWBOY 1: Herdin' cats…don't let anybody tell you it's easy.

COWBOY 2: Being a cat herder is probably about the toughest thing I think I've ever done.

VOICEOVER: You see the movies, ya hear the stories…I'm livin' a dream.

COWBOY 3: I wouldn't do nothin' else.

VOICEOVER: It ain't an easy job, but when you bring a herd into town and you ain't lost a one of 'em, ain't a feelin' like it in the world.

SFX: Music under.

SUPER: In a sense, this is what we do. We bring together information, ideas, and technologies and make them go where you want.

VOICEOVER: EDS. Managing the complexities of e-business.

SUPER: EDS solved. eds.com.

SUPER:	Sorry.
VOICEOVER:	I won't be home for dinner.
SUPER:	Sorry.
VOICEOVER:	My side of the bed's always cold.
VOICEOVER:	Sorry if I'm not the girl next door.
VOICEOVER:	If you think I've overstayed my welcome.
VOICEOVER:	I won't be home to put the kids to bed.
SUPER:	Sorry.
VOICEOVER:	If this seems a little Freudian.
VOICEOVER:	Sorry about your catscan.
SUPER:	Sorry.
VOICEOVER:	I won't be home to watch the late news.
VOICEOVER:	Sorry Premier Leagues.
SUPER:	Sorry.
VOICEOVER:	We don't have a cool nickname.
VOICEOVER:	Sorry I can't walk home from school with you.
VOICEOVER:	Sorry! Who do you feel sorry for?
VOICEOVER:	I'm not going to be home for a while. Sorry.
SUPER:	Just do it. Swoosh.

SFX:	Cheesy 80s Rock Music.
SUPER:	Music Chronicles Danger Kitty.
ANNOUNCER:	The year was 1983 and the metal band, Danger Kitty, released their hit single, Love Rocket. With it came instant fame and fortune…And the boys of Danger Kitty were quick to embrace the life of excess. They bought mansions…Cars… The finest women's clothing…Even gold-plated toilet seats.
ROCK CRITIC:	They spent, spent, spent. It was a rock n' roll dream.
ANNOUNCER:	But in 1984, the Love Rocket crashed. The fortune was gone…
SUPER:	Band broke: Kitty spent.
ANNOUNCER:	…and the dream was a distant memory. Desperate for money, Danger Kitty booked one last show in '96, at the Smukler Bar Mitzvah.
SUPER:	Discover Card logo. Some people just can't live within their means.
ANNOUNCER:	Some people just can't live within their means. The Discover Card with spending management tools. For the slightly smarter consumer.

TELEVISION MERIT

MERIT AWARD
Consumer Television Over :30
Single

ART DIRECTORS
Michael Simons
Liz Montgomery

WRITERS
Josh Gold
Joe Staples

AGENCY PRODUCERS
Craig Sloan
Debby Ross

PRODUCTION COMPANY
Film Graphics

DIRECTOR
Dave Denneen

CLIENT
Nike

AGENCY
Foote Cone & Belding/
Sydney

010484A

MERIT AWARD
Consumer Television Over :30
Single

ART DIRECTOR
Greg Bell

WRITER
Paul Venables

AGENCY PRODUCER
Tod Puckett

PRODUCTION COMPANY
Propaganda Films

DIRECTORS
Tom Kuntz
Mike Maguire

CLIENT
Discover Card

AGENCY
Goodby Silverstein &
Partners/San Francisco

010485A

TELEVISION MERIT

MERIT AWARD
Consumer Television Over :30
Single

ART DIRECTOR
Sean Farrell

WRITER
Colin Nissan

AGENCY PRODUCER
Tanya LeSieur

PRODUCTION COMPANY
Independent Media

DIRECTOR
Chris Smith

CLIENT
SBC Communications
Pacific Bell

AGENCY
Goodby Silverstein &
Partners/San Francisco

010486A

Also won:

MERIT AWARD
Consumer Television: Varying
Lengths Campaign

MERIT AWARD
Consumer Television Over :30
Single

ART DIRECTORS
Gary Robinson
Owen Lee

WRITERS
Gary Robinson
Owen Lee

AGENCY PRODUCER
Vicky Baldacchino

PRODUCTION COMPANY
Spectre

DIRECTOR
Daniel Kleinman

CLIENT
Britvic Soft Drinks-Tango

AGENCY
HHCL & Partners/London

010487A

FLANDERS: Laurel Lane used to be such a nice place to live. Um, everyone used to be friends in this neighborhood. But then everyone started sharing the same cable line for the Internet. That's when things online got slower and people started acting, well, downright unneighborly.

GUY: No, you're a web hog!

KIDS: You're a web hog!

MAILMAN: Every day I come into this neighborhood and I don't know what to expect. I'm scared…We used to use this mace for dogs.

COP: Occasionally, you get a situation like this with the overcrowding on the Internet. People try to take the law into their own hands.

JOHNSON: You've got to get them to log off, that is the whole point.

COP: The thing is these aren't bad people, and that's what breaks my heart.

KIDS: Web hog!

GUY: Oh, no, no you're a web hog!

SUPER: Don't share a cable line. Get Pacific Bell DSL. Always fast. Never shared. Pacific Bell logo.

VOICEOVER: The Internet is once again, your friend.

MUM: Four years…Jack and I married within six months of meeting one another, you know?

DAUGHTER: Mum!

(Jeremy takes a gulp from a can of Tango. A little face inside the stomach wall yawns and wakes up.)

TANGO INSIDE: Oh no. You're not still seeing her, are you? You've been wanting to get out of this relationship for years and now her mother speaks of marriage. You must do something drastic, my friend—make a pass at her father…Go on, just give his knee a little squeeze. Excellent.

(The girl's father reaches over and gently squeezes his knee in reply.)

TANGO INSIDE: Oh dear.

VOICEOVER: Feed the Tango inside.

(A soldier who has returned from war tells his father how his comrade saved his life. To celebrate, the father uncorks a bottle of wine, but his son and his comrade ask for Stella Artois. Distressed, the father pours a pint for his son. He begins to pour a second, but alas, nothing but froth splutters from the font. Apologetically, he once again reaches for the bottle of wine. At the end of the spot we see that the father has placed his foot on the pipe that supplies the brew.)

SUPER: Stella Artois. Reassuringly expensive.

SFX: "Zoom!" by Fat Larry's Band throughout.

(A dog walks from an empty house into Magicland. In the middle of a lake, a beautiful girl dog sits in a row boat. As if by magic, he is now sitting in the boat with her. Throughout the spot, we see fountains, helibabies in wigs, rainbows and surfing kittens. The commercial ends with the dogs watching fireworks that spell out magic 105.4fm.)

TELEVISION MERIT

MERIT AWARD
Consumer Television Over :30
Single

ART DIRECTOR
Vince Squibb

WRITER
Paul Silburn

AGENCY PRODUCER
Sarah Hallat

PRODUCTION COMPANY
Gorgeous Enterprises

DIRECTOR
Frank Budgen

CLIENT
Interbrew UK

AGENCY
Lowe Lintas/London

010488A

MERIT AWARD
Consumer Television Over :30
Single

ART DIRECTOR
Kim Gehrig

WRITERS
Caroline Pay
Paul Bruce

AGENCY PRODUCER
Zoe Bell

PRODUCTION COMPANY
400 Films

DIRECTOR
John Hollis

CLIENT
Magic FM

AGENCY
Mother Ltd./London

010489A

445

TELEVISION MERIT

MERIT AWARD
Consumer Television Over :30
Single

ART DIRECTOR
Robert Prins

WRITER
Jeff Spiegel

AGENCY PRODUCER
William O'Reilly

PRODUCTION COMPANY
Coppos Films

DIRECTOR
Mike Bigelow

CLIENT
Young & Co.'s Brewery

AGENCY
Prins/Spiegel/Venice

010490A

MERIT AWARD
Consumer Television Over :30
Single

ART DIRECTOR
Nik Studzinski

WRITER
Gavin Kellett

AGENCY PRODUCERS
Linsey Rogers
Clare Hunter

PRODUCTION COMPANY
Harry Nash

DIRECTOR
Fredrik Bond

CLIENT
Monster.com

AGENCY
Saatchi & Saatchi/London

010491A

WOMAN: Have you been a good boy?

MAN: Well, I, uh…

WOMAN: Shut up! I think you've been a bad boy. A very bad boy. Do you know what I do to bad boys?

MAN: Spank them?

WOMAN: No.

MAN: Take their temperature?

(She starts to pour a bottle of beer out.)

MAN: No! That's sick! Get out! Go on! What a freak.

SUPER: There's no greater pleasure than a Young's Old Nick.

VOICEOVER: So your salary negotiations are going badly. You loser. Think. What's going wrong? Can he smell your fear? No way. You're a tiger…Come on, what noise do tigers make? Now get back in there.

(He charges down the corridor to his boss' office, growling.)

VOICEOVER: Show them a tiger fears nothing! I smell money…

SUPER: Beware of the voices.

VOICEOVER: For career advice worth listening to and thousands of jobs, visit monster.co.uk.

MIKE:	The great thing about these collars is that they show off a fabulous figure. If you've got a great figure like, uh, Stacy obviously has, this is sort of the new one to wear. They really look great.
DEBBIE:	And I think it's true that you can wear one of these collars without looking remotely tarty.
MIKE:	You're absolutely right there, Debbie, because I don't think Stacy could look tarty if she tried. Could you, Stacy?
DEBBIE:	I'm sure you'd like to find out, Mike.
MIKE:	Oh, yes.
DEBBIE:	But even the more eloquent and refined cats will find one of these, uh, a very welcome accessory for uh, fashion, wardrobe…
MIKE:	Should we listen to some of the bells? Hold on, let's have a look. Did you hear that? Can you hear that? That is a lovely, well-crafted bell. I mean, that really does say, "I'm coming." Look out! Meow!
DEBBIE:	It really does.
MIKE:	Absolutely.

MIKE:	I think we've got a bit of a blast from the past for you, Debbie. Do you remember this everyone?
SFX:	Laughs.
MIKE:	Do you remember, those were the days, eh, Debbie?
DEBBIE:	Oh.
MIKE:	In those days I had a little bit of a *(whispers)* flea problem. I know we're not really meant to talk about it but, yeah, that's what I had. I was sort of host to a number of parasites. But now I got rid of it—and you can, too, if you have this problem— with this marvelous kit from Pets Pyjamas. It's the usual number, so call in for a catalogue and, uh, you wouldn't have to look like I looked there. Unless you look like you look there, Debbie. You were really something special in those days. That was when you were the sexiest cat on tele, wasn't it? So lovely…so lovely. I used to…
DEBBIE *(breaking down)*:	I'm going to my dressing room.
MIKE:	What was it? Did I…

TELEVISION MERIT

MERIT AWARD
Consumer Television Over :30
Single

ART DIRECTOR
Brian Connolly

WRITER
Paul Domenet

AGENCY PRODUCER
Tess Woodward

PRODUCTION COMPANY
Stark Films

DIRECTOR
Steve Reeves

CLIENT
Pets Pyjamas

AGENCY
Saatchi & Saatchi/London

010492A

MERIT AWARD
Consumer Television Over :30
Single

ART DIRECTOR
Brian Connolly

WRITER
Paul Domenet

AGENCY PRODUCER
Tess Woodward

PRODUCTION COMPANY
Stark Films

DIRECTOR
Steve Reeves

CLIENT
Pets Pyjamas

AGENCY
Saatchi & Saatchi/London

010493A

TELEVISION MERIT

MERIT AWARD
Consumer Television Over :30
Single

ART DIRECTOR
Jeff Labbe

WRITER
Chuck McBride

AGENCY PRODUCERS
Betsy Beale
Jennifer Wallrapp

DIRECTOR
Michael Haussman

CLIENT
Levi Strauss

AGENCY
TBWA/Chiat/Day/
San Francisco

010494A

MERIT AWARD
Consumer Television Over :30
Single

ART DIRECTOR
Jarbas Agnelli

WRITER
Alexandre Machado

PRODUCTION COMPANY
Ad Studio

DIRECTOR
Jarbas Agnelli

CLIENT
Editora Globo

AGENCY
W/Brasil/São Paulo

010613A

(Throughout the spot various women destroy the rooms of a building—swinging a large hammer at the sink, throwing a chair through a window, chainsawing through the wall. A maintenance boy moves from disaster to disaster.)

MAINTENANCE BOY: Hi, I got your page.

SFX: Solo violin.

(Blonde woman watches maintenance boy fix the sink.)

SFX: Pager beeps. Hammer smashing a sink…Pager beeps. Hammer smashing sink again…Glass breaking. Pager beeps…Axe hitting the wall.

(Office woman opens a door and lets the maintenance boy in.)

SFX: Pager beeps. Chainsaw noise. Pager beeps.

(Girl in the bathroom lights some sticks of dynamite and puts them in the toilet.)

SFX: Fire fizzing from the dynamite.

GIRL: Que Pasa?

MAINTENANCE BOY: Man, this place is falling apart.

SFX: An explosion. Pager beeps. Solo violin.

SUPER: Levi's 569, Loose Straight Jeans.

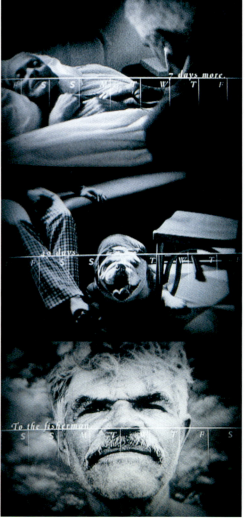

SUPER: To the prisoner, seven days or less. To the sick, seven days or more.

SUPER: To the happy, seven reasons. To the sad, seven remedies.

SUPER: To the rich, seven dinners. To the poor, seven hungers.

SUPER: To hope, seven new dawns. To the sleepless, seven long nights.

SUPER: To the lonely, seven chances. To the absent, seven guilts.

SUPER: To a dog, 49 days. To a fly, seven generations.

SUPER: To businessmen, 25% of the month. To economists, 0.019 of the year.

SUPER: To the pessimist, seven risks. To the optimist, seven opportunities.

SUPER: To the earth, seven turns. To the fisherman, seven returns.

SUPER: To meet a deadline, too little. To create the world, enough.

SUPER: To someone with the flu, the cure. To a rose on a jar, death.

SUPER: To history, nothing. To EPOCA everything.

SUPER: EPOCA. Every week.

SFX:	Music throughout.

(A woman in the bathroom shuts a medicine cabinet. In the reflection of the mirror is the face of a masked man, who revs a chainsaw in the air. She runs out of the house and through the woods, with the masked man pursuing her. The masked man can't keep up and falls to his knees.)

SUPER:	Why Sport?
SUPER:	You'll live longer.
SUPER:	Swoosh. Just do it.

DAD:	Okay, gang, I'll be doing the taxes. Dad's gonna get us a big, fat refund.
SUPER:	Tax Day 5.
DAD:	So you don't know if I should list it on schedule C. Okay, yeah, here she is. *(to daughter)* It's some boy from school. Brad or Chad or something.
SUPER:	Tax Day 6.

(Mom is wearing lingerie with rose in mouth.)

DAD:	Honey, do you know where your W-2 is?
MOM:	No.
DAD:	Okay.
SUPER:	Tax Day 8.
DAD:	Hey! Dad needs a quiet house, okay?
SUPER:	Tax Day 13.
MOM:	Bill?
DAD:	Who's out there?
SUPER:	Tax Day 17.
MOM:	I'm worried about Bill. Taxes. I think he might need professional help.
SUPER:	1-800-HRBLOCK. hrblock.com. H & R BLOCK.

TELEVISION MERIT

MERIT AWARD
Consumer Television Over :30
Single

ART DIRECTOR
Scott Vitrone

WRITER
Ian Reichenthal

AGENCY PRODUCER
Chris Noble

PRODUCTION COMPANY
Villains

DIRECTOR
Phil Joanou

CLIENT
Nike

AGENCY
Wieden + Kennedy/Portland

010495A

MERIT AWARD
Consumer Television Over :30
Single

ART DIRECTOR
Rick Casteel

WRITER
John Matejczyk

AGENCY PRODUCER
Lee Goldberg

PRODUCTION COMPANY
Coppos Films

DIRECTOR
Craig Gillespie

CLIENT
H & R Block

AGENCY
Young & Rubicam/Chicago

010496A

TELEVISION MERIT

MERIT AWARD
Consumer Television Over :30
Single

ART DIRECTOR
Javier Celentano

WRITER
Pablo Capara

AGENCY PRODUCERS
Luis Pompeo
Marcelo Fontao

PRODUCTION COMPANY
Oruga Films

DIRECTOR
Javier Nir

CLIENT
Pirelli/Institutional

AGENCY
Young & Rubicam/
Buenos Aires

010497A

MERIT AWARD
Consumer Television Over :30
Campaign

ART DIRECTORS
Dave Beverley
Tom Hudson

WRITERS
Rob Burleigh
Tom Hudson

AGENCY PRODUCER
Nerine Soper

PRODUCTION COMPANY
RSA

DIRECTOR
Tony Scott

CLIENT
Barclays

AGENCY
Leagas Delaney/London

010498A

450

(A truck cuts off a car. The driver barely misses hitting it. He gets out of the car, very angry, shuts the door and begins to walk toward the truck when he slips on the wet road.)

SUPER: Power is nothing without control. Pirelli logo.

ANTHONY HOPKINS VOICEOVER: What is this about "big?" You know, seeing the big picture, having the big idea, clinching the big deal. Nobody wants to clinch the little deal. Who wants to do that? You'd be a little deal clincher. A small shot.

I want my girlfriend to say, "good morning, big boy," to which I'll reply, I've got a big day today, big meeting with a big cheese from a big studio, it's the big time for the big bucks, and she'll turn to me and say: "big head."

I'll retort, "What's the big deal?" And give her a big kiss, she'll close the door of our big house, look in the mirror and ask herself, "does my bum look big in this?"

SUPER: Because we're big...we've become the largest online bank in the UK. Because we're big...more than half a million UK businesses work with us. Because we're big...you can access your money from over 45,000 places worldwide.

HOPKINS: And in my big meeting I'll turn to one of the big hitters and I'll say, "I love this movie, it's gonna be 'big.'" There's only one small problem, my fee...I'd like it to be...erm...what's the word?...

SUPER: A big world needs a big bank. BARCLAYS. www.barclays.com.

SFX: Happy song.

SUPER: This is Bob. Maybe he needs some help. Or a new car. The automobile market every Wednesday and Saturday. The Hamburger Abendblatt. If you really want to know.

(A male and female blow-up doll couple walk down the street in Levi's Engineered Jeans. He gives her a rose. Suddenly, a large truck races by, blowing the male doll into a barbed wire fence. The barbs puncture his body, causing him to slowly deflate. The female doll then takes her own life by puncturing herself on the thorn of her rose.)

SUPER: Levi's Engineered Jeans. The twisted original.

TELEVISION MERIT

MERIT AWARD
Consumer Television Over :30
Campaign

ART DIRECTOR
Jochen Mohrbutter

WRITER
Nicole Franz

AGENCY PRODUCER
Guntram Krasting

PRODUCTION COMPANY
Wunderfilm Hamburg

DIRECTOR
Guntram Krasting

CLIENT
Hamburger Abendblatt-
Daily Hamburgian
Newspaper

AGENCY
McCann-Erickson/Hamburg

010499A

MERIT AWARD
Consumer Television :30
Single

ART DIRECTORS
Matt Saunby
Adam Scholes

WRITERS
Adam Chiappe
Shawn Preston

AGENCY PRODUCER
Frances Royle

PRODUCTION COMPANY
Propaganda

DIRECTOR
Dante Ariola

CLIENT
Levi Strauss/Robert Hanson

AGENCY
Bartle Bogle Hegarty/
London

010500A

451

TELEVISION MERIT

MERIT AWARD
Consumer Television :30
Single

ART DIRECTORS
Matt Saunby
Adam Scholes

WRITERS
Adam Chiappe
Shawn Preston

AGENCY PRODUCER
Frances Royle

PRODUCTION COMPANY
Outsider

DIRECTORS
Dom & Nic

CLIENT
Levi Strauss/Robert Hanson

AGENCY
Bartle Bogle Hegarty/
London

010501A

MERIT AWARD
Consumer Television :30
Single

ART DIRECTOR
Guy Shelmerdine

WRITER
Grant Holland

AGENCY PRODUCER
Nick Felder

PRODUCTION COMPANY
HKM

DIRECTOR
Mike Mills

CLIENT
Finish Line

AGENCY
Cliff Freeman and Partners/
New York

010502A

(A couple begins tearing each other's clothes on. They dress each other passionately, especially when they reach for each other's Levi's Engineered Jeans. Suddenly, two parents and their younger son enter the apartment.)

SUPER   New Levi's Engineered Jeans. The twisted original.

(A Finish Line employee is following a runner. He starts playing "Eye of the Tiger" on his boom box. The runner shoves the employee to the ground, but then, concerned, helps him back on his feet. The employee then hits play again and continues to follow the runner.)

SUPER: Maybe we love runners too much.

ANNOUNCER: Air Max Deluxe by Nike. Available at Finish Line. The place to go for Nike running.

(A sports news commentator does a play-by-play in Turkish. A skinny Turkish diver in a Speedo dives off a cliff in a beautifully executed swan dive…into dirt—there is no water.)

SUPER: Sports news from the only region you care about. Yours. 11PM Regional Sports Report. Fox Sports Net.

(A sports reporter in a dark smoky room does a pre-game set up in Russian. Two large Russian men face each other at a small table. They begin to exchange slaps in the face. One powerful slap, which we see in slow-motion replay, causes the room to erupt.)

SUPER: Sports news from the only region you care about. Yours. 11PM Regional Sports Report. Fox Sports Net.

TELEVISION MERIT

MERIT AWARD
Consumer Television :30
Single

ART DIRECTORS
Rossana Bardales
Taras Wayner

WRITER
Dan Morales

AGENCY PRODUCERS
Claire Grupp
Catherine Abate

PRODUCTION COMPANY
Partizan/Cape Direct

DIRECTOR
Traktor

CLIENT
Fox Sports

AGENCY
Cliff Freeman and Partners/
New York

010506A

MERIT AWARD
Consumer Television :30
Single

ART DIRECTORS
Rossana Bardales
Taras Wayner

WRITER
Dan Morales

AGENCY PRODUCERS
Claire Grupp
Catherine Abate

PRODUCTION COMPANY
Partizan/Cape Direct

DIRECTOR
Traktor

CLIENT
Fox Sports

AGENCY
Cliff Freeman and Partners/
New York

010507A

Also won:

MERIT AWARD
Consumer Television :20 and
Under: Single

TELEVISION MERIT

MERIT AWARD
Consumer Television :30
Single

ART DIRECTORS
Rossana Bardales
Taras Wayner

WRITER
Dan Morales

AGENCY PRODUCERS
Claire Grupp
Catherine Abate

PRODUCTION COMPANY
Partizan/Cape Direct

DIRECTOR
Traktor

CLIENT
Fox Sports

AGENCY
Cliff Freeman and Partners/
New York

010508A

MERIT AWARD
Consumer Television :30
Single

ART DIRECTORS
Rossana Bardales
Taras Wayner

WRITER
Dan Morales

AGENCY PRODUCERS
Claire Grupp
Catherine Abate

PRODUCTION COMPANY
Partizan/Cape Direct

DIRECTOR
Traktor

CLIENT
Fox Sports

AGENCY
Cliff Freeman and Partners/
New York

010509A

Also won:

MERIT AWARD
Consumer Television :20 and
Under: Single

(A Chinese sports news announcer does the play-by-play as two Chinese lumberjacks chop down a large tree. An athlete then tries to catch the giant 200-foot tree falling toward him.)

SUPER: Sports news from the only region you care about. Yours. 11 PM Regional Sports Report. Fox Sports Net.

(Two Indian men banter on a news show set in Bombay. We see two blindfolded men swinging clubs at each other, but missing. All of a sudden, one of the men loses his bearings and starts pounding a gentleman in the crowd.)

SUPER: Sports news from the only region you care about. Yours. 11PM Regional Sports Report. Fox Sports Net.

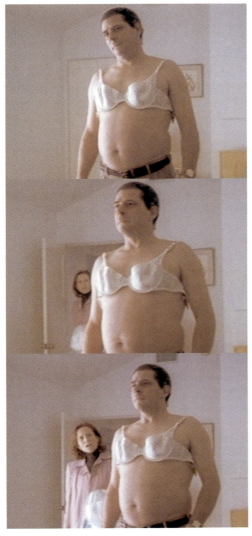

WIFE:	Scott?
MAN:	Hmm?
WIFE:	Who's the NBA's all time leader in blocked shots?
SUPER:	If only every question was a sports question. Sports Geniuses. The new game show premieres March 27. Fox Sports Net.

(A guy is staring at an attractive woman who is breast feeding her baby.)

WOMAN:	Excuse me? Who's the only Super Bowl MVP to play for a losing team?
SUPER:	If only every question was a sports question. Sports Geniuses. The new game show premieres March 27. Fox Sports Net.

TELEVISION MERIT

MERIT AWARD
Consumer Television :30
Single

ART DIRECTOR
Rob Carducci

WRITER
Richard Bullock

AGENCY PRODUCER
Catherine Abate

PRODUCTION COMPANY
MJZ

DIRECTOR
Rocky Morton

CLIENT
Fox Sports

AGENCY
Cliff Freeman and Partners/
New York

010510A

MERIT AWARD
Consumer Television :30
Single

ART DIRECTOR
Rob Carducci

WRITER
Richard Bullock

AGENCY PRODUCER
Catherine Abate

PRODUCTION COMPANY
MJZ

DIRECTOR
Rocky Morton

CLIENT
Fox Sports

AGENCY
Cliff Freeman and Partners/
New York

010511A

TELEVISION MERIT

MERIT AWARD
Consumer Television :30
Single

ART DIRECTOR
Chris Lange

WRITER
Michael Hart

AGENCY PRODUCER
Damian Stevens

PRODUCTION COMPANY
@radical.media

DIRECTOR
Errol Morris

CLIENT
Public Broadcasting System

AGENCY
Fallon/Minneapolis

010513A

MERIT AWARD
Consumer Television :30
Single

ART DIRECTOR
Matt Vescovo

WRITER
William Gelner

AGENCY PRODUCER
Melissa Miller

PRODUCTION COMPANY
Partizan

DIRECTOR
Traktor

CLIENT
Conseco

AGENCY
Fallon/New York

010512A

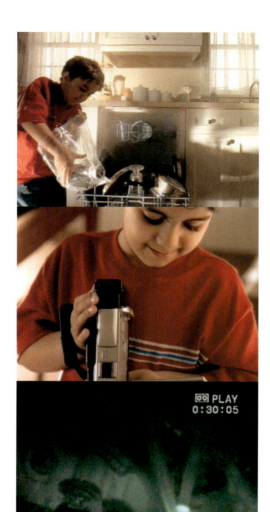

(A boy is staring at the dishwasher. When it stops, he opens it and pulls out a plastic bag. There is a video camera inside. He rewinds the recorder and watches footage from inside the dishwasher.)

SFX: Music under.

SUPER: 0:30:06 Play. 1:16 PM. JUN. 1, 2000

SUPER: Stay curious PBS logo.

DAD: Okay, sweetie, on your toes. Swing through the ball...through it. Eye on the ball, hon. We're working on a forehand. Okay, let's try backhand. We'll work backhand.

(A ball hits his daughter's racquet, knocking it clear out of her hand.)

DAD: Okay, we just need to connect with the ball. Let's stay in the game, sweetheart. Now, don't be afraid to charge the net.

VOICEOVER: How do you plan on financing your retirement?

SUPER: Financial Services.

VOICEOVER: Conseco's annuities have tax advantages that can help. Conseco. Step up.

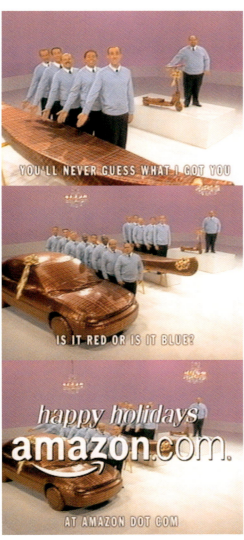
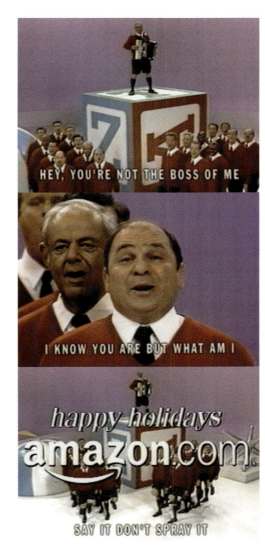

CHORUS: It could be a teddy bear,
a bike or smoke alarm.
Or possibly a new TV
or game on CD rom.

You'll never guess what I got you
at Amazon.com.

Looks like a telescope
Or a blender for the bar?
Guess again, a fountain pen?
Or teachin' tunes guitar?

You'll never guess what I got you
Is it red or is it blue?
You'll never guess what I got you
at Amazon.com.

CHORUS: Amazon.com is my favorite toy store.
Hey, you're not the boss of me.
The greatest selection of toys online.
I know you are but what am I?

Amazon.com. (Amazon.com.)
Makes me feel like a kid. (Makes me feel like a kid.)
Stop copying me. (Stop copying me.)

So if you need some toys, don't hesitate it's…
Amazon.com—say it don't spray it.

TELEVISION MERIT

MERIT AWARD
Consumer Television :30
Single

ART DIRECTORS
Matt Reinhardt
Ron Lim

WRITERS
Tom O'Keefe
Patrick Durkin

AGENCY PRODUCER
Jim Phox

PRODUCTION COMPANY
Headquarters

DIRECTOR
Joe Public

CLIENT
Amazon.com

AGENCY
Foote Cone & Belding/
San Francisco

010514A

MERIT AWARD
Consumer Television :30
Single

ART DIRECTORS
Matt Reinhardt
Ron Lim

WRITERS
Tom O'Keefe
Patrick Durkin

AGENCY PRODUCER
Jim Phox

PRODUCTION COMPANY
Headquarters

DIRECTOR
Joe Public

CLIENT
Amazon.com

AGENCY
Foote Cone & Belding/
San Francisco

010515A

TELEVISION MERIT

MERIT AWARD
Consumer Television :30
Single

ART DIRECTOR
Todd Grant

WRITER
Steve Dildarian

AGENCY PRODUCER
Cindy Epps

PRODUCTION COMPANIES
Gil Smith Studio
Innervision Studios

DIRECTOR
Tom Routson

CLIENT
Anheuser-Busch

AGENCY
Goodby Silverstein & Partners/San Francisco

010516A

MERIT AWARD
Consumer Television :30
Single

ART DIRECTOR
Greg Bell

WRITER
Paul Venables

AGENCY PRODUCER
Tod Puckett

PRODUCTION COMPANY
Propaganda Films

DIRECTORS
Tom Kuntz
Mike Maguire

CLIENT
Discover Card

AGENCY
Goodby Silverstein & Partners/San Francisco

010517A

LOUIE:	Ladies and gentlemen, I have disturbing news about the ferret.
FRANK:	What's this?
LOUIE:	In the summer of '79, the ferret posed nude.
FRANK:	Oh, that's revolting.
LOUIE:	The photos were tasteless.
FRANK:	Ohhhhh!
LOUIE:	They were vulgar.
FRANK:	Oh, that's grotesque.
LOUIE:	And this one was just obscene.
FRANK:	Hey, I know her.
LOUIE:	And I would like to ask for his resignation from this proud company called Budweiser.
FRANK:	Oh, what was he thinking?
LOUIE:	Yeah, there's one with a guinea pig that would make you pass out.

GIRL:	This one, Daddy, this one!
(Dad looks at price tag: "beagle—$600.")	
DAD:	I don't know, sweetie. He's kind of expensive.
(Dad looks at a different puppy cage. Price tag "hyena—$25.")	
CLERK:	No one seems to want him.
DAD:	Oh, look, sweetie, he needs a home.
SFX:	Chaos. Dog bowl flying out of cage. Rattling. Thuds. Food Flying. Clerk screaming throughout attack.
SUPER:	Some people know when to pay a little more.
VOICEOVER:	Some people know when to pay a little more....
SUPER:	Discover Card logo. For the slightly smarter consumer.

SFX:	Light, happy music throughout.
ANNOUNCER:	At Gene Enterprises, we've harnessed the power of the human gene, so you can say goodbye to your allergies forever. Nozulla may cause the following symptoms: itchy rashes, full body hair loss, projectile vomiting, gigantic eyeball, the condition known as hot dog fingers…
SUPER:	Gene powered. (Pearsonadine 8000 mg). Not appropriate for women. Not appropriate for women. Consult your attorney before taking.
ANNOUNCER:	Children born with the head of a golden retriever, seeing the dead, bone liquification, possession by the prince of darkness, tail growth, elderly pregnancy…

(A man watching from his living room sells 3,000 shares of Gene Enterprises.)

SFX:	Mouse click. Music.
SUPER:	Learn to identify trading opportunities. E*TRADE logo.
ANNOUNCER:	E*TRADE. It's your money.
SUPER:	It's your money. 1-800-ETRADE-1.

VOICEOVER:	If you don't watch a lot of movies, you may never learn certain valuable skills.
MOBSTER 1:	What are we gonna do with it?
VOICEOVER:	Like how to dispose of a body.
VOICEOVER:	But if you watch a lot of movies, you'd know.
MOBSTER 1 *(tossing body bag off bridge)*:	Arrivederci…
SFX:	Splash.
MOBSTER 1:	What do we do now?
MOBSTER 2:	Let's go eat.
MOBSTER 1 VOICEOVER:	You gotta touch me every time you talk to me?
VOICEOVER/SUPER:	netflix.com. Rent all the DVDs as you want for 20 bucks a month. Limit three DVDs at a time.

TELEVISION MERIT

MERIT AWARD
Consumer Television :30
Single

ART DIRECTOR
Stephen Pearson

WRITER
Tom Miller

AGENCY PRODUCER
J. D. Williams

PRODUCTION COMPANY
hungry man

DIRECTOR
Bryan Buckley

CLIENT
E*TRADE

AGENCY
Goodby Silverstein & Partners/San Francisco

010518A

MERIT AWARD
Consumer Television :30
Single

ART DIRECTOR
Greg Bell

WRITER
Paul Venables

AGENCY PRODUCER
Cindy Fluitt

PRODUCTION COMPANY
Headquarters

DIRECTOR
Joe Public

CLIENT
Netflix.com

AGENCY
Goodby Silverstein & Partners/San Francisco

010519A

TELEVISION MERIT

MERIT AWARD
Consumer Television :30
Single

ART DIRECTOR
Greg Bell

WRITER
Paul Venables

AGENCY PRODUCER
Khrisana Edwards

PRODUCTION COMPANY
Stiefel & Co.

DIRECTOR
Noam Murro

CLIENT
SBC Communications
Pacific Bell

AGENCY
Goodby Silverstein &
Partners/San Francisco

010520A

MERIT AWARD
Consumer Television :30
Single

ART DIRECTOR
Sean Ehringer

WRITER
Matt Elhardt

AGENCY PRODUCER
Adrienne Cummins

PRODUCTION COMPANY
@radical.media

DIRECTOR
Errol Morris

CLIENT
Adidas

AGENCY
Leagas Delaney/
San Francisco

010521A

VOICEOVER: Warden Whitman isn't worried about his bills. Because he's just combined his phone and high-speed Internet with Pacific Bell and now saves money. This allows the warden to worry about other things.

WARDEN (holding a pirate's sword): You know...I don't think we're going to allow you guys to make these letter openers anymore.

INMATES: Oh, man.

INMATE 1: This is unbelievable!

SUPER: Pacific Bell Simple Solutions.

VOICEOVER: Introducing Simple Solutions. Combine stuff, save money.

SUPER: Home phone + DSL. Save 44%.

BRUCE (holding wire cutters): And I'm not so sure about these toenail clippers either.

SFX: Logo.

(A boxer wearing Adidas shorts is getting a "Medicine Ball" heaved at his stomach by his trainer. We see the determination on the boxer's face as this continues.)

SUPER: Long Live Sport. Adidas.

(A weightlifter chalks his hands in preparation to lift. He bends and lifts the weights over his head. Once over his head he drops the weights and shouts in triumph.)

SUPER: Long Live Sport. Adidas.

(A couple is having sex. The man lies back, looking pleased with himself. The woman pulls on a gown and gets out of bed. In the kitchen, something is cooking in the microwave. As the digital display reaches two minutes, the woman opens the door and takes out a steaming bowl of Heinz Tomato Soup.)

SUPER: Heinz Microwaveable Soups. Ready in two minutes.

TELEVISION MERIT

MERIT AWARD
Consumer Television :30
Single

ART DIRECTOR
Sean Ehringer

WRITER
Matt Elhardt

AGENCY PRODUCER
Adrienne Cummins

PRODUCTION COMPANY
@radical.media

DIRECTOR
Errol Morris

CLIENT
Adidas

AGENCY
Leagas Delaney/
San Francisco

010522A

MERIT AWARD
Consumer Television :30
Single

ART DIRECTOR
Steve Jones

WRITER
Martin Loraine

AGENCY PRODUCER
Graeme Light

PRODUCTION COMPANY
Blink Productions

DIRECTOR
Dominic Murphy

CLIENT
Heinz

AGENCY
Leo Burnett/London

010523A

TELEVISION MERIT

MERIT AWARD
Consumer Television :30
Single

ART DIRECTORS
Dave Christensen
Ali Peaty

WRITERS
Lawrence Seftel
Nicky Bullard

AGENCY PRODUCERS
Thea Slevin
Suzi Wilson

PRODUCTION COMPANY
Garretts

DIRECTOR
Nicholas Barker

CLIENT
Birds Eye Walls

AGENCY
Lowe Lintas/London

010524A

MERIT AWARD
Consumer Television :30
Single

ART DIRECTOR
Vince Squibb

WRITER
Paul Silburn

AGENCY PRODUCER
Sarah Hallatt

PRODUCTION COMPANY
Outsider

DIRECTOR
Paul Gay

CLIENT
Weetabix

AGENCY
Lowe Lintas/London

010525A

SON: Dad, could you pass me the potatoes?

GRANNY: He's not your dad. We never knew who your dad was.

MOTHER VOICEOVER: There are some things you really shouldn't share and some things you definitely should. Like Carte d'or ice cream.

DAD: Good pud!

MOTHER: Come on, Mother.

GRANNY: Of course, after the wedding night, it was separate beds.

MOTHER VOICEOVER: Carte d'or.

SUPER: Don't keep it to yourself.

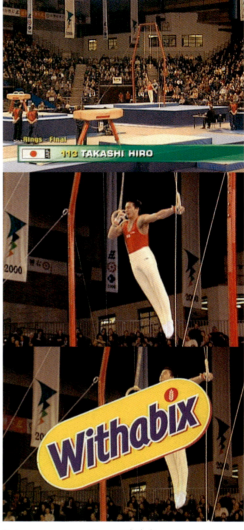

(A Japanese commentator can't hide his excitement as one of his countrymen performs breathtakingly on the rings. But even he is stunned to silence when the gymnast lets go with one hand midway through in order to scratch his nose.)

SUPER: Withabix.

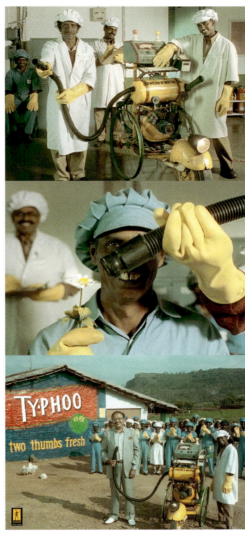

VOICEOVER:	Sleeping bag for his first sleepover: 40 dollars.
SUPER:	Sleeping bag: $40.
SUPER/VOICEOVER:	Backpack: $18.
VOICEOVER:	Sorry about that. Hey buddy, couldn't sleep, huh?
SUPER/VOICEOVER:	Walkie talkies: $25.
SUPER/VOICEOVER:	Going home: priceless.
SUPER/VOICEOVER:	There are some things money can't buy. For everything else there's MasterCard.
VOICEOVER:	Accepted for everything that makes home, home.

TOMMY:	Hello, Tommy Singh for extra fresh Typhoo tea. Tommy's fresh-o-meter will demonstrate various levels of freshness. This daisy scores well…very fresh. This chap's feet…dangerously unfresh. Normal tea is fresh…but only Typhoo tea is two thumbs fresh.
SFX:	Game show buzzer. Applause.

TELEVISION MERIT

MERIT AWARD
Consumer Television :30
Single

ART DIRECTOR
Kathy Kuhn

WRITER
Lisa Brandriff

AGENCY PRODUCER
Sally Hotchkiss

PRODUCTION COMPANY
Partizan

DIRECTOR
Dominic Murphy

CLIENT
Mastercard

AGENCY
McCann-Erickson/New York

010529A

MERIT AWARD
Consumer Television :30
Single

ART DIRECTORS
Mark Waites
Jim Thornton

WRITERS
Jim Thornton
Mark Waites
Markus Bjurman

AGENCY PRODUCER
Sarah Case

PRODUCTION COMPANY
Partizan

DIRECTOR
Traktor

CLIENT
Premier Brands

AGENCY
Mother Ltd./London

010526A

TELEVISION MERIT

MERIT AWARD
Consumer Television :30
Single

ART DIRECTORS
Mark Waites
Jim Thornton

WRITERS
Jim Thornton
Mark Waites
Markus Bjurman

AGENCY PRODUCER
Sarah Case

PRODUCTION COMPANY
Partizan

DIRECTOR
Traktor

CLIENT
Premier Brands

AGENCY
Mother Ltd./London

010527A

MERIT AWARD
Consumer Television :30
Single

ART DIRECTOR
Julian Pugsley

WRITER
Jim Garaventi

PHOTOGRAPHER
William Huber

AGENCY PRODUCER
Kim Burns

PRODUCTION COMPANY
Picture Park

DIRECTOR
Jonathan Bekemeier

CLIENT
Cozone.com

AGENCY
Mullen/Wenham

010528A

TOMMY: Hello, Tommy Singh for extra fresh Typhoo tea. Many times I'm saying the phrase, "Two thumbs fresh."

ASSISTANT: Tommy, what can this mean?

TOMMY: Well, first we pick only the freshest leaves. One thumb fresh. Then they are vacuum packed here on my plantation. Two thumbs fresh.

ASSISTANT 2: Tommy, I thought all the tea was fresh?

TOMMY: You blinking teddy boy. Tommy only sells his tea to Typhoo. Two thumbs fresh.

SFX: City noises.

(A young man rides a scooter up to a telephone pole, takes his lap top out of his bag, and duct tapes it to the pole. We see the screen as he rides away: "Have you seen my cat?")

SUPER: Need a printer? Cozone.com. Free Xerox laser printer. See site for details.

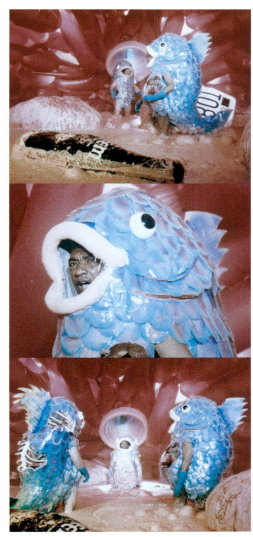

MOSQUITO 1: Buzz, buzz.

MOSQUITO 2: Buzz, buzz, buzz.

MOSQUITO 1: Hello, mosquito.

MOSQUITO 2: Hello, mosquito.

MOSQUITO 1: Have you heard about the website called Discovery.com?

MOSQUITO 2: No.

MOSQUITO 1: They have a very useful travel section.

MOSQUITO 2: I love to travel.

MOSQUITO 1: They can help you research and book your trip, and get local health warnings.

MOSQUITO 2: How interesting.

(A pink hand from above squishes mosquito 2.)

MOSQUITO 1: Buzz, buzz, buzz.

SUPER: Discovery.com. Discover something new every day.

MAN 1: Hello, fellow partially eaten fish.

MAN 2: Hello there.

MAN 1: Have you heard about the website called Discovery.com?

MAN 2: Why, yes. It has interesting facts about the world we live in and lots of practical information on stuff like health, traveling and pets.

MAN 1: Wow.

(A just-eaten fish comes splashing into the shark's stomach.)

MAN 3: They even have the news and weather.

SUPER: Discovery.com. Discover something new every day.

TELEVISION MERIT

MERIT AWARD
Consumer Television :30
Single

ART DIRECTORS
Roger Camp
Mike McCommon

WRITERS
Mike McCommon
Roger Camp

AGENCY PRODUCER
Kelly Green

PRODUCTION COMPANY
Partizan Films

DIRECTOR
Traktor

CLIENT
Discovery.com

AGENCY
Publicis & Hal Riney/
San Francisco

010530A

MERIT AWARD
Consumer Television :30
Single

ART DIRECTORS
Roger Camp
Mike McCommon

WRITERS
Mike McCommon
Roger Camp

AGENCY PRODUCER
Kelly Green

PRODUCTION COMPANY
Partizan Films

DIRECTOR
Traktor

CLIENT
Discovery.com

AGENCY
Publicis & Hal Riney/
San Francisco

010531A

TELEVISION MERIT

MERIT AWARD
Consumer Television :30
Single

ART DIRECTOR
Mike Mazza

WRITERS
Mike Mazza
Matt Ashworth

AGENCY PRODUCER
Kris Roberts

PRODUCTION COMPANY
Stiefel & Co.

DIRECTOR
Noam Murro

CLIENT
Webvan.com

AGENCY
Publicis & Hal Riney/
San Francisco

010532A

MERIT AWARD
Consumer Television :30
Single

ART DIRECTORS
Jeff Labbe
Jon Soto

WRITER
Stephanie Crippen

AGENCY PRODUCERS
Jennifer Golub
Jennifer Wallrapp

DIRECTOR
Traktor

CLIENT
Levi Strauss

AGENCY
TBWA/Chiat/Day/
San Francisco

010535A

(In a grocery store, people fondle, squeeze and smell a pile of nectarines. A bunch of them fall on the floor. A grocery clerk puts them back on the pile.)

ANNOUNCER: Same groceries...no store. Webvan. You may never go to the grocery store again.

SUPER: Webvan.

SFX: Noise of a man's cords rubbing together as he walks—a voop, voop sound. A badger's grunts, which is similar to the cords noise. (The badger pursues the man.) The noise of the cords and the badger's grunts as a pursuit quickens.

SUPER/VOICEOVER: Levi's Cords. Levi's, make them your own. Levi.com.

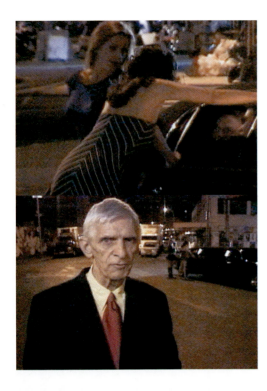

HOOKER:	So you guys want a date or what?
ADVERTISING EXECUTIVE:	Oh, we do. We're really lonely.
PITCHMAN:	Sure, this transaction looks innocent enough. But the truth is, these advertising executives plan to bill their client for these young ladies' services. But TDA is different. At TDA Advertising and Design, we never bill our prostitutes to your account.
SUPER:	TDA logo and phone number.
PITCHMAN:	TDA Advertising and Design…Where the client is never billed for prostitutes.

SUPER: Do not drink gasoline. Safety First. Winter X Games. February 2-6, Mount Snow, VT. ESPN.

TELEVISION MERIT

MERIT AWARD
Consumer Television :30
Single

ART DIRECTORS
Eric Liebhauser
Jonathan Schoenberg

WRITERS
Jonathan Schoenberg
Eric Liebhauser

AGENCY PRODUCER
Kathryn Kaufman

PRODUCTION COMPANY
Washington Square Films

DIRECTOR
Pete Sillen

CLIENT
TDA Advertising & Design

AGENCY
TDA Advertising & Design/Boulder

010536A

MERIT AWARD
Consumer Television :30
Single

ART DIRECTOR
Kim Schoen

WRITER
Kevin Proudfoot

ILLUSTRATOR
Geoff McFetridge

AGENCY PRODUCER
Tony Stearns

PRODUCTION COMPANY
Champion Graphics

DIRECTOR
Geoff McFetridge

CLIENT
ESPN

AGENCY
Wieden + Kennedy/
New York

010537A

TELEVISION MERIT

MERIT AWARD
Consumer Television :30
Single

ART DIRECTOR
Matt Stein

WRITER
Kevin Proudfoot

AGENCY PRODUCER
Gary Krieg

PRODUCTION COMPANY
hungry man

DIRECTOR
David Levin

CLIENT
ESPN

AGENCY
Wieden + Kennedy/
New York

010538A

MERIT AWARD
Consumer Television :30
Single

ART DIRECTOR
Kim Schoen

WRITER
Ilicia Winokur

AGENCY PRODUCER
Brian Cooper

PRODUCTION COMPANY
hungry man

DIRECTOR
Marc Klasfeld

CLIENT
ESPN

AGENCY
Wieden + Kennedy/
New York

010539A

STUART SCOTT: As an anchor you always want that complete show.

KENNY MAYNE (stumbling over words): And coming up, a Did You Know about sports...

PRODUCER: So, Kenny, how are you feeling?

KENNY MAYNE: I'm fine, never better. I'm great, I can go. Just let me finish.

PRODUCER: You'll get 'em next show.

STUART SCOTT: Sometimes you don't have your best stuff—and they have to bring in a closer. We usually handle it like professionals.

(Kenny storms off the set and kicks something on his way out.)

STUART SCOTT: It's all part of the game.

PRODUCER: You're on in 3, 2, 1...

TREVOR HOFFMAN: Welcome back to Sportscenter, the subject...

SUPER: This is Sportscenter. ESPN.

DAN: I'm Dan Patrick here in the ESPN Radio chopper. You know, radio marketing is all about promotions. That's why we're blanketing the country with these ESPN Radio bats. We've got live sporting events. We've got call-in shows. You can log onto espnradio.com to find out more about stations in your area or to listen online. So tune in. And if you happen to get lucky and catch one of these bats, enjoy.

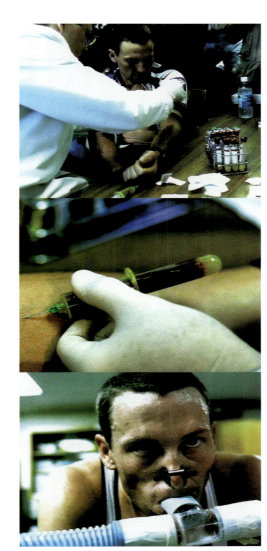

SUPER: Keep clothing away from machinery. Safety First. Winter X Games. February 2-6, Mount Snow, VT. ESPN.

LANCE VOICEOVER: This is my body and I can do whatever I want to it. I can push it and study it, tweak it, listen to it. Everybody wants to know what I am on. What am I on? I'm on my bike six hours a day. What are you on?

TELEVISION MERIT

MERIT AWARD
Consumer Television :30
Single

ART DIRECTOR
Kim Schoen

WRITER
Kevin Proudfoot

ILLUSTRATOR
Geoff McFetridge

AGENCY PRODUCER
Tony Stearns

PRODUCTION COMPANY
Champion Graphics

DIRECTOR
Geoff McFetridge

CLIENT
ESPN

AGENCY
Wieden + Kennedy/
New York

010540A

MERIT AWARD
Consumer Television :30
Single

ART DIRECTOR
James Selman

WRITER
Steve Skibba

AGENCY PRODUCER
Chris Noble

PRODUCTION COMPANY
@radical.media

DIRECTOR
Ralf Schmerberg

CLIENT
Nike

AGENCY
Wieden + Kennedy/
New York

010533A

TELEVISION MERIT

MERIT AWARD
Consumer Television :30
Single

ART DIRECTOR
Jeff Williams

WRITER
Jeff Kling

AGENCY PRODUCER
Tieneke Pavesic

PRODUCTION COMPANY
@radical.media

DIRECTOR
Errol Morris

CLIENT
Miller High Life

AGENCY
Wieden + Kennedy/Portland

010541A

MERIT AWARD
Consumer Television :30
Single

ART DIRECTOR
Jeff Williams

WRITER
Jeff Kling

AGENCY PRODUCER
Tieneke Pavesic

PRODUCTION COMPANY
@radical.media

DIRECTOR
Errol Morris

CLIENT
Miller High Life

AGENCY
Wieden + Kennedy/Portland

010542A

ANNOUNCER: Grandma's cooking for her boys tonight.

SFX: A "grunt" like someone is full.

ANNOUNCER: Good to know there's a light way to live the High Life.

SUPER: Miller High Life Light.

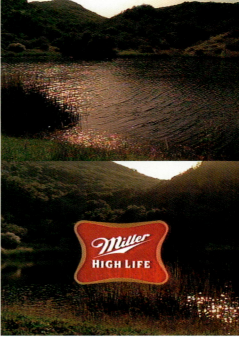

ANNOUNCER: Marvel at how many men have forgotten their calling. Used to be the prospect of some cold beer and some fishing would catch many a man on these shores packed shoulder to shoulder. When the last man turns in his Miller High Life for a "cappucinna," don't come crying if all you get is fishsticks.

SUPER: Miller High Life.

SFX: Music under throughout.

HUMAN CANNONBALL: She's stopped breathing. I think we've lost her.

RINGMASTER: Is there nothing we can do?

HUMAN CANNONBALL: I'm a human cannonball, not a doctor!

(Lance Armstrong gives the elephant CPR. The elephant's stomach rises with air.)

SUPER: Why sport? Healthy lungs. Nike Swoosh.

(As a woman runs through a neighborhood, the things that worry her most—her mother, her boss, her computer and washing machine—fall out from her back and land on the ground.)

BOSS: Don't forget about the meeting tomorrow.

MOTHER: When are you getting married?

SUPER: Just do it. Swoosh.

TELEVISION MERIT

MERIT AWARD
Consumer Television :30
Single

ART DIRECTOR
Andy Fackrell

WRITER
Kash Sree

AGENCY PRODUCER
Alicia Hamilton

PRODUCTION COMPANY
@radical.media

DIRECTOR
Dante Ariola

CLIENT
Nike

AGENCY
Wieden + Kennedy/Portland

010543A

MERIT AWARD
Consumer Television :30
Single

ART DIRECTOR
Joe Shands

WRITER
Jose Molla

AGENCY PRODUCER
Andrew Loevenguth

PRODUCTION COMPANY
Pytka and Flehner Films

DIRECTOR
Joe Pytka

CLIENT
Nike

AGENCY
Wieden + Kennedy/Portland

010544A

TELEVISION MERIT

MERIT AWARD
Consumer Television :30
Single

ART DIRECTOR
Andy Fackrell

WRITER
Simon Mainwaring

AGENCY PRODUCER
Alicia Hamilton

PRODUCTION COMPANY
Outsider

DIRECTOR
Rupert Sanders

CLIENT
Nike

AGENCY
Wieden + Kennedy/Portland

010545A

MERIT AWARD
Consumer Television :30
Campaign

ART DIRECTOR
Rob Carducci

WRITER
Richard Bullock

AGENCY PRODUCER
Catherine Abate

PRODUCTION COMPANY
MJZ

DIRECTOR
Rocky Morton

CLIENT
Fox Sports

AGENCY
Cliff Freeman and Partners/
New York

010546A

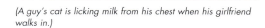

ANDRE:	Jeopardy.
PETE:	Seinfeld.
ANDRE:	Eggs.
PETE:	Butter and Jam.
ANDRE:	Jesus.
PETE:	Princess Diana.
ANDRE:	I like the coyote. I hope he gets that little…
PETE:	…Road Runner.
ANDRE:	Boxers.
PETE:	Briefs.
ANDRE:	I don't know.
PETE:	The death of my coach.
ANDRE:	Sinner.
PETE:	Saint.
ANDRE:	Backhand.
PETE:	Forehand.
ANDRE:	Wear down.
PETE:	Demolish.
ANDRE:	I don't know.

(A guy's cat is licking milk from his chest when his girlfriend walks in.)

GIRLFRIEND: Jeff? Which U.S. hockey team has won the most Stanley Cups?

SUPER: If only every question was a sports question. Sports Geniuses. The new game show premieres March 27. Fox Sports Net.

VOICEOVER: ...killing a pig is an important right of passage to manhood.

BOY: Maybe I don't even want to be a hunter! Did you ever think of that? I hate you, Dad—I hate you!

PIG: Want me to go talk to him?

ANNOUNCER: Documentaries, coming of age stories or family movies. Find them all at Hollywood Video.

CLERK: Can I help you?

WOMAN: Yeah, hi, um, do you have that band I like? I was here a few years ago. I bought their last CD. I'm just looking for their new one.

SUPER/VOICEOVER: Amazon.com changed the way people shop.

MALE CUSTOMER: I'm sorry. Where do I click on this to hear a sample?

SUPER/VOICEOVER: HP technology makes it happen.

TELEVISION MERIT

MERIT AWARD
Consumer Television :30
Campaign

ART DIRECTOR
Wayne Best

WRITER
Steve Zumwinkel

AGENCY PRODUCER
Maresa Wickham

PRODUCTION COMPANY
Tate & Partners

DIRECTOR
Baker Smith

CLIENT
Hollywood Video

AGENCY
Cliff Freeman and Partners/
New York

010547A

MERIT AWARD
Consumer Television :30
Campaign

ART DIRECTORS
Amy Nicholson
Kilpatrick Anderson

WRITER
Albert Kelly

AGENCY PRODUCER
Khrisana Edwards

PRODUCTION COMPANY
@radical.media

DIRECTOR
Frank Todaro

CLIENT
Hewlett-Packard

AGENCY
Goodby Silverstein &
Partners/San Francisco

010548A

TELEVISION MERIT

MERIT AWARD
Consumer Television :30 Campaign

ART DIRECTOR
Greg Bell

WRITER
Paul Venables

AGENCY PRODUCER
Cindy Fluitt

PRODUCTION COMPANY
Headquarters

DIRECTOR
Joe Public

CLIENT
Netflix.com

AGENCY
Goodby Silverstein & Partners/San Francisco

010549A

MERIT AWARD
Consumer Television :30 Campaign

ART DIRECTOR
Arnie Presiado

WRITER
Steve O'Brien

AGENCY PRODUCER
Heidi Hawkings

PRODUCTION COMPANY
A & R Group

DIRECTOR
David Frankham

CLIENT
ESPN

AGENCY
Ground Zero/Los Angeles

010550A

VOICEOVER: If you don't watch a lot of movies, you may never learn certain valuable things. Like what to do when an animal talks to you.

CRITTER: Hey, kids, Jimmy needs your help down by the lake!

Boy 1: It talks!

Boy 2: Squish it!

CRITTER: No, wait, Jimmy needs...

BOY 3: Let's make a hat out of it!

CRITTER: Hold on. Hold on. Everybody take a deep breath.

GIRL: Let's cook it and eat it.

VOICEOVER: But if you watch a lot of movies, you'd know.

CRITTER: Hey, kids, Jimmy needs your help down by the lake!

Boy 3: Let's go help Jimmy!

Boy 1: Thanks, prairie dog!

VOICEOVER/SUPER: netflix.com. Rent all the DVDs you want for 20 bucks a month. Limit three DVDs at a time.

SFX: Hammering. Mumbling in distance.

(A man discovers Answer and chases him.)

ANSWER: Ninety-two goals, single season. Ninety-two goals, single season. *(jumping off rooftop and running away)* Ninety-two goals, single season. Ninety-two goals, single season. Ninety-two goals, single season. Ninety-two goals, single season. Ninety-two goals, single season.

SUPER: Have you got the answer? ESPN's Two Minute Drill. The ultimate sports quiz show.

VOICEOVER: ESPN's Two Minute Drill. The ultimate sports quiz show.

(A man falls down on the ground and rolls around like an injured football player. He feigns agony, then gets up and looks around in an accusing manner.)

SUPER: Ninety minutes is not enough. eurofootball.com.

YOUNG GUY: Hello, flying doctor? It's Billy, I think grandpa's just carked it. *(pause)* What!? You can't get here for three days?

SUPER 1: Large capacity refrigerators delivered in 24 hours. Rentlo. 13 23 11.

TELEVISION MERIT

MERIT AWARD
Consumer Television :30
Campaign

ART DIRECTOR
Carl Dalin

WRITER
Johan Nilsson

AGENCY PRODUCER
Mark Baughen

PRODUCTION COMPANY
Stink

DIRECTOR
Laurence Hamburger

CLIENT
Eurofootball.com

AGENCY
Lowe Brindfors/Stockholm

010551A

MERIT AWARD
Consumer Television :30
Campaign

ART DIRECTOR
Oliver Devaris

WRITER
Oliver Devaris

AGENCY PRODUCER
Rod James

PRODUCTION COMPANY
Renegade Films

DIRECTORS
Anthony Alenka
Matthew McCaughey

CLIENT
Rentlo

AGENCY
M&C Saatchi/Sydney

010552A

TELEVISION MERIT

MERIT AWARD
Consumer Television :30 Campaign

ART DIRECTORS
Roger Camp
Mike McCommon

WRITERS
Mike McCommon
Roger Camp

AGENCY PRODUCER
Kelly Green

PRODUCTION COMPANY
Partizan Films

DIRECTOR
Traktor

CLIENT
Discovery.com

AGENCY
Publicis & Hal Riney/
San Francisco

010553A

MERIT AWARD
Consumer Television :30 Campaign

ART DIRECTOR
Tia Lustig

WRITER
Jeremy Postaer

AGENCY PRODUCER
Betsy Beale

DIRECTOR
Roman Coppola

CLIENT
Gameshow Network

AGENCY
TBWA/Chiat/Day/
San Francisco

010554A

METEOR 1:   Hello, meteor.

METEOR 2:   Hello, meteor.

METEOR 1:   Have you heard about the website called Discovery.com?

METEOR 2:   Discovery.com is my guidebook for life. I learned how to plant an herb garden, train my dog and cure my dandruff.

METEOR 1:   I learned that most meteors burn up in Earth's atmosphere…The atmosphere. Ahh!

METEOR 2:   Ahh! The atmosphere. Ahh!

SUPER: Discovery.com. Discover something new every day.

ELDERLY MAN ON HOSPITAL BED: Botulism.

CLERK AT A MARKET: Botulism.

LITTLE GIRL IN PAJAMAS WITH A COUPLE BEHIND HER ON A COUCH: Botulism.

TWO MILITARY GUYS: Botulism.

COCKTAIL WAITRESS: Botulism.

GROUP OF EMPLOYEES IN AN EMPLOYEE LOUNGE DRINKING COFFEE: Botulism.

CLERK: Botulism.

COUPLE EATING BURGERS: Botulism.

CLERK WITH ROBBER STEALING MONEY: Botulism.

DORKY GUY IN BAKERY: Botulism.

WOMAN IN A LAUNDROMAT: Botulism.

ELDERLY COUPLE IN FRONT OF THEIR TRAILOR: Botulism.

CONTESTANT ON A GAMESHOW: Salmonila.

SUPER: You Know You Know. Gameshow Network.

SUPER:	Never Ski With Scissors. Safety First. Winter X Games. February 2-6, Mount Snow, VT. ESPN.

FAN 1: C'est Pete Sampras.

FAN 2: Agassi.

FAN 3: No, Pete's my favorite player.

FAN 4: Andre.

FAN 5: Maybe Pete Sampras.

FAN 6: Andre Agassi.

FAN 7: He's lovely.

FAN 8: I think Sampras.

FAN 9: Sampras can't beat him.

FANS 10 & 11: Andre...

FAN 12: Pete.

FANS 13, 14 & 15: ANDRE!

FANS 16 & 17: PETE!

FANS 18 & 19: I don't know what I'd scream!

FAN 6: An...

FAN 20: ...dre!!

JOHN McENROE: Uh, is there a third option?

TELEVISION MERIT

MERIT AWARD
Consumer Television :30
Campaign

ART DIRECTOR
Kim Schoen

WRITER
Kevin Proudfoot

ILLUSTRATOR
Geoff McFetridge

AGENCY PRODUCER
Tony Stearns

PRODUCTION COMPANY
Champion Graphics

DIRECTOR
Geoff McFetridge

CLIENT
ESPN

AGENCY
Wieden + Kennedy/
New York

010555A

MERIT AWARD
Consumer Television :30
Campaign

ART DIRECTOR
Andy Fackrell

WRITER
Simon Mainwaring

AGENCY PRODUCER
Alicia Hamilton

PRODUCTION COMPANY
Outsider

DIRECTOR
Rupert Sanders

CLIENT
Nike

AGENCY
Wieden + Kennedy/Portland

010556A

TELEVISION MERIT

MERIT AWARD
Consumer Television :30 Campaign

ART DIRECTOR
Monica Taylor

WRITER
Jose Molla

AGENCY PRODUCER
Jennifer Smieja

PRODUCTION COMPANY
Harry Nash

DIRECTOR
Fredrik Bond

CLIENT
Nike

AGENCY
Wieden + Kennedy/Portland

010557A

MERIT AWARD
Consumer Television :30 Campaign

ART DIRECTORS
Jason Black
Mark Watson

WRITERS
Dean Saling
Michael McCullough

AGENCY PRODUCER
Craig Potter

PRODUCTION COMPANY
Ober/Lenz Films

DIRECTOR
Tony Ober

CLIENT
Azteca Mexican Restaurants

AGENCY
WONGDOODY/Seattle

010558A

(A young man climbs in a parked car and lets the brake off, so that the car slides into another in front of it. He gets out, sits on one car, and leg presses with the other.)

SUPER: Entrena Come Se Te Ocurra. *(Train Any Way You Want.)* Swoosh.

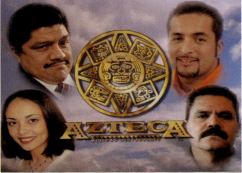
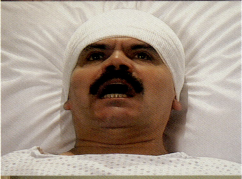
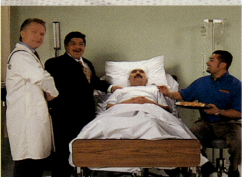

ANNOUNCER: Join the Ramos family on "Azteca!"

PEPE: Teto! Hector has been hurt in a horrible accident! He can't remember who he is or even his recipe for fajita burritos! He got...amnesia!

SFX: Heart monitor beeps slowly.

DOCTOR: I'm afraid there's little chance he'll snap out of it.

TETO: Here, Hector, *(voice breaking)* I brought you a fajita burrito.

SFX: Heart monitor starts beeping rapidly.

HECTOR: Need...more...cilantro.

PEPE: He remembered!

SFX: Heart monitor flatlines.

SUPER: Azteca Mexican Restaurants logo.

ANNOUNCER: Azteca. Obsessed with great food.

VOICE FROM TV: We the jury, find the defendant charged with three counts of murder in the first degree not guilty.

(The factory workers, munching on BiFi, cheer.)

SUPER: VW logo. The new Caravelle TDI Synchro. The Family 4x4.

TELEVISION MERIT

MERIT AWARD
Consumer Television :20 and Under: Single

ART DIRECTORS
Matt Saunby
Adam Chiappe

WRITERS
Adam Chiappe
Matt Saunby
Tom Kuntz
Mike Maguire

AGENCY PRODUCER
Julia Methold

PRODUCTION COMPANY
Propaganda

DIRECTORS
Tom Kuntz
Mike Maguire

CLIENT
Andreas Ostermayr/
UDL Foods

AGENCY
Bartle Bogle Hegarty/
London

010559A

MERIT AWARD
Consumer Television :20 and Under: Single

ART DIRECTOR
Jonathan Lang

WRITER
Wayne Lubbe

AGENCY PRODUCER
Nicola Martin

PRODUCTION COMPANY
Giant Films

DIRECTOR
Miles Goodall

CLIENT
Volkswagen South Africa

AGENCY
Ogilvy & Mather/Cape Town

010562A

TELEVISION MERIT

MERIT AWARD
Consumer Television :20 and Under: Single

ART DIRECTOR
Simon Tuplin

WRITER
Chris Taciuk

AGENCY PRODUCER
Dave Medlock

PRODUCTION COMPANY
Radke Films

DIRECTORS
Tom Kuntz
Mike Maguire

CLIENT
Ikea Germany

AGENCY
Roche Macaulay & Partners/Toronto

010563A

MERIT AWARD
Consumer Television :20 and Under: Single

ART DIRECTOR
Rick Casteel

WRITER
John Matejczyk

AGENCY PRODUCER
Lee Goldberg

PRODUCTION COMPANY
Coppos Films

DIRECTOR
Craig Gillespie

CLIENT
H & R Block

AGENCY
Young & Rubicam/Chicago

010564A

SUPER: Swedish Solutions. IKEA logo.

(A man is deciding where to hang his framed picture when a wrestler's head crashes through the wall.)

SFX: Smash!

(He hangs the picture over the hole that was made.)

SUPER: $45

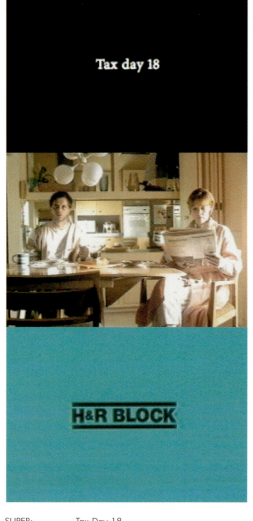

SUPER: Tax Day 18.

DAD: I'm sorry, what'd you say?

MOM: You're scaring me.

SUPER: Get help. 1-800-HRBLOCK. H&R Block. Available at most larger Sears Stores.

SUPER:	Irritating eyes? Fast relief from hay fever eyes.

SUPER:	Brett Hull's day with the Stanley Cup.
WOMAN:	So you're locked out of your car. Is that the Stanley Cup?
BRETT HULL:	Yeah, yeah.
WOMAN:	Oh, man.
SUPER:	Who will win it this year? What will they do with it? The Stanley Cup playoffs on ESPN.

TELEVISION MERIT

MERIT AWARD
Consumer Television :20 and Under: Campaign

ART DIRECTOR
Stuart Mills

WRITER
Rupert Jordan

AGENCY PRODUCER
Jackie Tyson

PRODUCTION COMPANY
Winkle Films

DIRECTORS
David Knight
Rupert Jordan
Stuart Mills

CLIENT
Johnson & Johnson

AGENCY
Saatchi & Saatchi/London

010565A

MERIT AWARD
Consumer Television :20 and Under: Campaign

ART DIRECTOR
Kim Schoen

WRITER
Mike Byrne

AGENCY PRODUCER
Gary Krieg

PRODUCTION COMPANY
RSA

DIRECTOR
Jake Scott

CLIENT
ESPN

AGENCY
Wieden + Kennedy/New York

010566A

TELEVISION MERIT

MERIT AWARD
Consumer Television :20 and Under: Campaign

ART DIRECTOR
Monica Taylor

WRITER
Dylan Lee

AGENCY PRODUCER
Jennifer Smieja

PRODUCTION COMPANY
Oil Factory

DIRECTOR
Richard Kenworthy

CLIENT
Nike

AGENCY
Wieden + Kennedy/Portland

010567A

MERIT AWARD
Consumer Television: Varying Lengths Campaign

ART DIRECTOR
Richard Flintham

WRITER
Andy McLeod

AGENCY PRODUCER
Kirsty Burns

PRODUCTION COMPANY
Harry Nash

DIRECTOR
Fredrik Bond

CLIENT
Skoda UK

AGENCY
Fallon/London

010569A

SFX: Music. Music stops. Unintelligible yelling.

(The dancing panda blows up to fill the screen, his head disjoints and bubbles come from his mouth. Then panda suddenly returns to normal size and continues happy dancing.)

SFX: Music resumes.

VOICEOVER: Rabid Panda. Presto!

OFFICIAL: Wo wo wo, oi oi oi! What do you think you're doing, eh? Who d'you think you are, the Silly Brothers? That car does not go on this stand. Oh, yeah, they're gonna be dead chuffed when they see their car on the Skoda stand, aren't they?

(The men loading the Fabia then carry on with what they were doing.)

SUPER: The new Fabia. It's a Skoda. Honest.

(A boy is staring at the dishwasher. When it stops, he opens it and pulls out a plastic bag. There is a video camera inside. He rewinds the recorder and watches footage from inside the dishwasher.)

SFX: Music under.
SUPER: 0:30:06 Play. 1:16 PM. JUN. 1, 2000
SUPER: Stay curious PBS logo.

JEFF: Yes, it does give quite a sensual, quite a very, very, very heady pleasant atmosphere in the hutch and creates quite an interesting scenario.

MIKE: For you and what, uh, your wife? Oh, sorry, wives, Jeff?

JEFF: Yeah.

DEBBIE: And there's a number along the bottom there to get your catalogue and order your bedding—and they will deliver it direct to your door.

JEFF: Yes, and I say it's no problem. It's very convenient. You literally just—the packet comes straight open—and it's gently placed into the hutch and used as convenient, luxurious bedding.

DEBBIE: So you too can smell as irresistible as Jeff does.

JEFF: Thank you. You smell very good yourself.

DEBBIE: Thank you.

JEFF: What is that smell?

DEBBIE: Oh, it's just a…

MIKE (angry): It's my scent, mate, all right? She smells of me.

JEFF: Very good. You obviously have a very feminine smell.

TELEVISION MERIT

MERIT AWARD
Consumer Television: Varying Lengths Campaign

ART DIRECTOR
Chris Lange

WRITER
Michael Hart

AGENCY PRODUCER
Damian Stevens

PRODUCTION COMPANY
@radical.media

DIRECTOR
Errol Morris

CLIENT
PBS

AGENCY
Fallon/Minneapolis

010568A

MERIT AWARD
Consumer Television: Varying Lengths Campaign

ART DIRECTOR
Brian Connolly

WRITER
Paul Domenet

AGENCY PRODUCER
Tess Woodward

PRODUCTION COMPANY
Stark Films

DIRECTOR
Steve Reeves

CLIENT
Pets Pyjamas

AGENCY
Saatchi & Saatchi/London

010571A

TELEVISION MERIT

MERIT AWARD
Consumer Television: Varying Lengths Campaign

ART DIRECTOR
Tom Burnay

WRITER
Stef Jones

AGENCY PRODUCER
James Letham

PRODUCTION COMPANY
James Garrett & Partners

DIRECTOR
Nicholas Barker

CLIENT
Reckitt Benckiser

AGENCY
WCRS/London

010572A

MERIT AWARD
Consumer Television: Under $50,000 Budget: Single

ART DIRECTORS
Mercedes Tiagonce
Sebastian Garin

WRITER
Guillermo Castañeda

AGENCY PRODUCER
Carlos Volpe

PRODUCTION COMPANY
Andon Films

DIRECTOR
Ruben Andon

CLIENT
Mercado

AGENCY
CraveroLanis EURO RSCG/Buenos Aires

010573A

MAN: What!

WOMAN VOICEOVER: Quick, the Vanish ad's on.

MAN: What?

WOMAN VOICEOVER: It's the Vanish Tablet ad.

(The man sprints to the TV. Moments later he emerges, having missed it again.)

WOMAN VOICEOVER: Sorry, luv.

MAN WITH GLASSES: Crossing?

BLIND MAN: Yes.

(As one helps the other cross the street, we realize the men are actually both blind.)

SUPER: Even worse than not being informed is to believe that you are. Mercado Business Magazine.

SALESMAN: So, this is the lightest wheelchair in its category. As you can see, it has a very small wheelbase, thus giving you very, very sharp turns. Jump in. Give it a try. And also, being titanium, you get a lifetime warranty on the frame...So, when is this big party of yours happening?

GUY: Tomorrow. Probably get totally hammered... drive home.

SUPER: If you're going to drink and drive, plan ahead. Molson logo. Don't drink and drive.

MAN FROM WINDOW 1: Twenty pounds.

FIREMAN WITH BULLHORN: Twenty pounds on my left.

WOMAN FROM WINDOW 2: Thirty pounds!

FIREMAN: Thirty on my right.

MAN FROM WINDOW 3: Fifty pounds!

FIREMAN: Fifty!

WOMAN FROM WINDOW 4: Seventy!

MAN FROM WINDOW 5: Ninety!

WOMAN FROM WINDOW 6: Two hundred pounds!

FIREMAN: Two hundred pounds up there! Anyone else? Going, going, gone!

(The woman climbs out of the window and jumps.)

MAN FROM WINDOW 7: Two hundred and ten!

(The firemen move to catch the higher bidder. We hear the thud of the woman from window 6 landing.)

SUPER: Everything can be bought, it's just a question of price. Aucland.com. Auctions on line.

TELEVISION MERIT

MERIT AWARD
Consumer Television: Under $50,000 Budget: Single

ART DIRECTOR
Paul Lavoie

WRITER
Zak Mroueh

AGENCY PRODUCER
Louise Blouin

PRODUCTION COMPANY
Avion

DIRECTORS
Zak Mroueh
Paul Lavoie

CLIENT
Molson Canada

AGENCY
TAXI/Toronto

010574A

MERIT AWARD
Non-Broadcast Cinema: Single

ART DIRECTORS
Fred Raillard
Farid Mokart

WRITERS
Fred Raillard
Farid Mokart

AGENCY PRODUCERS
Pierre Marcus
Erinn Lotthe

PRODUCTION COMPANY
Quad

DIRECTOR
Remy Belvaux

CLIENT
Aucland

AGENCY
CLM/BBDO/
Issy Les Moulineaux

010575A

TELEVISION MERIT

MERIT AWARD
Non-Broadcast Out-of-Home: Single

ART DIRECTOR
Niko Courtelis

WRITER
Doug James

AGENCY PRODUCER
Steven Ford

PRODUCTION COMPANY
Tate & Partners

DIRECTOR
Baker Smith

CLIENT
Heineken

AGENCY
Lowe Lintas & Partners/New York

010576A

MERIT AWARD
Foreign Language Television: Single

ART DIRECTOR
Pachaya Rungrueng

WRITER
Suthisak Sucharittanonta

AGENCY PRODUCER
Naree-sara Ajchariyakul

PRODUCTION COMPANY
Matching Studio

DIRECTOR
Suthon Petchsuwan

CLIENT
United Winery and Distillery

AGENCY
BBDO/Bangkok

010577A

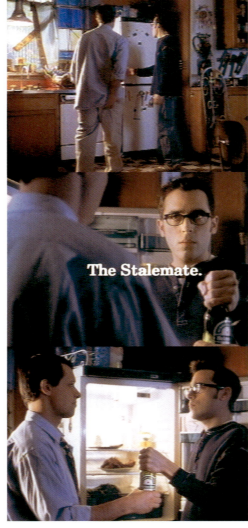

SFX: "The Good, The Bad & The Ugly."
SUPER: The Stalemate.

(Two guys both reach up for a Heineken in the fridge. They both hold the beer in front of open fridge. The Stalemate lasts for days.)

SUPER: It has to be Heineken.

DRUNK HUSBAND: Told you many times don't wait up. You know I'm always late. What's this? *(talking to an ornate jug, which he thinks is his wife)* You've got a dragon tattoo, sick. Forget it...Hey...Who put this huge jar here? C'mon give me a hand.

SFX: Man being punched by wife.
VOICEOVER: Sorry, this has got nothing to do with us.
SUPER: Black Thai, good Thai whisky.

(A line of people dance the conga through the streets. All but one of them get on a bus. The person who remains tries to joke with a man in front of him in the bus queue—to no avail.)

SUPER: Itineris—There are times when we'd like to spend one more hour with the people we love.

(A woman stops in front of a closed storefront and takes a coin and a tube of adhesive from her purse. She glues the coin to the sidewalk in front of the storefront. We realize as she unlocks the door and windows that the store is her own.)

SUPER: Loctite. The most effective instant adhesive.

TELEVISION MERIT

MERIT AWARD
Foreign Language Television: Single

ART DIRECTOR
Vincent Behaeghel

WRITER
Bernard Naville

AGENCY PRODUCERS
Pierre Marcus
France Monnet

PRODUCTION COMPANY
Quad

DIRECTOR
Remy Belvaux

CLIENT
France Telecom Itineris

AGENCY
CLM/BBDO/
Issy Les Moulineaux

010578A

MERIT AWARD
Foreign Language Television: Single

ART DIRECTOR
Julian Montesano

WRITER
Martin Jalfen

AGENCY PRODUCER
Maximiliano Pocino

PRODUCTION COMPANY
Antidoto Films

DIRECTORS
Julian Montesano
Carolina Riveros

CLIENT
Henkel-Loctite

AGENCY
DDB Argentina/
Buenos Aires

010579A

487

TELEVISION MERIT

MERIT AWARD
Foreign Language Television: Single

ART DIRECTORS
Blanca Maldonado
Mauricio Davila
Alejandro Vazquez

WRITERS
Raul Cardos
Gustavo Duenas
Yosu Aranguena

AGENCY PRODUCER
Sara Martinez

PRODUCTION COMPANY
Z Films

DIRECTOR
J. Aguilera

CLIENT
Volkswagen of Mexico

AGENCY
Gibert DDB/Mexico City

010580A

SFX: Refrigerator door closes. Blender at a low speed. Blender at medium speed.

(The guy is reminded of something.)

SFX: Blender at high speed. Blender at very high speed.

SUPER: You never stop driving your Golf. Volkswagen.

COLLEGE

COLLEGE MERIT

MERIT AWARD
College Competition

ART DIRECTOR
Rudi Anggono

WRITER
Ariel Lustig

COLLEGE
The Academy of Art College/San Francisco

010586A

ASSIGNMENT:
To promote track and field as a spectator sport.

MERIT AWARD
College Competition

ART DIRECTORS
Gail Randall
Christie Cruz

WRITERS
Christie Cruz
Gail Randall

COLLEGE
The Book Shop/Culver City

010587A

COLLEGE MERIT

MERIT AWARD
College Competition

ART DIRECTORS
Chuck Matzker
Kelly Smith

WRITER
Jon Yasgur

COLLEGE
Brainco/Minneapolis

010588A

MERIT AWARD
College Competition

ART DIRECTOR
John Tso

WRITER
John Tso

COLLEGE
California State University/
Long Beach

010589A

COLLEGE MERIT

MERIT AWARD
College Competition

ART DIRECTORS
David Johnson
Philip Ramage

WRITERS
David Johnson
Philip Ramage

COLLEGE
Central Saint Martins
College of Art and Design/
London

010590A

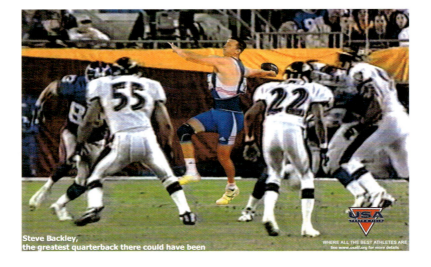

MERIT AWARD
College Competition

ART DIRECTOR
Tom Becka

WRITER
Tom Becka

COLLEGE
Columbus College of Art
and Design/Columbus

010591A

 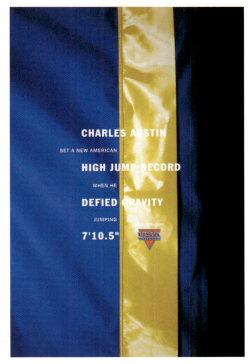

A seven foot, spiral strip of paper can be pulled off the image on the left, revealing the image on the right.

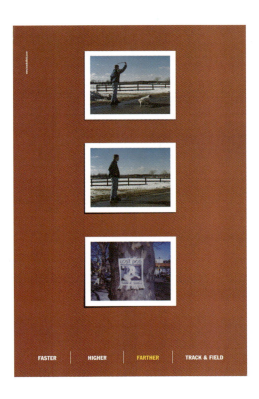 

MERIT AWARD
College Competition

ART DIRECTOR
Andrew Novak

WRITER
Andrew Novak

COLLEGE
The Creative Circus/Atlanta

010592A

MERIT AWARD
College Competition

ART DIRECTOR
Diogo Mello

WRITER
Chris La Rocque

COLLEGE
Miami Ad School/New York

010593A

COLLEGE MERIT

MERIT AWARD
College Competition

ART DIRECTOR
Phil Mimaki

WRITER
Ricardo Gandolfi

COLLEGE
Portfolio Center/Atlanta

010594A

MERIT AWARD
College Competition

ART DIRECTOR
Mike Hanley

WRITER
Matt Covington

COLLEGE
Portfolio Center/Atlanta

010595A

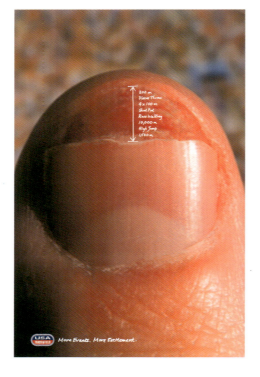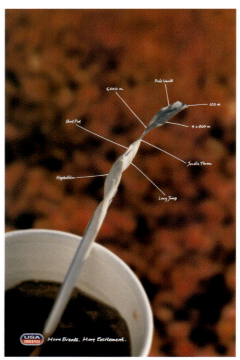

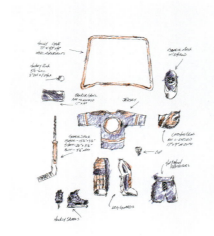

— Labor disputes you will never read about —

TRACK STRIKE CONTINUES. SCABS STRUGGLE THROUGH THE OLYMPICS.

The purest form of sport.

www.usatf.org

— Demands we will never make —

BUILD US A NEW STADIUM OR WE'LL GO RUN FOR THE RUSSIANS.

The purest form of sport.

www.usatf.org

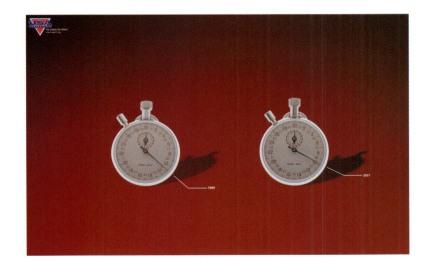

COLLEGE MERIT

MERIT AWARD
College Competition

ART DIRECTOR
Anthony Lane

WRITER
Miguel Fernandez

COLLEGE
Portfolio Center/Atlanta

010596A

MERIT AWARD
College Competition

ART DIRECTOR
Mike Hanley

WRITER
Matt Covington

COLLEGE
Portfolio Center/Atlanta

010597A

COLLEGE MERIT

MERIT AWARD
College Competition

ART DIRECTOR
Greg Wilson

WRITER
Nicole Rayburn

COLLEGE
Portfolio Center/Atlanta

010598A

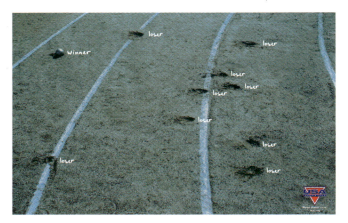

MERIT AWARD
College Competition

ART DIRECTOR
Allison Gill

WRITER
Jason Hoff

PHOTOGRAPHER
Jared Anderson

COLLEGE
University of Colorado/Boulder

010599A

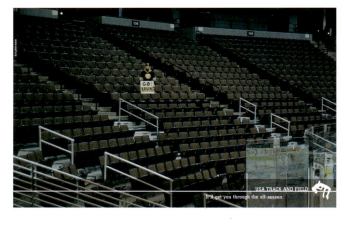

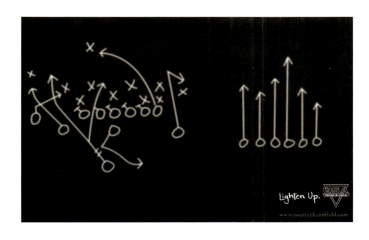

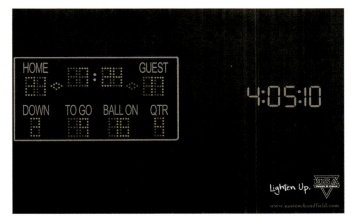

COLLEGE MERIT

MERIT AWARD
College Competition

ART DIRECTORS
Nikki DeFeo
Shelly Rangsiyakul

WRITERS
Nikki DeFeo
Shelly Rangsiyakul

COLLEGE
University of Delaware/
Newark

010600A

MERIT AWARD
College Competition

ART DIRECTOR
Charla Olmsted

WRITER
Dalel Serda

COLLEGE
University of Texas/
Texas Creative/Austin

010601A

COLLEGE MERIT

MERIT AWARD
College Competition

ART DIRECTOR
Michael Ashley

WRITER
Dinesh Kapoor

COLLEGE
VCU Adcenter/Richmond

010602A

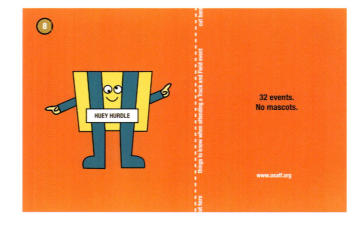

MERIT AWARD
College Competition

ART DIRECTOR
Eider Suso

WRITER
Karen Walker

COLLEGE
VCU Adcenter/Richmond

010603A

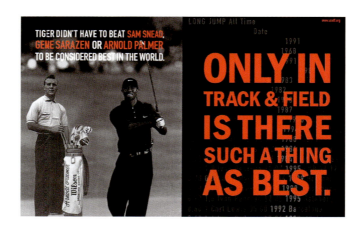

COLLEGE MERIT

MERIT AWARD
College Competition

ART DIRECTOR
Tracey Morgan

WRITER
Pat McKay

COLLEGE
VCU Adcenter/Richmond

010604A

MERIT AWARD
College Competition

ART DIRECTOR
Jason Ward

WRITERS
Dave Perks
Jason Smith

COLLEGE
VCU Adcenter/Richmond

010605A

501

COLLEGE MERIT

MERIT AWARD
College Competition

ART DIRECTORS
Rachel Scott Everett
Jason Smith

COLLEGE
VCU Adcenter/Richmond

010606A

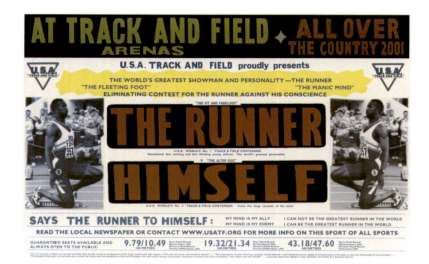

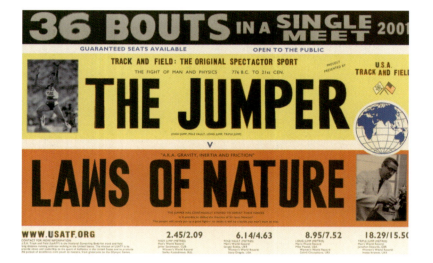

MERIT AWARD
College Competition

ART DIRECTOR
Ping Li

WRITER
Jynelle Herbert

COLLEGE
VCU Adcenter/Richmond

010607A

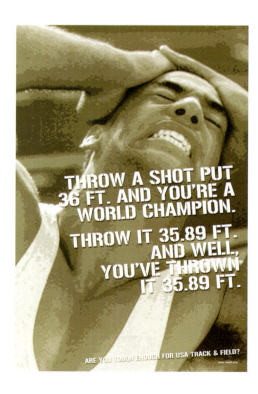

This is an ad placement. A series of still images would be placed in succession along the side of a subway train. From the vantage point of the stationary spectator, the motion of the train would cause the images to animate in a "flipbook" effect.

COLLEGE MERIT

MERIT AWARD
College Competition

ART DIRECTORS
Jon Bunning
Greg Desmond

WRITERS
Nicole Santucci
David Fredette

COLLEGE
VCU Adcenter/Richmond

010608A

MERIT AWARD
College Competition

ART DIRECTOR
Greg Desmond

WRITER
David Fredette

COLLEGE
VCU Adcenter/Richmond

010609A

COLLEGE MERIT

MERIT AWARD
College Competition

ART DIRECTOR
Michael Ashley

WRITER
Dinesh Kapoor

COLLEGE
VCU Adcenter/Richmond

010610A

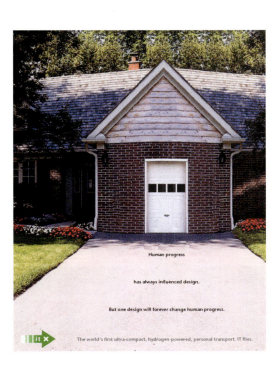

YOUNG CREATIVE
PROFESSIONAL
COMPETITION
Print

TEAM
Chemical X

MEMBERS
Amy Butterworth
Rahul Bhatia

TEAM SPONSOR
Pratt Institute/New York

ASSIGNMENT:
To create a campaign for "Ginger," a revolutionary mode of transportaion.

YOUNG CREATIVE
PROFESSIONAL
COMPETITION
Print

TEAM
Frogs

MEMBERS
Mike Brooks
Nick Gebhardt

TEAM SPONSOR
The Creative Circus/Atlanta

YOUNG CREATIVE PROFESSIONAL COMPETITION
New Media

TEAM
Riker's Island

MEMBERS
Jason S. Ambrose
Gray Luckett
Kris Wixom

TEAM SPONSOR
University of Texas/
Texas Creative/Austin

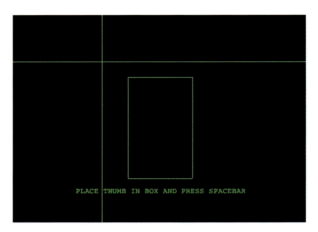

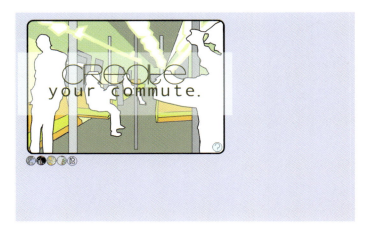

YOUNG CREATIVE
PROFESSIONAL
COMPETITION
New Media

TEAM
Akarei

MEMBERS
Adam Dachis
Jarrod Riddle

TEAM SPONSOR
Brainco/Minneapolis

YOUNG CREATIVE
PROFESSIONAL
COMPETITION
Print Honorable Mention

TEAM
Two Sensitive Mans

MEMBERS
Ryan O'Hara Theisen
Jon Yasgur

TEAM SPONSOR
Brainco/Minneapolis

YOUNG CREATIVE
PROFESSIONAL
COMPETITION
Print Honorable Mention

TEAM
Vinny's Angels

MEMBERS
Soo Mean Chang
Molly Sheahan

TEAM SPONSOR
School of Visual Arts/
New York

INDEX

AGENCY

180/Amsterdam   60, 298, 440
*, S, C, P, F/Barcelona   34
Abbott Mead Vickers.BBDO/London
   21, 47, 128, 232, 250, 374, 385, 440
Adworks/Washington   45
Age./São Paulo   299
Almap/BBDO Comunicacoes/
   São Paulo   149, 159, 160, 161
Ames Design/Seattle   79
Ammirati Puris/Toronto   422, 433
AND/Salt Lake City   299, 300
Archrival/Lincoln   301
Arian Lowe & Travis/Chicago   128
ARNOLD Worldwide/Boston   8, 9, 12,
   141, 161, 162, 163, 164, 189, 190, 225,
   251, 261, 301, 302, 386, 415
ARNOLD Worldwide, Crispin Porter
   Bogusky/Boston   374, 414
Axiom Creative Group/Charlotte   303
Barnhart/CMI/Denver   284
Bartle Bogle Hegarty/London   375,
   387, 441, 451, 452, 479
Bates/Hong Kong   226
Bayless Cronin/Atlanta   285
BBDO/Bangkok   486
BBDO Denmark/Copenhagen   303
BBDO/Guerrero Ortega/
   Makati City   273
BBDO/Hong Kong   304
Beast/Hong Kong   191
Black Rocket/San Francisco
   50, 422, 434
Black Sheep/Singapore   221
BMP DDB/London   60, 165, 166, 192,
   441, 442
Borders Perrin Norrander/Portland
   36, 285, 375, 376, 388, 404
Brazen Communications/
   Singapore   305
Bryant Fulton & Shee/Vancouver
   149, 273
The Buntin Group/Nashville   306, 307
Butler Shine & Stern/Sausalito   274,
   280, 281
Cahan & Associates/San Francisco
   74, 308, 309
Carmichael Lynch/Minneapolis
   310, 311
Cartoon Network/Atlanta   311, 312
Clarity Coverdale Fury/Minneapolis
   193, 239, 404, 405
Clarke Goward/Boston   70, 150,
   154, 219
Clemenger BBDO/Wellington   377
Clemenger Harvie Edge/
   Melbourne   415

Cliff Freeman and Partners/New York
   52, 55, 56, 57, 86, 167, 194, 423, 424,
   425, 452, 453, 454, 455, 472, 473
CLM/BBDO/Issy Les Moulineaux
   485, 487
Cole and Weber/Red Cell/Portland
   226, 227
Cole and Weber/Red Cell/Seattle   377
Colenso BBDO/Auckland   24, 44,
   227, 228
Colle + McVoy/Minneapolis   42, 389,
   405, 406
Connelly Partners/Boston   312
Contract Advertising/Mumbai   239
CONTRAPUNTO/Madrid   390
Copper/Kalamazoo   426
Cramer-Krasselt/Chicago   262, 286
CraveroLanis EURO RSCG/
   Buenos Aires   484
Crispin Porter & Bogusky/Miami
   34, 48, 167, 168, 195, 196, 286, 287, 418
DDB Argentina/Buenos Aires   487
DDB/Chicago   49, 50, 426, 427
DDB/Paris   63
DDB/Seattle   129, 416
Dentsu/Tokyo   233
Dentsu Young & Rubicam/Singapore
   240, 288, 391
Design Asylum/Singapore   75, 313, 314
DeVito/Verdi/New York   41, 142, 392,
   406, 407
DGWB/Santa Ana   314
Di Zinno Thompson/Coronado   71
DM9DDB/São Paulo   393
Duffy/Minneapolis   315, 316, 317
Duffy/New York   318, 319, 320
Duncan|Channon/San Rafael   321
Dupla Design/Rio de Janeiro   321
DVC Group/Morristown   322
dweck!/New York   50
Enterprise Nexus Communications
   Private Limited/Mumbai   322
Euro RSCG McConnaughy Tatham/
   Chicago   43
Euro RSCG Wnek Gosper/
   London   197
F/Nazca Saatchi & Saatchi/São Paulo
   63, 378, 394
Fallon/London   21, 130, 169, 252,
   258, 482
Fallon/Minneapolis   26, 31, 54, 129,
   168, 198, 252, 253, 258, 263, 264, 442,
   456, 483
Fallon/New York   456
FCB/Seattle   408
Foote Cone & Belding/San Francisco
   55, 57, 457
Foote Cone & Belding/Sydney   443
Fort Franklin/Boston   323, 324

Gabriel Diericks Razidlo/
   Minneapolis   131
Gibert DDB/Mexico City   488
GMO Hill Holliday/San Francisco
   36, 378, 379, 395, 396, 435
Goodby Silverstein & Partners/
   San Francisco   16, 18, 20, 170, 171,
   172, 199, 200, 201, 202, 228, 234, 428,
   443, 444, 458, 459, 460, 473, 474
Graham Clifford Design/New York
   325, 326
Grant Scott & Hurley/Francisco   203
Grey/Copenhagen   204, 229
Grey Worldwide/London   7, 8, 11
Grey Worldwide/Melbourne   46
Ground Zero/Los Angeles   27, 35, 61,
   143, 235, 265, 419, 474
GSD&M/Austin   288, 327, 328, 416,
   429, 436
Happy Forsman & Bodenfors/
   Gothenburg   329, 331, 332, 333
HHCL & Partners/London   444
Hill Holliday Connors Cosmopulos/
   Boston   6, 275, 417
Holland Mark Advertising/Boston
   131, 379
Hornall Anderson Design Works/
   Seattle   334, 335
Huey/Paprocki/Atlanta   397
Hunt Adkins/Minneapolis   336
icecream!/Singapore   144
The Integer Group/Lakewood   275
J. Walter Thompson de Mexico/
   Mexico City   22
J. Walter Thompson/Detroit   240
J. Walter Thompson/Houston   336
J. Walter Thompson Italia/Milan
   380, 398
J. Walter Thompson/London   47, 253
JACK/Venice   35
JDA/Perth   276
The Jupiter Drawing Room (South
   Africa)/Johannesburg   5, 25, 64,
   80, 172
Kirshenbaum Bond & Partners/
   New York   173, 174, 205, 241
Kowloon Wholesale Seafood Co./
   Santa Monica   276, 436
Kruskopf Olson Advertising/
   Minneapolis   32, 151, 219, 222
Leagas Delaney/London   450
Leagas Delaney/San Francisco   9, 14,
   174, 175, 176, 177, 178, 206, 207, 208,
   460, 461
Leo Burnett/London   56, 59, 229, 242, 461
Leo Burnett/Singapore   254, 380
Lift Communications/Portland   337
Loeffler Ketchum Mountjoy/Charlotte
   289, 337

Lowe Brindfors/Stockholm   475
Lowe Lintas & Partners/Bangkok   243
Lowe Lintas & Partners/New York   486
Lowe Lintas/London   10, 209, 445, 462
M & C Saatchi/Singapore   338
M & C Saatchi/Sydney   475
Mad Dogs & Englishmen/San Francisco
   281, 282
mass/New York   339
The Martin Agency/Richmond
   132, 155, 179, 210, 294, 381, 399, 400
matthews/mark/San Diego   429
McCann-Erickson/Hamburg   451
McCann-Erickson/Madrid   39, 401
McCann-Erickson/New York   463
McClain Finlon Advertising/Denver   289
McHugh Worldwide/Edina   29, 254
McKinney & Silver/Raleigh   156
Merkley Newman Harty/New York   259
The Miller Group/Santa Monica   42
Mother Ltd./London   23, 30, 33, 76, 77,
   179, 211, 340, 445, 463, 464
Mullen/Wenham   2, 3, 7, 17, 19, 132,
   151, 212, 220, 464
Myrtle/London   266
Net#work BBDO/Benmore   213, 243
Nickelodeon Creative Resources/
   New York   341
Octagon/Singapore   236
Odiorne Wilde Narraway & Partners/
   San Francisco   277, 430
Ogilvy/London   37, 244, 245
Ogilvy & Mather Argentina/
   Buenos Aires   40, 255, 267, 382
Ogilvy & Mather/Bangalore   133, 145
Ogilvy & Mather/Cape Town   137, 246,
   247, 479
Ogilvy & Mather/Frankfurt   26, 43,
   290, 417
Ogilvy & Mather/Hong Kong   230
Ogilvy & Mather/New Delhi   147, 343
Ogilvy & Mather/New York   342
Ogilvy & Mather/Singapore   2, 4, 133,
   134, 135, 136, 137, 146, 180
Ogilvy & Mather/Toronto   181
onemanbrand.com/Singapore   33
Pagano Schenck and Kay/Boston
   159, 223
Pages/BBDO/Santo Domingo   344
Palmer Jarvis DDB Downtown/Toronto
   247, 430
Palmer Jarvis DDB/Vancouver   224,
   255, 382, 409, 414
Platinum Design/New York   345
Prins/Spiegel/Venice   446
Pronto Design/New York   345
Publicis & Hal Riney/San Francisco
   15, 181, 182, 465, 466, 476
Publicis/Singapore   346

Pullar Smith/Minneapolis   410
R & R Partners/Las Vegas   290, 347
rain/Elmhurst   291
RATTO/BBDO S.A./Buenos Aires   183
Rethink/Vancouver   52, 138, 348, 431
The Richards Group/Dallas   282
Rick Johnson & Company/
   Albuquerque   349
Roche Macaulay & Partners/Toronto
   349, 480
Ron Foth/Columbus   350
Roundel/London   350, 351
Saatchi & Saatchi New Zealand/
   Auckland   237
Saatchi & Saatchi/Cape Town   248
Saatchi & Saatchi/Hong Kong
   62, 214
Saatchi & Saatchi/London   25, 45, 53,
   249, 446, 447, 481, 483
Saatchi & Saatchi/Madrid   44, 215
Saatchi & Saatchi/Singapore   148,
   256, 268, 277, 352, 411
Saatchi & Saatchi/Torrance   138
Salles D'Arcy Publicidade/
   São Paulo   216
Sandstrom Design/Portland   81, 353, 354
Sawyer Riley Compton/Atlanta   278,
   355, 411, 412
SciFi Channel/New York   18
Slaughter Hanson/Birmingham   71, 81,
   356, 357
SSC&B Lintas/Mumbai   257
Tango Design/London   358, 359
TAXI/Toronto   360, 437, 485
TBWA Hunt Lascaris/Johannesburg
   13, 61, 139, 140, 183, 184
TBWA Hunt Lascaris/Sandton   54
TBWA/Chiat/Day/Los Angeles   6, 66,
   140, 152, 231, 238
TBWA/Chiat/Day/New York   157, 230
TBWA/Chiat/Day/San Francisco   185,
   448, 466, 476
TBWA/London   38, 139, 383, 384, 402
TDA Advertising & Design/Boulder
   283, 291, 292, 293, 467
Team One Advertising/El Segundo   361
Tequila/Johannesburg   362
Tom O'Connor Worldwide/Roswell   283
The Tracey Edwards Company/
   Manchester   363
Trollback & Company/New York   364,
   365, 366
Turner Duckworth/San Francisco   72, 78
USA Networks/Scifi Channel/
   New York   367
VH1 Off Air Creative/New York   367, 368
VITROROBERTSON/San Diego
   185, 217, 257, 269
Viva Dolan/Toronto   369

W/Brasil/São Paulo   448
WCRS/London   45, 270, 484
WestWayne/Atlanta   370
Whitney Morse/Minneapolis   432
Wieden + Kennedy/Amsterdam   73
Wieden + Kennedy/New York   67, 82,
   83, 186, 187, 218, 278, 279 370, 467,
   468, 469, 477, 481
Wieden + Kennedy/Portland   449, 470,
   471, 472, 477, 478, 482
Wonderlust Industries/New York   371
WONGDOODY/Seattle   52, 259,
   279, 432, 478
WORK/Richmond   153, 158, 280, 412
Young & Rubicam Brasil/São Paulo   272
Young & Rubicam/Buenos Aires   188, 450
Young & Rubicam/Chicago   27, 28,
   58, 59, 188, 260, 271, 293, 449, 480
Young & Rubicam/Miami   413
Young & Rubicam/New York   384, 403

AGENCY PRODUCER

Abate, Catherine   57, 453, 454, 455, 472
Adler, Jackie   60, 440
Ajchariyakul, Naree-sara   486
Anderson, Molly   430
Andrade, Daniela   63
Baldacchino, Vicky   444
Barber, Jo   61
Baughen, Mark   475
Beale, Betsy   448, 476
Bell, Zoe   445
Blouin, Louise   437, 485
Brink, Judy   442
Brown, Dan   429
Burgmann, Jacqueline   52, 431
Burns, Kim   151, 464
Burns, Kirsty   482
Carek, Susanne   435
Case, Sarah   463, 464
Chambers, Johnny   430
Clarke, Suzanne   435
Cole, Susie   46
Collister, Sue   436
Cooper, Brian   468
Cummins, Adrienne   460, 461
Curzon, Henrietta   47
Dacker, Karena   435
Davis, Mila   66
Dezen, Keith   48
Diller, Kevin   55, 56, 86
Edwards, Khrisana   460, 473
Epps, Cindy   428, 458
Eus, Nicolette   414
Farmer, Richard   419
Felder, Nick   452

Fluitt, Cindy   459, 474
Fogarty, Danae   415
Fontao, Marcelo   450
Ford, Steven   486
Forsyth, Fiona   436
Francis, Mary   47
Fuchs, Leigh   52, 423, 424, 425
Gatsky, Charlie   56
Goldberg, Lee   58, 59, 449, 480
Golub, Jennifer   466
Green, Kelly   465, 476
Grupp, Claire   57, 453, 454
Gulliman, Andy   441
Hallat, Sarah   445, 462
Hamilton, Alicia   471, 472, 477
Hawkings, Heidi   61, 474
Hotchkiss, Sally   463
Hudson, Wendy   417
Hunter, Clare   53, 446
James, Rod   475
Jenkins, Brian   45
Johnson, Jeff   416
Kaufman, Kathryn   467
Kennedy, Jenny   294
Krasting, Guntram   451
Krause, Amy   429
Krieg, Gary   468, 481
Lazarus, Susan Clark   436
LeSieur, Tanya   444
Letham, James   484
Lieberman, Frank   440
Light, Graeme   461
Loevenguth, Andrew   471
Lopez, Olga   44
Lotthe, Erinn   485
Mahney, Jon   415
Marcus, Pierre   485, 487
Martin, Nicola   479
Martinez, Sara   488
McClain, Stacy   50, 422, 434
Medlock, Dave   480
Methold, Julia   479
Miller, Melissa   456
Mislang, Sandy   45
Monnet, France   487
Murray, Hannah   434
Narine, Deb   416
Netts, Jonathan   45
Noble, Chris   449, 469
O'Reilly, William   446
Paulsen, Corinne   45
Pavesic, Tieneke   470
Persch, Corinne   63
Phox, Jim   55, 57, 457
Pillsbury, Sam   49, 50, 426, 427
Pocino, Maximiliano   487
Pompeo, Luis   450
Potter, Craig   62, 432, 478
Puckett, Ted   443, 458

Roberts, Kris   466
Rogers, Linsey   53, 446
Rolfe, David   418
Ross, Debby   443
Royle, Frances   451, 452
Sautter, Cat   429
Shufelt, Erika   50
Slevin, Thea   462
Sloan, Craig   443
Smieja, Jennifer   478, 482
Smith, Jonathan   59
Soper, Nerine   450
Spivey, Howard   60, 441, 442
Stearns, Tony   67, 467, 469, 477
Stevens, Damian   54, 456, 483
Storey, Jen   44
Sweeney, Brian   414
Tan, Christina   431
Tan, Magie   62
Tong, Alesa   44
Tyson, Jackie   481
Vernon, Ali   24
Volpe, Carlos   484
Wallrapp, Jennifer   448, 466
Wetherall, Marty   442
Whitney, Michael   432
Wickham, Maresa   473
Williams, J. D.   459
Wilson, Suzi   462
Wood, Ginny   45
Woodfine, Helena   54
Woodward, Tess   447, 483

ART DIRECTOR

Agnelli, Jarbas   448
Albright, Gary   311, 312
Alden, Aaron   284
Alves, Rui   243
Amadeo, Jim   150, 154, 219
Anderson, Jack   334, 335
Anderson, Kilpatrick   473
Anderson, Tammy   411, 412
Anggono, Rudi   492
Araujo, Sidney   378, 394
Arrowood, Scott   300
Arteaga, Borja   34
Ashley, Michael   500, 504
Ayriss, David   377
Azula, Andy   18, 20, 201, 202, 228, 234
B., Haridas   145
Back, Steve   7, 8, 11
Backhouse, Margie   362
Baldacci, Roger   168
Baran, Joe   291
Bardales, Rossana   57, 453, 454
Barrie, Bob   253, 258

Barry, Karin   13
Bateson, John   351
Becka, Tom   494
Behaeghel, Vincent   487
Belford, Paul   38, 383, 384, 402
Bell, Greg   443, 458, 459, 460, 474
Benjafield, Jana   276
Berger, Amanda   128
Best, Wayne   473
Beverley, Dave   450
Bianchi, Valdir   160, 161
Bjurman, Markus   23, 76, 179, 211, 340
Black, Jason   62, 478
Blood, Andy   237
Boccassini, Cristiana   380
Bond, Michael   25, 64
Borrell, Rodolfo   344
Braun, Greg   42, 392
Brazier, Paul   440
Brenek, Gene   328
Broadhurst, Carl   139
Brown, Amber   363
Brown, Jonathan   314
Brown, Ron   385
Brown, Shawn   143, 235
Bryant, Dan   263
Bull, Ashley Coursey   282
Bunning, Jon   503
Burnard, Alex   48, 168, 196
Burnay, Tom   484
Busk, Merete   73
Cahan, Bill   74, 308, 309
Calcao, Tony   195, 286, 287, 374
Camp, Roger   15, 175, 176, 181, 182, 206, 465, 476
Caporn, Oliver   197
Caputo, Gerard   220
Carducci, Rob   167, 194, 455, 472
Caro, Guillermo   255, 267, 382
Casteel, Rick   58, 59, 449, 480
Celentano, Javier   450
Cerveny, Lisa   335
Chee, Melvin   305
Chiappe, Adam   479
Chila, Mark   185, 217
Choo, Kenny   240
Christensen, Dave   462
Chu, Calvin   18, 367
Cinquepalmi, Luca   398
Clausen, Debra   247
Clifford, Graham   325, 326
Cohen, David   241
Cohen, Mark   285
Cohen, Michael   285
Cochran, Steve   227, 228, 281
Collins, Reed   55, 56, 86
Colliss, Mick   276
Colvin, Alan   317

Conner, Richard 229
Connolly, Brian 447, 483
Courtelis, Niko 486
Coverdale, Jac 193, 404, 405
Covitz, Phil 16, 170, 171
Cronin, Markham 168, 196
Crowe, Mike 244, 245
Cruz, Christie 492
Cullen, Steve 323, 324
Daley, Kevin 159, 223
Dalin, Carl 475
Dalin, Matt 282
Davila, Mauricio 488
Dearden, Douglas 299, 300
DeChausse, Jeff 43
Deeksha 147
DeFeo, Nikki 499
Delagorce, Nathali 364, 366
DeLana, Libby 2, 3, 132
Denberg, Josh 199
Desmond, Greg 503
Devaris, Oliver 475
Devers, Wade 161, 251, 261
DeVito, Sal 41, 392
Dewsbury, Neil 391
Dickey, Ryan 408
Diehl, Paulo 393
Dinetz, Bob 74
Doar, Tia 36, 375, 376, 388, 404
Dooley, Thomas 291, 292
Dow, Rob 46
Driggs, Steve 26, 31, 252, 264
Duckworth, Bruce 72, 78
Dufils, Cecilia 76, 179, 211
Durban, Mike 232
Dye, Dave 21, 128, 232
Edens, Michel 282
Ehringer, Sean 9, 14, 174, 175, 460, 461
Eibel, Barbara 392, 407
Ellis, Adele 163, 164, 190, 225
Elterman, Eileen 345
End, Jackie 230
English, Crystal 202
Evans, Jason 255
Everett, Rachel Scott 502
Fackrell, Andy 471, 472, 477
Fago, Joe 240
Fairbanks, Mark 244
Farrell, Sean 16, 170, 171, 444
Fauchère, Laurent 364, 365, 366
Felix, Jesus 288
Ferrer, David 273
Figone, John 259
Fink, Brian 303
Fishcakes 226, 227
Flintham, Richard 21, 169, 252, 482
Foulkes, Paul 27, 35, 61, 265
Francilia, Lisa 149, 273
Frank, Jens 26

Frey, Larry 60, 440
Fund, Jack 35
Gaikwad, Vikram 257
Gallo, Marino A. 342
Gallucci, Marc 323, 324
Gardiner, Dave 417
Garin, Sebastian 484
Garthwaite, Steve 377
Gatto, Peter 18, 367
Gaxiola, Robert 221
Gehrig, Kim 23, 445
Gerda, Randy 416
Gibson, Tom 381, 399, 400
Giglio, Mark 74
Gill, Allison 498
Gill, Slade 248
Golomb, Andrew 157
Grais, Ian 348, 382, 409, 431
Grant, Todd 458
Greenspun, Mark 45
Grewal, Sonya 262
Haak, Chris 366
Hahn, Mike 174
Hanley, Mike 496, 497
Hanson, Dean 442
Harms, Sharon 307
Harris, Cabell 153, 158, 280
Harris, Pat 419
Harrison, Glenn 358, 359
Hartmann, Lars 303
Hernandez, Lara 401
Hicks, Russel 341
Higgs, Sue 37
Hilland, Thomas 77
Hin, Tay Guan 380
Hirsch, Paul 172, 199, 200
Hobbs, Dave 249
Hofbeck, Thomas 26, 43
Hoffman, Thomas 204
Hope, Jane 360
Hopfer, Jeff 282
Howalt, Paul 153, 158, 280
Hudson, Tom 450
Hurd, Tom 379
Hussein, Saad 144
Jack, Rob 60, 441
Jacobs, Chris 69
Jacobs, Heloise 5, 64
Jacobs, Jan 54, 61
Jahara, Guilherme 216
Jayram, Mani 147
Jenner, Graeme 213
Jex, Andy 130, 258
Johnson, Amy 337
Johnson, David 494
Johnson, Jamie 340
Jones, Colin 25
Jones, Steve 461
Jorge, Carlos 390

Joyce, Mike 345
Kai 314
Kakazu, Denis 272, 413
Kamble, Raj 257
Kann, Martin 138
Kaplan, Scott 142
Keister, Paul 34, 167, 418
Khaotong, Addy 277
Kiefer, Dan 275
Kilmer-Purcell, Josh 173, 205
King, Eric 18, 20, 185, 202, 228, 234
Kinghorn, Janet 80
Kingston, Robert 349
Kittel, Andreas 329, 330, 331, 332
Kornestedt, Anders 333
Kuhn, Kathy 463
Kung, Yu 270
Kwan, Lavin 226
Labbe, Jeff 448, 466
Ladd, Brent 416
Laffy, Paul 17, 19, 220
Lane, Anthony 497
Lang, Jonathan 479
Lange, Chris 54, 456, 483
Lavoie, Paul 485
Lear, Kelley 370
Lebron, Bob 322
Lee, Christopher 75, 313, 314
Lee, Dean 224
Lee, Owen 444
Leusink, Alan 320
Li, Ping 69, 502
Liebhauser, Eric 467
Lim, Ron 55, 57, 457
Lincoln, Luciano 159
Lloyd, Melanie 141
Lockett, Matt 289
Lok, Andrew 33
Lollo, Jose Carlos 149
Loo, Martin 33
Lorente, Tomas 299
Lubensky, Dean 367, 368
Lubow, Jeff 18, 367
Luckin, Frances 139
Lustig, Tia 476
Lyons, Mike 286
Macarelli, Susanne 407
Mackersey, David 253
Malan, David 246
Maldonado, Blanca 488
Mapp, Steve 178, 208
Martinez, Andres 39
Martins, Eduardo 63
Marucci, Jerome 274
Maryon, Dean 60, 298, 440
Mason, Mark 248
Matzker, Chuck 493
May, Stacey 345
Mazza, Mike 466

McCommon, Mike 15, 181, 182, 465, 476
McConnachie, Mark 350
McGlennon, Joseph 288
McGrath, Tim 349
McGuinness, Troy 181
McQueen, Billy 24
McQueen, Simon 250
Mello, Diogo 495
Meng, Tham Khai 134, 135, 136, 146
Messeter, Rob 244, 245
Migliore, Rachel 282
Mills, Stuart 481
Milner, Duncan 140
Mimaki, Phil 496
Minchan, Amabel 215
Minisman, Andy 259
Mirabelli, Richard 29, 254
Mizgala, Mark 382, 409
Moffet, Sarah 72
Mohrbutter, Jochen 451
Mokart, Farid 485
Montesano, Julian 487
Montgomery, Bill 230
Montgomery, Liz 443
Morgan, Tracey 501
Morris, Ed 165
Mowat, Matt 36, 378, 379, 395, 396
Murray, Patrick 282
Myers, Randall 301
Myrtle 266
Nakata, Robert 73
Nathane, Betsy 361
Nations, Greg 291
Neale, Todd 366
Neibert, Dana 71
Newman, Carpender 79
Newman, Julian 301, 302
Nichols, Josh 18, 367
Nicholson, Amy 473
Nielsen, Rob 242
Norcutt, Mark 59
Nordfors, Ardy 408
Norman, Vanessa 64, 172
Novak, Andrew 495
Nynas, Tom 282
O'Brien, Jim 131
O'Donnell, Dan 6
O'Keefe, Tom 55
O'Kelly, Mariana 139
Oliver, Robert 232, 374
Olmsted, Charla 499
Olsen, Jon 353
Otremba, Liz 42, 389, 405, 406
Owerko, Lyle 371
Paino, German 255, 267
Pang, Vincent 62
Paprocki, Joe 397
Paterson, Ewan 60, 441
Pathak, Sweta 239

Pawych, Dan 247
Pearson, Stephen 459
Peaty, Ali 462
Peck, Jessica 363
Pedersen, Doug 289, 337
Peng, Koh Hwee 254
Pfiszter, Quentin 24
Pierno, Adam 275
Pinkham, Chris 70
Poulin, Chris 2, 3, 132
Powers, Marion English 71, 81, 356, 357
Pratt, Steve 189
Prayongyam, Prapaipim 2
Presiado, Arnie 474
Prins, Robert 446
Pugsley, Julian 7, 151, 464
Quah, Raymond 221
Raillard, Fred 485
Ramage, Philip 494
Ramnathkar, Bhupal 322
Rand, Jason 368
Randall, Gail 492
Rangsiyakul, Shelly 499
Rao, Maya 6, 66, 153, 231, 238
Rautenbach, George 362
Reddy, Mark 192
Redman, Helena 330, 331, 332, 333
Reid, Kevin 282
Reinhardt, Matt 57, 457
Renneker, Jeanne 81
Rich, Mary 212
Richards, Grant 203
Richardson, Dan 293
Riddle, Tom 315
Riley, Sean 179, 210
Robb, Chris 42
Roberson, Kevin 74
Robinson, Gary 444
Rodgers, Rich 283
Rosen, Jon 318
Rosenberg, Tobias 229
Rossi, Adrian 375, 387
Roth, Will 257, 269
Rotondo, Anne 336
Royer, Ted 40, 255, 267, 382
Runge, Clint! 301
Rungrueng, Pachaya 486
Russoniello, Patricia 341
Sage, Steve 129, 198
Salleh, Rashid 236
Sanches, Luiz 160, 161
Sandstrom, Steve 81, 353, 354
Saunby, Matt 451, 452, 479
Scharpf, Tom 29, 254
Scharr, Brandon 303
Schoen, Kim 67, 82, 83, 186, 187, 278, 279, 370, 467, 468, 469, 477, 481
Schoenberg, Jonathan 467
Schoenhoff, Hans-Friedrich 290

Scholes, Adam 451, 452
Schrod, Joerg 26
Schutte, Eric 392, 406
Selman, James 469
Shade, Claude 199
Shands, Joe 471
Shelford, Don 8, 9, 12, 162, 163, 164
Shelmerdine, Guy 452
Shultz, David 350
Silburn, Paul 56
Simmons, Haven 290, 347
Simon, Annette 327
Simons, Michael 443
Skinner, Jason 306
Smith, Craig 4, 133, 134, 136, 137, 180, 367
Smith, Jason 502
Smith, Kelly 493
Smith, Kevin R. 410
Smith, Paul 18, 367
Soady, Paul 276
Sorah, Cliff 381, 399
Sorensen, Mark 239
Soto, Jon 466
Soudan, Laura 40
Souter, Peter 47
Squibb, Vince 445, 462
Stechshulte, Paul 404, 405
Stein, Matt 218, 468
Stout, Shelley 285
Studzinski, Nik 53, 446
Sucharittanonta, Suthisak 2
Suso, Eider 500
Suter, Kent 36, 375, 376, 388, 404
Suvongse, Kobe 316
Szabo, David 191
Tan, Alvin 305
Tan, Jackson 305
Tan, Michael 346
Taylor, Chuck 188
Taylor, Mark 277
Taylor, Monica 478, 482
Tench, Hal 132
Teng, Vancelee 243
Tham, Grover 214
They, Patrick 417
Thoem, Kevin 278, 355, 411, 412
Thompson, Wayne 131
Thornton, Jim 463, 464
Tiagonce, Mercedes 484
Tindall, Justin 165, 166
Tinguely, Antoine 364, 366
Tinning, Andrew 237
Tokuda, Yuji 233
Toland, Christopher 177, 207
Tom, Steve 386
Tomato 266
Toro, Alyssa D'Arienzo 312
Trujillo, José 69

Tso, John 493
Tuplin, Simon 480
Turner, Chris 142
Turner, David 72, 78
Turner, Ryan 282
Turpin, Miles 138
Tutssel, Mark 59
Underwood, Jerry 280, 281
V, Sunil 343
Valle, Ney 321
Valter, Stephan 339
Vazquez, Alejandro 488
Vazquez, Maximo 183
Veleda, Demian 188
Verbrugge, Moe 6, 66, 152, 231, 238
Vervroegen, Erik 13, 140, 183, 184
Vescovo, Matt 456
Vicksten, Peter 33, 77
Vitrone, Scott 449
Viva, Frank 369
Waites, Mark 463, 464
Waldron, Ken 350
Walker, Sam 30
Wan, Daniel George 338
Wang, Conan 314
Waraksa, David 412
Ward, Jason 501
Watson, Mark 279, 478
Watson, Ralph 156
Wayner, Taras 57, 453, 454
Webb, David 81
Webb, Otis 68
Weber, Marco 43, 290
Wee, Maurice 256, 268
Welsh, Alasdair 441
Wenley, No 442
Whitney, Bill 32, 151, 219, 222
Williams, Jeff 470
Williams, Steve 10, 209
Williamson, John 129
Willig, Lew 185
Wilson, Greg 498
Withers, Mike 384, 403
Wittich, Pat 155, 294
Wong, Annie 230
Wong, Clif 301, 302
Wong, Tracy 259
Wong, Willis 304
Wood, Bradley 9, 14, 174, 175
Wood, Gavin 137
Wootton, Nick 47
Wright, Michael 179, 210
Wyville, Jon 27, 28, 188, 260, 271, 293
Yaacop, Zainal 144
Yaffe, Steve 301
Yeo, Simon 148, 411
Zanini, Sebastien 63
Zunini, Alvaro 22

CLIENT

180 298
3M 133, 145
A.T. Cross Pens 310
AAR 266
About Magazine 272
The Absolut Company 230
ACLU 41, 392, 406, 407
Acushnet/FootJoy/Titleist/Pinacle/Cobra 189
Ad Club of Greater Boston 323
Adidas 9, 14, 174, 175, 176, 177, 206, 207, 460, 461
Adidas International 60
Adidas International BV 440
Adidas Philippines 273
Adventure World 276
Advertising Club of Los Angeles 27, 35, 265
Afrodita TV 255, 267
Ajay Salvi 322
Åkes Locksmith & Security 329
Alan Beacham 248
Alliance to Save Energy 416
Allied Model Trains 138
Alzheimers Association 404, 405
Amazon.com 55, 57, 457
American Express 342
American Heritage Dictionary 17, 19, 220
American Legacy Foundation 48, 374, 414
Ameristar Casinos 435
Amibika Pillai 343
Amnistia International 390
Amnesty International 413
Andreas Ostermayr/UDL Foods 479
Andrew Lok 33
Andrew Nebel/Barnardo's 375, 387
Anheuser-Busch 49, 50, 192, 426, 427, 428, 458
Apple 140
Arjo Wiggins Fine Papers 369
Art Director's Club of Denver 283
Asia Pacific Breweries 4, 133, 134, 180
AT&T 322
Atlanta History Center 397
Auckland Regional Council 237
Aucland 485
Audi/Rawdon Glover 441
AWNY (Advertising Women of New York) 318
Azteca Mexican Restaurants 62, 478
Backbone NYC 325
Barclays 450
Bell Helmets 203
Belvedere Vodka 193

Bianco Shoes 204
The Big Issue Foundation 38, 383
Bill & Melinda Gates Foundation 377
Birds Eye Walls 462
B-Line Snowboards 284
BMW 54, 129, 168, 198, 270
BMW Iberia 34
Boeri 212
Borders Bookstore 134, 135, 136, 146
Boston Fund For The Arts (BARBER) 379
Boston Globe 131
Boston Herald 6
BP/Sanccob 246
Brazen Communications 305
Brazilian Post Service 216
Britart.com 23, 340
British Council 221
Britvic Soft Drinks-Tango 444
Brunswick Lanes 278
Bulmers America 323, 324
Burke Museum of Natural History & Culture 408
Burti Graphics 299
Business Leaders for Sensible Priorities 417
Business Pages 250
Cannondale 291, 292
Cape Talk 247
Carfax 132
Cartoon Network 311, 312
Casa França-Brazil Foundation 321
Centrepoint-Young Homelessness 45
Chapters 437
Checkered Past Records 27, 28, 260, 271, 293
Cia das Letras 159
CKF, Royal Chinet 181
COI/The Army 45, 249
Columbia Sportswear 285
Conin (Malnutrition Fighting Association) 382
Conseco 456
Consolidated Papers 74
Coronet Books 25
Costa Coffee 76
Cozone.com 7, 151, 464
Creative Club Of Atlanta 370
Crimestoppers 414
Crown Motors-Lexus 214
Cruz Roja (Spanish Red Cross) 401
Cult Films 149
Cumberland Science Museum 306
DDB, Seattle 129
Design Asylum 75, 313
Discover Card 443, 458
Discovery Asia 256, 268
Discovery.com 15, 181, 182, 465, 476
Do Asia 136, 137

Drinks.com   2, 3, 132
E*TRADE   459
Earl's Restaurants   52, 431
The Economist   21, 128, 230, 232
Editora Globo   448
Effem   160, 161
Electronic Arts   277
Electronic Data Systems   442
Embassy Suites Hotels   157
ESPN   67, 82 83, 218, 278, 279, 370, 467, 468, 469. 474, 477, 481
ESPN NFL Preseason   61
ESPN Tour de France   285
Eurofootball.com   475
Fallon   252
Fastreader   355
Fila   259
Findus   7, 8, 11
Finish Line   452
Flix Television Networks   364
Florida Department of Health   418
Foodline   50
Ford of Britain   244
Fox Sports   55, 56, 57, 86, 453, 454, 455, 472
France Telecom Itineris   487
FreeAgent.com   173, 205
Fuji Ya   32, 151, 219, 222
Full Circle   169
Fundacao SOS Mata Atlântica   378, 394
Gameshow Network   476
Gartner Group   308
Georgia Tech   411, 412
Giro Sport Design   34, 167, 195, 286, 287
Glenpak Foods   191
Gold's Gym International   35
Goodwill   70
Gordo Snowboards   426
Graphic Arts Center   353
Greater Alabama Boy Scouts Council   356
GSD&M/Idea University Press   327
GT Bicycles   168, 196
Gufic Healthcare   257
Guinness   2
Gum Joy Records   321
H & R Block   58, 59, 449, 480
Hamburger Abendblatt-Daily Hamburgian Newspaper   451
Hand-It-Back Bookstore   275
Harry Knowles   288
Harry Roser   349
Harvey Nichols   179, 211
Headmint   326
He'Brew (Shmaltz Brewery)   241
Heineken   486
Heinz   242 461
Henkel-Loctite   487
Hewlett-Packard   473

Hi Fi Corporation   61
Hill Country Ride for AIDS   328
Hollywood Video   52, 353, 423, 424, 425, 473
Hunger Free America   419
Hunt Adkins   336
iArchives   299
ICRF   374
Ikea Germany   480
ILGA (International Lesbians & Gays Association)   44
Interbrew UK   445
International   263
International Truck & Engine Corp.   315
Iowa Beef Producers   316
J Records   345
Jack in the Box   276, 436
Japan Lighting Design   233
Joe Jackson Society   286
John F. Kennedy Library Foundation   381, 399, 400
John West   56, 229
Johnson & Johnson   481
Kansas Workwear   229
Kryptonite   312
L. L. Bean   220
Labatt Breweries of Canada   247, 422, 430, 433
Land Rover North America   429
Land Transport Safety Authority   377
Landeszentrale f. Gesundheitsförderung/IBM   290
Lega Per La Lotta Contro I Tumori (Cancer League)   398
Levi Strauss   448, 466
Levi Strauss/Robert Hanson   451, 452
Lexus   361
Logo   364
Los Angeles Dance Invitational   42
Los Angeles Times   143, 235
Lotto News Plus   236
Louder Music & Sound Design   29, 254
Loyola University Health System   128
Mad Dogs & Englishmen   281, 282
Magic FM   445
MASP-São Paulo Art Museum   393
mass.com   339
Massachusetts Department of Public Health   386, 415
Mastercard   463
Mattell/Scrabble   244, 245
Mazda   346
McDonald's   59, 224
McKinsey & Company   358, 359
Médecins Sans Frontières   39
Melvin Mark Development   337
Mercado   484
Miller High Life   470

Minneapolis League of Women Voters   42, 389, 405, 406
Molson Canada   485
Monaco   227
Monster.com   53, 446
Mother Ltd.   33, 77
Museo de la Ciudad (Museum of the City)   40
The Museum of Contemporary Art   6, 66, 152, 231, 238
Mutual UFO Network Museum   289
Myownshirt.com   303
Nascar   188
National Congress of American Indians   407
National D-Day Museum   36, 378, 379, 395, 396
Nebraska Wesleyan University   301
Nestle Rowntree   253
Netflix.com   459, 474
New Hope Democrats For Al Gore   410
New York University   324
Newseum   45
Nickelodeon Creative Resources   341
Nike   5, 16, 25, 64, 73, 170, 171, 172, 186, 187, 199, 288, 443, 449, 469, 471, 472, 477, 478, 482
Nike Mexico   22
Nike Retail   226, 227
Nike SA   183
Nordstrom   317
North Carolina Songwriters Cooperative   156
North Carolina Travel & Tourism   289
Ogilvy & Mather Frankfurt   26
The Olive Room   81
Olympus Optical Co.   10, 209
Open Table   430
Orange County Ad Club   314
Oscar de la Renta   344
OurHouse.com   50, 422, 434
Palmer Jarvis DDB   255
Parke-Davis   239
PBS   54, 456, 483
Peace Council   416
Pearl Jam   79
Performer   159
Pets Pyjamas   447, 483
Peugeot UK   197
Pharmacia & Upjohn   165
Pharmacia & UpJohn/Regaine   226
Physicians for Human Rights   43
Pierside Kitchen & Bar   314
Pirelli   188, 450
Plain Clothes   71
Playland   431
PlayStation   185
Potlatch   310
Premier Brands   30, 463, 464

Princeton Architectural Press 309
Professional Bull Riders 290, 347
Pronto Design 345
PruLink Realty 148
Pub Tours of Ireland 291
Public Service 415
Quantel 350
Quixi 167, 194
Radio K 239
Ragged Mountain 150, 154, 219
Reckitt Benckiser 484
Rentlo 475
Reptilian Haven 275
Republic of Singapore Air Force 254
Republic of Singapore Navy 352
Rethink 348
The Richards Group 282
Richmond Ballet 412
Richmond Savings 138
Rick Johnson & Company 349
Röhsska Museet 330, 331, 332
Royal Caribbean 161
RSPCA 385
Ruth Chowles 80
Salomon 178, 208
The Samaritans 37
Samaritans of Singapore 391
San Diego Ad Club 71
Sara Lee Singapore 338
Saturday Star Property Guide 139
Sauder 262
SBC Communications Pacific Bell 444, 460
SCA Hygiene Products 333
The Science Museum 384, 402
SciFi Channel 18, 367
SCMP Book Publishing 304
Seattle SuperSonics 279, 432
Seychelles 13, 140, 183, 184
Seychelles Tourism & Marketing Authority 362
Shell Oil 336
Singapore Cancer Society 240
Skoda UK 169, 482
Skol Beer 63
Slaughter Hanson 357
Smoke Free Singapore 411
Sony Asia Pacific 277
Sony España, S.A. 215
Sony Singapore 144
Space Needle 334
Special Olympics 47
Specialized 172, 200, 201
Sports Illustrated 26, 31, 252, 264
The Spy Store 149, 273
SSL Healthcare 243
St. John Ambulance 382, 409
St. Paul Pioneer Press 432
Star Tribune 131

Steven Stankiewicz 280, 281
Sumus Interactive 300
Superdrug 78
Survival International 380
SWR Television Station 417
Target 174
Tattoo Direct & Digital 360
Taylor Guitars 185, 217, 257, 269
Tazo 81, 354
TDA Advertising & Design 467
TELCO 147
Television 3 24
Television National Network 366
Tennessee Repertory Theatre 307
TheStreet.com 142
Thule 293
Tibor Nemeth Photography 251, 261
The Timberland Company 179, 210
Time 253
The Times 223
Timebank 47
Tom O'Connor 283
Tracey Edwards Company 363
Transamerica 303
Transport Accident Commission 46
Trick Dog Cafe 319
Trollback & Company 365
TV Land 155, 294, 366
UJA Federation 258
UK Time-Timex 21, 130, 258
UNICEF 62
United Negro College Fund 384, 403
United Winery and Distillery 486
US Weekly 436
Velux Skylights 337
VH1 367, 368
Viant 320
Viejas Casino 429
Virgin Atlantic 72, 213, 243
Volkswagen 60
Volkswagen France 63
Volkswagen Group 165, 166, 441, 442
Volkswagen of America 8, 9, 12, 141, 162, 163, 164, 190, 225, 301, 302
Volkswagen of Mexico 488
Volkswagen South Africa 137, 479
Wabedo 311
Wall Street Journal 18, 20, 202, 228, 234
Waterstone's Booksellers 139
Webvan.com 466
Weetabix 462
Westerville North High School 350
White Castle Restaurants 240
Wiffle Ball 274
Willamette Week/BPN 36, 375, 376, 388, 404
Wonderlust Industries 371
WONGDOODY, LA 259
WORK Beer 153, 158, 280

Wrangler 440
WWF Germany 43
WWF ITALIA ONLUS 380
XOW! 335
Young & Co.'s Brewery 446
Youthline 44
Zanders Fine Papers 351

COLLEGE

Academy of Art College/San Francisco 492
The Book Shop/Culver City 492
Brainco/Minneapolis 493, 507, 508
California State University/Long Beach 493
Central Saint Martins College of Art and Design/London 494
Columbus College of Art & Design/Columbus 494
The Creative Circus/Atlanta 68, 495, 505
Miami Ad School/New York 495
Portfolio Center/Atlanta 496, 497, 498
Pratt Institute/New York 505
School of Visual Arts/New York 508
University of Colorado/Boulder 69, 498
The University of Delaware/Newark 499
University of Texas/Texas Creative/Austin 499, 506
VCU Adcenter/Richmond 69, 500, 501, 502, 503, 504

DESIGNER

Ament, Barry 79
Ang, Cara 313
Arrowood, Scott 299
Atherton, Mark 79
Bateson, John 350
Blankely, Erin 341
Blom, Mikael 333
Borrell, Rodolfo 344
Bowling, Belinda 334
Branson-Meyer, Bruce 335
Burgoyne, Andre 353
Cerveny, Lisa 335
Chu, Calvin 367
Clifford, Graham 325, 326
Cole, Tim 358
Colvin, Alan 317
Cook, Gretchen 334
Craven, Holly 334
Crouch, Matt 311

Cusson, Natalie   360
Davis, Tanya   350
Davison, Janice   78
Day, David   352
Dela Cruz, Elmer   334
Delagorce, Nathalie   366
Dinetz, Bob   74, 309
Duffney, Craig   317
Dufils, Cecilia   340
Elterman, Eileen   345
Erhart, Marty   328
Escobedo, Jacob   311, 312
Estrada, George   79
Fauchère, Laurent   365, 366
Fawcette, Amy   334
Fisher, Bob   311, 312
Fitzgerald, Kevin   311
Foelske, Sarah   82, 83, 370
Gallo, Marino A.   342
Gallucci, Marc   323, 324
Gamboa, Claudia   321
Gehrig, Kim   340
Giglio, Mark   74
Gorder, Genevieve   318
Grais, Ian   348
Haak, Chris   366
Hanrahan, Rory   320
Hartmann, Lars   303
Henderson, Alan   357
Hermes, Mary   334
Hutchinson, Mary Chin   335
Ingle, Paul   351
Johnson, Amy   337
Joyce, Mike   345
Kai   313, 314
Kinghorn, Janet   80
Kittel, Andreas   329, 330, 331, 332
Lee, Christopher   75, 313
Levite, Adam   367, 368
Lindvall, a'Tony   310
Lock, Julie   334
Lorente, Tomas   299
Lubow, Jeff   367
Lundberg, Britt   336
Maryon, Dean   298
Matz, Starlee   337
McDonough, Brian   300
McFetridge, Geoff   82, 83, 370
Mitchell, Steve   336
Moffet, Sarah   72
Molloy, Kieron   359
Monnens, Joe   316
Myers, Randall   301
Nakata, Robert   73
Neale, Todd   366
Neibert, Dana   71
Newman, Julian   302
Nichols, Josh   367
Nishi, Jana   335

Oeth, Luke   336
Olsen, John   353
Parra, Greg   353
Pedersen, Doug   337
Peh, Larry   313
Powell, Neil   319
Powers, Marion English   81
Purcer, Pam   367, 368
Ramnathkar, Bhupal   322
Rand, Jason   368
Randall, Andrew   354
Rautenbach, George   362
Redman, Helena   330, 331, 332
Renneker, Jeanne   81
Riddle, Tom   315
Roberson, Kevin   74, 308
Rotondo, Anne   336
Runge, Clint!   301
Sakurai, Ken   317
Sandstrom, Steve   81, 353, 354
Schoen, Kim   82, 83, 370
Schrimpf, David   310, 311
Schultz, Coby   79
Simon, Annette   327
Smith, Andrew   334
Smith, Paul   367
Staples, Chris   348
Staples, Mark   371
Stayner, Don   335
Suvongse, Kobe   316
Tan, Michael   313, 346
Tatham, Jennifer   357
Thompson, Carol   345
Tinguely, Antoine   364, 366
Valter, Stephan   339
Van Keuren, Jacquie   321
Vela, André   321
Viva, Frank   369
Wang, Conan   314
Webb, David   356
Weiping, Liew   313
Wong, Clif   301, 302
Wong, Willis   304
Yaffe, Steve   301

DIRECTOR

Agnelli, Jarbas   448
Aguilera, J.   488
Alenka, Anthony   475
Amon, Sergio   63
Andon, Ruben   484
Ariola, Dante   451, 471
Barker, Nicholas   462, 484
Bekemeier, Jonathan   464
Belvaux, Remy   485, 487
Bigelow, Mike   446

Bond, Fredrik   53, 60, 440, 446, 478, 482
Buckley, Bryan   459
Budgen, Frank   445
Coppola, Roman   476
Denneen, Dave   443
Dom & Nic   452
Filgate, Gus   59
Frankham, David   474
Gay, Paul   462
Geldenhuys, Kim   54
Gillespie, Craig   58, 59, 449, 480
Glazer, Jonathan   440
Goodall, Miles   479
Hamburger, Laurence   475
Haussman, Michael   448
Hendley, Charles   47
Hoagland, Christian   48, 418
Hollis, John   445
Humphrey, Mat   46
Ichilcik, Derek   61
Joanou, Phil   449
Jordan, Rupert   481
Kenworthy, Richard   482
Klasfeld, Marc   468
Kleinman, Daniel   56, 441, 444
Knight, David   481
Krasting, Guntram   451
Kuntz, Tom   55, 56, 86, 443, 458, 479, 480
Lavoie, Paul   485
Levin, David   468
Maguire, Mike   55, 56, 86, 443, 458, 479, 480
McCaughey, Matthew   475
McCollum, Marcus   61, 419
McCoy, Harry   417
McFetridge, Geoff   67, 467, 469, 477
McWatters, Gord   416
Miller, Peter Darley   416
Mills, Mike   452
Mills, Stuart   481
Montesano, Julian   487
Morris, Errol   54, 456, 460, 461, 470, 483
Morton, Rocky   60, 441, 455, 472
Mroueh, Zak   485
Murphy, Dominic   461, 463
Murro, Noam   460, 466
Nemeta, François   63
Nir, Javier   450
Ober, Tony   62, 478
O'Hagan, John   442
Petchsuwan, Suthon   486
Public, Joe   55, 57, 457, 459, 474
Pytka, Joe   471
Reeves, Steve   447, 483
Ren, Lee Wei   62
Riveros, Carolina   487
Routson, Tom   458
Sanders, Rupert   472, 477
Schmerberg, Ralf   469

Scott, Jake 481
Scott, Tony 450
Seifert, Christian 417
Sillen, Pete 467
Smith, Baker 473, 486
Smith, Chris 444
Stark, Jeff 59
They, Patrick 417
Todaro, Frank 473
Traktor 57, 453, 454, 456, 463, 464, 465, 466, 476
Weiland, Paul 47
Zacharias, Ivan 442

ILLUSTRATOR

Alden, Aaron 284
Ambler, Barbara 178, 208
Ament, Barry 79
Ang, Cara 313
Archive 393
Arteaga, Borja 34
Atherton, Mark 79
Baker, Alan 320
Baynes, Saddington 169
Beauchamp, Greg 27, 35, 265
Berzins, Ingrid 237
Bjurman, Markus 76
Boisineau, David 294
Burgoyne, John 9, 14
Caton, Tim 14, 175
Chan, Henry 214
Chu, Calvin 367
Coe, Wayne 300
Coffey, Floyd 337
Cohen, David 241
Cole, Tim 358
Colvin, Alan 317
Cook, Gretchen 334
Crespa, Steve 341
Cuan, Sergio 341
Day, David 352
Dell, Julian 25, 64
Dell, Steve 166
Dinetz, Bob 74
Duffney, Craig 317
Edens, Michel 282
Ehringer, Sean 14, 174
Estrada, George 79
Fabricatore, Carol 309
Fleck, Tom 370
Foell, Hayden 178, 208
Foster, Jeff 353
Franco, Mario 40, 382
Fusion 214
Giglio, Mark 74
Goodall, Jasper 270
Hadley, Sam 78

Ho, Kirby 144
Horita, Hugo 183
Hussey, Steve 308
Jastrebski, Erik 322
Joe, D. I. 144
Johnson, Amy 337
Kakazu, Denis 413
Kann, Martin 138
Keystone Studios 247
Kin, Yau Wai 4, 133, 134, 180
Kinghorn, Janet 80
Kubal, Mahesh 257
Lear, Kelley 370
Lee, Christopher 313
Leung, Samson 191
Lucas, John 30
McFetridge, Geoff 67, 82, 83, 278, 279, 370, 467, 469, 477
Molloy, Kieron 359
Myers, Randall 301
Neideigh, Sherry 283
Nemeth, Tibor 251, 261
Newman, Julian 301, 302
Niah, Lim Seng 277
Nina, Debbie 243
Orcavision Digital Art Studio 332
Persson, Fredrik 333
Peters, George 32, 151, 219, 222
Phenomenon 148
Procolor 136, 137, 254, 277, 338, 380, 411
Quirk, Mike 408
Riddle, Tom 315
Roberson, Kevin 74
Ross, Graziano 380
Ruane, Peter 72
Runge, Clint! 301
Sakurai, Ken 317
Schultz, Coby 79
Schwab, Michael 161
Simon, Annette 327
Singer, Leah 186
Singh, Bhim 343
Smith, Andrew 334
Stankiewicz, Steven 280, 281
Stock 336, 370
Stone, Dylan 187
Teo, Ali 237
Walden, Jason 408
Watson, Ralph 156
Webb, David 356
Weiping, Liew 313
Wong, Willis 304
Zuiderwik, Meek 377

PHOTOGRAPHER

Ackerman, Daniel 188, 382

Ahlgren, Steven 308
Alex Kaikeong Studio 254
Allbritton, Randy 377
Allison, Glen 74
Ammirati, Robert 41, 392, 406, 407
Artist's Archive 321
Avila, Joao 272
Barbieri, Coppi 21, 130, 258
Barcellos, Ricardo 299
Barnum, Cameron 175, 176, 206
Beck, Robert 31, 264
Behar, Leon 149, 273
Belford, Paul 38, 383
Bergengren, Ola 330, 331
Biever, John 252, 264
Biondani, Willy 299
Blinkk, 169
Blue, Greg 255
Borges, Phil 377
Borthwick, Mark 9, 14, 174, 175
Brauneis, Keith 202
Bridgman, Lorne 29, 254
Brown, Peter 74
Burnard, Alex 168, 196
Butera, Gus 18, 367
Caetano, Joao 378, 394
Calcao, Tony 374
Cappa, Robert 36, 378, 379, 395, 396
Carnegie, Rory 253
Cash, Bill 8, 9, 12, 162, 163, 164, 301, 302
Catan, Alexandre 299
Chan, Paul 304
Cheng, Lars 304
Chesley, Paul 74
Cheung, Nelson 304
Ching, Lawrence 304
Chu, Almond 304
Chua, Charles 236
Cipriani, Aldo 369
Clang 175, 176, 206
Clemmens, Clint 129, 161, 198
Collier, Keith 376, 388
Cook, Anthony 143
Coverdale, Jac 193
Crispino, Luis 299
Crosta, Laura 208
Dato, Maribel 318
Davis, Chris 411, 412
Dawkins, Kip 155, 294
Day, James 165, 166
Debold, Bill 288
Derrick Lim Photography 338
Doman, Jakob 139
Donaire, Roberto 299
Eastman, Michael 185, 217
Elisabetsky, Claudio 299
Erickson, Jim 179, 210
Esparza, Philip 328
Esperón, Marco 22

Esteban, Santiago 39
Feiler, Tom 180
Ferrari, Pierpaolo 398
Fiscus, Jim 285
Flores, Miguel 22
Fowelin, Johan 179, 211
Freehill, Brooks 291, 292, 293
Freeman, Hunter 18, 20, 228, 234
Fun, Po 191
Ganem, Steve 150, 154, 219
Georghiou, Nick 375, 387
Goddard, Wade 74
Gonzalez, Luis Enrique 215
Gray, Sebastian 196
Greenfield, Lauren 15, 181
Griffith, Christopher 402
Guan, Teo Chai 144
Guider, John 307
Gutierrez, Marcos 401
Halim, Jen 191, 226
Hall, Stuart 163, 190, 225
Harbor, Don 71, 356
Harting, Christopher 275
Haskell, Laurie 139, 385, 402
Hawthorne, Dean 412
Heimo, 188, 196
Heiniger, Andreas 299
Henry, Morgan 226, 227
Hill, Jackson 36, 378, 379, 395, 396
Hooper, Mark 353
Howard, William 309
Huber, William 7, 16, 151, 170, 171, 220, 262, 464
Hubrigste, Jim 189
Iwaya, Hiroshi 354
Jacobs, Joe 241
Jacobson, Christian 342
Jensen, Gary M. 290, 347
Johnson, Curtis 42, 389, 404, 405, 406
Jones, Matt 218
Jones, Deborah 316
Jorde, Sara 310
Kai 313
Kennedy Library Archives 381, 399, 400
Keong, Alex Kai 2
Kerr, Vikki 284
King, Carol 291
Klein, Richard 317
Kovar, 276
Laita, Mark 195, 286, 287
Learoyd, Richard 351
Ledner, Catherine 308
Lee, Christopher 313
Lee, Dean 224
Lee, Lester 191
Lee, Roy 214
Legaspi, Caloy 273
Leong, Nicholas 256, 268
Leung, Himson 191

Lewis, Mike 13, 140, 183, 184, 362
Liamkyle, David 31
Lockett, Matt 289
Loh, Edward 148, 240
MacIndoe, Graham 74, 218
Magni, Tiziano 7, 8, 11
Mahany, Brian 280, 281
Mahayni, Sam 244, 245
Manninen, Mika 257, 269
Martín, Abelardo 22
Martinelli, Pedro 299
Mascaro, Cristiano 299
Mason, Don 408
Master, Kiran 165
McCorry, Kitty 244, 245
McCurry, Steve 74
Meeks, Raymond 193
McLeod, William Mercer 309
Mermelstein, Jeff 8, 12
Mex, Anthony 335
Michenzi, Shawn 167, 168, 194, 198
Mikos, Joe 155
Millan, Manny 264
Millennium 255, 267
Minchin, James 143, 235
Miro 299
Mitchell, Willabel Cole 374
Mitteldorf, Klaus 299
Moran, Manolo 160, 161
Moretti, Luis Otavio 159
Mother 340
Muna, R. J. 263
Murray, Steve 289
Nahas, Mauricio 299
Naik, Prasad 257
Necessary, Kevin 138
Neff, David 303
Nelson, Tom 35
Nemenov, Alexander 253
Nemeth, Tibor 251, 261, 355
Neto, João Henrique 299
Nicholls, Steve 244
Nivek, Yelad 159
Nourie, Dan 17, 19, 220
Nowitz, Richard 74
One Twenty One 236, 277
Opcao Fotoarquivo 216
Orsini, Craig 212, 312
Pape, Lygia 321
Pappalardo, Arnaldo 299
Peh, Larry 313
Peixotto, Steve 36, 378, 379, 395, 396
Peterson, Bruce 386
Peterson, Charles 409
Picture Farm 391
Plienpairojana, Tawatchai 243
Politis, Spiros 169
Posey, Carl 384, 403
Preutz, David 209

Prior, David 5, 25, 64, 172, 213
Probst, Ken 74
Proctor, Daniel 203
Quackenbush, Russ 141, 379
Richmond, Jack 161
Roberts, Andy 229
Robertson, Dave 382
RSN Archives 352
Rubin, Steffany 341
Ruiz, Stefan 15, 181, 182
Russ, Gary 288
Salvi, Ajay 322
Schlatter, Robert 74, 309
Schrameck, Chris 322
Schulke, Flip 129
Seo, Takashi 233
Seow, Eric 411
Shade, Claude 201
Sheenan, Chris 315
Shooting Gallery 346
Sikka, Bharat 147
Sipma, Hans 138
Skogsberg, Ulf 2, 3, 132
Smari 164, 190, 225
Sonic Stock Photography 279
Sonne, Claus 204
Staub, Pat 289
Steele-Perkins, Chris 10
Steinbrenner, Karl 132, 294
Stevenson, Aaron 303
Stewart, Dave 165
Stock 8, 9, 12, 27, 34, 35, 131, 137, 143, 155, 162, 163, 164, 172, 178, 200, 208, 235, 258, 259, 265, 277, 286, 288, 376, 380, 404, 409
Stoddart, Tom 184
Stone, Dylan 187
Stromberg, Tony 309
Swanson, Marcus 408
Sygmal, Corbis 132
Szuba, Tom 247
Taira, Karina 174
Tam, Sam 148
Telegraph Colour Library & Corbis Images 192
Tielemans, Al 26, 31
Tinguely, Antoine 365
Toma, Kenji 199
Tunbjork, Lars 74, 308
Turnley, David 74
US Army Corps 36, 378, 379, 395, 396
V, Sunil 343
Vainer, Paulo 299
van Deventer, Jacko 24, 227, 228
Van Overbeek, Will 177, 207
Van Sommers, Jenny 197, 250
Vasconcellos, Cassio 299
Vaughn, Joe 240
Veasey, Nick 72

Walsh, Sam   285
Warren, Vinny   291
Watson, Graham   172, 200
Wilder, Brian   34, 167
Wong, Willis   304
Yarbrough, Will   321
Yee, Tang Kim   391
Zhang, Roy   4, 133, 134, 136, 137, 180
Zuiderwik, Meek   377

PRODUCTION COMPANY

@radical.media   54, 456, 460, 461, 469, 470, 471, 473, 483
2AM Films   59
400 Films   445
A & R Group   474
Academy   440
Ad Studio   448
Andon Films   484
Antidoto Films   487
Audio Master   45
Avion   485
Blink Productions   442, 461
Champion Graphics   67, 467, 469, 477
Coppos Films   58, 59, 446, 449, 480
Egg Productions   54
Filmgraphics   46, 443
Fusion Films   61
Garretts   462
Giant Films   479
Gil Smith Studio   458
Gorgeous Enterprises   445
H3O Films   47
Harry Nash   53, 60, 440, 446, 478, 482
Headquarters   55, 57, 457, 459, 474
HKM   452
hungry man   442, 459, 468
Independent Media   444
Innervision Studios   458
James Garrett & Partners   484
La Base   63
Lizard Post Production   61
Matching Studio   486
Mindfield   61, 419
MJZ   455, 472
One Union Recording   430
Ober/Lenz Films   62, 478
Oil Factory   482
Oruga Films   450
Outsider   452, 462, 472, 477
Partizan   60, 441, 456, 463, 464, 465, 476
Partizan/Cape Direct   57, 453, 454
Paul Weiland Film Co.   47
Picture Park   417, 464
Pirate Radio   422, 433, 437
Propaganda   55, 56, 86, 443, 451, 458, 479
Pytka and Flehner Films   471
Quad   485, 487
Radke Films   480
Redtree Productions   48, 418
Renegade Films   475
RSA   450, 481
Spectre   56, 441, 444
Spy Films/Toronto   416
Stark Films   59, 447, 483
Stiefel & Co.   416, 460, 466
Stink   475
Tate & Partners   473, 486
Villains   449
Visual Impact   62
Washington Square Films   467
Winkle Films   481
Wunderfilm Hamburg   451
Z Films   488
Zero Filme   63

WRITER

Aal, Scott   203
Abrahamson, Joan   311
Adams, Julie   229
Ahern, Brian   50
Alberola, Jose Luis   215
Alexander, Joe   381, 399
Allen, Aaron   50, 422, 434
Anderson, Christy   300
Angkasupornkul, Sirirut   243
Aranguena, Yosu   488
Arteaga, Borja   34
Asbek, Thomas   229
Ashworth, Matt   466
Atkinson, Michael   404, 405
B., Haridas   133, 145
Back, Steve   7, 8, 11
Baldacci, Roger   198, 263
Barger, Scott   316
Becka, Tom   494
Bell, Nick   59
Bellotti, Fernando   40
Benjafield, Jana   276
Berkeley, Joe   417
Bertelli, Bruno   398
Best, Wayne   50
Betancourt, Carlos   22
Bianco, Joe   341
Bildsten, Bruce   54, 168
Biskin, Lisa   45
Bjurman, Markus   179, 211, 463, 464
Blandford, Tom   426
Blank, Ryan   174
Blood, Andy   237
Bollinger, John   384, 403
Bone, Eric   311
Borrell, Rodolfo   344
Brandriff, Lisa   463
Braneckey, Lynn   157
Bruce, Paul   445
Brunelle, Tim   141
Brunnström, Lasse   330
Buckhorn, Dean   253, 258
Bueno, Miguel   401
Bullard, Nicky   462
Bullock, Richard   52, 423, 455, 472
Burke, Pat   426
Burleigh, Rob   450
Buss, Michael   429
Byrne, Mike   481
Cahan, Bill   309
Callaghan, Peter   64, 172
Calvo, Ray   345
Camp, Roger   15, 181, 182, 465, 476
Campbell, Michael   25
Campopiano, Javier   255, 267, 382
Capara, Pablo   450
Cardos, Raul   488
Casarotti, Flavio   393
Castañeda, Guillermo   484
Cawley, Kim   223
Cawley, Tim   159
Chan, Paul   304
Charney, Paul   434
Chasnow, Adam   52, 167, 194, 423, 424, 425
Cheong, Eugene   136, 137
Chiappe, Adam   451, 452, 479
Chiavegato, David   430
Chitayat, Eitan   301, 302
Chochran, Bill   282
Christensen, Greg   128
Christmann, Tom   173, 205
Cimino, Bill   50, 426
Clarke, Lawson   150, 154
Clayton, Antonia   250
Cochran, Steve   227, 228
Cohen, Amy   300
Cohen, Mark   285
Cohen, Michael   285
Cohen, Nick   281
Cole, Glenn   73
Colliss, Mick   276
Comar, Daniel   255, 267, 332
Compton, Brett   411, 412
Conde, Paco   44
Connelly, Steve   312
Connolly, Simon   380
Cooney, Scott   29, 254
Cooper, Rich   349
Cooperrider, Stu   386
Corp, Dominic   270
Coupland, Ken   309
Covert, Steve   153, 158, 280, 412

Covington, Matt   496, 497
Craigen, Jeremy   442
Crawford, Craig   361
Crawford, Paul   397
Crippen, Stephanie   466
Cronin, Markham   370
Crowe, Mike   244, 245
Cruz, Christie   492
Cullen, Steve   323, 324
Daga, David   247
Davenport, John   243
Davis, Katy   411, 412
Dawson, Nigel   46
De Rita, Lorenzo   60, 440
De Souza, Joe   23, 30, 76, 340
DeCarlo, Chris   6, 150, 154
DeFeo, Nikki   499
del Valle, Felix   390
Delmonte, Warwick   24
Denberg, Josh   172, 199, 200
Devaris, Oliver   475
DeVito, Sal   41, 392
Dhalia, Heitor   272
di Paulo, JoAnna   309
Dildarian, Steve   428, 458
Dillon, Leslee   337, 353
Dinetz, Bob   74, 309
Dolan, Doug   369
Domenet, Paul   447, 483
Domingos, Carlos   299
Doyle, Sean   21, 128, 232
Duchon, Scott   185
Duenas, Gustavo   488
Dufils, Cecilia   23, 179, 211
Dunbar, Don   286
Duncan, Robert   321
Durkin, Patrick   55, 57, 457
Ebling, Susan   220
Edwards, Chris   414
Einstein, Harold   18, 20, 202, 228, 234
Elhardt, Matt   175, 176, 206, 460, 461
Elkjer, Thom   309
Elliott, Kent   426
Emerick, Patrick   429
Emslie, Ruth   351
End, Jackie   230
Erdem, Erhan   407
Erke, Ken   27, 28, 260, 271, 293
Escobar, Saul   22
Esses, Barbara   188
Evans, Craig   71
Evans, Jason   255
Fago, Joe   240
Fahrenkopf, Erik   282
Fair, Diana   322
Fairbanks, Mark   244
Faussurier, Pierre Marie   63
Fernandes, Fabio   63
Fernandez, Miguel   497

Fisher, Mark   137
Foster, Donna   50
Foth Jr., Ron   350
Frank, Jens   26
Franson, Katie   310
Franz, Nicole   451
Fredette, David   503
French, Neil   2, 134, 135, 136, 146
Frey, Larry   298
Fund, Jack   35
Fury, Jerry   193
Gandolfi, Ricardo   496
Garaventi, Jim   7, 151, 464
Gardiner, Neil   247
Gardner, Geraldine   350
Garthwaite, Steve   377
Gassman, Dave   436
Gaxiola, Robert   221
Gelner, William   456
Gettins, Dom   197
Gibbs, Mike   198
Giglio, Mark   74
Gill, Slade   248
Gillan, Martin   45
Gillingham, Tim   163, 164, 190, 225
Ginés, Rigoberto   22
Girouard, Bill   415
Gold, Josh   443
Goldberg, Barney   436
Goldberg, Jon   218
Goldenberg, Rob   436
Graham, Ian   241
Graham, Kerry   306, 307
Greenaway, Andy   4, 134, 136, 137, 180
Grieve, Alex   375, 387
Gross, Mark   50, 426
Grossman, Alex   280, 281
Guisande, Carolina   344
Gutierrez, Eric   416
Hagan, Merril   311
Hagar, Jim   131
Hage, John   42
Hahn, Greg   26, 31, 252, 264, 442
Hall, Jenna   318
Halling, Siggi   253
Hamiter, Jimmy   312
Hampton, Tyler   27, 35, 61, 265
Handford, Simon   230
Harges, Chris   309
Hart, Michael   54, 129, 198, 456, 483
Haselton, Hilary   69
Haven, Jim   18, 20, 202, 228, 234
Hayes, Brian   17, 19, 220
Helfand, Glen   309
Henthorne, David   350
Herbert, Jynelle   502
Hernandez, Gloria   401
Higgs, Sue   37
Hipp, Courtney   303

Hirsch, Paul   199
Hite, Anne Marie   400
Hoff, Jason   498
Holland, Grant   452
Hower, Reuben   69
Hudson, Tom   450
Hunter, Bernard   25, 64
Husband, Eric   42, 389, 405, 406
Idle Industries   77
Immesoete, John   49, 427
Jack, Brendan   5, 64
Jack, Rob   60, 441
Jackson, Al   2, 189, 278, 355, 411, 412
Jakob, James   30
Jalfen, Martin   487
James, Doug   486
Jeffers, Crockett   274
Jendrysik, Ted   2, 3, 132, 133
John, Jonathan   47
Johnson, David   259, 494
Jones, Stef   484
Jordan, Rupert   481
Jorgensen, Scott   32, 151, 219, 222
Kaplan, Scott   142
Kapoor, Dinesh   500, 504
Kapur, Priti   254
Keepper, Dave   42, 389, 405, 406
Kellett, Gavin   53, 446
Kelly, Albert   473
Kelly, Tom   154, 219
Kerstetter, Bob   434
Khazanchi, Ashish   147
King Jr., Martin Luther   131
Kinney, Beth   408
Kling, Jeff   470
Knight, Natalie   44
Krassner, Deb   341
Kuntz, Tom   479
La Rocque, Chris   495
Labaton, Dana   382
Lai, Ming   71
Landrum, Steve   138
Lang, Dave   45
Law, Lucien   227, 228
Lear, Mike   370, 397
LeBrecht, Eric   335
Lee, Dylan   482
Lee, Owen   444
Lehmann, Rafiq   352
Leighton, Tony   308
Lichtenfeld, Sharon   309
Liebhauser, Eric   283, 293, 467
Lim, Adrian   10, 209
Lim, Daniel   62
Lim, Justin   136, 137
Lim, Renee   256, 268
Lim, Troy   277
Lima, Eduardo   378, 394
Linardatos, Andy   138

Lisko, Tim   158
Lok, Andrew   33, 240
Loomis, Alex   430
Loraine, Martin   461
Lowe, Greg   129
Lubars, David   54
Lubbe, Wayne   479
Lubow, Jeff   18, 367
Luckin, Frances   139
Lustig, Ariel   492
MacDonald, Geoff   18, 367
Machado, Alexandre   448
Maciolek, Dave   341
Macomber, Anne   289
Madariaga, Miguel   390
Maguire, Mike   479
Mahney, Jon   415
Mainwaring, Simon   472, 477
Marcus, Ken   156
Martin, Greg   45
Martins, Jose Luiz   159
Mason, Mark   248
Matejczyk, John   58, 59, 449, 480
Mazza, Mike   466
McAllister, Cal   279
McBride, Chuck   448
McCarley, Laura   436
McCommon, Mike   15, 181, 182, 465, 476
McCullough, Michael   62, 478
McHugh, Peter   29, 254
McHugh, Rick   379
McKay, Michael   20
McKay, Pat   501
McKenna, Mike   45
McKinney, Raymond   132
McKinsey & Company   358, 359
McLean, Patrick   303
McLeod, Andy   21, 169, 252, 482
McNally, Clare   54
Meagher, Bob   155, 294
Meehan, Chuck   36, 378, 379, 395, 396, 435
Merkin, Ari   34, 48, 167, 168, 196
Messeter, Rob   244, 245
Mietelski, Stephen   212
Miller, Tom   459
Mokart, Farid   485
Molla, Jose   471, 478
Monroe, Dan   357
Montaquila, Christine   262
Montgomery, Bill   230
Moorcroft, Wendy   13, 140, 183, 184
Morales, Dan   57, 453, 454
Morris, Steve   9, 14, 174, 175, 177, 207
Mother Ltd.   77
Moyse, Peter   236
Mroueh, Zak   437, 485
Myhren, Tor   259
Myrtle   266

Navarro, Vicente   44
Naville, Bernard   487
Neibert, Dana   71
Neumeier, Marty   309
Nilsson, Johan   475
Nissan, Colin   444
Nogueira, Marcelo   159
Norman, Vanessa   5
Novak, Andrew   495
O'Brien, Steve   419, 474
O'Bryan-Tear, Nick   441
Ocampo, Dino   273
O'Connor, Tom   283
Oelofse, Petra   362
O'Keefe, Tom   57, 457
O'Kelly, Mariana   139
Oldham, Kathy   71, 356
Owerko, Lyle   371
Oyasu, Tohru   188
Paterson, Ewan   60, 441
Patten, Thomas   226, 227
Pay, Caroline   445
Pegors, Tim   349
Pereira, Roberto   160, 161
Pereira, Tony   322
Perks, Dave   501
Piccolo, Joe   52, 431
Pierce, Bobby   320
Pierce, Brian   282
Postaer, Jeremy   476
Potts, Rob   130, 258
Preston, Shawn   451, 452
Proudfoot, Kevin   67, 82, 83, 278, 279, 370, 467, 468, 469, 477
Pryce-Jones, Rich   430
Pullar, Dave   410
Quah, Raymond   221
Quinn, Laurence   59
Raff, Larry   70
Raillard, Fred   485
Ramage, Philip   494
Ramos, Anselmo   413
Randall, Gail   492
Rangsiyakul, Shelly   499
Rao, Maya   6, 16, 66, 152, 170, 171, 231, 238
Ray, Gordon   246
Ray, Mark   436
Rayburn, Nicole   498
Rea, Chad   33, 77
Reichenthal, Ian   52, 424, 449
Reid, Peter   139
Reilly, Brad   213
Renfro, Mike   282
Riley, Tim   232, 374
Rivitz, Matt   178, 208
Robbins, Josh   44
Roberson, Kevin   74, 309
Roberts, Nigel   38, 383, 384, 402

Robertson, John   185, 217, 257, 269
Robinson, Gary   444
Robinson, Ginger   36, 375, 376, 388, 404
Rodriguez, Jaume   34
Roe, Mike   408
Roper, Tim   418
Ross, David   181
Ross, Jeff   179, 210
Roth, Jay   275
Russell, Alan   382, 409, 414
Saling, Dean   432, 478
Saltmarsh, Ron   377
Sampaio, Rodolfo   216
Samuel, Ron   276
Sandoz, Steve   81, 353, 354
Sant'Anna, Victor   378, 394
Santucci, Nicole   503
Saunby, Matt   479
Scherk, Dan   149, 273
Schildkraut, Josh   68
Schmidt, Jim   43
Schoenberg, Jonathan   291, 292, 293, 467
Schoenhoff, Hans-Friedrich   290
Schofield, Chris   24
Schrod, Joerg   26
Schwartz, Rob   140
Seftel, Lawrence   462
Seidenberg, Lee   392, 406
Seifert, Christian   417
Serda, Dalel   499
Shaikh, Parveez   239
Sherring, Matt   325, 326
Shipley, Alex   380
Shoval, Alon   416
Shunker, Pio   342
Silburn, Paul   56, 445, 462
Silver, Eric   55, 56, 86
Simon, Jack   327
Simpson, John   161, 251, 261
Sinclair, James   165
Singh, Satbir   343
Sittig, Dick   436
Skibba, Steve   469
Slade, Kristina   143, 235
Smith, Chris   282
Smith, Curtis   289, 337
Smith, Dave   357
Smith, Jason   501
Sola, Augusto   183
Sorensen, Mark   239
Souter, Peter   47, 385
Speed, Paul   427
Spiegel, Jeff   446
Squid   266
Sree, Kash   471
Srinath, M.   148, 411
Staples, Joe   443
Stark, Delores   288
Stein, Randy   224

Steinberg, Hayes   422, 433
Stephens, Jack   242
Stephenson, Charles   282
Stern, Aaron   201
Stern, Andy   276
Stern, Tony   277
Stoney, Richard   249
Strasberg, Rob   195, 286, 287, 374
Strong, Tony   232
Sucharittanonta, Suthisak   486
Sullivan, Troy   230
Swisher, Kevin   282
Szabo, David   191
Taciuk, Chris   480
Tan, Evelyn   313
Tan, Jackson   305
Tarry, Rob   52, 431
Tavares, Ana   321
Tembulkar, Parag   346
Teng, Vancelee   243
Teo, Mikael   144
Teringo, Mark   392, 407
Terril, Traci   367, 368
Tham, Grover   214
Thompson, Chip   282
Thompson, Wayne   131
Thornton, Jim   463, 464
Tinning, Andrew   237
Tipton, Franklin   263
Titus, Jennifer   311
Tractenberg, Joel   41, 392
Trewartha, Kelly   193
Tsang, K. C.   304
Tsao, Robert   391
Tso, John   493
Tucker, Adam   165, 166
Turner, Chris   142
Ueland, Eivind   6, 275
Valter, Stephan   339
Van Huyssteen, Leon   25, 64
Van Ness, Tom   284
Vanderbilt, Tom   309
Vathiyar, Anand Arumugam   288
Vázquez, Alex   22
Veltroni, Enrica Ficai   380
Venables, Paul   443, 458, 459, 460, 474
Verbrugge, Moe   6, 66, 152, 231, 238
Viva, Frank   369
Vogel, Dr. Stephan   26, 43
Vohra, Vidur   145
Waites, Mark   23, 463, 464
Walker, Karen   500
Wan, Daniel George   338
Ward, Mike   285
Warren, Vinny   291
Warsop, Graham   64
Webb, Dean   92
Webster, Deacon   281, 282
Weiland, Paul   47

Weinstein, Josh   363
Weiss, Ari   411, 412
Weisser, Karolin   43
Weist, Dave   8, 9, 12, 162, 163, 164
Werner, Larry   336
Whitney, Michael   432
Whitney, Tom   432
Wild, Scott   177, 185, 207
Williams, Gavin   5, 64
Wilson, Leon   227, 228
Winokur, Ilicia   186, 187, 468
Wirt, Mark   316
Wolfe, Tim   73
Wong, Alvin   240
Wood, Glenn   44
Worthington, Nick   440
Wright, Bill   414
Xue, Jiang Wu   62
Yasgur, Jon   493
Yeung, Ronnie   226
Zanatta, Cassio   149
Zulawinski, Mike   290, 347
Zumwinkel, Steve   473

YOUNG CREATIVE PROFESSIONAL COMPETITION

Ambrose, Jason S.   506
Bhatia, Raul   505
Brooks, Mike   505
Butterworth, Amy   505
Chang, Soo Mean   508
Dachis, Adam   507
Gebhardt, Nick   505
Luckett, Gray   506
Riddle, Jarrod   507
Sheahan, Molly   508
Theisen, Ryan O'Hara   508
Wixom, Kris   506
Yasgur, Jon   508